```
BIOG WAS

Clary, David A.

George Washington's first
 war
```

**Please check all items for damages
before leaving the Library.
Thereafter you will be held
responsible for all injuries
to items beyond reasonable wear.**

Helen M. Plum Memorial Library

Lombard, Illinois

A daily fine will be charged for
overdue materials.

JAN   2011

GEORGE WASHINGTON'S FIRST WAR

His Early

Military Adventures

DAVID A. CLARY

Simon & Schuster • New York   London   Toronto   Sydney

Simon & Schuster
1230 Avenue of the Americas
New York, NY 10020

First Simon & Schuster hardcover edition January 2011

Designed by Jill Putorti

Illustration Sources
1: From a copy of the original at the New-York Historical Society
2: Artist unknown, from a copy of the original in the collection at Mount Vernon
3: Artist unknown, from a copy of the original in the National Portrait Gallery,
London
4: Engraving after Alonzo Chappell, from John Frederick Schroeder, *Life and Times
of Washington* (1857)
5: From a copy of the original in the Union League of Philadelphia
6: Photographer unknown, from *Handbook of North American Indians* (1907)
7, 8, 9, 10, 11: David A. Clary
12, 13, 15, 16, 17, 19, 22: Author's Collection
14: From *Scribner's Magazine* (May 1893)
18: Library of Congress
20: From a copy of the original at the Virginia Museum of Fine Arts, Richmond
21: From a copy of the original at Washington and Lee University, Lexington, Virginia

Manufactured in the United States of America

10 9 8 7 6 5 4 3 2 1

Library of Congress Cataloging-in-Publication Data
Clary, David A.
George Washington's first war : his early military adventures / David
A. Clary.—1st Simon & Schuster hardcover ed.
  p. cm.
Includes bibliographical references and index.
1. Washington, George, 1732–1799—Military leadership. 2. United States—History—
French and Indian War, 1755–1763—Campaigns. 3. Washington's Expedition to the
Ohio, 1st, 1753–1754. 4. Washington's Expedition to the Ohio, 2nd, 1754. 5. Fort
Necessity, Battle of, Pa., 1754. 6. Braddock's Campaign, 1755. 7. Forbes Expedition
against Fort Duquesne, 1758 I. Title.
 E312.23.C53 2011
 973.2'6—dc22

                                                              2010046455

ISBN 978-1-4391-8110-2
ISBN 978-1-4391-8112-6 (ebook)

To the memory of Benjamin Robinson, the wisest man I ever knew

Of Arms, and the Man, I sing!

—Virgil

To the memory of the Man, first in war, first in peace, and first in the hearts of his countrymen.

—Henry "Light-Horse Harry" Lee,
eulogy on the death of George Washington

CONTENTS

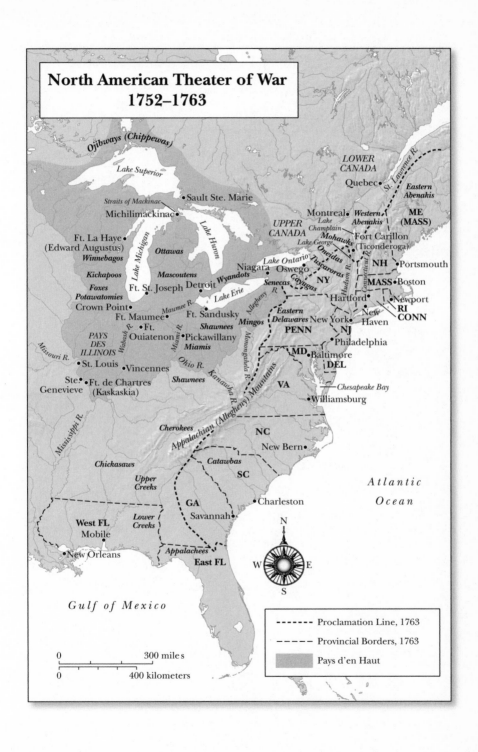

North American Theater of War
1752–1763

Ojibways (Chippewas)

Lake Superior

Straits of Mackinac
Sault Ste. Marie
Michilimackinac•

Ft. La Haye•
(Edward Augustus)
Winnebagos

Lake Michigan

Lake Huron

Ottawas

Kickapoos
Mascoutens
Foxes
Ft. St. Joseph• Detroit•
Potawatomies
Crown Point•
Maumee R.
Ft. Maumee•
Wabash R.
•Ft.
Miami R.
Ft. Sandusky•
Shawnees
Mingos

PAYS
DES
Ouiatenon•
Pickawillany
ILLINOIS
Miamis
Missouri R.
•St. Louis
•Vincennes
Ohio R.
Shawnees
Ste.• •Ft. de Chartres
Genevieve (Kaskaskia)

Lake Erie
Wyandots
Niagara•
Allegheny R.
Lake Ontario
Oswego•
Senecas
Cayugas

LOWER
CANADA
Quebec•
St. Lawrence R.
Eastern
Abenakis

Montreal• *Western*
UPPER *Lake* *Abenakis*
CANADA *Champlain*
Mohawks
Lake George
Fort Carillon
(Ticonderoga)
ME
(MASS)

Oneidas
Tuscaroras
NY
NH •Portsmouth
MASS •Boston
Hartford•
•Newport
RI
New *CONN*
New York• Haven
Eastern
Delawares
PENN
NJ
•Philadelphia
MD •Baltimore
DEL
VA
—*Chesapeake Bay*
•Williamsburg

Cherokees
NC
New Bern•

Chickasaws
Catawbas
SC
Upper
Creeks
GA
•Charleston
Lower
Savannah•
Mississippi R.
West FL
Creeks
Mobile
•New Orleans
Appalachees
East FL

Atlantic
Ocean

N
W E
S

Gulf of Mexico

0   300 miles
0   400 kilometers

- - - - - - - Proclamation Line, 1763
- - - - Provincial Borders, 1763
        Pays d'en Haut

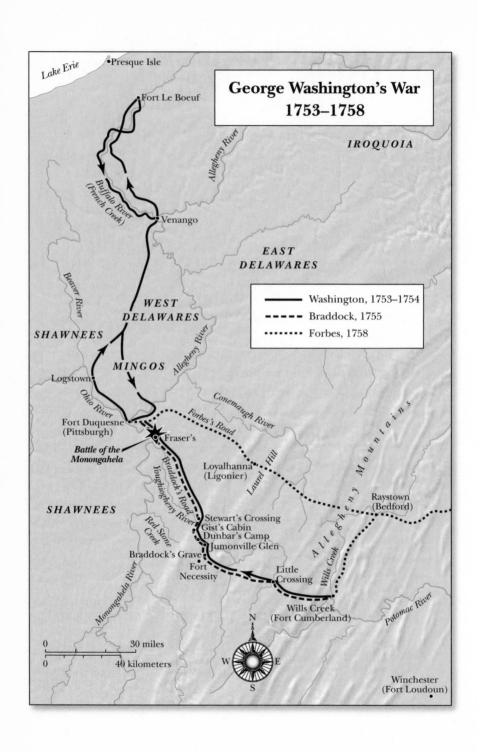

**George Washington's War
1753–1758**

Lake Erie

•Presque Isle

•Fort Le Boeuf

Allegheny River

IROQUOIA

*Buffalo River
(French Creek)*

•Venango

*EAST
DELAWARES*

——————	Washington, 1753–1754
– – – – –	Braddock, 1755
··········	Forbes, 1758

*WEST
DELAWARES*

Beaver River

Allegheny River

SHAWNEES

MINGOS

Logstown•

Ohio River

Conemaugh River

Fort Duquesne
(Pittsburgh)•

Forbes's Road

•Fraser's

**Battle of the
Monongahela**

Loyalhanna
(Ligonier)•

Laurel Hill

Allegheny Mountains

Raystown
(Bedford)•

SHAWNEES

Braddock's Road

Youghiogheny River

Stewart's Crossing•
Gist's Cabin•
Dunbar's Camp•
•Jumonville Glen

Red Stone Creek

Braddock's Grave•
Fort
Necessity•

Little
Crossing•

Wills Creek

Monongahela River

Wills Creek
(Fort Cumberland)•

Potomac River

0		30 miles
0		40 kilometers

N
W E
S

Winchester
(Fort Loudoun)
•

A Word about Words

The letters and documents quoted in this book are presented as they were originally written, with one exception. I have eliminated the eccentric capitalization common during that age, which is tolerable in handwriting but distracting when set in type. Otherwise, spelling, grammar, syntax, and punctuation are in original form, and bracketed clarifications are inserted only when necessary.

The term "English" identifies people of Britain's colonies in North America, whatever their national origins. "British" identifies those in or from Great Britain. The modern term "Anglo" refers to both. "Canadian" and "French" are used interchangeably, as they were historically.

The various collectivities of Indians are "nations," a European term that is inexact when applied to the cultural identities of North American peoples but less so than "tribes." Modern members of the nations prefer the term. The misnomer "Native American" does not appear. Indians today generally prefer the term "Indian," although historically pan-Indian identities appeared after the time period of this book. Nor are there "braves" or "squaws" in this account; Indian men and women are "men" and "women."

Names of individual Indians were historically rendered into English with a variety of spellings. I have adopted the most common versions in recent literature. Collectively, Indians take regular English plurals ("Shawnees," "Delawares") or accepted French ("Iroquois," "Illinois").

Cast of Characters

Abercromby, James (1706–81), commander in chief, British forces in North America, 1757–58

Amherst, Jeffrey (1717–97), commander in chief, British forces in North America, 1758–63

Atkin, Edmund (1697–1761), superintendent of Indian affairs for southern colonies

Beaujeu, Daniel-Hyacinthe-Marie Liénard de (1711–55), led attack on Braddock at the Monongahela

Bigot, François (1703–78), notoriously corrupt royal *intendant* of New France, 1748–59

Bouquet, Henry (1719–65), deputy to Forbes in expedition against Fort Duquesne

Braddock, Edward (ca. 1695–1755), commander in chief, British forces in North America; defeated at the Monongahela, 1755

Cèleron de Bienville, Pierre-Joseph (1693–1759) French marine officer, commanded force in Ohio Valley, 1749, warned French government of English incursions into territory

Coulon de Villiers, Louis (1710–57), French marine officer, defeated Washington at Fort Necessity; older brother of Jumonville

Contrecoeur, Claude-Pierre Pecaudy sieur de (1705–75), French marine officer, commanded troops who occupied the Forks of the Ohio in April 1754

Croghan, George (?–1782), land speculator, Indian trader, and ally of William Johnson

Demoiselle (see Memeskia)

Dinwiddie, Robert (1692–1770), lieutenant governor of Virginia, 1751–58

Dumas, Jean-Daniel (1721–94), commanded at Monongahela after Beaujeu's death; later commanded at Fort Duquesne

Dunbar, Thomas (?–1767), Braddock's deputy, 1755

Duquesne de Menneville, Ange, marquis (1700–78), naval officer, governor of New France, ordered construction of fort at the Forks of the Ohio

Fairfax, George William (1729–87), William's son, Washington's friend, husband of Sally

Fairfax, Thomas (1693–1781), sixth baron Fairfax of Cameron, largest landowner in Virginia

Fairfax, William (1691–1757), nephew of Lord Fairfax, master of Belvoir, Lawrence Washington's father-in-law

Fauquier, Francis (1703–68), succeeded Dinwiddie as lieutenant governor of Virginia

Forbes, John (1707–59), negotiator with Indians, commander of expedition against Fort Duquesne, 1758

Gage, Thomas (1721–87), battalion commander under Braddock; commander in chief, British forces in North America, 1763–76

Galissonière, Roland-Michel Barrin, marquis de la (1693–1756), governor of New France, 1746–49

George II (1683–1760), king of Great Britain, 1727–60

George III (1738–1820), king of Great Britain, 1760–1820

Gist, Christopher (1706–59), land speculator and surveyor, Indian trader, accompanied Washington to the French forts, 1753; later a captain and Indian agent in Washington's regiment

Glen, James (1701–77), governor of South Carolina

Halkett, Francis (?–1760), son of Peter, Forbes's brigade major

Halkett, Sir Peter (1695–1755), colonel of 44th Regiment of Foot, killed at the Monongahela

Johnson, William (1715–74), British superintendent of Indian affairs for northern colonies

Joncaire Chabert (Daniel-Marie Chabert de Joncaire de Claussonne, 1714–71), French Indian agent

Jonquière, Jacques-Pierre de Taffanel, marquis de la (1685–1752), governor of New France, 1749–52

Jumonville, Joseph Coulon de Villiers de (1718–54), French marine officer, killed at Jumonville Glen, 1754; younger brother of Coulon de Villiers

Langlade, Charles-Michel Mouet de (1729–1801), led attack on Pickawillany, 1752

Legardeur de Saint-Pierre, Jacques (1701–55), French marine officer commanding forces in the Ohio country, received Washington at Fort de la rivière aux Boeufs (Fort Le Boeuf), 1753

Lignery, François-Marie le marchand de (1703–59), French marine officer, commanded Fort Duquesne as Forbes approached, 1758

Longueuil, Charles le Moyne, baron de (1687–1755), acting governor of New France, 1752

Louis XV (1710–74), king of France, 1715–74

Loudoun, John Campbell, earl of (1705–82), succeeded Shirley as commander in chief, British forces in North America

Marin, Pierre-Paul de la Malgue, sieur de (1692–1753), French marine officer, commanded the troops sent into the Ohio Valley to build forts, 1753

Memeskia, aka Old Briton or la Demoiselle (1695–1752), Miami chief who defied the French; killed and eaten at Pickawillany, 1752

Mercer, George (1733–1784), aide-de-camp then company commander under Washington

Montcalm de Saint-Véran, Louis-Joseph de Montcalm-Grozon, marquis de (1712–59), French military commandant in North America, 1756–59; killed at Quebec

Newcastle, Thomas Pelham-Holles, duke of (1693–1768), prime minister of Great Britain, 1757–62

Orme, Robert (?–1790), Braddock's principal aide-de-camp, wounded at Monongahela

Péan, Michel-Jean-Hugues, chevalier de Saint-Michel (1723–82), succeeded Marin in command of Ohio forts

Pépin, Michel *dit* La Force (1721–64?), French commissary in Ohio, captured at Jumonville Glen

Pitt, William (1708–78), prime minister of Great Britain, 1757–61

Pompadour, Jeanne-Antoinette Poisson le Normant d'Etoiles, madame de (1721–64), Louis XV's mistress

Pontiac (1712?–69), Ottawa leader in a pan-Indian rebellion against British that began in 1763 and took on his name

Robinson, John (1705–66), speaker of the Virginia assembly, treasurer of the colony

St. Clair, Sir John (?–1767), deputy quartermaster general, British forces in North America, 1754–67

Scarouady (?–1758), Oneida sachem who succeeded Tanaghrisson as Half-King

Shirley, William (1694–1771), governor of Massachusetts, commander in chief after Braddock

Stanwix, John (ca. 1690–1765), British commander in southern district, 1756–58

Stephen, Adam (ca. 1718–91), with Washington at Fort Necessity; lieutenant colonel of Virginia Regiment

Stobo, Robert (1727–70?), officer in Virginia militia, one of two who stayed with the French as hostage against the return of the French prisoners taken at Jumonville Glen

Tanaghrisson, aka Half-King (?–1754), Mingo leader of Iroquois affiliates in Ohio Valley

Teedyuscung (1700–63), Delaware leader, famous orator, occupied middle ground between French and English, involved in several dubious land deals

Van Braam, Jacob (1725–1784), Washington's translator in 1753, company commander 1754, held hostage by French six years under terms of capitulation of Fort Necessity

Vaudreuil-Cavagnal, Pierre-François, marquis de (1698–1778), governor of Louisiana, succeeded Duquesne as governor of New France

Washington, Augustine (1694–1743), George's father

Washington, George (1732–99), Virginia military commander in the 1750s; married Martha Custis (1732–1802), 1759

Washington, Lawrence (ca. 1718–52), George's half brother

Washington, Mary Ball (c. 1708–89), George's mother

A PORTRAIT OF THE HERO AS A YOUNG MAN

But we are like the leaves that flowery spring puts forth, quick spreading in the sun's warm light: for a brief span of time we take our joy in our youth's bloom, the future, good or ill, kept from us.

— MIMNERMUS

The name George Washington evokes for many Americans the old man on the dollar bill, the "Father of His Country," his face benign but expressionless, a mysterious figure as unreadable as a sphinx. For others, the sanctimonious cherry-tree killer invented by Mason Weems comes to mind, a miniature version of the wise and solemn man he would become. Both images are false.

Washington was a human being, who started out as a baby. So do we all, yet we shirk from picturing our great men (or women) suffering teething pains, throwing tantrums, becoming boys (or girls) with snot on their faces and scrapes on their knees, storming through adolescence, and maturing in the hardest school of all—life. If we are really to understand the Founding Fathers, we must grant them the one thing they shared with us—their humanity. They were not superheroes armed with powers beyond those of mere mortals, but people who achieved greatness despite their all-too-human flaws.

George Washington towered over his generation, and still towers over American history, but he was not born a great man. He became one during a long life of learning from trial and error—especially error. That continual self-education made him, in the end, the outstanding figure of his age. But if it is difficult to picture him as a toddler, it is harder to grasp that he—just like us—passed through adolescence before he became a man. This book follows him on that journey.

It began with an epic trek into a howling wilderness late in 1753, when Washington was twenty-one years old. He carried a message from the governor of Virginia to the French commandant in the Ohio Country, ordering him to leave territory claimed by Virginia, although as Washington himself admitted, he was not trained as a diplomat. The next year, having no military training either, he was placed in command of Virginia's troops aiming to enforce the colony's territorial claim in Ohio. This ended in a horrible disaster. Washington's Virginians and his Indian allies attacked a French diplomatic party and massacred the wounded; this bloody affair was credited at the time and ever since as igniting the first real world war, called the Seven Years War in Europe and the French and Indian War in America. Vengeful French and Indians ran Washington's little army down and nearly destroyed it before he surrendered.

Facing demotion in the aftermath, Washington resigned his commission, then in 1755 attached himself as a volunteer to General Edward Braddock, who was leading a new force of redcoats and provincials against the French on the Ohio. This ended with the Battle of the Monongahela, which Americans called "Braddock's Defeat." Yet Washington emerged from the debacle as the "Hero of the Monongahela," earning him promotion to colonel in command of all Virginia forces. He spent the next two and a half years dreaming of winning honor and glory at the head of an army, but confined to life as that little army's chief bureaucrat, begging for material support from his government while his starving men deserted in mobs. He at last took the field in 1758 in a new campaign commanded by a British general, but he earned neither honor nor glory.

This may well be called "A Portrait of the Hero as a Young Man." Washington's introduction to public affairs, in particular war, occurred while he struggled through his long adjustment from boyhood to manhood. He was self-focused, uneasy about his responsibilities, anxious about what others thought of him, and inclined to shade the truth—hardly the qualities of a good leader. He felt isolated and frustrated, so he lashed out against his superiors, both civilian and military. This portrait is an unfamiliar one to most Americans, and it is sometimes unflattering. But Washington's behavior at the time was understandable for someone at his stage of life, deprived of the guidance of an experienced mentor. He was not incompetent, just young, a boy struggling to become a man, carrying responsibilities that should not have been placed on someone so young. Understanding this period is essential to understanding the future Father of His Country.

Washington survived a five-year ordeal unlike that endured by any other Founding Father. He emerged from it not yet the steady supreme commander of the army of the Revolution, but he had started on the road to that end. The former boy colonel of the French and Indian War became the great soldier and statesman of his age. How he began his remarkable life's journey is what this book is about.

GEORGE
WASHINGTON'S
FIRST WAR

PROLOGUE

PICKAWILLANY

(June 21, 1752)

Cry *Havoc!* and let slip the dogs of war.
—WILLIAM SHAKESPEARE

The river gurgled. The only other sounds came from the rustle of leaves, the chattering of squirrels, the mating calls of birds, and the occasional barking of dogs. The men crept silently in small groups through the towering forest until they nearly surrounded the town, a collection of pole-and-bark wigwams and log huts and the Pennsylvania traders' stockaded storehouse. The silent figures carried muskets and tomahawks, with ammunition and scalping knives on cords slung from their shoulders; some of them also had cutlasses. They wore, most of them, no more than moccasins and loincloths, some not even that much, and they had coated themselves with bear grease—a defense against mosquitoes and biting flies, and against an enemy getting a solid grip during a tussle. Each had painted himself in colored patterns according to his own way of projecting fierceness, and most had adorned their hair with feathers and other objects.

The town was Pickawillany, the main English trading post in the

Ohio Country. Beside the Great Miami River, it was also the capital of the Miami (Twightwee) Federation, which was in rebellion against the great alliance among the French and the Great Lakes nations. The raiders' aim was to end the rebellion, drive the English traders out of the country, and teach a lesson about getting in league with *l'Anglais* to the Miami leader, Memeskia—whom the French called "la Demoiselle" ("Maiden," in the derisive sense of "Old Maid") for his perfidy and the English called "Old Briton" for his loyalty.

There were about 250 men in the raiding party, Ottawa and Ojibway (Chippewa) fighters from around Michilimackinac, at the northwest end of Lake Huron, and a few Canadian militia. They followed a handsome and charismatic young man—really little more than a boy but already a proven leader. He was a *métis* (mixed blood) who had inherited his French father's flowing black hair and his Ottawa mother's glittering black eyes. Charles-Michel Mouet de Langlade was his name, a grand one reflecting his status among the *habitants* of western New France. He enjoyed even higher status among the Indians of the northern Great Lakes.

Langlade had led his men in a flotilla of canoes down the lakes to the French post at Detroit, which they reached in early June. There they gathered intelligence and whipped their spirits up for the campaign. They then paddled on to the Maumee River, stopping at the French post at the head of the portage to the Great Miami before crossing overland to Pickawillany. They ate the boiled meat of sacrificial dogs the night before the attack, their ritual way of acquiring strength, loyalty, and determination.

They had timed their assault well. Ordinarily there would be as many as fifty Pennsylvanians at the town this time of year, but there were only eight because most of the Miami men were out hunting for meat instead of bartering furs. Not enough land had been cleared for farming to feed the town's population of about 2,000, and the previous year's crops had failed because of drought. Only about two dozen Miami men, including Memeskia, guarded the place.

The town's women were in the surrounding cornfields, pulling weeds and planting squash and beans, when the attackers exploded out of the forest, screaming war whoops and firing their muskets. The terrified women fled into the town. Langlade's men tore across the fields behind the women, pouring into the settlement with hatchets drawn, still screaming. The first rush took down three English traders, two dead, one wounded, before the other five escaped into their stockade. Fourteen Miamis went down before gunfire and slashing blades, among them Memeskia. The women and a few men were prisoners.

After some ineffective sniping back and forth, the raiders called to the English in the stockade, offering to swap the women for the traders, whom they promised not to harm. There was no water in the stronghold, so the Englishmen agreed, and the exchange took place. The trader wounded outside the fort, however, was not worth saving as far as the Indians were concerned. They finished him off, cut open his chest, and passed his heart around, each taking a bite out of it. During this distraction, two of the surrendered traders escaped into the woods, along with a few Miamis.

Ritual cannibalism was a sacred custom among Langlade's people, and he honored it, formally presenting Memeskia's corpse to his men. They cut it up, boiled it in a large iron pot, and ate the great chief to ingest his spiritual energy. They also, in this peculiar way, reincorporated him into the French alliance. When they had concluded their feast, they torched part of the town and the trading post, rounded up their captives, and set off back to Detroit and eventually Montreal with scalps and a pile of loot. Pickawillany was left to the blowflies, the buzzards, and its dogs.[1]

Shock waves spread out in all directions, changing the alliances and attitudes of Indian nations great and small, revising the imperial policies of the French, and rattling the colonies of Pennsylvania and Virginia. In the Old Dominion the news was received with special alarm because Virginians believed that Pickawillany had stood in their own colony. Virginia's charter claimed its borders ran west to the Pacific and northwest to, in theory, the Bering Strait. The hundreds of traders dealing with the Indians of the Ohio Country had been mostly Pennsylvanians, and Virginians had begun to take steps to counter the "invasion" of Virginia territory by men from the other province.

Now French-allied Indians had taken matters into their own hands, and this was interpreted in Virginia as foreboding a French invasion of the Old Dominion. What should be done about that? The colony's leaders considered that question for more than a year until they settled on a solution. Implementing that decision fell upon the shoulders of an energetic and ambitious young man—really little more than a boy. His name was George Washington.

CHUISING RATHER TO SLEEP IN THE OPEN AIR

(1732–1753)

The imagination of a boy is healthy, and the mature imagination of a man is healthy; but there is a space of life between, in which the soul is in a ferment, the character undecided, the way of life uncertain, the ambition thicksighted.

—JOHN KEATS

The expedition had turned into an utter disaster. Men ashore and those in transports off Cartagena, on the northern shore of South America, were dying as fast as their bodies could be thrown to the sharks, the easiest way to dispose of the corpses. It was not supposed to be like this. The fleet was commanded by a proven winner, the bad-tempered but capable Admiral Edward "Old Grog" Vernon, who had captured Portobello, Panama, in November 1739. The trouble was, he commanded only the fleet. The army it carried was led at first by Major General Charles, Viscount Cathcart, who dropped dead in December 1740. He was succeeded by the pigheaded Brigadier Thomas Wentworth, a mediocrity who had risen in the British army thanks to connections and enough money to buy a commission.

The present war was an outgrowth of a colonial dispute between Britain and Spain in the Caribbean, which started when a Spanish ship stopped a British merchantman skippered by Robert Jenkins, who lost an ear in a fight with the boarding party. The War of Jenkins' Ear gave London an excuse to pluck some wealth from the Spanish Empire. After Portobello, Cartagena should fall easily under the Union Jack, and then the big prize: Havana, Cuba.

London had ordered the colonial governors in North America to raise a regiment of volunteers commanded by American officers to reinforce the regulars. Volunteers, however, did not exactly flock to the king's colors. Virginia provided 400 men in four companies: vagabonds, drunkards, thieves, highwaymen, and convicts, the dregs of society more or less forced into service to get rid of them. Wentworth inspected the 3,000 Americans in Jamaica in January 1741 and described them as "all the banditry the colonies afford." They were a dirty lot, undisciplined and sometimes mutinous, and shabby; very few had anything resembling a uniform.

Still, the brigadier thought they had potential under the right leadership, as redcoat privates were notorious for being the same sort of material. If the men served under regular officers, they might amount to something. But the ragamuffin colonials would have no part of it; they liked their own officers and refused to serve under any others. Wentworth decided that they would play no role in the campaign, but instead of sending them home or leaving them in Jamaica, he took them along when the expedition sailed for Cartagena in February 1741.

The fleet carried about 8,000 regulars and marines along with the Americans. The redcoats went ashore in March, invested the harbor's fort, then bogged down while Vernon and Wentworth wrangled over how to proceed. Sunstroke, malaria, and other tropical killers felled men one after the other. Finally, on April 9, Wentworth launched an attack that was so poorly conducted, the Spanish defenders shot it to pieces. The redcoats retreated, leaving behind 700 of their own to feed the local insects. They returned to the transports, where the idle Americans had also been dying en masse. Then the *vómito negro* ("black vomit," or yellow fever) paid its annual visit to the region.

The expedition returned to Jamaica with only about 2,000 redcoats and 1,000 Americans still present and fit for duty. Two-thirds of some regiments were dead, including dozens of officers. "Our regiment has not recd that treatment we expected," a Virginia captain wrote home in May 1741, "but I am resolved to persivere in the undertaking. War is horrid in fact, but much more so in imagination; we there learn'd to live on ordinary diet, to watch much, & disregard the noise, or shot of cannon." He glossed over the fact that his men had not died fighting but instead doing nothing aboard ship.

Along with the other survivors of the catastrophe, this captain returned home during the summer of 1742. His name was Lawrence Washington, and he had a younger brother who welcomed him as a conquering hero.[1]

He Knew Little of His Father

Lawrence's brother was born February 22, 1732, at Popes Creek Plantation, a snow-covered tobacco farm beside a wide, glittering tributary of the lower Potomac River in Virginia, and was christened George Washington. He was part of the fourth generation of Washingtons in Virginia, reaching back to 1657. His male forebears were an ambitious lot, each an orphan who expanded his estate through talent and hard work, only to die young and leave something for his own orphans.[2]

George's father, Augustine, had continued that pattern after his father died in 1698, when "Gus" was four years old. He grew up to buy Popes Creek Plantation, another called Epsewasson upriver, and Ferry Farm across the Rappahannock from an iron mine he had bought near Fredericksburg. He married in 1715 and produced three sons (one of whom died an infant) and a daughter before his wife died in 1729. He remarried in 1731, to Mary Ball, who gave him four sons and a daughter.

The first was George, a stocky little fellow with reddish brown hair and blue eyes. He took after his father. One of Augustine's friends remembered that Gus presented a "noble appearance, and most manly proportions, with the extraordinary development of muscular power for which his son was afterward so remarkable." Gus had a reputation "for the mildness, courtesy, and amiability of his manners," the friend continued. His strength was legendary, because he could pick up and load into a wagon a "mass of iron that two ordinary men could barely raise from the ground." He may have stamped his physique on his son but little else. Years later George told an interviewer that "he knew little of his father, other than a remembrance of his person, and of his parental fondness."[3]

That vague impression was owing to the fact that Augustine was a mostly absentee father; his first wife died when he was on a trip to England to round up backing for the iron mine. He was a nervous businessman, devoted to land speculation, prone to inviting lawsuits, and, as the years went on, increasingly hesitant and a procrastinator. He also deprived his younger children of a stable home. The family moved from Popes Creek to Epsewasson before George was three; there Gus built a story-and-a-half timber farmhouse on the foundations of an earlier structure. Within another three years, with the iron mine showing signs of playing out, Gus decided he needed to be on site if the operation stood any chance at all. So he bought 260 acres and leased about 300 more on the Rappahannock near the mine, called the land Ferry Farm, and moved his family there in 1738. He built yet another timber farmhouse, four rooms below, two above, ample but crowded, and definitely not elegant.[4]

This repeated shifting, followed by George's own wandering during his teen years, may help to explain his fierce attachment to Mount Vernon once it became his. In the meantime, he gained a stable prop in his life in 1738 as the family was settling into Ferry Farm. His older half brother, Lawrence, age twenty, returned home from school in England, a model of grace, bearing, and manners. George was just six, but Lawrence became his instant hero, and others noticed that from the outset he emulated his brother.

Lawrence was a tall, dark, handsome young man who soon established a reputation in Virginia as likable, a genuine intellectual beyond his schooling, with good political sense but average business sense. He was properly deferential to his social betters and courteous to inferiors, the model of a Virginia gentleman. He had a lantern jaw, an oval face, big eyes, a curved mouth, and a high, broad brow. His thin neck and shoulders suggested weakness, but he was really very strong. He preferred horses to books, yet he was a cultured man who gave off an impression of wide learning.[5]

Lawrence did not stay at Ferry Farm long, because he went off to war in 1740, leaving George consumed by loneliness. When he returned in 1742, he established himself at Epsewasson overlooking the Potomac. It was destined to be his inheritance anyway, and it needed attention. Lawrence renamed the estate Mount Vernon, in honor of Admiral Vernon. George visited as often as he could, soaking in his brother's tales of exotic places, the roar of cannons, and the incompetence of British generals and their disdain for provincials. Lawrence became adjutant of the Virginia militia, confirming his brother's notions that he was a great military hero. Then calamity struck.

Even by the age of eleven, George had developed a pattern of staying away from home—meaning his domineering mother—as much as he could, visiting Lawrence and other relatives far and wide. In April 1743 he was with cousins on the lower Potomac when a messenger rode up with news that his father was suddenly very sick. By the time George reached Ferry Farm on April 12, his father was stretched out on a bed pending his burial. He may have been an absentee parent, but his sudden loss left an emptiness in George's life, a vacuum that needed to be filled.[6]

Augustine's will was probated in May. He left behind 10,000 acres of land in seven tracts, forty-nine slaves, and the iron mine. Lawrence, as the eldest son, got the lion's share, including Epsewasson and the mine. George's other half brother, Augustine, gained title to Popes Creek Plantation. George's part included Ferry Farm, half a tract of 4,360 worthless acres on Deep Run, three town lots in Fredericksburg, and one-fifth interest in the residuary estate, divided among his mother, Mary, and her four sons. George and the others should receive control of their property when they turned twenty-one. As it turned out, George battled his own mother for three decades to get what belonged to him.[7]

Let Your Countenance Be Pleasant
but in Serious Matters Somewhat Grave

This was not Washington's only conflict with his mother. When Gus died, she had five children still at Ferry Farm. George was the eldest, and his hopes for education in England were dashed by his father's death. Mary would not have let him leave anyway, because from the time they were born she scarcely let the children out of sight, forbidding them from playing or doing chores farther than she could see them.

Mary Washington was a large, uneducated, frenetic woman with a foul mouth and an explosive temper; George probably inherited his own temper from her. She was also selfish and tyrannical. She lived into George's presidency and gave every sign of being jealous of his fame. She made it widely known that she felt herself neglected when he was off fighting wars or governing the country.

She was once seen in Fredericksburg standing up in her carriage, beating her driver (a slave) with a whip, cursing him in language that would shame a sailor, for allegedly mishandling his horse. She made Washington's home life a terror. One of his cousins called her "the presiding genius of her well-ordered household, commanding and being obeyed." He added that he was "ten times more afraid" of her than he was of his own parents. When she was around, the boys, including George, "proper tall fellows," were all "mute as mice." George found every excuse to stay away from her. With Lawrence's help, he even looked into joining the Royal Navy as a midshipman, but Mary put a stop to that.[8]

Mary Washington's tyranny aside, Ferry Farm was typical of those Virginia farms whose owners occupied the midlevel of the colony's social pyramid. The interior walls were whitewashed, but there were no pictures. There was, however, one mirror, a rare luxury in those days. The inventory at Gus's death listed eleven leather-bottomed chairs, two tables, and one armchair. For meals there was plenty of china of modest value but no silver plate. Besides the four bedrooms housing eight beds, the parlor provided space for three more beds and storage. The meals were heavy on johnnycake and meat, with garden produce in season; everything eaten was grown on the property. The consumption of rum, beer, and wine was heavy—normal for the age and something Washington continued all his life.[9]

The atmosphere was more inviting at Mount Vernon, where Lawrence was building a new house. Lawrence more or less adopted George as a son, so the boy was welcome at his place. Social graces were always on display, along with books and a growing stock of fine furnishings. Lawrence's next-door neighbor William Fairfax, master of Belvoir Plantation, was a frequent guest, and George soaked up their conversations about war and the future. They talked about their hopes of extending Virginia to the west beyond the Blue Ridge Mountains, aiming to get rich together speculating in frontier lands. Lawrence's prospects brightened in 1743, when he married Fairfax's daughter Anne, pretty and vivacious, a charming hostess, and thus established his connection to one of the Old Dominion's great fortunes and its political power.[10]

George became a frequent guest at Belvoir and fell under the tutelage of William Fairfax. William was first cousin to Thomas Fairfax, sixth baron Fairfax of Cameron, born in 1693 and the proprietor, by royal grant, of the entire Northern Neck of Virginia (the area between the Potomac and Rappahannock rivers), along with other lands to the west, about 5 million acres in all. His claims faced constant attack by the Virginia legislature, which objected to one man's controlling so much of the colony's patrimony. Lord Fairfax fought his challengers at a distance until 1735, when he moved to Virginia. In 1747 he built a "castle" in the Shenandoah Valley and hired surveyors to perfect his claims. He was a case study in British aristocratic eccentricity because he had only two passions: He hated all women, and he loved horses. He was a bulky man with a thoughtful face that belied his peculiar notions. He dressed as a buckskinned frontiersman when he was at his own place, but when he visited Belvoir he was a model of English dress and deportment. William Fairfax, two years older than his cousin, had experience in the army and royal appointments in the colonies, and he was a proven administrator. In 1734 he accepted His Lordship's offer to manage his Virginia properties. He built Belvoir in 1741.

William took an instant liking to George and dedicated considerable energy to watching over the boy's development. He was a dignified, fatherly man, of middling height and build, whose elegant ways masked the fact that he was one of the most powerful political forces in the colony. George soon realized that the Fairfaxes were a clan he should cultivate if he wanted to get ahead.

Washington also became fast friends with George William Fairfax, William's English-educated son and heir, just seven years older than himself. He was slightly built, with a square jaw, a hooked Roman nose, deep, wide-set dark eyes, and an unusually dark (for an Englishman) complexion. This sparked rumors that he was mulatto, his mother being born in the Bahamas, which may have contributed to his relative timidity compared to the rest of his family. The friendship of the two boys—and that of Washington with the older Fairfaxes—was real. It lasted through the Revolution and beyond, as Washington took over the management of the Fairfax properties after the family returned to England.[11]

Then there was Belvoir itself, the great mansion overlooking the Potomac, just visible from Mount Vernon. It was aristocratic England transplanted to the American wilderness—the materials, workmen, and splendid furnishings all brought over from the old country. In contrast to Ferry Farm's parlor, which served as an extra bedroom, that at Belvoir was a large room filled with expensive mahogany and plush furniture and dominated by an enormous mirror above the mantel. Washington described the house as "of brick, two stories high, with four convenient rooms and a large passage on the lower floor; five rooms and large passage on the second; servant's hall and cellar below." It was the centerpiece of a large and productive complex that included offices, stables, and a coach house. A "large and well-furnished garden" yielded "a great variety of fruits all in good order."[12]

Washington wanted to live like that, in a splendid house adorned with splendid decor, inhabited by people with impeccable manners and an air of natural superiority. He also wanted to dress as well as the Fairfaxes, their garments tailor-made in England, and so he became meticulous about his appearance. Proper dress and grooming contributed to the commanding presence and air of dignity—some said nobility—that so impressed everyone who saw him in his later career.[13]

Lawrence and William set out to turn young George into a member of Virginia's ruling class. There were two avenues to follow: formal education and social grooming. Schooling in England was foreclosed by Augustine's death—the family did not have enough money for that—and there were limited opportunities in Virginia, especially in the isolated Northern Neck. Washington attended a country school for a while, and Lawrence hired a tutor who did not stay long. His education in the formal sense was over by the time he was fifteen, its most notable influence a solid grounding in mathematics, especially geometry and trigonometry. Otherwise, supported by the libraries at Mount Vernon and Belvoir, and with guidance from his brother and William Fairfax, Washington established his lifelong habit as a self-educator. Virginia grandees were greatly influenced by the classics, especially the Romans, and Washington read such works as the *Morals* of Seneca. That first-century Stoic emphasized the virtues of sacrifice, along with courage, persistence, and self-control; he called anger "the most outrageous, brutal, dangerous, and intractable of all passions." Given Washington's volcanic temper, he took that to heart.

Another influence was Joseph Addison's play *Cato*, about the Roman republican who chose suicide over bowing to the will of Caesar, a lesson about service and devotion to one's country. Washington saw it performed several times in later life, and he often quoted from it. It is also likely that during this period he first read Caesar's *Commentaries on the Wars in Gaul*, a readable adventure in its own right, which in the eighteenth-century was regarded by military men as a valuable treatise on their art. Along with British literature and other classics, Lawrence and William steered George's reading to inspire him to emulate Roman models of patriotism and virtue, so he would know the public responsibilities of landed gentry and the nobility of character expected of a man of high station. This was not scholarly learning so much as training for aristocratic leadership.[14]

Lawrence and Fairfax also gave George copybook exercises, which produced the most famous work in his childish hand, copied from *The Rules of Civility & Decent Behaviour in Company and Conversation*, a boy's guide to good manners. It had been assembled in the previous century by Jesuits providing guidance to young French nobles, and in translation it served British nobles and American would-be nobility. The rules began: "Every action done in company ought to be with some sign of respect to those that are present." They continued through decent comportment ("In the presence of others, sing not to yourself with a humming noise nor drum with your fingers or feet"; and "Kill not vermin, as fleas, lice, ticks, etc., in the sight of others") and such subjects as table manners ("Cleanse not your teeth with the tablecloth"), to general instructions on treating people considerately. George learned to show deference to superiors and kindness to inferiors. As for those in the middle, "Keep to the fashion of your equals." And there was this: "Let your countenance be pleasant but in serious matters somewhat grave," advice Washington followed his whole life.[15]

That Washington took these rules to heart there is no doubt; in later years he often coined or repeated maxims when he advised the young. Not as well known was another copybook exercise aimed at preparing him for the practical aspects of being an aristocrat. This was "Forms of Writing," from which he copied templates for twenty-eight legal or financial documents, including a receipt for a hogshead of tobacco, a land patent, a warrant, a bail bond, a contract between a master and an indentured servant, and something else useful in his family tradition, "a general release by a minor to the administrators of his father's estate." It was not a complete education in the law, but it was as much as a gentleman might need.[16]

Washington was clearly driven by social ambition by the time he reached his teens. He learned that he must above all aim to earn his country's honor if he wanted to advance. This was not just a matter of behaving properly, but of being approved of by honorable gentlemen. Getting rich or owning a lot of land would not elevate him to the top. He had to earn the respect of those already there.

The top was where the rulers were in Virginia's stratified society, and subjects were below. The upper class indulged in various rituals to reinforce the principle that hierarchy was the natural order of things. The notion of honor, Washington discovered, applied only to white gentlemen, not to women, poor whites, or slaves; these were all regarded as irresponsible and childlike, so their betters should look after them as fathers would. Hence, only the top tier of Virginia society should hold sway in public affairs.

The Virginia gentleman saw himself as independent on his estate, lord over his tenants, servants, slaves, and women. From that base he could assume political office and power, and that was what young Washington aimed for: enough land and wealth to join that rarefied circle, buttressed by an honorable reputation however earned. He did not yet realize, however, that the Virginia aristocracy was more dominated by outside powers, especially British politicians and businessmen, than its denizens could admit. Washington was preparing to take high place in a dream world.[17]

Part of what he had to learn to enter the upper reaches of society was how to control the explosive temper he had inherited from his mother. He cultivated a sternly reserved manner, bordering on iciness, and trained himself (with only partial success) to not take public offense at what others said or did. He wanted to be admired, respected by honorable men, but outside of his small circle he did not crave popularity.

He acquired another skill during this period. Thanks to the stables at Mount Vernon he became a superb horseman; several observers in later years called him the best they had ever seen. This ability was improved further when Fairfax imported a pack of foxhounds, and Washington developed a passion for foxhunting. He seemed to come by his equestrian talents almost naturally. His wife's grandson related a family yarn about how he overcame a "fierce and ungovernable" horse. When George leaped aboard, the horse began bucking ferociously, and onlookers feared the rider would be killed. However, "the gallant horse, summoning all his powers to one mighty effort, reared, and plunged with tremendous violence, burst his noble heart, and died in an instant." Washington usually took good care of his animals, and the grandson's tale evoked one about the boy who became Alexander the Great, but it might have been true.[18]

As his education continued, Washington underwent a teenage growth spurt, almost reaching his final rawboned height of six foot three. He was shaving by the age of sixteen, and already he showed signs of becoming a clothes horse. In the parlor at Belvoir he became adept at the card games whist and loo (his favorite, and he usually won) and billiards, and in 1748 he also took dancing lessons. But he knew he had much yet to learn. He was still a boy, but close enough to manhood to begin looking for an honorable profession to support himself and his ambitions. William Fairfax pointed the way.[19]

There Was Neither a Cloth Upon the Table nor a Knife to Eat With

Fairfax needed a surveyor, and he would continue to need one for the foreseeable future. The royal grant of land to the Fairfaxes had been a source of contention since it was made in 1649. As Virginia's population and its hunger for "unimproved" lands grew in the eighteenth century, the dispute only became more bitter. However, land-hungry grandees might cease their battle with the Fairfaxes if they could get access to other lands in the west, leaping over the Fairfax proprietary claims.

In 1744, the Virginia government sent a delegation to a conference at Lancaster, Pennsylvania, involving the governments of Pennsylvania and Maryland and delegates from the Six Nations of the Iroquois League. This was the culmination of eight years of negotiations between Pennsylvania and the Iroquois, founded on a claim in the Treaty of Utrecht in 1713 that the Iroquois were subjects of the British crown. They never accepted that, but over the decades they had worked out a "Covenant Chain" of understandings with royal authorities in New York that was just short of an alliance. The British acknowledged Iroquois claims to sovereignty over—and hence to being spokesmen for—the Shawnees, Delawares, and several other nations they claimed as clients, who in turn refused to accept that status.

By the terms of the bargain worked out in 1744, Virginia granted the Iroquois the right to pass through the province to make war against the Cherokees and Catawbas of South Carolina, a deal sweetened by a hefty diplomatic gift. In return, the Iroquois ceded all the League's lands within Pennsylvania, Maryland, and Virginia; the lands the Iroquois ceded belonged to other nations. Moreover, the Iroquois intended to surrender to Virginia only lands in the Shenandoah Valley, believing that Virginia's boundaries extended no farther. The Virginians, on the other hand, interpreted the cession to include lands beyond the Allegheny Mountains, in particular those in the Ohio Valley.

The Treaty of Lancaster was a swindle all around. When the Ohio Indians learned of it, they were outraged. So were the French, who had their own claims to the disputed lands. But it was a happy event for Lord Fairfax and other land-hungry Virginia aristocrats. In 1745 the King's Council (the upper house of the Virginia assembly) recognized the Fairfax land grant in its entirety and shortly began making expansive grants of Ohio lands to syndicates of grandees.[20]

No gentlemen at the time foresaw trouble emerging from these developments. Instead, they spied opportunity. Virginia's gentry depended on land speculation, because the mainstay of their economy—tobacco growing—mined the land, leaving it nearly sterile. Virginia planters typically ignored the English custom of primogeniture and entail: the passing on of estates undivided to only the eldest sons. Eldest sons, such as Lawrence Washington, did get the major parts of estates, but most gentry passed on some land and slaves to younger offspring, as happened with George.

The need to find unimproved land to replace that worn out by tobacco—not to mention places to keep slaves productively employed—the dividing of estates among younger sons, and the growth of the population created a demand for new lands. Since getting a land grant required approval by the governor and Council, wealthier Virginians cultivated political influence by holding offices in new counties and getting themselves elected to the House of Burgesses, the lower house of the assembly. From those positions they could gain vast grants of royal lands for fairly small sums, providing they promised to settle farmers on their new holdings. This in turn meant collecting rents and selling off both improved and unimproved plots. Steady acquisition of large landholdings, therefore, provided a more reliable source of wealth and future income than farming alone.

There was a catch: All grants and purchases had to be platted by a licensed surveyor who was paid according to an official schedule of fees, or the claims could not be recorded and patented. Surveyors had no trouble collecting their fees, because without their plats and reports the speculators' claims were worthless. Moreover, surveyors in newly opened lands were ahead of the market when it came to finding the best properties, and therefore they could acquire lands of their own. Surveying, accordingly, was a respectable, honorable, and rewarding occupation. Small wonder that Lawrence encouraged George to take it up.[21]

Augustine Washington had been a surveyor, and George had access to his father's instruments: a circumferentor (an eighteenth-century predecessor of the theodolite and an expensive precision instrument), chains, drawing boards and instruments, and so on. He began taking lessons from local surveyors as early as 1746 and passed his first tests on simple tasks on August 18, 1747. Soon he passed more complicated ones, and he worked as an assistant to licensed surveyors, for the first time in his life earning pocket money.[22]

In March 1748, William Fairfax hired James Genn, surveyor of Prince William County, to plat some of the Fairfax lands in the Shenandoah Valley. The party included two chainmen, a marker, and a pilot. Washington and George William Fairfax tagged along, their roles not specified, but there was always something for extra hands to do. Washington recorded this journey in the first of his diaries, a habit he continued for the rest of his life.[23]

It was a grand adventure, and Washington not only learned more about surveying but also that he loved being in wild country. It was a rough trip, over a month in cold, early spring weather, and the sixteen-year-old enjoyed almost every minute of it. The first day the party covered forty miles on horseback, and the next day it crossed the Blue Ridge to the Shenandoah River. "Nothing remarkable happen'd," he recorded. The journal filled up with descriptions of the landscape, especially its agricultural potential. Already his eye was that of a land speculator.

There was a lot of hard work in cold, wet weather. On March 15, after an especially rough day, the party stayed in a squatter's shack. "I not being so good a woodsman as the rest of my company," Washington said, he stripped himself "very orderly" and went to his bed "as they call'd it," which turned out to be "nothing but a little straw—matted together without sheets or any thing else but only one thread

bear blanket with double its weight of vermin such as lice fleas &c."
Predictably, he was glad to get up, put on his clothes, and join his
companions on the bare floor. He vowed that he would not again
sleep indoors, "chuising rather to sleep in the open air before a fire."
But the next night the party stayed in Frederick, where they had a
good dinner with "wine & rum punch in plenty & a good feather bed
with clean sheets which was a very agreeable regale."

Unexpected events made the trip an adventure. After traveling
up the upper Potomac on "the worst road that ever was trod by man
or beast" on March 21, there followed two days of heavy rain. When
the sky cleared on the afternoon of the 23rd, the party was "agreeably surpris'd at the sight of thirty odd Indians coming from war with
only one scalp." They gave them some liquor, "elevating there springs
[and] put them in the humour of dauncing of whom we had a war
dauncing." The Indians performed a circle dance choreographed in
advance by a "speaker." Washington called it "comicle."

The party trudged on, fording swollen rivers and cursing the
wretched weather. On the 26th, the surveyors were invited to supper
by a justice of the peace of Frederick County. "When we came to supper," said the horrified youngster, "there was neither a cloth upon the
table nor a knife to eat with but as good luck would have it we had
knives of [our] own." Belvoir this backwoods judge's house was not.

So young Washington was a snob. He showed greater disdain a
few days later when he encountered German settlers on the South
Branch of the Potomac. He called them "as ignorant a set of people
as the Indians." They would "never speak English but when spoken
to they speak all Dutch [German]." The weather was the worst burden of the journey, however. April 2 ended with a "blowing & rainy
night. Our straw catch'd a fire that we were laying upon & was luckily
preserv'd by one of men awaking." The next night was worse, "much
more blostering . . . we had our tent carried quite of[f] with the wind
and was obliged to lie the latter part of the night without covering."
The tent blew away again on April 4, and so it went until the group
headed home. "This day," said the last entry in the journal, "see a
rattled snake the first we had seen in all our journey."

Washington was hooked on the surveyor's life. His background
in mathematics was reflected in his survey plats and later drawings
for forts to be constructed on the frontier. Neat, clear, free of distractions, they reveal him as a born engineer. He continued training

under established surveyors and gained experience supervising others, usually older than he was but of a lower social status.

A stroke of fortune hit in May 1749 when the Virginia assembly appointed trustees to oversee the establishment of a port city at Bellhaven near the head of navigation on the Potomac; the new city would be named Alexandria. Three Fairfaxes were among the trustees, and they wanted to get the town platted and sold quickly. The surveyor was John West Jr., but the Fairfax connection made Washington West's assistant, and he actually did most of the work. By the middle of July Washington had platted the town, and the lots went on the market. Then on July 31, Washington accepted appointment as the surveyor of Culpeper County, after receiving his commission from the president and masters of the College of William and Mary and swearing the required oath. He began earning more money than he had ever seen, enough within a year to buy his first plantation, a thousand acres in two parcels on Bullskin Creek in the Shenandoah.

Further acquisitions followed as Washington surveyed furiously for profit. And profit there should be, because his principal client, thanks to William Fairfax, promised to be the Ohio Company of Virginia, which had grand ideas about opening the west.[24]

His Movements and Gestures Are Graceful, His Walk Majestic

Lawrence Washington, William Fairfax, and other Virginians began talking as early as 1747 about forming a "company of gentlemen and adventurers," as joint-stock corporations were called, to speculate in Ohio lands and take the Indian fur trade away from the French and the Pennsylvanians. Lawrence brought his brother Augustine and other Virginians into the deal, while Fairfax became a silent partner, his son George William representing the family. What they aimed at required royal authority, so the Virginians brought prominent Londoners into the picture, in particular the three Hanbury brothers, who were rich merchants, and the duke of Bedford, who had an in at court. Thomas Lee of Virginia was the first president of the company, and before it formally came into existence its members already included others bearing names to reckon with in the colony. When a new lieutenant governor, Robert Dinwiddie, arrived from England in 1751, he also received a seat at the table.

John Hanbury presented the petition of the Ohio Company of Virginia at court in London on January 11, 1749, seeking a grant of 200,000 acres and asking for another 300,000 if the company met the terms of the original grant. The terms were to settle 100 families in the requested lands, "free of quit rent [a feudal fee for occupation of land] for ten years" on condition that they erected a fort and maintained a garrison to protect the settlement. Hanbury passed shares in the company around in the right places, so this offer was too good for the crown to pass up, promising reward at home while the Virginians bore any risk. On March 16 the Privy Council recommended granting the petition, the king agreed, and the acting governor of Virginia, William Good, was instructed to transfer to the company 200,000 acres "to the westward of the great mountains within the colony of Virginia." Good made the transfer on July 12, 1749.[25]

At the same time, Good and his Council made another grant of Ohio lands to the Loyal Company, whose investors included John Robinson, speaker of the House of Burgesses. As always in Virginia, one faction or another used the power of government to feather its own nest. But other Virginians were not the Ohio Company's biggest challenge, because it faced competition from the well-established network of Pennsylvania Indian traders in the Ohio Valley, objections from the government of New France, and most of all resistance from Delaware (Leni-Lenape) Indians who did not much care for the idea of English settlements in their territory.

The Ohio Company had naively believed that it could take over the west on the cheap, building a trading storehouse at Wills Creek, Maryland, across the Potomac from the Shenandoah Valley, and a fort at the "Forks of the Ohio" (present-day Pittsburgh), where the Allegheny and Monongahela join to form the Ohio River. The flock of hoped-for settlers did not materialize, and securing advanced posts would require investments in fortifications and armed men, not to mention diplomatic gifts to the Indians.

Faced down by the Delawares, the company postponed going as far as the Forks and settled on a strong storehouse at Wills Creek. Pennsylvania traders and French agents may have played some role, but the Delawares were masters of their own fate. They had already been cheated out of much of their lands in eastern Pennsylvania, and they quite reasonably interpreted the company's plans as an invasion and potential loss of what remained to them. "Those very Indians that had encouraged [the company] at first," Thomas Lee complained, "had been persuaded that our design was to ruin, not to trade with them; and such a spirit of jealousy is raised among them that without a treaty and presents we shall not be able to do anything with them." That was part and parcel of Indian diplomacy, but either the company leaders did not understand that, or they were too stingy to follow established customs. A discouraged Lee gave up the Ohio Company presidency in 1750, handing it to Lawrence Washington.[26]

Virginia politics also complicated anything these "adventurers" wanted to do. Landowners elected the House of Burgesses, which in turn elected most of the members of the King's Council; in effect, picking the most powerful members of the gentry to cooperate with the governor in running the colony.

In reality there was no governor, except in name. The governorship was a sinecure for high nobles fluttering around the British throne. The earl of Albemarle held that position from 1737 to 1754, when he resigned to become ambassador to France; he was succeeded by Lord Loudoun. Neither ever set foot in the colony. The lieutenant governor, therefore, held the reins of power, or as much power as the burgesses did not snatch from him. He bought his office from the nominal governor but received a salary of £2,000 and perquisites of £400, along with a brick house in Williamsburg grandly called the "governor's palace." He had many titular powers, among them serving as "commander-in-chief and vice-admiral" of the colony, and appointed all but the lowest militia officers, but he did not have authority to declare war. The lieutenant governor could extract fees and kickbacks from his official duties, but he was in a constant struggle with the burgesses, who jealously guarded their power of taxation.[27]

The Ohio Company had received its grant during a power vacuum. Long-time lieutenant governor Sir William Gooch died in June 1749 and was succeeded by local officials acting in the position. Robert Dinwiddie bought the post from Albemarle in July 1751 and arrived in Williamsburg in November. Born in Scotland in 1693, he prospered there as a merchant before becoming an imperial bureaucrat in a succession of royal offices in Bermuda and on the American mainland. He knew how to make money, and it showed in his amply padded frame and heavily brocaded, elegantly tailored London suits. His face had an unusually high and broad forehead, balanced at the other end by multiple chins, between which sat a straight mouth reflecting his determination to have his way, a long nose, and deep-set, almost philosophical gray eyes closely guarded by curving eyebrows. It was the face of a man who liked to eat, accented by apple cheeks. He favored gray court periwigs, an English fashion going out of favor in America.[28]

Dinwiddie could be a gruff man, and he guarded his prerogatives, so he had one conflict after another with the House of Burgesses, which he usually prorogued (dismissed) if it did not do his bidding. A newcomer who failed to fit into the existing high society, he was often accused of favoring fellow Scots too much in patronage, appointments, and contracts. Yet he stayed in office until poor health sent him home late in 1757, and he kept Virginia afloat financially through its first foreign war.

One dispute persisted throughout his years in the colony. He discovered early on that men of influence received "orders" from the King's Council issuing land patents in a manner that dodged the required fee for the patent and for quitrent on the land; there were also cases where some of Virginia's finest gamed this system to swindle less fortunate men out of their land. The lieutenant governor was entitled by law to a fee of one pistole (a small gold coin) for validating each patent. This was one of his office's most rewarding benefits, so Dinwiddie demanded that a patent be issued when orders were approved, and that he be paid the authorized fee for each patent he signed and validated with the colony's seal. This position put him into extended and almost violent conflict with burgesses involved in speculation, often interrupting the colony's business.[29]

Washington steered mostly clear of the muddy little village of Williamsburg while he was building an estate that would let him run for a seat in the Burgesses, for which he would first be legally old enough in 1753. His hoped-for surveys in the Ohio Company land grant were frustrated by the failure of the company to establish itself there. Still, William Fairfax had plenty for him to do, and he continued surveying and staking claims of his own in the Shenandoah Valley. He hated the settlers he dealt with, calling them "a parcel of barbarians . . . an uncouth set of people." He was still a snob where the "lower" classes were concerned. So he tended to his own affairs, making enough money to loan some to relatives and to necessitate the start of the financial ledgers he would compile for the rest of his life.[30]

Pursuing a high place in society might consume his consciousness, but Washington was still a boy. Everything old was new to the adolescent, hence confusing. One of life's facts that came upon him at this time was sex. The other was death, still frightening after the loss of his father.

Sex reared its lovely head late in 1748, when Washington was sixteen, in the form of George William Fairfax's new bride, Sarah (Sally) Cary, the beautiful eighteen-year-old daughter of one of Virginia's richest families, which had other beautiful daughters and cousins at home in Alexandria. Slim, dark-haired, with a striking long face, rosy cheeks, deep-set eyes, a noble nose, and a wide mouth set in a Mona Lisa smile, she radiated intelligence and sex appeal, making her the object of male attention from a very early age. She was an accomplished flirt—but then, this was the golden age of flirting among the highborn on both sides of the Atlantic. She used her coquetry to dominate the men around her; into old age she was an accomplished tease who enjoyed tormenting as well as manipulating.

Washington suffered his first crush when he saw her. Ever since a 1758 letter to her (discussed below) was discovered in 1877, historians and gossips have speculated that George had an affair with Sally. That seems unlikely—no contemporary evidence suggests such a thing—on several accounts. First, all his life he enjoyed flirting with pretty girls. (He was flirting with Peggy Arnold when her husband, Benedict's, treason came to light in 1780.) Second, in the small society of the Virginia gentry, an affair could not escape notice, and even a hint would generate gossip. Third, the high ethical standards he cultivated would not let him cheat on his friend. Fourth, if all that drove him was an urge to empty his prostate—and with sixteen-year-old boys that is usually what it amounts to—he had the ancient option of self-treatment. And, finally, for a member of the slaveholding class, sexual release was as close as the nearest slave cabin, although evidence that Washington took advantage of that is also lacking.

In fact, Belvoir was always host to pretty girls. Washington occasionally visited the Cary household with its collection of beauties, and in his travels during the 1750s he encountered many other eligible, lovely daughters of his hosts. Washington made halfhearted efforts through the 1750s to court several young women and was not greatly disappointed by his failures. His libido may have been low, or he may have been too shy, or he was so absorbed in his advancement that he could think of little else, or he may have been on the watch for a match that suited his own interests. In any case, it appears that the young Washington simply behaved himself as a gentleman should.[31]

Death crept back into Washington's life more gradually. His brother Lawrence came down with a serious cough in the spring of 1749. When he went to the session of the Burgesses in May, the cough was so violent that the speaker sent him home. Worse, at about the same time the third of his children followed the first two to the grave. Lawrence recovered some, and the next year George took him to some hot springs (now Berkeley Springs, West Virginia) that he had surveyed in 1748. The place was mobbed by other sufferers, and George thought it was too shaded and gloomy, but Lawrence got better. George, meanwhile, spent the time there taking on lucrative surveying jobs, then returned to surveying in Fairfax County.

Lawrence had come down with tuberculosis, which in its early stages can come and go. It returned again in the summer of 1751, and the brothers made another trip to the hot springs, during which time George spent another profitable season surveying and claiming lands. But Lawrence did not recover this time, so in September the two of them went to Barbados. George loved the island but hated ocean travel; while there he came down with smallpox, fortunately a mild case that left only a few scars and gave him immunity to this killer. Later that winter the brothers split up, George returning to Virginia, Lawrence moving to Bermuda. They were together again at Mount Vernon by spring—that is, when George was not out surveying.

Lawrence died on July 26, 1752, leaving behind a daughter and his wife. George became one of six executors of the estate, its affairs so tangled that it took much of the next decade to sort them out. George and his half brother Augustine split the residuary estate. If Lawrence's widow and daughter died, or the daughter if the widow remarried (she did), Mount Vernon and other Fairfax County properties would go to George. He got title to Mount Vernon in 1761.[32]

Washington's continued pursuit of his own interests during his brother's illness did not reflect callousness so much as his drive and ambition. Still, he was orphaned again, deprived of the closest thing to a father he had ever known. There remained his patron William Fairfax, but he had children and concerns of his own, although he offered Washington guidance on every manner of subject for the next decade. Nevertheless, the emptiness that followed Gus's death had returned. Washington was on his own.

He continued his drive to society's top. One step was to join the Freemasons, although he was still a minor and technically ineligible. On November 4, 1752, he was initiated in Fredericksburg Lodge No. 4. He passed his exams on March 3, 1753, and was raised to the Sublime Degree of Master Mason ("Third Degree") on August 4. This was a social organization that every gentleman felt obliged to join. Washington attended only one more meeting in 1753 and another in 1755, and although he remained a member he was inactive until the 1770s. He was more active thereafter, but as with church he seldom attended meetings. His funeral, however, was Masonic.[33]

A more important avenue into Virginia's hierarchy was through the militia. With Fairfax's support, Washington started lobbying for Lawrence's position as adjutant, a supervising inspector, even before his brother died. The colony had spread out far enough that the single adjutancy should be divided among districts. On November 6, the governor and Council established four militia districts. Washington wanted the one for the Northern Neck where he lived, but he had a powerful rival for that post, although the man actually lived in Maryland. The governor gave him instead the southern district, from the James River to the North Carolina line, with pay of £100 per year. This was purely a result of political influence, because Washington had absolutely no military experience, not even in the militia. It was, for him, the honor of the thing.

His commission from the governor, dated December 13, appointed him "major and adjutant of the militia, horse and foot," in ten southern counties. Washington took his oath before the court of Spotsylvania County on February 10, 1753. His duties were not much, as least at first. The governor and Council had ordered a general muster for September, before which the adjutants must exercise the county officers so they could exercise their men. Washington had not the slightest clue what to do and began reading tactical manuals.[34]

George never visited any of the counties in his district that year. Events intervened. News of Pickawillany reached Williamsburg during the early summer of 1752, in the form of letters from the Miami survivors to the governors of Virginia and Pennsylvania asking for help in their struggle against the French. They described themselves as "lost people, fearing that our brothers will leave us, but before we will be subject to the French, or call them our fathers, we will perish here." Pennsylvania, alarmed that its traders had been driven out of the west, voted some monetary assistance but little else. Virginia's government hesitated. Word arrived the following winter that the Miamis had concluded an alliance with the French, and in the spring of 1753 it became known that the French were building forts in the Ohio Country. Rumors spread that Dinwiddie would send an ultimatum to the French, ordering them to leave British territory, so as early as spring (before that decision had been made), Washington showed up in Williamsburg volunteering to deliver the message. He got the job at the end of October.[35]

Who was this young man in the red uniform of a militia major, who thought he could challenge a foreign power? George Mercer, who served with Washington through the 1750s, left a vivid portrait:

> Straight as an Indian, measuring six feet two inches in his stockings and weighing 175 pounds . . . His frame is padded with well-developed muscles, indicating great strength. His bones and joints are large, as are his hands and feet. He is wide shouldered but has not a deep or round chest; is neat waisted, but is broad across the hips and has rather long legs and arms. His head is well-shaped, though not large, but is gracefully poised on a superb neck. A large and straight rather than a prominent nose; blue gray penetrating eyes which are widely separated and overhung by a heavy brow. His face is long rather than broad, with high round cheek bones, and terminates in a good firm chin. He has clear though rather colorless pale skin which burns with the sun. A pleasing and benevolent though a commanding countenance, dark brown hair which he wears in a cue. His mouth is large and generally firmly closed, but which from time to time discloses some defective teeth. His features are regular and placid with all the muscles of his face under perfect control, though flexible and expressive of deep feeling when moved by emotions. In conversation he looks you full in the face, is deliberate, deferential, and engaging. His demeanor at all times composed and dignified. His movements and gestures are graceful, his walk majestic, and he is a splendid horseman.[36]

Two

TWO

THE NATIONS OF
THESE COUNTRIES ARE
VERY ILL-DISPOSED

(1600–1753)

It was a feature peculiar to the colonial wars of North America
that the toils and dangers of the wilderness were to be encountered before the adverse hosts could meet.

—JAMES FENIMORE COOPER

The English believed that North America was a "desert," which before
the nineteenth century meant an uninhabited region, what moderns
call "wilderness." The Indians did not count; or, as a British officer
said in the 1750s, the western lands were "a desolate country uninhabited by anything but wild Indians, bears and rattlesnakes."[1]

The forest was what is now called an oak-hickory type of mixed
hardwoods, with islands of pines. In the eighteenth century it was a
chestnut-oak-hickory type, because the majestic American chestnut,
which became extinct from imported disease during the twentieth
century, was the Emperor of the Forest. There were also American
elm (now extinct), walnut, locust, poplar, laurel, larch, hemlock, and
a dazzling wider array including sugar maple along with the oaks and
hickory. The actual mix of species on any one plot depended on local
environmental conditions. These were mostly old-growth trees that
measured ten and even twenty feet in diameter. Much of the forest

was choked at ground level by thick tangles of understory—much, but
not all. "After quitting that camp we came upon a more open country," Captain Francis Peyton of the Virginia Regiment wrote in 1755,
"and our roads were less difficult, for there was no undergrowth."
Christopher Gist explored beyond the mountains in the early 1750s
and raved about the "good level farming land, with fine meadows"
interrupting the "great thickets."[2]

This rich and varied plantscape supported an equally rich and
varied animal population: bear, deer, woodland buffalo, wolves, wild-
cats, wolverines, groundhogs, beavers, squirrels, turkeys, buzzards, an
astounding variety of songbirds, ducks and geese in season, and great
flocks of passenger pigeons. There were also ticks, flies in wondrous
variety, mites, biting gnats, and other little critters. Algae-covered
ponds breathed out clouds of mosquitoes and dragonflies and hosted
swarms of leeches. The rivers teemed with trout, catfish, sturgeon,
shad, eels, and other edible fish.

This abundant animal life reflected variations in forest cover, with
game animals thriving on the edges of woods growing the kinds of
trees that littered the ground with seeds and nuts. The many "meadows," grassy open areas, kept the forest from being a solid mass of
trees; the extent of meadows was so great that much of the eastern
part of the continent was open. Travelers in the Ohio Valley described
the landscape as "park-like" or "savannah." Meadows were products of
various causes. Beavers felled substantial areas of trees, then flooded
the open space with their dams. Soil conditions, especially moisture,
inhibited tree growth in some places. Violent thunderstorms, including tornadoes, felled great swaths of timber, which after it dried
caught fire; soils baked in such fires might not produce trees for decades, just grass, forbs, and brush.

The principal agents in opening the forests, however, were Indians
who had actively managed the landscape of North America for more
than 10,000 years. Their chief tool was fire, and with it they cultivated
nature as actively as they tended their crops. They had several objects
in view, the chief one in the east being to increase forest-grassland
edges favored by game. Another aim was to clear out underbrush,
promoting the growth of berries that fed man and beast. Burning also
reduced populations of poisonous snakes, ticks, and mosquitoes, and
such annoyances as poison ivy.

Captain Peyton described the change in ground cover he trudged through; he did not understand that he had passed from forest that might be in contention between nations into an active hunting ground. He and other English did not understand the forest, and accordingly they did not understand the Indians. The Indians knew the landscape intimately, and how to use it in warfare.[3]

Pays d'en Haut

Washington knew a little about the geography in 1753 but next to nothing about the history and interests of the people inhabiting it. The century following the "discovery" of America by Christopher Columbus in 1492 devastated the natives, especially through diseases to which the people had no resistance. The population north of the Rio Grande shrank from somewhere between 4 and 16 million to a few hundred thousand by 1600, after which it recovered in part.[4]

The great Mississippian culture that had dominated the Mississippi and Ohio drainages had collapsed, leaving behind new nations engaged in ceaseless warfare with each other. Still, there was by 1600 a general pattern of relatively stable new societies living off a combination of farming, hunting, and gathering, although many of them shifted their locations occasionally. Then non-Hispanic Europeans showed up on the edge of this world and stayed—the French in the northeast, the English southward along the coast. Smallpox and other European plagues drove through the Ohio Valley again, followed by the trade in furs, especially beaver pelts. Indians became increasingly dependent on European manufactured goods, from blankets to pots and weapons. Trade also introduced alcohol and started an arms race in Indian country.[5]

There were wars between Indians and the English and French invaders, with important differences. The numerous English colonists wanted land and viewed the Indians as obstacles, so wars of the seventeenth century became wars of extermination. The English burned Indian towns and crops and killed or enslaved women and children, slaughtering males while they were at it. The aim was to drive the natives away with superior firepower.[6]

The French arrived in fewer numbers, seeking trade more than land, and in the early years they were most interested in spreading their religion. They formed alliances with selected nations but learned that to uphold their side of a partnership they had to help fight their allies' enemies. To avoid getting too embroiled in wars among the Indians, the French presented themselves as mediators, inviting all nations to call them "father," a term in many Indian societies for a respected elder who resolved disputes.[7]

Warfare among some nations was nearly constant, but before white colonization the Indians engaged in highly ritualized conflicts that limited carnage. Usually the goal was to take captives and high-status trophies (scalps or heads) or booty. Especially among Iroquoian-speaking peoples, these were "mourning" wars, aimed at taking captives to replace lost loved ones with the newcomers adopted into the families that held them. The taking of captives also cemented kinship relations among nations. Captives were typically women and children, although not always. Dangerous adult male captives were often tortured to death. This honored them with a chance to demonstrate their bravery and ability to withstand pain, spiritual virtues absorbed by the captors. The pattern of raid and captivity was general all across North America.[8]

There were differences between Indian and white styles of warfare, but the two groups had much in common, and they learned from each other the better to kill each other. The social distinction between them was not as sharp as that between colonials and officials in their home countries.[9]

It was against this background that international rivalry burst into the Ohio Country, what the French called the *pays d'en haut*, or "upper country." By the mid-1700s it encompassed the lands around the Great Lakes except for those near eastern Lake Ontario, which was part of Iroquoia. It included territory north of the Ohio River and westward to the Mississippi River, or *pays des Illinois*. This vast region had been all but depopulated during the 1600s, owing to epidemics and a series of wars launched by the Iroquois League against any nations that did not bow to its will. The Iroquois believed they had a sacred mission to unite the peoples of the world under their system, but they were also materialistic. The conflicts were known as the Beaver Wars, aimed at funneling the fur trade into Iroquoia, whence the Five (later Six) Nations could control all trade with Europeans. Some nations were all but exterminated, and by 1700 the Ohio Country was surrounded by nations with bitter grievances against the Iroquois.[10]

The Iroquois were masters of international power politics. They had maintained a strong trade relationship with New France during the Beaver Wars, but the English made them the focus of their own diplomacy in the northern colonies. They supported Iroquois claims to sovereignty over the Ohio Country by right of conquest. The Iroquois saw the English as a growing rival to French power in America and so adroitly played the two against each other.[11]

They were not alone in this game: Several other nations had discovered that being between the French and English could be profitable, gaining them access to trade goods and gifts from the rival white powers. French or English connections could also free them from Iroquois domination, or so they hoped. Since 1700 the Ohio Country had been repopulating. The Delawares, shoved west from Pennsylvania, the Shawnees, the Mingos (expatriate Iroquois, mostly Senecas), and the Miami Confederation moving in from the Illinois Country had planted themselves in the Ohio Valley, and together the nations defied Iroquois claims to dominance. They often flew both French and British flags over their towns. By the 1740s the region was a stew of contests and struggles between Europeans, European colonies, white traders, various nations, and factions within nations.[12]

The Iroquois felt threatened by the rise of rivals in territory where they claimed sway. They could not depend on the English after the latter interpreted the Treaty of Lancaster in 1744 as an Iroquois cession of the Ohio Country. The French reacted to this land grab by trying to separate the Iroquois League from the English during meetings with Iroquois delegates at Quebec in 1748. The French warned the Indians against becoming "vassals" of the English, while the Indians answered (not altogether honestly) that the English had continually solicited them to "take up the hatchet against the French, which they constantly refused to do," and that they had not ceded their lands to anyone. The French concluded that the Iroquois would not fight for their interests, so they must rule Ohio themselves.[13]

The Iroquois remained formidable, so both the French and the English, via their agents Joncaire Chabert and Sir William Johnson, continued negotiations with them. Mostly, each side told the Indians how evil the other side was. Johnson complained to New York governor George Clinton about the "confounded wicked things the French had infused into the Indians' heads," including the charge that the English "were determined, the first opportunity, to destroy them all." Joncaire said much the same to his superiors about the devious *Anglais*.[14]

As Washington would soon discover, few Englishmen could speak any of the huge variety of Indian tongues. The French had many Canadian officers and *métis* who were fluent in the local dialects, but interpreters for the English were scarce. "As to the interpreting, tis most extream bad," complained a British officer in 1754; "at best the interpreter is a most extream stupid, ignorant & illeterate person." Yet the Indians expected the colonists to provide interpreters as a sign of respect; many nations asserted superiority by forcing the other side to speak a foreign language. The few translators available to the English were men captured young by Indians, or traders who had learned the languages while conducting business.[15]

As You Threaten Us with War in the Spring, We Tell You That We Are Ready

Those very traders drew France and Great Britain to the brink of war in America. About 300 a year were crossing the Appalachian Mountains by the late 1740s. The authorities of New France overreacted, not understanding that English traders did not represent London projecting its power into the Ohio Country. French traders were strictly controlled agents of their government, but English traders were free spirits, packing their goods on horseback over the mountains and going from village to village. They had a low odor in the colonies. "They appear to me to be in general a set of abandoned wretches," Virginia lieutenant governor Robert Dinwiddie sniffed to Pennsylvania governor James Hamilton, who replied, "I concur with you in opinion that they are a very licentious people."[16]

The most aggressive Pennsylvania trader was George Croghan, a steel-hard man of the wilderness, land speculator, merchant, and accomplished diplomat who spoke several Indian languages. In the late 1740s he established a trading post at Logstown down the Ohio from the Forks, then another on the south shore of Lake Erie at present-day Cleveland, then shifted his base to Pickawillany. Since 1727 the French had tolerated an English trading post at Oswego, in Iroquois country on the southeast shore of Lake Ontario, but it had been ineffective in competing with the French-Indian trade. Now the combination of

Oswego and Pickawillany, in the French view, threatened to detach the Ohio Algonquians from the French and attach them to the English and the Iroquois.[17]

Oswego was operated out of New York, and Pickawillany by Pennsylvanians. The French did not appreciate the rivalries among the English colonies, so they were doubly alarmed by the formation of the Ohio Company of Virginia in 1749. The new company quickly built a storehouse at Wills Creek on the Potomac (present-day Cumberland, Maryland). The next year the company commissioned veteran Indian trader Christopher Gist to survey its granted lands.[18]

Gist would become thoroughly familiar with the western lands, and accordingly he was the best choice to conduct Washington into the territory in 1753. His instructions in 1750 ordered him to explore and select sites for farming settlements. They must be "good level land; we had rather go quite down to the Mississippi than take mean, broken land," his employers declared. At Logstown, Gist ran into a "parcel of reprobate Indian traders" from Pennsylvania. At the Wyandot village of Muskingum, he met Croghan, sent by the governor of Pennsylvania to treat with the western Indians. "Croghan," said Gist, "is a mere idol among his countrymen, the Irish traders."

With Croghan was Andrew Montour, grandson of a French officer and an Indian woman; his *métis* mother had been kidnapped and adopted by Iroquois, and he still lived in Iroquoia. His face was "like that of a European," a Moravian missionary said, "but marked with a broad Indian ring of bear's-grease and paint drawn completely round it." Montour was highly respected among several Indian nations, and Gist was delighted when he and Croghan agreed to accompany him down the Ohio and on to Pickawillany. It sat in country that, Gist said, was "fine, rich, level land, well timbered . . . well watered with a great number of little streams and rivulets, full of beautiful natural meadows." A French expedition the previous year had been rebuffed by Miami leader Memeskia, but the Old Maid and his followers greeted Gist's party joyfully, smoked the peace pipe with them, and welcomed them into town with a volley of musketry.

There was a series of councils, and Gist and Croghan distributed gifts and made friendly speeches. The result was a peace treaty between the Miamis and the English. Then four Ottawas showed up from Detroit with brandy and tobacco and an invitation from the French commandant for the Miamis to visit him. Memeskia rose and told the Ottawas to take this message to their French master: "Fathers, we have made a road to the sun-rising, and have been taken by the hand by our brothers the English, the Six Nations, the Delawares, Shawnees, and Wyandots . . . and as you threaten us with war in the spring, we tell you that we are ready to receive you."[19]

The French alliance in Ohio was dead if the Old Maid was taken at his word. This was what the powers in New France had dreaded since the end of the last war with Britain in 1748. The governor based at Quebec, the marquis de Galissonière, like other governors was a naval officer, later famous for his victory over the British fleet near Minorca. A hunchback, he had a fighting spirit and a powerful intellect, and he warned his superiors at Versailles that unless France acted promptly she would lose all of America. He wanted more French settlers and a line of forts to hold back the English. He was ignored, so in 1749 he sent Captain Céleron de Bienville at the head of a party of soldiers, militia, and Indians to the Allegheny River, then down the Ohio and up the Great Miami, to post lead-plate notices declaring that this was French territory.

That message was for the English, as if they would notice. Joncaire Chabert, a French-Iroquois *métis*, went along to win over the Indians. They mostly ran away when the party approached, but Joncaire made a few speeches, warning against the perfidious *Anglais* and urging the nations to stay loyal to the French "father" in Canada. Though the Delawares, Shawnees, Mingos, and others accepted Céleron's gifts, they remained determined to trade with the English. The weak French expedition earned contempt.

Céleron met his final defeat late in the summer at Pickawillany. Memeskia gracefully told him to leave the Ohio Country, so the party struggled back to Montreal. "All I can say," he reported when he got there, "is that the nations of these countries are very ill-disposed towards the French, and devoted entirely to the English." Pickawillany's population grew eightfold over the next two years, becoming one of the greatest Indian towns in the west, a center of English trade and influence and the target of French strategic thinking. Céleron was ordered to Detroit, to expand it into the main French post in the west.[20]

As Céleron made his way there, the marquis de la Jonquière replaced Galissonière as governor general of New France. He was another naval officer with a high reputation, a tall and imposing man with ability and courage, but he was old. Two years later, in 1751,

Robert Dinwiddie took the helm in Virginia. He invested in the Ohio Company and decided to protect its interests by allying with the Six Nations. His delegates met with theirs in 1752, showering the Iroquois with presents. They said they would accept the Treaty of Lancaster and let the Virginians build trading posts on the Ohio. This was too little too late, because affairs in the west had already boiled over.[21]

This Business Troubles Me;
It Robs Me of Sleep; It Makes Me Ill

Events focused on Pickawillany. By the time Céleron passed through, it had become a gathering place for Algonquian and Iroquoian peoples from the whole Ohio Country, most with grudges against the Six Nations, the French, or both. It had a French rival, Fort Miami on the Maumee River, whose commandant complained that "the English spare nothing to keep them [the Indians] and draw away the remainder of those who are here." The French were losing the competition, he reported: "The excessive price of French goods in this post, the great bargains which the English give, as well as the large presents which they make to the tribes, have entirely disposed those tribes in their favor." The English, he charged, "do not cease working to make war on us by means of the Indians and to bring them into a general revolt against the French."[22]

The English traders were simply better businessmen than the French, and war would be bad for business. The French, however, viewed commercial rivalry as war by another name. The government of New France faced an additional burden: interference from the ministry of the marine 4,000 miles away in Versailles, which demonstrated abject ignorance of American realities. In particular, the ministry concluded that the real threat was the fortified trading post at Oswego on Lake Ontario, and it overestimated the willingness of the Iroquois—who traded there—to shed blood for the king of France.

Oswego should be wiped out, the ministry ordered in 1749, but this could not be accomplished directly because France and England were not at war. Instead, Governor Jonquière should get the Iroquois to do the job, "but act with great caution." Versailles prodded the governor again in 1750. He should persuade the Iroquois that Oswego was "opposed to their liberty, and, so to speak, a usurpation by which the English mean to get possession of their lands." But he should exercise "circumspection" and "labor to accomplish it in a manner not to commit himself." As for roving English traders, the ministry advised using every means to fend them off but treat them "with the greatest politeness."[23]

The governor did what his budget allowed, pushing small posts forward and sending out patrols. By 1750 jabbing at each other was becoming a regular occupation among the governors of New York, Pennsylvania, and New France. New York governor George Clinton complained to Jonquière about the establishment of a new French post at the Niagara portage; he also raised a fuss over the arrest of four traders. Niagara, he claimed, was in the land of the Iroquois, whom the Treaty of Utrecht, which ended the War of the Spanish Succession in 1713, had declared "subject to the dominion of Great Britain." The treaty had also said that subjects of France and Britain "shall enjoy full liberty of going and coming on account of trade," so the French should release the traders. Jonquière denied that the Iroquois were British subjects and said the arrests were justified.

Then the governor offered bounties for the scalps of George Croghan and another trader. Sir William Johnson told Clinton, "If the French go on so, there is no man can be safe in his own house; for I can at any time get an Indian to kill any man for a small matter." Jonquière meanwhile examined the four captive traders, and one of them said that Croghan had urged Indians to kill Frenchmen. The New York and Pennsylvania governments leveled similar charges at the French. With Virginia entering the Indian trade, it was just a matter of time before it joined the chorus.[24]

New France cost France a lot of money, but by 1750 Versailles was in a cost-cutting mood. Jonquière advised building forts near Lake Erie, but the ministry declared that Niagara and Detroit would "secure forever our communications with Louisiana." That was beside the point, because the governor wanted new forts to hold back the English. The next year the minister of marine told him that the king had thought that expenses would diminish after the peace of 1748 but, on the contrary, they had increased. "There must be great abuses. You and the intendant must look into it." Much of the money the government sent to Canada for royal service did end up in the pockets of highly placed thieves, and the worst malefactor was the intendant, François Bigot, whose job it was to prevent peculations, not to commit them. Jonquière answered, "I have reached the age of sixty-six years, and . . . I will not conceal from you that the slightest suspicion on your part against me would cut the thread of my days." This situation was not likely to produce an effective response to the disorganized incursions by English traders.[25]

Jonquière was wearing down by the fall of 1751, as panic spread among those under him. Versailles finally agreed that having the Iroquois attack Oswego would not work and told him to shift his focus to the Ohio Country. The governor ordered Céleron at Detroit to wipe out Pickawillany in October, but the man would not or could not budge. "I cannot express," the governor told him, "how much this business troubles me; it robs me of sleep; it makes me ill." The comte de Raymond, commanding Fort Miami, added his own contribution to what was verging on hysteria in the government. His people were leaving him for Detroit, he complained. "Nobody wants to stay here and have his throat cut. All the tribes who go to the English at Pickawillany come back loaded with gifts. I am too weak to meet the danger." He claimed that all the Indians in the territory were "leaguing together to kill all the French, that they may have nobody on their lands but their English brothers. . . . If the English stay in this country we are lost. We must attack, and drive them out."

As if that was not discouraging enough, Jonquière received yet another blast from Versailles. The previous year, the minister of marine groused, the governor had promised to drive the English from the Ohio soon, but "private letters" said that he had "done nothing. This is deplorable. . . . Send force enough at once to drive them off." That was the last straw. The governor meekly complained about Céleron's failure to act and begged for a recall on account of exhaustion. He took to bed early in 1752 and died on March 6; he was replaced by the baron de Longueuil until a new governor arrived.[26]

New France was leaderless. The vacuum drew the Ohio Company deeper into the west, to keep Pennsylvanians and New Yorkers from reaping all the fruits of trade. Gist spent the winter at Pickawillany and left in March 1752 to report to Williamsburg, dodging scalp hunters until he was east of the mountains. He and Croghan had firmed up alliances with the Miamis and tentatively the Shawnees, but the Delawares still bore old grudges against the Pennsylvanians and the Iroquois. Both Gist and Croghan advised their governments to build more trading posts and seal alliances with the nations. This advice was rejected in Pennsylvania and only halfheartedly received in Virginia. The boundary between the two colonies had never been settled, so both claimed territory also claimed by France. Until the line was run between the two provinces, Dinwiddie told the Lords of Trade in London, he could not appoint "magistrates to keep the traders in good order." Neither the crown nor the colonies would cough up money for western affairs, in effect inviting the French to set things right on their own terms.[27]

With Dinwiddie's support, the Ohio Company pursued its interests among the Indians. Virginia sent commissioners to Logstown in June 1752 to meet with the chiefs of the Ohio nations, promising cheaper trade goods, handsome gifts, and protection against the French in return for permission to build a fort at the Forks. These agreements furthered those arranged by Gist and Croghan with the Delawares, Shawnees, and Mingos, whose "Half-King," as the English called him, a wily man named Tanaghrisson, wanted English support against the French and Iroquois. The Delawares received recognition of their independence, further weakening Iroquois control in the region.[28]

The French also were losing their grip. Acting governor Longueuil complained to Versailles that English traders were winning over the Indians by selling at low prices and making plenty of gifts, including unlimited gunpowder. The commander at Vincennes, on the Wabash River in the *pays des Illinois*, predicted a "storm" about to break over the country. Joncaire declared that all the Ohio Indians had gone over to the English. The Miamis had scalped two soldiers, the Piankashaws had killed seven Frenchmen, and reliable sources said that the nations of the Wabash and Illinois valleys would join the Osages in an uprising. Every dispatch brought news of killings. Smallpox had broken out at Detroit. "It is to be wished," Longueuil told the ministry, "that it would spread among our rebels; it would be fully as good as an army." He predicted that soon the English on the Miami would win over all the surrounding nations and cut Canada's communications with Louisiana. That was the voice of panic, and panic makes men do desperate things.[29]

Virginia, via the Ohio Company, now claimed a stake in the west. But after its delegates finished their work at Logstown, word arrived of the destruction of Pickawillany. This drove all English traders out of the territory, terrorized the Pennsylvania frontier, and forced the Miamis to return to the Iroquois fold. The French thought they had scored a great triumph; they had really miscalculated in every way. They assumed there was a unified English campaign to take over the Ohio Country, but actually there were three colonies competing against each other. They assumed the English were behind every revolt against the French, but Pickawillany represented conflicts between the Miamis and other nations. And although they had driven the traders out, there was too much profit in the fur trade for them to stay away for long, especially with new competition from Virginia. The French could have offered cheaper goods and better gifts to the nations, cementing alliances with them, but they did not. Instead, they decided to lord it over Ohio and its peoples.[30]

As for those foreign traders, it was merely a matter of fortifying the eastern boundary of the *pays d'en haut* and sending out patrols to arrest and strip any who ventured into French territory. Such a program required a steadier hand at the tiller of New France than the colony had known in a long time. In July 1752, such a man arrived, his name Ange, marquis Duquesne de Menneville.

There Are So Many Rascals in This Country

Duquesne was a career naval officer from a long line of naval heroes. He arrived in New France early in July 1752 and conducted a general review of his troops and militia. His lofty bearing offended some, but he soon showed that he was born to command. Exploiting the failure of the English colonial assemblies to protect their western interests, he planned to occupy the upper Ohio Valley, using forts and troops to keep English traders out, and depriving the Indian nations of the guns, powder, and other goods the English supplied them. The nations would become entirely dependent on the French, because he hoped also to muscle the Iroquois aside. Duquesne would exert control over the west and choke off all English pretensions there.[31]

Duquesne's orders from the minister of marine stressed the importance of protecting communication between the Canadian and Illinois settlements by way of the Ohio. He should "make every possible effort to drive the English from our lands . . . and to prevent their coming there to trade." The governor should "make our Indians understand . . . that we have nothing against them, that they will be at liberty to go and trade with the English in the latter's country, but that we will not allow them to receive [the English] on our lands."[32]

Langlade and his Indians had stripped the traders taken at Picka-willany and paraded them through Indian towns and French forts all the way to Montreal, in time for Duquesne to hear about what had happened in April. The governor offered the highest praise for Lan-glade's leadership and recommended that the ministry reward the man, but he advised against being too generous. "As he is not in the king's service, and has married a squaw," Duquesne said of Langlade, "I will ask for him only a pension of two hundred [livres], which will flatter him infinitely."[33]

It was not long before the ministry's caution caught up with it, especially regarding new military posts. "Be on your guard," the min-ister of marine warned, "against new undertakings; private interests are generally at the bottom of them. . . . The expenses of the colony are enormous." Later the minister relented, but only in part. Build on the Ohio "such forts as are absolutely necessary, but no more," he advised. "Remember that His Majesty suspects your advisers of interested views." Duquesne had already learned that every govern-ment undertaking in Canada was an opportunity for official thievery. "There are so many rascals in this country," he complained.[34]

The governor pressed ahead with his plans. By early 1753 he had developed a program to occupy the upper Ohio with about 2,000 men under Pierre-Paul de la Malgue, sieur de Marin. An advance party left Montreal on February 1. By early May it had built a fort at Presque Isle on the southeastern shore of Lake Erie and started a road south. Marin was ready to march out of Niagara by the end of May. In Virginia, Dinwiddie and his business partners were outraged at this French "invasion."[35]

Duquesne's advance threatened to open a colonial theater for a war that had gone on and off between England and France for 700 years. Neither country had a national military presence in America, preferring to fight most battles in Europe and on the seas. French authorities in America had already concluded that the activities of English traders represented a British imperial offensive. English co-lonial governors decided that Duquesne was doing the same thing in reverse.

There were barely 80,000 Frenchmen, including Catholic *métis*, in North America, concentrated in Louisiana, a small settlement in

Acadia, and about 55,000 in Canada. English colonists numbered more than a million. The French were unified in language and religion under an authoritarian feudal structure. The English (so-called, though many were Irish, Scots, Scots-Irish, Dutch, French Huguenots, Germans, Swedes, and others) were divided among thirteen often quarreling colonial governments.

Canadian settlements were guarded by the rugged wilderness that confined the English to the seacoast. New France controlled North America's river system, and thereby communications between Canada and Louisiana. English settlers were stuck in the coastal belt by want of good rivers inland and by the Appalachian Mountains. In Canada the government and society aped the rigid social structure at home; there were many Canadians with noble titles. The rest of the population was mostly poor, illiterate, and cowed by dogmatic priests.

The English colonies varied greatly in forms of government and character of their inhabitants. New Englanders, dominated by their Puritan religion, were literate, captains of industry and trade, flinty, and used to firearms. Virginians, except for the ruling class, were generally poor and illiterate, their economy agricultural, their society limited by its copying the aristocracy of the old country. Between these two extremes was Pennsylvania, with its quarreling nationalities, creeds, and political factions. If there was one common outlook in English America, it was that each colony identified itself as its own "country," with little attachment to Britain or each other. Nor was there a common religion.

English Americans and French Americans were generally not eager to go to war against each other. Some of their leaders, however—most notably Duquesne and Virginia's Dinwiddie—welcomed the prospect. Nor did their mother countries appear ready to pick up the sword. Britain, on the one hand, had reduced its army to 18,000 men after 1748, including garrisons at Minorca and Gibraltar and half a dozen understrength "independent companies" in the West Indies and on the American mainland. The navy had fewer than 17,000 sailors. At the top was the Hanoverian King George II, who could not speak English and who was surrounded by ministers and courtiers feathering their nests and stabbing each other in the back. The government, however, was parliamentary, more or less representing popular will, and capable of financing a war.

France, on the other hand, was part of a Bourbon family enterprise that held the thrones of France, Spain, and Naples; the nation dominated the European continent and was second only to Spain in the extent of its colonial acreage. This was an absolutist monarchy, founded by Louis XIV, with all power vested in the throne. The country had a powerful navy and large army, but its best generals were foreigners. On the throne was the Great Louis's grandson, Louis XV, weak and self-indulgent. France wallowed at its lowest point, nobles dissipating themselves in the vices of Versailles, the people seething with rage at oppression and high taxation. Never was a French king so despised by his subjects. The real ruler of the country was madame de Pompadour, Louis's mistress, who filled the prisons with her opponents and imposed her vain and frivolous policies on all institutions of government, including the army and the navy.[36]

There was one area where the French were definitely superior to the English in America, and that was military power. The English essentially had none. Virginia and New England had developed effective, if often savage, volunteer forces during the Indian wars of the 1600s, but these were long gone. The militia was supposed to provide a ready response to military threats, but decades of peace had eroded it away. Where it survived at all, it was as a social institution, especially in New England.[37]

France's overseas colonies were supervised by the *Ministère de la Marine* (ministry of the marine), organized in 1669 to administer both the navy and the colonies. It had its own army, *troupes de la Marine*, distinct from marines serving aboard ships and recruited and paid by the ministry. The forces were first assembled in the 1670s as *compagnies franches de la Marine*, independent companies, and had been in New France since 1683. Numbers and sizes of companies varied through the decades, and in the early years all officers and men were recruited in France. After 1722, while the men continued to come from France, the officers were recruited in Canada.

These were the only regular troops in New France until 1756, armed with swords and flintlock muskets with bayonets similar to those issued to shipboard marines and regular army troops. The independent companies wore gray-white uniforms with blue cuffs and lining, brass buttons, blue breeches and stockings, and hats laced with false gold. In practice, decades of hard service in the wilderness had simplified field uniforms, which gave way to faded colors, and by the 1750s the enlisted men campaigned in Indian dress: moccasins, leggings, breechclouts, and a hooded *capot* similar to the "hunting shirt" of Virginia. Officers had traded swords and spontoons for hatchets and knives.

These were crack troops. They were supplemented by Indian allies and by the *milice*, the Canadian militia. This echoed the militia of the English colonies but was better trained and organized. In appearance these men were anything but uniform, and they and the Indians preferred a hunting musket, light but sturdy.[38]

This was the armed force bearing down on the Ohio Country in 1753. This formidable array was what Dinwiddie proposed to challenge via a young militia major named George Washington.

THREE

YOU SEE BROTHERS I HAVE GOT THUS FAR ON MY JOURNEY

(1753–1754)

> Fortification, or military architecture, is no other thing than an art, which teaches men to fortify themselves . . . to the end the enemy may not be able to attack . . . without great loss of his men; and that the small number of soldiers which defend the place may be able to hold out for some time.
>
> —SÉBASTIEN LE PRESTRE DE VAUBAN

A fort, in the eyes of the French, was an emblem of empire. They had centuries of experience fortifying their borders, communications, and towns in war-torn Europe. The British lived safely on an island, guarded by the sea. When the French projected themselves into America, they built forts wherever they went. The English did not.

The greatest military engineer in history was a Frenchman, Sébastien le Prestre de Vauban (1632–1707). Under his influence the French government established a corps of engineers with its own academy in 1690, producing engineers, manuals, and other guidance for building forts in the colonies. Some were elaborate masonry works, but most forts in the wilderness were simple, following a Vaubanesque model: the square fort with corner bastions. This adaptable form could be erected fairly cheaply with native timber, supplemented by earthworks where necessary.

Forts were placed at the mouths of rivers, on natural harbors, and on major lakes. It was theoretically possible to control wide areas with comparatively few posts. There was a drawback, however, because this system sometimes failed to take advantage of good defensive positions; forts could be more vulnerable than they looked. Troops slept together on benches built into barracks walls, two or three to a bench. Many advanced posts were abandoned in winter because it was too difficult to supply them.[1]

The English in America, unlike the French, had no engineers. English settlement began, however, with a stockade at Jamestown in 1607, and wars with the Indians made fort-building habitual until the Indians died out from disease or moved westward; the forts of the 1600s were crude timber stockades. When settlement spread toward Indian territories in the mid-1700s, there was renewed interest in fort-building. These pioneer forts were intended only for emergencies and soon fell apart for want of maintenance. Washington found out in 1754 that he did not know the first thing about designing a defensible post. The English learned from the French, however, building square stockades with corner bastions and crude barracks and storehouses, the men sleeping in pairs or trios head-to-foot, belabored by bedbugs, fleas, flies, ticks, and lice.[2]

This Sort Are Worse Than Useless

The marquis Duquesne probably did not realize early in 1753 that he was about to upset a balance of power among the Iroquois, French, and English that had existed for more than half a century. He was new to the country, and he was surrounded by high officials he could not trust. The balance may have been in its last stages anyway, owing to the defection of Ohio nations from the Iroquois, growing population in the English colonies, and intrusions by English traders.

The Six Nations were confident they could control other nations by sending "Half-Kings," as the English called sachems or village chiefs, to represent Iroquois interests locally. The restive Ohio nations trusted none of the other parties. The English acted without policy, hoping to expand their range without getting into a war with either Indians or the French. Without really understanding the complexities of North American geopolitics, Duquesne replaced a century and a half of French diplomacy with a show of military power.[3]

Duquesne mustered his *compagnies franches*, of whom he had a low opinion, and the Canadian militia, whom he praised for their obedience and eagerness. He had "not the least trouble in getting them to march," he told the minister of the marine. The expedition set out as the ice began breaking up early in 1753, about 1,000 men, later increased to 1,500. It impressed the Indians as a mighty host; the lakes and rivers were covered with boats and soldiers from Montreal to Presque Isle.[4]

Excitement advanced before the mighty flotilla like a giant bow wave. An English lieutenant at Oswego saw the spectacle and heard from a passing Frenchman that it carried an army of 6,000 men, headed to the Ohio "to cause all the English to quit those parts." The craft put in at Presque Isle (*presqu'isle*, or "peninsula," now Erie, Pennsylvania) in April 1753 and began to build a fort.

The expedition was not as mighty as it appeared. Its commander was Pierre-Paul de la Malgue, sieur de Marin, hard-bitten marine veteran of the wilderness, a gruff, quarrelsome, but energetic and capable officer despite his sixty-one years. He promptly came down with dysentery but refused to go back to Montreal. Second in command was Michel-Jean-Hugues Péan, chevalier de Saint-Michel, thirty-one years old, also a veteran of marine service in New France but a grossly immoral man. Like so many Canadian officials, he was an embezzler. Moreover, the colony's embezzler in chief, Intendant François Bigot, reportedly lusted after Péan's wife and had arranged for him to have the position under Marin. This was, it appears, not an isolated happening.[5]

Alarm over the Ohio expedition spread even before it sailed out of Montreal, generating correspondence during the winter and spring among the English colonial governors, Virginia's Robert Dinwiddie being the lead writer. He told James Glen of South Carolina that the French force was designed to "take possession of these lands, & to build forts on that river, a step not precedented in the time of confirm'd peace."[6]

Duquesne and his predecessors had interpreted the actions of English traders as a military threat. Dinwiddie couched his objections to the French expedition in similar terms, glossing over what really bothered him: that French domination of the Ohio Country would scuttle the Ohio Company's ambitions. So he was suitably alarmist when he complained to Pennsylvania governor James Hamilton in

May about "the French designs to settle the Ohio. I have sometime ago heard of their robberies & murders," and he predicted that if the French took the territory without opposition, the result would be "the ruin of our trade with the Indians & also in time will be the destruction of all our settlemts. on the continent."[7]

Dinwiddie wanted to wage war against the French, although a declaration of war was beyond his authority. He wanted other colonies to support him with men and money, but the other governors failed to share his alarm. Nor would their assemblies pay for an intercolonial expedition. Moreover, there was widespread suspicion that Dinwiddie's real strategic aim was to further the interests of the Ohio Company.

The French prosecuted their designs unmolested. The landing at Presque Isle opened a better route to the Ohio than Céleron had followed. Marin deployed his men to clear the forest to at least 100 yards (beyond musket range) from the fort, trim timbers, and lay out the fort's trace, while another party began clearing a road south toward *riviére aux Boeufs* (Buffalo River, now called French Creek). From there the expedition could float down to the Allegheny River, then on to the Forks.

This involved an incredible amount of labor portaging baggage, most of the heavy lifting falling on the backs of the Canadian militia. Then there was construction of the fort itself, begun May 15. It was about 180 feet square, with four corner bastions, intended to house 150 men and twelve guns. The walls were of squared chestnut logs, and—very unusual for American forts—they were laid flat on top of each other instead of the usual pattern of a vertical stockade planted into a trench in the ground (*en pile*). Four buildings stood inside the enclosure, and a masonry powder magazine was added later. Fort Presque Isle's purpose was to act as a supply depot between forts to the east and the new ones to the south.[8]

The expedition was a victim of corruption and poor management. Charles Bonin, called "*Jolicoeur*" ("Sweetheart"), arrived at Presque Isle in April to serve as a commissary clerk. The fort's trace was already laid out, most timber had been cleared, and the cannons had been hauled ashore. Marin was driving his troops hard. They had only salt meat and hardtack to eat, and scurvy ravaged the garrison. By late April about 200 men were down with it, and according to Bonin a hospital had been established to prevent the sickness from spreading to the remainder of the detachment. Scurvy was curable by foods containing vitamin C, but the French had not yet figured that out. Officers ate bread, fresh game, wine, and brandy, so they were protected from scurvy.[9]

Work at Presque Isle was far enough along that gangs could be shifted southward down the new nine-mile portage road to what became Fort Le Boeuf (present-day Waterford, Pennsylvania). This was a smaller work about 90 feet square, built of beech logs with the backs of buildings acting as walls; the bastions were made of logs planted *en pile*. Eight guns were on hand by the end of the year, the place a communications link and supply depot on the route to the Ohio.[10]

Work started in August on Fort Machault (also called Fort Venango, now Franklin, Pennsylvania) on the Allegheny below the mouth of Buffalo River, next to the Delaware village of Venango. The location had been occupied since 1741 by a Pennsylvania trader and blacksmith, John Fraser, who fled at the French approach. He left behind a complex of stone buildings including a storehouse and forge, which Marin's crew incorporated into their layout. This was planned as a major supply depot, so it was big, a rectangle with large bastions armed with six swivel-mounted guns. Long, squared-timber buildings formed the northern and southern walls, with stockades *en pile* making up the eastern and western walls and the bastions. An outer stockade added later provided a defense in depth.[11]

A fourth fort at the Forks of the Ohio would have to wait until spring 1754; winter was approaching, and the ceaseless labor told on the men. The project had been expensive, costing 4 million livres and 400 deaths from accidents, scurvy, dysentery, and other diseases. Duquesne thought the cost was justified, because the alleged danger from the English was so great. Marin and Péan were able drivers, but their junior officers were a generally bad lot. They hated service in the wilderness, and their complaints had reached Montreal by late summer. Duquesne told Marin, "This sort are worse than useless." He advised sending grumblers to Montreal, "that I may make an example of them."[12]

Duquesne's expedition had accomplished much, or so it appeared. Among other things, the sheer scale of the enterprise had intimidated Indians of every nationality. Iroquois, Delawares, and Shawnees on the Allegheny came into the French camps and offered to help. Tribes in the west were also impressed. A delegation of Miamis presented two English scalps as tokens of their good faith. Sacs, Potawatomies, Ojibways, and others declared their loyalty to France. Duquesne thought he could win over every nation from the mountains to the Mississippi, so he ordered Péan to take a corps down the Ohio, terrorize any nations that wavered, and bring them into the fold. But winter approached, and this did not happen.

At the end of September Péan reported that Marin was dying. Duquesne was not only alarmed at the pending loss of that sturdy old officer, but he wanted somebody with more experience (and honesty) than Péan to command. He appointed yet another grizzled veteran, Jacques Legardeur de Saint-Pierre, fifty-two years old and just returned from an expedition toward the Rocky Mountains. He reached Fort Le Boeuf late in the fall, after Marin's death on October 29.

Chilly rain, gloom, and snow promised to hang over the troops through a long season. The whole force could not be supplied or even kept alive so far from Montreal in the winter. Duquesne ordered Marin to keep 300 of the fittest men to garrison Presque Isle and Le Boeuf and send the rest home. The governor was appalled when he inspected them. He "could not help being touched by the pitiable state to which fatigues and exposures had reduced them," he reported to the ministry. "Past all doubt, if these emaciated figures had gone down the Ohio as intended, the river would have been strewn with corpses."[13]

The English had not resisted the expedition's advance, and although most Indians had made a show of bowing to its strength, not all did. Mingo Half-King Tanaghrisson and other representatives of the Ohio nations had gone to Presque Isle in September to warn Marin against French intrusion into their country. Presenting a wampum peace belt—beads made from polished seashells, woven into patterns indicating intent—Tanaghrisson addressed the Frenchman: "With this belt we . . . ask you to have them [your men] cease setting up the establishments you want to make. All the tribes have always called upon us not to allow it. We have told our brothers the English to withdraw. They have done so."

Marin, who was active up to his death, was not impressed, and he did not think Tanaghrisson enjoyed much support from other nations. He answered with a peroration tracing French ownership of the Ohio Country to explorations by René-Robert Cavelier, sieur de la Salle, in the previous century. He dismissed the Indian with open contempt, and Tanaghrisson left in tears of rage and frustration.[14]

Arrogance had gotten the better of Marin, as well as Duquesne. They assumed that they had created a new and permanent diplomatic order in the *pays d'en haut,* and that thereafter all the Indians would dance to the French tune. They did not recognize that the various nations would do what it took to safeguard their own independence, and so would continue to bob and weave between the French and the English and the Iroquois as circumstances required. Tanaghrisson in particular played a game of his own, and for all his emotionalism he kept to himself just what his aim was.

The English understood this even less than the French. Duquesne was satisfied that, up to the fall of 1753, they also had bowed to the might of New France. He saw no threat from New York or Pennsylvania. He did not reckon, however, on the newest players in this game, Virginia and the Ohio Company.

We Do Hereby Strictly Charge, & Command You, to Drive Them Off

While the French built their forts early in 1753, and Dinwiddie fumed, Washington was anything but consumed by his duties as district adjutant. The Virginia militia had been established by the assembly in 1623, following a bloody war with the Powhatan Nation. Three years later the lawmakers extended a military obligation to all free males between seventeen and sixty. As settlement spread over the next decades, the governor assumed the role of commander in chief, appointing higher officers who selected subordinates with the governor's approval. These officials were to see that all freemen had arms, drill their companies, and guard public stores of gunpowder.

By the end of the 1600s, the militia had lost touch with its roots and its purpose. So long as the colonial population was close to Indian country, most men were skilled with muskets, and most were Indian fighters. As the frontier receded, older communities lost both interest and practice. Where training was attempted, officers relied on manuals from Europe, tactics not suitable for "bush fighting," as it was called. At the same time, the Indian nations became better armed and increasingly superior to colonial militia. By the 1750s leaders had forgotten that militias were training, not fighting, units, a source of manpower for a crisis. Washington would soon find himself vexed by militias called up in their home units, unfit to deal with the enemy or conditions on the frontier. Militia were less effective the farther they were from home.[15]

Washington made his own contributions to militia deterioration by dodging his duties as adjutant, other than to order his red major's uniform from a tailor while he pursued surveying and land acquisition. Dinwiddie and the Council had hoped to overcome decades of neglect by instituting the four inspection districts and prescribing both county musters and at least one general muster a year. Washington made some effort to educate himself in tactics and instruction, but mostly he strove to win transfer from the southern district to the northern district, where he lived, riding around the Northern Neck politicking for appointment.

He also exploited his connections, via the Fairfaxes, among the colony's leadership. That involved beseeching people with political influence, such as William Nelson of York, who in February gave him a typical response. "I have received yours of the 12th instant," Nelson said, "in which you express a desire to be removed to the adjutancy of the Northern Neck. I think the thing so reasonable, that I wish you may succeed." There were, however, two other applicants, "both strongly recommended; yet, reason, I hope, will always prevail at the board over interest & favour." Of course, it was "interest & favour" that Washington cultivated, and his persistence paid off. He received the northern district in November 1753.[16]

That was as far as he could climb in the militia, so he looked around for other opportunities. He had made himself familiar to Lieutenant Governor Dinwiddie by the spring of 1753, if not before. Dinwiddie's chief interest at the time was the French "invasion." In that interpretation of what was going on, however, the governor failed to understand that the contest was not over European land claims but over the allegiance of the Ohio nations. Washington never understood that either.

It was even more complicated than that, because along with the struggle between European powers there were the various international tussles among the Indians, each nation wanting white support in settling scores with others. The Iroquois, especially, played on their economic and military advantages to the white colonizers, maintaining their freedom of action in conflicts with other nations. New York Indian affairs secretary Peter Wraxall put his finger on the truth when he declared that "to preserve the balance between us and the French is the great ruling principle of modern Indian politics." Now both Duquesne and Dinwiddie were determined to butt heads, oblivious to the fact that they would do so not in the white man's world, but in that of the Indian nations.[17]

Dinwiddie was British, not American, and he reflected the outlook of his government. French activities in America had raised alarms in the king's cabinet since the treaty of 1748, because the British ministers saw anything the French did in America as complementary to events in Europe. With France trying to become more powerful in the eastern continent, anything it gained in the western one would take pressure off its side in the next European war. Conversely, countering the French in America would strengthen the United Kingdom's position in the Old World. The earl of Halifax, president of the Board of Trade, supervisor of the English colonies, piled up dossiers on French "encroachments" on English colonial frontiers. Dinwiddie obligingly fed Halifax's files.[18]

Halifax had powerful allies in the duke of Newcastle, secretary of state for the northern department, and the duke of Bedford, secretary of state for the southern department, between them the makers of British foreign policy. They believed that with France pursuing dual policies of expansion in Europe and America, Great Britain needed dual counterpolicies in both places. With alarming letters arriving from colonial governors claiming that the French intended to seal off the Ohio Country, in August 1751 the cabinet had ordered the governors "to prevent, by force, these and any such attempts that may be made by the French, or by the Indians in the French interest."[19]

The loudest and most insistent of the governors was Dinwiddie, who routinely passed on alarms from, among others, company traders reporting French activities in Ohio. "The French told the Indians their army when collected will make up 15,000 men," one declared, "that the country belongs to them & that they will build when they like." This was a gross exaggeration, but no worse than Dinwiddie's own. On June 16, 1753, frustrated by a lack of concern in other colonies, he pointedly told the Board of Trade that he hoped its members would "think it necessary to prevent the French taking possession of the lands on the Ohio." In his "private opinion," the French "ought to be prevented making any settlements to the westward of our present possessions."[20]

Dinwiddie's letter reached the Board of Trade on August 11 and was forwarded to the king and cabinet on the 18th. At about the same time, the cabinet was alarmed by a new danger in the northern colonies, where the Mohawks were the staunchest allies of the English. That did not prevent crooked speculators from trying to swindle them out of millions of acres of land. Chief Hendrick (Theyanoguin) met with the governor and Council of New York on June 16 and declared that "the Covenant Chain is broken between you and us," meaning a break in relations. Alarmed, the Board of Trade told all colonial governors to attend a conference with the Mohawks, scheduled for the following June, to arrive at a new general treaty with the Indian nations. Dinwiddie declined to send a delegation, however, on several grounds. One was that he thought he had power to make his own frontier policy. Another was that he did not want to ask the Burgesses to pay for a diplomatic mission, because they included shareholders in syndicates competing with the Ohio Company.[21]

The main reason Dinwiddie charted his own course was that he had separate instructions from the government in London. On August 28, Bedford's successor in the southern department, the earl of Holderness, sent a circular to all the governors ordering them to "repell force by force [within] the undoubted limits of His Majesty's dominions." Dinwiddie received orders aimed solely at him, also sent on August 28. He was "warranted by the king's instructions," the document began, "to repell any hostile attempt by force of arms; and you will easily understand, that it is his majesty's determination, that you should defend to the utmost of your power, all his possession with your government, against any invader." At the same time, the king did not want to be the "aggressor," so the governor was enjoined "most strictly" not to use the force under his command, "excepting within the undoubted limits of his majesty's province." This suggested that the cabinet in London did not really know what lands were in Virginia and which were not. In any case, Dinwiddie was sure he knew.

The lieutenant governor now had His Majesty's orders, the letter continued, to erect forts "within the king's own territory." If he was "interrupted therein, those who presume to prevent you . . . are the aggressors, and commit an hostile act. And this is one case, in which you are authorized to repell force by force." Another such case would be if "persons not subjects to his majesty" were discovered "presuming to erect fortresses upon the king's land." If they refused Dinwiddie's summons to cease and desist, that would be "an hostility," and he was required by his instructions to "inforce by arms, (if necessary) a compliance with your summons." This was repeated: If the invaders persisted, "We do hereby strictly charge, & command you, to drive them off by force of arms." To that end, the government sent Virginia thirty pieces of artillery to bolster its defenses.[22]

Dinwiddie received this authority—essentially a delegation of power to declare war, if the cabinet had thought about it—in mid-October 1753. He did not move hastily against the French because he did not want to ask the Burgesses for money to finance an expedition. The feud over the pistole fee for land patents dragged on, preventing action on almost anything the lieutenant governor wanted. Dinwiddie was a businessman, so negotiation was more in his style than military action. On November 17 he told the Board of Trade that he had sent one of the adjutants of the militia to the commander of the French forces, "to know their intentions, & by what authority they presume to invade His Majesty's dominions in the time of tranquil peace."[23]

It is doubtful that the ministers realized that they had committed their government to doing the Ohio Company's dirty work for it. It is also unlikely that they expected Dinwiddie to send a twenty-one-year-old to confront the French commandant. But he did; the adjutant was George Washington. "It was deemed by some an extraordinary circumstance," Washington admitted later, "that so young and inexperienced a person should have been employed on a negotiation with which subjects of the greatest importance were involved." The Ohio Company's owners trusted him to serve the interests of the government without harming those of the company. There was another reason Washington got the job: He wanted it, and nobody else did.[24]

Dinwiddie had shared his orders with only a few members of his Council and with other colonial governors. Washington learned the secret, possibly through William Fairfax, and showed up in Williamsburg on October 26. The taverns were full because the governor had called the assembly to meet on November 1. Washington went directly to Dinwiddie, who told the Council on October 27 that the young adjutant "had offered himself to go properly commissioned to the commandant of the French forces." The Council approved Washington's appointment and assigned a committee to prepare his instructions. Dinwiddie did not tell the Burgesses what was going on until November 8, by which time the emissary was gone.[25]

Washington had no diplomatic experience or knowledge of French, but he was eager to go. He wanted to see new country and to prove himself worthy of trust; he was too young to have a sense of prudent caution. Dinwiddie's first order to him was to find Christopher Gist and give the company explorer a written request to serve as the young man's guide. Washington later said of Gist, "He has had extensive dealings with the Indians, is in great esteem among them; well acquainted with their manners and customs, is indefatigable, and patient: most excellent qualities indeed, where Indians are concerned!"[26]

There was no one better prepared than Gist to teach Washington the ways of the frontier and of Indians. The youngster needed all the guidance he could get, because the route before him ran from the Ohio Company storehouse at Wills Creek westward over ridges as much as 3,000 feet high, crossing out of the Potomac watershed into that of the Ohio. Once across the Youghiogheny River 34 miles from Wills Creek, he faced a trek over a long ridge, down the Monongahela River to the Forks of the Ohio, then thirteen miles downstream to the town and trading post of Logstown. There he had to find Indians to guide him to the French posts. Washington recalled that it was "a most inclement season," and he trekked through rough country in the depth of winter when "the face of the Earth was covered with snow and the waters covered with ice." Whether he realized before he set off just how challenging it would be is impossible to say.[27]

Dinwiddie had presented him a pile of diplomatic paperwork on October 30. First were his instructions. Referring to "a body of French forces being assembled in an hostile manner" with plans to build forts within Virginia territory "& contrary to the peace & dignity of our sovereign the King of Great Britain," Dinwiddie ordered Washington first to learn where the French were posted. When he reached the French station, he was to present his credentials and a letter from Dinwiddie to the officer in charge, "& in the name of His Britannic Majesty, to demand an answer from him thereto."

At Logstown, Washington should meet with sachems of the Six Nations, telling them about his orders and "desiring the said chiefs to appoint you a sufficient number of their warriors to be your safeguard, as near the French as you may desire, & to wait your further direction." This undiplomatic advice was followed by orders to learn all he could about French numbers, dispositions, and intentions. He was to identify any forts and where they were, and discover why the French had invaded Virginia territory. Once the French commandant had handed over his reply to the governor's message, Washington should ask him that, "agreeable to the Law of Nations, he wou'd grant you a proper guard, to protect you as far on your return, as you may judge for your safety, against any stragling Indians, or hunters, that may be ignorant of yr. character, & molest you."[28]

Washington's credentials included a cover letter for Dinwiddie's message to the French commandant and a separate "passport." Whereas the lieutenant governor, it began, had appointed Washington "by commission under the Great Seal" to carry a message to the commandant of the French forces, "I do hereby command all His Majesty's Subjects, & particularly require ALL IN ALLIANCE AND AMITY WITH THE CROWN OF GREAT BRITAIN, & all OTHERS to whom this PASSPORT may come, agreeable to the Law of Nations," to aid, assist, and protect Washington and his party on their journey to the Ohio and back.[29]

Dinwiddie's message to the French officer was under seal, but Washington probably read it before he left. "The lands upon the River Ohio are so notoriously known to be the property of the Crown of Great Britain," it began, "that it is a matter of equal concern and surprise to me, to hear that a body of French forces are erecting fortresses and making settlements upon that river." The governor had received many reports of "acts of hostility," and so he was compelled to complain to the commandant "of the encroachments thus made, and of the injuries done to the subjects of Great Britain." The message demanded to know by what authority French forces had invaded British territory, "that according to the purport and resolution of your answer I may act agreeable to the commission I am honored with from the King, my master." It was Dinwiddie's duty to demand the French officer's "peaceable departure."

This was not diplomacy but an ultimatum. Yet Washington traveled under diplomatic cover. "I perswade myself," Dinwiddie ended, "you will receive & entertain Major Washington with the candour & politeness natural to your nation; & it will give me the greatest satisfaction, if you return him with an answer suitable to my wishes, for a very long & lasting peace between us."[30]

Washington packed the papers in an oilskin pouch and headed out alone on October 31. At Fredericksburg he hired as a translator

Jacob van Braam, who had once given him fencing lessons. Born in Holland in 1729, van Braam had arrived in America in 1752 and set himself up as a French teacher. Washington stopped in Alexandria to pick up "necessaries," then in Winchester to get packhorses, and reached Wills Creek on November 14. Gist readily agreed to come along. So did John Davison, a translator of Indian tongues. Three others signed on as packers. The party supplied itself with match coats (woolen ponchos) and other Indian winter dress.

Washington kept a journal, the basis of his report to Dinwiddie; his writing had improved since 1748, although it had become deadpan. Gist also was a diarist. They set out from Wills on November 15, and according to Washington "the excessive rains & vast quantity of snow that had fallen" kept them from reaching Turtle Creek on the Monongahela until November 22.[31]

I Excused It in the Best Manner I Was Capable

At Turtle Creek Major Washington wanted to press on to the Forks, but "the waters were quite impassable, without swimming our horses, which oblig'd us to get the loan of a canoe." He sent two of his men with the baggage down the Monongahela to rendezvous at the Forks, where they all met on November 24. This was Washington's first look at the object of the Ohio Company's affections—the site of its proposed fortified trading post. It was "extreamly well situated for a fort; as it has the absolute command of both rivers."

The party reached Logstown after dark on the 24th. There Washington met Shingas, principal chief of the Unalachtigo band of the Delawares, allied to the English but wavering under French pressure. The Half-King Tanaghrisson was away hunting. The Virginian turned to Scarouady, sent by the Six Nations to superintend the Shawnees at Logstown. Speaking through Davison, Washington told Scarouady of his mission, giving him wampum and a twist of tobacco, and asking him to send for the Half-King, "which he promis'd to do by a runner in the morning, & for other sachems." Washington invited Scarouady and the "other great men present" to his tent, where they stayed an hour.

On the next day there came "to town four of ten French men that deserted from a company at the Cuscusas [Kaskaskia, Illinois]."

They gave Washington a description of French posts on the Ohio and Mississippi rivers before they took off for Philadelphia. Tanaghrisson arrived late in the afternoon. Washington had heard about the meeting between the Ohio Indians and Marin in September, and he invited the Half-King and Davison into his tent to provide details. This violated the Indian tradition of giving weary travelers a break before conducting business, but the sachem was indulgent. His account recalled that the French formerly tried to win the Indians over by trade and gifts. That had changed. "NOW FATHERS," he had complained to the French, "it is you that is the disturber in this land, by coming & building your towns." At Montreal in 1732, the nations had asked the French not to intrude on their land, which was "our land, & not yours."

The Half-King was not through. "FATHERS," he had told Marin further, "both you & the English are white. We live in a country between, therefore the land does not belong either to one or the other; but the GREAT BEING above allow'd it to be a place of residence for us; so Fathers, I desire you to withdraw, as I have done our brothers the English, for I will keep you at arm's length." He intended to play the two white nations against each other. "I lay this down as a tryal for both," he had told the Frenchman, "to see which will have the greatest regard to it, & that side we will stand by."

Then he related Marin's reply. "NOW MY CHILD," the French officer began, "You spoke first . . . but you need not put yourself to the trouble of speaking for I will not hear you: I am not affraid of flies or musquito's; for Indians are such as those." He declared further that "down that river I will go, & will build upon it according to my command." This was not the end of Marin's insults: "Child, you talk foolish; you say this land belongs to you, but . . . it is my land."

Washington accepted whatever Tanaghrisson said without question. The fifty-year-old sachem posed himself as a friend of the English and an enemy of the French. That was enough for the Virginian, but he missed the clear signal in Tanaghrisson's account: that he made demands of both white nations and would tilt toward whichever side suited his people's interests. The major, fortunately, did not confess that his mission was to stake an English claim to the Ohio.

Two Virginia traders had been captured at Venango in August by French soldiers, who confiscated their goods and dragged them away in irons. Washington asked about that, and the Half-King claimed he also had asked Marin about them and received this reply: "CHILD you think it is a very great hardship that I made prisoners of those two people at Venango, don't you concern yourself with it we took & carried them to Canada to get intelligence of what the English were doing in Virginia."[32]

The next day, November 26, Washington had his first chance to perform the formal rituals of Indian diplomacy, so he put on his uniform for a council in the longhouse. Gist must have explained to him that the longhouse was the social, spiritual, and political center of many Indian communities. Washington faced the leading men of several nations, wearing deerskin leggings and moccasins and upper garments of furs or trade blankets, their clothing and turbans decorated in a variety of styles.

The English had long since addressed Indians as "brothers," as opposed to the "fathers" and "children" of the French. Gist or Davison no doubt coached the Virginian on this. "BROTHERS," Washington began, "I have call'd you together in council, by order of your brother the governor of Virginia, to acquaint you that I am sent with all possible dispatch to deliver a letter to the French commandant of very great importance to your brothers the English: & I dare say to you their friends & allies." He had been "desir'd" by "your brother the governor" to ask their advice and assistance. "You see brothers I have got thus far on my journey." The governor, Washington continued, also wanted him to ask the nations to supply provisions and a guard of "young men" to protect him from attack. As a sign of his good faith, he gave them a string of wampum.

The sachems consulted each other, and Tanaghrisson rose to respond. "I rely upon you as a brother ought to do," he told Washington, "as you say we are brothers & one people." They would go with him to the French to protest Marin's insults, "& you may depend that we will endeavour to be your guard." His main point was that Washington should not leave yet, as it would take three days to retrieve the "French speech belt," which Tanaghrisson would give back to the French to break relations, and to assemble a "guard of Mingoes, Shanesse, & Delawar's, that our brothers may see the love and loyalty we bear them."

Washington was young and impatient, and knew that the weather would only get worse. He thanked the sachem in the "most suitable manner," but he really had to hurry along on his journey. The Half-

King flatly refused to let the English party leave without protection, and, as the major put it, "etc etc." He gave in, because it was "impossible to get off without affronting them."

Washington had no choice but to cool his heels in Logstown while runners went out to bring in the Shawnees, and Tanaghrisson went to his cabin to get the speech belt. The Indians provided plenty of food, but Gist complained that the Virginians stayed until November 29, "when the Indians said, they were not ready. They desired us to stay until the next day, and as the warriors were not come, the Half-King said he would go with us himself, and take care of us." Tanaghrisson, Scarouady, and two other sachems had entered Washington's tent late on the 28th and asked him flatly what business he had going to the French. He had expected this question all along, the major said, and "provided as satisfactory answers as I cou'd, which allay'd their curiosity a little." He did not record those answers.

Word had arrived from Venango, where French Indian agent Joncaire Chabert had called in Mingos, Delawares, and other nations and advised them that the French had intended to go on to the Forks that fall, but the weather prevented it. But according to Joncaire, the Indians "might assuredly expect them in the spring, with a far greater number." The French demanded that the nations "not intermeddle, unless they had a mind to draw all their force upon them." This was a bald threat, uncharacteristic of French diplomacy until after Pickawillany. Tanaghrisson was inclined to sever ties with the French and ally with the English, but making such a choice depended on which Europeans appeared more powerful. The parties continued negotiating at Logstown through November 29, with the sachems now promising to retrieve wampum peace belts from all the Ohio nations and return them to the French. When he "found them so pressing in their request," Washington said, "& knew that returning of wampum, was the abolishing of agreements; & giving this up was shaking off all dependence upon the French," he agreed to stay. Offending the sachems "at this crisis," he realized, might have been "attended with greater ill consequence than another day's delay."

The Virginian had exceeded his authority by entering diplomatic negotiations. The Ohio nations, on the other hand, saw before them one English boy, as against a large French force to the north. Washington had entered Logstown to find the nations evidently leaning toward breaking their French connection. By the 29th, the Indians were again weighing their options. The wampum belts never came in. As Washington recorded in his journal, the sachems held a meeting that night and decided that only three of them and a hunter would escort him. He did not understand that the nations would bide their time to see how things worked out among the Europeans.

The party left on November 30, accompanied by Tanaghrisson and three other sachems. They were hampered, Washington said, by "a continued series of bad weather," although Gist remarked that the hunting was good. They reached Venango on December 4, after trudging seventy miles from Logstown. The major presented himself at headquarters, meeting three French officers. Captain Joncaire Chabert, who commanded on the Ohio, told him that there was a general officer at the next fort, where he should go for an answer to the governor's letter.

The Indians vanished into the Delaware town, while the French officers invited the "*rosbifs*" (as the French called the English) to dinner. The "frog eaters" (as the English called the French) treated their guests with a combination of Gallic courtesy and Canadian bravado. The wine flowed, said Washington, and "as they dos'd themselves pretty plentifully with it, soon banish'd the restraint which at first appear'd in their conversation" and therefore loosened their tongues to "reveal their sentiments more freely." They told him that it was their "absolute design" to take possession of the Ohio, "& by G__ they wou'd do it, for tho' they were sensible, that the English cou'd raise two men for their one; yet they knew their [the English] motions were too slow & dilatory to prevent any undertaking of theirs." The French "pretended to have an undoubted right" to the Ohio by right of discovery, and they would prevent the English from "settling on the river or waters of it."[33]

It rained all the next day and Washington and his party brooded in their tent until Joncaire sent for him, complaining that he had not let his French hosts know that Tanaghrisson was with him. He excused that in the best manner he could, he recorded, "& told him I did not think their company agreeable, as I had heard him say a good deal in dispraise of Indians." He had a private reason for keeping the Half-King and the French apart. Joncaire, he knew, was "a person of very great influence among the Indians," who had lately used "all possible means" to lure them into the French sphere of influence. Mostly, he did not want to give Joncaire a chance to get his Indian companions drunk. The French agent summoned Tanaghrisson anyway, making a great fuss over him and asking why he had not let him know he was in the town. Joncaire offered several presents and "applied liquors so fast, that they were soon render'd incapable for the business they came about."

Gist kept a close eye on the sachems, who held a council with the local Delawares, urging them to provide their peace belt to return to the French. "Our Indians," Gist reported, "could not prevail with them to deliver their belt but the Half-King did deliver his belt, as he had determined." Joncaire did everything he could to get the Indians to abandon the Virginians, but Gist "took all care to have them along with us." If Washington had been more perceptive, he would have realized that Tanaghrisson was trying to engineer a break between the French and the Ohio Indians, under his leadership, but the others were not about to risk French retaliation.

That should have been more clear to the Virginian the next day, when the Half-King came to Washington's tent "quite sober," insisting that he "shou'd stay & hear what he had to say to the French." When the major learned that there was a council fire kindled, he agreed to stay, but he sent his horses and packers up Buffalo River to make camp. The council met at ten o'clock, and Tanaghrisson spoke, offering "the French speech belt which had before been demanded." Joncaire refused to accept the belt, asking the sachem to take it to the commandant at Fort Le Boeuf.

Michel Pépin, known as "la Force," the French commissary, arrived from Fort Le Boeuf with three soldiers on December 7 to accompany Washington and his party to that post. The Virginians found it "extreamly difficult" to get the Indians to leave, Washington complained, because the French had used "every stratagem" to keep them at Venango. Gist had to go fetch them, "which he did with great perswasion." It took four days to reach the fort, because of "excessive rains, snows, & bad traveling, through many mires & swamps" and high water in all the creeks. The party lost a horse. On the 11th, the group traveled about fifteen miles to the French fort, arriving after dark. Van Braam, said Gist, "gave the commandant notice of our being over the creek; upon which he sent several officers to conduct us to the fort, and they received us with a great deal of complaisance." A heavy snowstorm did not prevent Commandant Legardeur from greeting his visitors warmly. He was a case-hardened veteran who had commanded posts as far-flung as Beaubassin in Acadia, Fort Assumption at present Memphis, and Fort La Jonquière 350 miles northwest of present Winnipeg, along with several Indian campaigns. Young Washington said the fifty-two-year-old was "an elderly gentleman" who had "much the air of a soldier."[34]

Early on December 12, Washington presented himself to the commandant, told him his business, and offered his "commission letter" and Dinwiddie's message. Legardeur said he would send for a captain who knew English and asked him to wait. The translator got there in the afternoon and retired to another room to work. After that was done, he invited Washington's translator van Braam to "peruse & correct" the translation.[35]

Legardeur summoned his officers to consider how to reply to Dinwiddie, giving Washington free run of the post, which gave him an opportunity to take "the dimensions of the fort, & making what observations I cou'd." He prepared a detailed description of the fort's location and layout, listing all the buildings and cannons. This strongpoint was like nothing he had ever seen. He could not get a "certain account of the number of men" there, he reported, but he estimated "an hundred exclusive of officers," of which there were many. He told his men to count the canoes assembled at the place to convey the French forces downriver in the spring. They numbered "50 of birch bark, & 170 of pine; besides many others that were block'd out, in readiness to make." The French clearly planned to move out in force.

Washington "found many plots concerted to retard the Indians business, & prevent their returning" with him. "I endeavour'd all in my power to frustrate their schemes, & hurry them on to execute their intended design," meaning the return of the wampums. The Indians gained an audience with Legardeur late on the December 14, and Tanaghrisson told the Virginian that he had tried to hand over the wampum but the commandant "evaded taking it, & made many fair promises of love & friendship; and said he wanted to live in peace & trade amicably with them." He promised to send a party bearing goods to Logstown, but Washington suspected that the real object was to round up the English traders there, so he asked Legardeur by what authority he had made prisoners of several English subjects. He told the Virginian that "the country belong'd to them, that no English man had a right to trade upon them waters."

The snow continued to fall, and the horses were getting weaker. Believing that he would soon receive Legardeur's reply, Washington sent them off unloaded under the care of three of his men, telling them to get to Venango as fast as possible. They should wait for him there if it looked like the rivers would freeze, otherwise go on to the Forks. He intended himself to go down by water, "as I had the offer of a canoe or two."

Legardeur handed his reply to Dinwiddie, dated December 15, to Washington late on the previous day. He acknowledged that the major had fulfilled his duty to deliver the letter of October 31, and expressed a wish that Washington had been ordered to go to Canada to see the governor general, "to whom it belongs, rather than to me, to set forth the evidence and the reality of the rights of the king, my master, to the lands situated along the Belle Rivière [Ohio River], and to contest the pretensions of the king of Great Britain thereto." The commandant would forward Dinwiddie's message to the marquis Duquesne. "His reply will be a law to me, and, if he should order me to communicate it to you, Sir," Legardeur would do so promptly.

"As to the summons you send me to retire," he told Dinwiddie, "I do not think myself obliged to obey it. Whatever may be your instructions, I am here by virtue of the orders of my general, and I entreat you, Sir, not to doubt for a moment" that the commandant would follow his orders "with all the exactness and determination which can be expected of the best officer." As to Dinwiddie's blunt accusations, "I do not know that anything has happened in the course of this campaign which can be construed as an act of hostility, or as contrary to the treaties between the two crowns." Last, "I have made it a particular duty to receive Mr. Washington with the distinction owing to your dignity, his position, and his own great merit!"[36]

Dinwiddie's letter soon reached Duquesne, who declared the claims of the Virginian baseless, because the Ohio Country belonged to the French. The news created a stir in Quebec, according to "Sweetheart" Bonin. Rumors spread that Virginia was preparing to attack the French "under the pretext of protecting the savages." Bonin was soon busy organizing another expedition, aiming to go all the way to the Forks.[37]

Are You Shot?

His mission completed, Washington tried to leave on December 15, when Legardeur ordered "a plentiful store of liquor, provisions & ca."

to be put into his canoe. The French also plied the Indians, in particular the Half-King, with liquor, presents, flattery, and ultimately guns
and powder if they would stay at the fort. "I can't say that ever in my
life I suffer'd so much anxiety as I did in this affair," Washington complained. He finally prevailed on Tanaghrisson, who left with him, van
Braam, and Gist on the 16th. The voyage down the creek was "tedious
& very fatiguing," several times the party nearly foundered on rocks,
and many times all hands had to get out and wade in the water half
an hour or more to get over the shoals. Legardeur had sent a party of
Canadians and Indians to shadow the English, Gist spotting them on
the 22nd, just outside Venango. The packers and horses were waiting
at Venango, as ordered.

Washington spent three days trying to persuade Tanaghrisson to
continue, before he gave up and left the Half-King behind with a
promise that they would rejoin at the Forks. With the creeks frozen
and the horses worn out, Washington wanted to set out on foot, carrying supplies in packs and wearing "Indian walking dress." He left
van Braam to supervise the packers and get the horses to Wills. Gist
objected: He did not think Washington was ready to travel overland
because he "had never been used to walking before this time." The
two of them set out anyway on the 26th, and Washington showed signs
of wearing out by the first night. The next day they met an Indian who
offered himself as a guide, shouldering Washington's pack to ease his
burden. Gist did not trust the man, who "made a stop, turned about;
the major saw him point his gun toward us and fire. Said the major,
'Are you shot?' 'No,' said I." Gist tackled the man as he reloaded. "I
would have killed him; but the major would not suffer me to." They
let their prisoner go at nightfall and made a forced night march to
elude pursuit. Washington left a different account, saying that "we fell
in with a party of French Indians, which had laid in wait for us, one
of them fired at Mr. Gist or me." The rest of the tale was the same as
Gist's, and he did not mention the other Indians again.

They reached the Allegheny on the 29th, found it choked with ice
floes, and built a raft "with but one poor hatchet," Washington said.
After floating halfway across they were pummeled by ice, Washington was thrown into roaring water, and they waded to an island. The
major was soaked, and Gist's fingers were frostbitten. They huddled
on the island overnight. It was so cold that the river froze over, and
they walked across the next morning. They reached a trading post on

the 30th. Washington made a goodwill visit to "Queen Aliquippa," an old Delaware woman with longstanding ties to the English. She was revered in the neighborhood, so the major gave her a match coat and a bottle of rum, "which was thought much the best present of the two."

Horses and saddles were available at Gist's own post, which the pair reached January 2, 1754. They continued on, passing a train of horses loaded with materials and stores the packers said were for a new fort at the Forks. They reached Wills Creek on January 6, according to Washington, "after as fatiguing a journey as it is possible to conceive, rendered so by excessive bad weather: From the first day of December 'till the 15th, there was but one day, but what it rain'd or sno'd incessantly & throughout the whole journey we met with nothing but one continued series of cold wet weather."

Washington was boasting, but it had been an epic trek. Leaving Gist behind, he went on alone, resting a day at Belvoir and reaching Williamsburg on January 16. There he visited "his honour the governor with the letter I had brought from the French commandant," along with his own account of the journey. His journal, he said, contained "the most remarkable occurrences that happen'd to me. I hope it will be sufficient to satisfy your Honour with my proceedings; for that was my aim in undertaking the journey: & chief study throughout the prosecution of it." So ended the journal of Washington's adventure.

The story did not end there. Dinwiddie told both the Council and the Burgesses about the French claims to the Ohio Country and their arrests of English traders. He sent Washington's journal to the Board of Trade on January 29, warning the board that the French planned to occupy the Forks in the spring.[38]

Dinwiddie also sent the journal to a printer. Washington prefaced it with an "Advertisement." "I think I can do no less than apologize, in some measure, for the numberless imperfections of it," he began. Then he excused any "imperfections" by claiming he had had only one day to prepare his report and that he did not know it would be published until it was already in press. Any shortcomings, in other words, were the fault of others.[39]

The journal was reprinted in newspapers all over the colonies, giving Washington a continental reputation. The Burgesses voted £50 to the major "to testify our approbation of his proceedings on his journey to the *Ohio*." The assembly had been in session from November 1 to December 19, most of the time wrangling over the pistole fee. Din-widdie had tried to get funds for defense against the French, but the Burgesses flatly refused. He hoped that the major's report would encourage them to grant money to stop the French "encroachment."[40]

Dinwiddie's friends heaped praise on the major, but the governor's enemies declared that he had exaggerated the dangers of his mission to further the interests of the Ohio Company. There were questions that were not raised at the time. Why did Dinwiddie send his emissary out at the worst time of year rather than wait for better weather? It seems apparent that he fully expected the French to reject his ultimatum so he would have grounds to "repell force by force." Getting that rejection in winter gave him time to organize an expedition in the spring. To that end, Washington had served the lieutenant governor's interests—and those of the Ohio Company—well.

FOUR

I HEARD THE BULLETS WHISTLE

(1754)

> We do not approve the judgment of those who call it a just cause for war, when our neighbor, being hindered by no treaty, builds a fortress in his own country. . . . It is equally wrong to claim for oneself on the ground of discovery what belongs to another . . . for discovery means that the property belongs to no one else.
>
> —HUGO GROTIUS

When Dinwiddie sent Washington to the Ohio, the messenger enjoyed the "Right of Embassy" under the Law of Nations. This was a body of western practices since ancient times, codified in 1625 by Dutch jurist Hugo Grotius, who believed that even wars should be governed by certain principles. His rules defined war and combatants, and virtually everything else involving relations between nations, in war or peace.

The Right of Embassy, he maintained, was part of the "voluntary law of nations," as compelling as the "law of nature." "In this class the Right of Embassy is a most important subject," Grotius declared in *The Law of War and Peace.* "Everywhere we read of the sanctity of embassies and of ambassadors, the law of nations appointed for them, divine and human law, the right of embassy sacred among nations, alliances sacred to principles, the alliance of mankind. To violate this right is, by universal admission not only lawless, but . . . impious."

The Right of Embassy guarded not only ambassadors between nations but also "deputies sent from provinces, cities, and other places." Emissaries were to be protected from violence, from collection of debts, even from prosecution for crimes. Protection extended to the emissary's aides and servants. "Profane histories abound," Grotius warned, "of wars undertaken because of the ill-treatment of ambassadors."

Grotius's work remained influential more than a century later, and every high official in Europe heeded its principles. This extended to officers in New France, who scrupulously safeguarded Washington and his party, allowed them to spy (which was expected of emissaries), and even provisioned them for their trek home. They did not attack the Virginians—the Indian who shot at Washington and Gist acted on his own. When the French sent their own emissary to the English, they expected him to be treated according to the Law of Nations.[1]

It Is a Charge Too Great for My Youth and Inexperience

Washington must have suspected before he returned to Williamsburg that Dinwiddie was taking action. He had passed a pack train carrying supplies for what the packers said would be a new fort at the Forks. The lieutenant governor had been busy. In January 1754 he sent ten cannons and ammunition to Alexandria to forward to the Forks. He told the Council that the French refusal to leave the Ohio Country constituted "an hostility" within the earl of Holderness's instructions the previous fall, so Virginia must stop the French or drive them out.

Dinwiddie had planned to send an expedition west in the spring, but he pushed the schedule up. He advanced the next assembly's meeting from April 18 to February 14, then set in motion anything he thought the Council had power to do on its own. He was sure that the Burgesses would ratify his actions after that body read Washington's report of his trip to the French forts. Under existing law, the governor's authority extended only to raising 200 volunteers. He thought that 100 would be enough to defend a separate party of 100 fortifying the Forks, and he hoped that the Burgesses would pay for another 400 troops. Meanwhile, he asked other colonies to help out.[2]

Dinwiddie appointed the Ohio Company's superintendent of construction, William Trent, as a captain in the Virginia militia and ordered him to recruit 100 men to build a fort at the Forks. Trent was an experienced frontiersman, Indian diplomat, and western trader in partnership with Pennsylvanian George Croghan. John Fraser, who had lost his property at Venango to the French, became Trent's lieutenant. Edward Ward, another refugee trader, was commissioned the company's ensign; he was Croghan's half brother. Virginia's campaign to repel the French "invasion" looked increasingly like an Ohio Company project, in partnership with Croghan's enterprises.[3]

Dinwiddie ordered Washington to raise fifty men each from Augusta and Frederick counties. He did not consider that the adjutant would compete for recruits with Trent. In any case, the governor assumed that by the time the combined 200 men reached the Forks, the additional 400 would be on their way. If other colonies sent troops, he told William Fairfax, Virginia forces "with the conjunction of our friendly Indians" would, he hoped, drive the French from the Ohio.[4]

Dinwiddie ordered the county lieutenants to have their quotas in Alexandria by February 20, ready for Washington to train. He assumed militiamen would flock to the colors; otherwise, men would be drafted by lot. "Having all things in readiness," the governor told Washington "to use all expedition in proceeding to the Fork of Ohio." There he should use his troops to complete a fort he presumed had already been started by the Ohio Company—a clear implication that the company's business had become the government's as well. Washington was to act on the defensive, but if anyone interfered he should "restrain all such offenders" or "kill and destroy them."[5]

The lieutenant governor had gotten ahead of himself, because nobody volunteered. Resistance was so strong that a draft was out of the question. Then debate broke out in the Council, because the law was unclear on whether militia could serve outside of Virginia. Was Ohio in Virginia? Many men not invested in the Ohio Company thought it was in Pennsylvania. That ended the mobilization.[6]

Backing Virginia's claim in the west with armed force proved more complicated than either Dinwiddie or Washington had imagined. There had never been training for militia officers, and the citizen-soldiers had neither training nor experience. Nobody in Virginia could say how long it would take to march a couple of hundred men to the Ohio, how many wagons they needed, let alone food, horses, or anything else. Nor had anyone thought up a plan for enlisting allies among the Indians.

Challenging a professional French-Canadian army with a handful of amateurs was not a promising idea. Washington's report had said that the other side could project as many as 6,000 troops into the Ohio Country; some Ohio Company traders had suggested even greater manpower. Washington had seen well-designed French fortifications entirely outside his experience. If Virginia built its own post at the Forks, could it do as well, and defend it? In short, neither the governor nor his adjutant had any idea what they were getting into.

Ignorance was no deterrence to Robert Dinwiddie. The determined Scot addressed the Burgesses when the assembly met on February 14, warning that French troops and Indians intended to advance in the spring and "build many fortresses," and he called on the members to vote a "proper supply" for defense. They were still enraged over the pistole dispute and irked that the lieutenant governor had already launched a campaign. Several members declared that it was all a plot to promote the interests of the Ohio Company, or another attempt to aggrandize the governor's powers.

The lawmakers appropriated funds, but they cut the requested 400 men to 300; to encourage enlistment, Dinwiddie proclaimed that 200,000 acres in the Ohio Country would be distributed later to men who signed up. The Burgesses granted £10,000 but established a committee of fourteen "leading men" who would "direct and appoint how the said money shall be applied." A military operation, in other words, would be commanded by a "military committee." The Council thought parts of the bill were unconstitutional. Dinwiddie said that the emergency was so great that he had to assent to the act as passed; he did so on February 23 and then prorogued the assembly yet again.[7]

Washington and Dinwiddie were both outraged by the way things worked out. The adjutant fumed about suggestions that he had been an Ohio Company stooge when he reported that the French planned to extend their presence in the Ohio Valley. "These unfavourable surmises caus'd great delays in raiseing the first men and money," Washington groused later. Dinwiddie was annoyed that the Burgesses had voted to send a delegation to London to complain about the pistole fee dispute. As for controlling the appropriation by committee, the governor said, "I am sorry, to find them too much in a republican way of thinking."[8]

While Dinwiddie and the Burgesses jousted with each other, on February 17 Trent and less than fifty men reached the Forks. This was a boost to the Mingo Half-King Tanaghrisson, who now saw evidence that the English would do more than talk about resisting the French. Tanaghrisson might have backing to rebuild his authority over the Ohio Indians. He himself set the first timber, declaring that the new fort would belong to the Ohio nations as well as the English, and together they would fight the French. The Shawnees, Delawares, and his own Mingos ignored him, however. They had suffered a hard winter, and they wanted to wait and see what a conflict between the white nations might offer.

Nations up the Allegheny sent word that once the water was clear of ice the French would advance to the Forks in strength. This reinforced cautious neutrality. The Virginian fort-builders ran low on food by March, and the Delawares refused to hunt for them, despite Trent's offer to pay for any game brought in. The party was soon down to handfuls of corn and flour, and although the French were approaching, Trent went east to beg for provisions, leaving Ensign Ward in command.[9]

Back in Virginia, Dinwiddie and the Council decided to raise six companies of fifty men each. The governor told a business associate on March 1 that he hoped these troops would be on the march to the Ohio before early April. These soldiers would need competent officers, and there were few of those in Virginia. Most company officers were unemployed Scots or young men of the planter class looking for adventure. Dinwiddie confessed to Maryland governor Horatio Sharpe, "We are in much distress for proper officers, but have taken all possible care of choosing the best we have, but not so well acquainted with the arts of war as I could wish, but as our cause is just, I hope for the protection of Heaven."[10]

The first duty of company officers was to recruit their men. They needed a colonel to command them, and for that Dinwiddie decided that the obvious candidate was himself, extra chins and all. He asked governors of other colonies to provide money for his expedition along with men to serve under his command. He also asked his London partner John Hanbury to get his tailor to make him "a proper suit of regimentals."[11]

Clothes may make the man, but Dinwiddie was slow to realize that they do not alone make the soldier. Besides, if he rode off to glory, his enemies in Williamsburg would take advantage of his absence. Washington approached Richard Corbin, a member of the Council and a chief voice in the selection of officers. He had told the ambitious major that he could expect "to be ranked among the chief officers of this expedition," as Washington reminded him. However, the young adjutant continued, "the command of the whole forces is what I neither look for, expect, nor desire; for I must be impartial enough to confess, it is a charge too great for my youth and inexperience to be entrusted with." He became lieutenant colonel in March.[12]

It is difficult to read beneath the surface of this statement. It might have been modesty, a style Washington cultivated when the occasion demanded. Or it might reflect ambition, because the colonel actually appointed—Joshua Fry, a mathematics instructor at the College of William and Mary—was too old and fat to move fast, putting Washington in effective command, but if the expedition marched into disaster blame would fall on the colonel.

Washington, as always, looked after his own interests. He had asked Corbin and colony treasurer John Robinson, also speaker of the House of Burgesses, what a lieutenant colonel's pay would be. He was told fifteen shillings per day and objected that that was too little. Then Robinson told him officers would receive their provisions without charge, and he accepted. When he got his commission in March, however, his pay had been cut to "12s 6d [pence] per day without any trouble of commanding a company"—ten shillings less than a British lieutenant colonel. The promised provisions equaled one private's ration per day. Not for the last time, Washington threatened to resign. William Fairfax talked him out of that and promised to seek higher compensation.[13]

Washington had gone ahead to Alexandria early in March to supervise recruitment and logistics. He formed a business partnership with the merchant John Carlyle, appointed commissary of supply, a man of status and a son-in-law of William Fairfax. But the weather was bad, and few recruits signed up. Those who showed interest asked only about the pay. Washington told Dinwiddie on March 9 that he had raised only twenty-five men, "loose, idle persons, that are quite destitute of house, and home, and, I may truly say, many of them of cloaths . . . in short, they are as illy provided as can be well conceiv'd." Their pay was eight pence per day, about a third of what a common laborer earned. The recruits were often described as "vagabonds," what would today be called "homeless," society's dropouts.[14]

Dinwiddie's appeals to other colonies brought mixed results.

North Carolina's assembly voted £12,000 and promised to recruit 750 men. Maryland was no help, and Pennsylvania was paralyzed by factional quarrels. Washington had urged Dinwiddie to recruit Cherokees, Catawbas, and Chickasaws from the Carolina frontier, to make up the shortfall in manpower. South Carolina's governor James Glen objected, "What benefit then do you propose by sending so many pressing messages to prevail" on these nations to go to Virginia? Dinwiddie was promised independent companies (royal troops not part of regiments) from South Carolina and New York; they should provide veteran manpower.[15]

The lieutenant governor pressed Washington on March 15 to make haste, because before he left to round up provisions Trent had sent word that the French were bearing down on the Forks. Dinwiddie told Washington that the other side was moving into Ohio more rapidly than expected, which made it "necessary for you to march what soldiers you have enlisted, immediately to the Ohio, and escort some waggons with the necessary provisions." Colonel Fry, his nominal commander, would march with others "as soon as possible."[16]

Washington received this message in Alexandria on March 20. He had only about seventy-five recruits, and shortages of money and credit hampered efforts to clothe, equip, and feed them and provide transportation. Dinwiddie told him, "You are to conduct yourself as the circumstances of the service shall require and to act as you shall find best for the furtherance of His Majesty's service and the good of his dominion." With that grant of discretion, Washington advertised the offer of land grants after the campaign. This was enough to raise his strength by the end of the month to 160 untrained volunteers. He needed more officers, wagons, and supplies, the roads were muddy, and the artillery from Britain was too heavy to move. But the governor wanted him to head out. From Wills Creek, the Ohio Company post on the Potomac opposite the Shenandoah Valley, he would go forward light if he could get enough pack animals. He asked Trent to send some to Wills.

Washington began a new journal on March 31, 1754, noting that his orders were to march his troops "towards the *Ohio*, there to help Captain *Trent* to build forts, and to defend the possessions of his Majesty against the attempts and hostilities of the *French*." Wearing his Virginia militia uniform—red coat with white lace cuffs, red vest and breeches, black boots, a black tricorn—on April 2 Washington climbed atop a tall horse and rode out at the head of a corps of men wearing cloth coats, breeches, and hunting shirts. It was his first independent military command.[17]

March Gently Across the Mountains, Clearing the Roads as We Go

He marched out of Alexandria with what he grandly styled two "companies of foot," commanded by Captain Peter Hog and Lieutenant Jacob van Braam, along with five subalterns, two sergeants, six corporals, a drummer, 120 privates, a surgeon, and one "*Swedish* gentleman, who was a volunteer." Hog was a Scotsman, fifty-one years old, who would later take charge of frontier fort construction. Van Braam was Washington's translator from the year before. The surgeon was Dr. James Craik, another Scot, twenty-three years old, who would attend at Washington's deathbed. The corps was trailed by two wagons and made just six miles the first day.[18]

The party slogged into Winchester on April 10, where Washington was joined by Captain Adam Stephen, his future second in command. Stephen was also Scottish, thirty-three, a university-trained medical doctor, veteran of the Royal Navy, somewhat of a braggart, who made important friends when he set up practice in Virginia. He was a muscular man, full of jovial self-confidence, but given to occasionally erratic behavior. That grew out of a fondness for the jug noticeable even in that hard-drinking age.[19]

Washington first confronted at Winchester what would be his greatest military headache: desertion. Four of his men had plotted to go over the hill, and they would have gotten away except another soldier reported them. He rewarded the snitch, and probably had the culprits whipped in front of the other troops. He was shocked to discover such disaffection in his ranks.[20]

Christopher Gist came into Winchester a week after Washington arrived, "sent from Oyo [Ohio] on express by the Half King in order to find out when the English could be expected there," Washington recorded in his journal. He said that Gist told him that the Indians were "very angry at our delay, and that they threaten to abandon the country; that the French are expected every day at the lower part of the river; that the fort is begun, but hardly advanced."[21]

Washington was stuck at Winchester without supplies or wagons. Commissary Carlyle had authority to impress civilian transport if he could not hire any at reasonable rates, but he had not done so. Washington impressed seventy-four wagons and teams, but only ten wagons came in, without enough horses. Gist's news alarmed him, so on April 18 he marched out for Wills with 159 men and a pitiful supply train. Washington rode ahead to find camps and scout the route, hoping to speed his troops along. On the 19th, nearing the Potomac, he got a frantic message from Trent, "demanding a reinforcement with all speed," because at least 800 French troops were on their way. Washington sent word back to Williamsburg, urging Colonel Fry to forward reinforcements and transport to him. He then went on to the South Branch of the Potomac to await his corps, which joined him on the 20th. Rumors swirled among civilians in the area that the French had taken the Forks.[22]

The rumors were true. Ensign Ward—Trent was still off looking for food—got word on April 13 that a large French force was nearby. Ward proclaimed to the world that he would "hold out to the last extremity before it should be said that the English retreated like cowards." His forty hungry men had just hung the gate on their little stockade on April 17 when the French advance force of 500 men and eighteen cannons debarked from pirogues and canoes, formed ranks, and marched toward the fort.

The French leader was Captain Claude-Pierre Pecaudy, sieur de Contrecoeur, a forty-nine-year-old veteran of frontier marine service, who had succeeded Legardeur as commandant. He was hard as iron, determined to oust the English from the territory, and in no mood to dicker. He told Ward that he had a choice between immediate surrender or a fight. Contrecoeur added that the English could march out with their goods and full military honors, so Ward surrendered his post. That evening Contrecoeur hosted the entire starving garrison to a lavish French dinner. Ward led his men out the next day. Behind him, he later testified, Tanaghrisson "stormed greatly at the French" and told them "it was he order'd that fort and laid the first log of it himself, but the French paid no regard to what he said."[23]

The Half-King understood that French control of the Forks meant the end of his fading influence over the Ohio nations. Contrecoeur knew that as well. He ordered Ward's shabby amateur stockade cleared away, and over the next few weeks he replaced it with a professional work named for the governor general of New France. Fort Duquesne was a 160–foot square with corner bastions, two ravelins, and a dry ditch. It was protected by rivers and a steep incline on the water side, so the north and west curtains, the northwest bastion, and half the northeast and southwest bastions were stockades *en pile*. On the land side, the curtains and bastions were built of two parallel walls of squared timbers laid horizontally, ten feet apart, tied together by heavy cross timbers; the space between was filled by earth. Embrasures for cannons were cut into the parapet. The fort soon included quarters and other buildings, an interior well for sieges, and an elaborate sewerage system. It could house only 200 men, so a stockaded hornwork with barracks was added later. The French were at the Forks to stay, but their system had weaknesses. If the English mounted a determined assault, the place was both too small to defend itself and commanded by high ground.[24]

Washington, meanwhile, had reached Wills Creek, where he found no pack animals or anything else useful. A rapid advance to the Forks was put off while he sent back for provisions and wagons. Then Ensign Ward, riding ahead of his retreating garrison, showed up on April 22. He told Washington "that the *Indians* kept stedfastly attached to our interest. He brought two young *Indian* men with him, who were *Mingoes*, that they might have the satisfaction to see that we were marching with our troops to their succour." They also carried a message from Tanaghrisson, by an Indian tradition of having a runner memorize a formal speech to deliver to its addressee. The Half-King begged Washington to come to his people's support. "Have good courage," Tanaghrisson advised, "and come as soon as possible; you will find us as *ready to encounter with them as you are yourselves*." He ended in torment: "If you do not come to our assistance now, we are intirely undone, and imagine we shall never meet together again. I speak it with a heart full of grief."[25]

Washington composed a speech in reply, carried back by one of the Mingo boys. "We return you our greatest thanks, and our hearts are fired with love and affection towards you," he began, praising Tanaghrisson for his "gracious speech, and your wise counsels." The English army was on its way; the first young messenger, he said, would go to the governor of Virginia to deliver the Half-King's speech. "We know the character of the treacherous *French*," Washington continued, "and our conduct shall plainly shew you, how much we have it at heart." He would "not be satisfied" until he and Tanaghrisson met, and he asked that the Half-King or a delegate meet the army on the road, "to assist us in council." He sent along wampum as earnest of his good faith, clearly worried that he would lose the only Indian allies he hoped to have.[26]

After hearing Ward's report and the Half-King's speech, and reading Contrecoeur's summons to Ward to surrender, Washington called his officers to a council of war to plan the next move. His information was that the French had a thousand men and eighteen guns at the Forks, with 600 Indians on the way from the Great Lakes. His detachment numbered about 150 men. Because it was "impracticable" to march toward the Forks with such a small force, but "being strongly invited by the Indians," the officers decided to advance to Red Stone Creek on the Monongahela, build a fort, and clear a road for artillery and wagons.

Red Stone was the "first convenient place" on the river, and supplies were there in a new Ohio Company storehouse. "We may easily (having all these conveniences)," Washington wrote, "preserve our people from the ill consequences of inaction, and encourage the *Indians* our allies, to remain in our interest." Washington sent Ward to Williamsburg with this information, the Mingo bearing Tanaghrisson's speech, and a letter for Dinwiddie. He sent a similar package to the governor of Maryland, saying he planned to "march gently across the mountains, clearing the roads as we go."[27]

Trent's men, meanwhile, had arrived from the Forks. Washington tried to recruit them for his command, but because "the officers having imprudently promised them *two shillings* per day, they now refuse to serve for less pay." The two-shilling rate for building the fort was usual for volunteers, but the Virginia militia paid only eight pence per day of active service. The difference resulted in unrest among other privates. Trent's men caused trouble until they finally ran off.[28]

To get to Red Stone Creek, Washington's men had to widen an existing trail. He sent sixty men forward, but they got only to Little Meadows, about twenty miles short of Red Stone, and stopped to build a bridge. Progress had slowed to under four miles a day, and reports continued to come in that the French were on the move.[29]

Washington was trying to advance over a narrow track more than eighty miles to a place less than forty miles from the Forks—within easy striking range of troops from Fort Duquesne. The racket of cutting through the forest, along with the foul curses of the hungry, sweating, fly-bitten men, told Contrecoeur's scouts where the corps was. Washington's strength was not enough to challenge the French, and he lacked enough transport, provisions, and even ammunition. His enterprise, in other words, was hopeless.

Why did he continue? As usual, he kept his motives to himself, but it was apparent that he was touched by the Half-King's plea for help. More important, Washington would not confess that he had not carried out his orders to secure the Forks. An older man with command experience might see that it was time to stop and take stock—and tell the governor that he needed to rethink the whole business. The youthful Washington was afraid that others would look on him as a failure, and that could cost him his command and his reputation. He was not incompetent, however, just young. Dinwiddie had sent a boy to do a job no sensible man would have taken on.

I Quite Despair of Success

Washington fretted about his reputation, but it remained high in Williamsburg. Ward and the Mingo boy got there May 4, and Dinwiddie summoned the King's Council, which asked him to "signifie by a letter to Col. Washington that his conduct in general has been approved of, more particularly the caution he has taken in halting at Red Stone Creek" until he had assembled enough men, supplies, and artillery to resume the advance. He need not, therefore, press on with inadequate resources; but even after hearing from the governor and Council, press on was what Washington intended to do.[30]

The French were evicting English traders, who fled through Washington's camp and told him his plan to clear a road to the Forks was impossible. A trader who came in on May 10 brought news from Tanaghrisson and other Ohio sachems, who had just received the speech the lieutenant colonel had sent them. "The Half King showed the pleasure it had given him and, before the trader left, a detachment of 50 men was sent to meet us," he recorded. Washington was sure that Tanaghrisson and his followers were staunch allies of the English. Croghan, who was on the Pennsylvania frontier, was one of the few Englishmen who knew better. The government might have its own opinion of the Ohio Indians, he told the governor of Pennsylvania, "butt I ashure your honour they will actt for themselves."[31]

Whatever the Indians did, Washington assumed the French were actively patrolling. He was stalled at Little Meadows by bad weather, but the rain fell also on the French. On May 11 he sent Adam Stephen with a detachment to Red Stone Creek to see what was afoot. Stephen struggled through terrible downpours that raised all the rivers. He reached Red Stone, where traders told him that all French parties had returned to the Forks because of the weather.[32]

Washington received encouraging news on May 12, when a letter from Dinwiddie informed him that Colonel Fry was at Winchester with over 100 men and would set out in a few days. Colonel James Innes was leading 350 troops from North Carolina, and Dinwiddie expected Maryland to raise 200 men. The Pennsylvania assembly had voted £10,000 to pay soldiers from other colonies in lieu of recruiting its own, and the governor of Massachusetts had sent 600 men to harass the French in Canada. "I hope," Washington recorded in his journal, "that will give them some work to do, and will slacken their sending so many men to the *Ohio*."[33]

Ward and the Mingo boy returned on May 17, bearing a letter from Dinwiddie, "wherein the governor is so good as to approve of my proceedings. . . . The governor also informs me, that Capt. *Mackay*, with an independant company of 100 men, excluding the officers, were arrived, and that we might expect them daily." Dinwiddie said that James Mackay "appears to be an officer of some experience and importance," and he hoped that he and Washington would cooperate instead of squabbling over who had the higher rank.[34]

Dinwiddie had reason to expect trouble. Mackay commanded the South Carolina Independent Company and had commanded others in several colonies. These units were part of the regular establishment, the officers commissioned by the king. Washington and his officers held provincial commissions. British regulars regarded their rank as superior to those of provincials whatever their grade, and this royal captain would surely claim precedence over a Virginia lieutenant colonel.[35]

News of the independent company's approach blew up an issue festering among Washington's officers: their pay. Mackay's officers and men were paid as regular troops, far more than Virginians, and they were better supplied and uniformed. Worse, Virginia paid its soldiers less than other colonies. Even worse than that, as Washington had already complained, the military committee had reduced pay from what it had originally promised, and it cut compensation for recruitment so sharply that officers had raised men at their own expense. Limiting provisions to one private's rations was taken as further abuse, because officers had many extra expenses.

The officers signed a protest and presented it to Washington on May 17, asking that he forward it to the governor. It included a threat to resign en masse. He could not refuse to accept the document, because the officers had a right to complain through channels. Besides, he agreed with them, and in one area—not allowing enough non-commissioned officers—he thought the committee had committed a real blunder. On May 18, rain pouring down, Washington huddled in his tent and wrote a letter to Dinwiddie forwarding the officers' petition. "I am heartily concerned," he said, "that the officers have such real cause to complain . . . and still more to find my inclinations prone to second their just grievances." He would "prefer the great toil of a daily labourer . . . than serve upon such ignoble terms; for I really do not see why the lives of his Majesty's subjects in Virginia should be of less value, than of those in other parts of his American dominions." He concluded, "I find so many clogs upon the expedition, that I quite despair of success."[36]

This last was the telling point, because the little army was becoming demoralized from top to bottom. Dinwiddie could not recognize that, because he was not a military man. He was a businessman, devoted to the sanctity of contracts. He answered on May 25, refuting the officers point by point. He was, he said, surprised by "such ill timed complaints. . . . The gent. very well knew the terms on w'ch they were to serve." As for their commander, he was surprised that Washington, from whom he had "so great expectat's and hopes," concurred "with complaints in general so ill-founded."[37]

Washington sent a speech to the Half-King and other sachems, via the memory of the Mingo who had returned with Ward. "*My Brethren,* It gives me great pleasure, to learn that you are marching to assist me with your counsels," he began; "be of good courage, my Brethren, and march vigorously towards your Brethren the *English*; for fresh forces will soon join them, who will protect you against your treacherous enemy the *French*." Washington said he was held up by "great waters," but he would march soon. He had just promised more than he was likely to deliver.[38]

After the rain stopped Washington took a small party out to

scout the Youghiogheny River, hoping that he might float down to the Monongahela rather than hack out a road. It was a rough and variable waterway, and a trader told him it was not passable even by canoes. He was back in camp on May 23 and sent Colonel Fry that bad news. He had learned from Indians, however, that there were only 700 or 800 French at the Forks, "and by a late account we are informed, that one half of them were detached in the night, without even the Indians knowledge, on some secret expedition," although he could verify none of this.[39]

Washington was not the only one receiving hazy intelligence. Contrecoeur had scouts out trying to size up the Virginia command, because his information was contradictory. The commandant had to keep the English away from his fort, but his orders forbade attacking without provocation. On May 23 he sent out Ensign Joseph Coulon de Villiers de Jumonville, thirty-six years old, a well-liked veteran from a large and distinguished military family. With him were Michel Pépin, the commissary called "la Force" by the English, and another experienced officer, Pierre Jacques Drouillon de Macé, two cadets, a volunteer, an interpreter, and twenty-eight privates, making thirty-five in all. Jumonville's orders echoed Washington's in the fall of 1753: locate the English, determine if they had entered French territory, then meet with their commander and summon him to withdraw. The aim was to present an ultimatum, not start a fight.[40]

The first Washington heard of this was on May 24, when Indians came in with a message from Tanaghrisson, written by his interpreter John Davison. "*To any of his Majesty's officers whom these may concern,*" it began in a decidedly English style. "As 'tis reported that the French army is set out to meet M. *George Washington*, I exhort you, my Brethren to guard against them; for they intend to fall on the first *English* they meet." The Half-King wanted to make Washington think he was about to be attacked; he did. The Virginian grilled the Indian messengers, and what they said should have calmed him. They reported two French parties out of the Forks, but none coming his way. The French were still working on their fort, many of them were sick, and, Washington told his journal, "they cannot find any *Indians* to guide their small parties towards our camp these *Indians* having refused them."[41]

Late in May, Washington led an advance party from Little Meadows to Great Meadows (now Fort Necessity National Battlefield, Pennsylvania), about halfway between Wills and Red Stone, ordering the rest of his corps to come up. It was a boggy prairie about a mile long and a quarter-mile wide, flanked all around by hills and by two mountains. It was bisected by a creek with a small tributary, and it offered good grazing for his livestock. There were also two natural trenches, shallow but improvable. "We have, with natures assistance made a good intrenchment," Washington told Dinwiddie, "and by clearing the buishes out of these meadows prepar'd a charming field for an encounter."[42]

Washington remembered three decades later that the place was "convenient for the purpose of forming a magazine & bringing up the rear—and to advance from (if we should ever be in force to do it) to the attack of the post [Fort Duquesne] which the enemy now occupied." His men extended the natural entrenchments, and Washington decided to erect a stockade, despite its being commanded by wooded high ground. He also sent out parties to prowl for the French, but all returned without finding anything. Everyone was jittery, kept awake with a constant alarm all night on May 26. The commotion was not caused by the French but by six deserters. "Be it as it will," Washington reported, "they were fired at by the centrys, but I belive without damage."[43]

On May 27 Christopher Gist arrived from his trading post about twelve miles to the north, saying that the French had been at his place the day before, when he was away. He had crossed their tracks five miles back, and he claimed that the party was fifty soldiers under la Force. Washington sent out sixty-five of his 150 men under two officers, to intercept the French between the Meadows and the Monongahela, assuming that they had canoed up the river. His report to Dinwiddie raised the French party to seventy-five men. Just after sunset, a messenger came in from Tanaghrisson, camped with some Mingos a few miles away. The Half-King had found the French camp about seven miles northwest of the Meadows. Washington had sent his men in the wrong direction.[44]

Tanaghrisson said that he was on his way to join Washington when he saw tracks and followed them "to a low obscure place; that he was of opinion the whole party of the *French* was hidden there." Washington recorded that he told the young Indians who had carried this message "that the *French* wanted to kill the *Half King*; and that had its desired effect. They thereupon offered to accompany our people to go after the *French*." To show his resolve, Washington led forty-seven men—half his strength still at Great Meadows—in a heavy rain, "and in a night as dark as pitch," along a narrow path toward Tanaghrisson's camp. They arrived at dawn, seven men having gotten lost on the way.[45]

Washington had no evidence that the French planned to attack the Half-King. He was not above straying from the truth when it suited his purposes, and he had been deluding himself the last several days. Thanks to Tanaghrisson's earlier message, he had persuaded himself that the French intended to strike him, and he had decided to get in the first blow. Since he also believed that Tanaghrisson served the English interest rather than his own, he expected his Indian ally to help. That was not a vain expectation, because once Washington and Tanaghrisson got together it was probably inevitable that they would go after the French party. What Washington could not understand, however, was that they would do so with entirely different motives.

There Is Something Charming in the Sound

Washington was driven by youthful uncertainty and a selective memory. He ignored the fact that ever since the evacuation of the Forks the French had driven off Englishmen but not attacked them. He ignored Dinwiddie's admittedly ambiguous orders to strike the French only if they refused to leave English territory. Moreover, France and Britain were not at war, and despite a requirement of the treaty of 1748 the two countries had not sorted out their respective claims in America; armed invasion by both sides was illegitimate. That did not close off diplomacy, however. Washington had carried his message to Legardeur, and now Jumonville bore a similar one to him. But Washington had decided that the Indian who had shot at him and Gist had been under French orders, and he would return the favor. He reached Tanaghrisson's camp at about daylight, and the rain ceased. Stephen said that the Virginians "put our arms in the best order we could," meaning that they drew out their ball and powder and reloaded with fresh cartridges.[46]

Washington led his forty men out behind Tanaghrisson and a dozen or so Mingos. The French were in a glen in the forest, surrounded on nearly three sides by a rock shelf about fifteen feet high in the center, tapering off as it curved toward its ends. The Indians silently went around to close off the rear while Washington spread his Virginians along the shelf. The camp was a collection of pole-and-bark wigwams, shelter against the recent rains. The French were just rousing from sleep about seven in the morning, men pulling their shoes on and getting ready for breakfast.

Washington's account of what happened neglected those details: "We were advanced pretty near to them, as we thought, when they discovered us; whereupon I ordered my company to fire." He claimed there was an exchange of volleys between the two sides, which nobody else remembered. He also said that his men killed outright ten to fourteen (his figures varied), while he lost one man killed and three wounded. Given that his men were green troops, who tend to shoot high, especially when aiming down, this would have been an amazing accomplishment in dimness and smoke. The action "only lasted a quarter of an hour, before the enemy was routed." He marched off twenty-one prisoners, while the Indians scalped and plundered the dead.[47]

It had not been that simple, or clean. Washington claimed that the French fired first, and his volleys were return fire. The French claimed that the Virginians fired first and without warning. What likely happened was that some French sprang for their arms, which drew fire from the jittery English—without a command from Washington. Most of the French retreated to the rear under the cover of trees but ran back when the Indians stopped them. The wounded Jumonville called for quarter, and Washington ordered a cease-fire, his first command of the action.

Jumonville had an English translator, although not a very good one. He explained that he came in peace, to deliver a message telling the Virginians to leave his king's country. As this parley proceeded, the other Frenchmen, a dozen of them wounded, formed ranks around their commander. Washington had brought his men down into the glen; he took Jumonville's message and handed it to van Braam. Tanaghrisson came forward, tomahawked Jumonville, and tore his brain out of his head, blood gushing. The other Mingos slaughtered the wounded, until the shocked Washington came to himself; he ordered the twenty-one surviving prisoners surrounded and herded them to safety. The Indians finished scalping and mutilating thirteen corpses, decapitating one and mounting the head on a stick, then left the glen. The wigwam camp was a ghastly mess, blowflies swarming, buzzards circling overhead, wolves closing in.

Washington's attempts to paper over the horror that he had witnessed are understandable. As he led his party away with the prisoners, he was likely shocked and embarrassed by his failure to exercise command; events simply happened. This was his first taste of combat, itself unsettling enough; he was excited and probably horrified, and he did not exert control until the end. When he calmed down, however, his main worry was the danger to his reputation as a military leader if the truth of what happened came out. Unfortunately, there were other witnesses, French and English.[48]

One of them was a Canadian named Monceau, who when the Virginians surrounded the French had been outside the glen answering the call of nature, leaving his shoes behind. Barefoot, hungry, and in rags, he reached Fort Duquesne on June 1 and told his story to Contrecoeur. He said that about seven in the morning the party found itself surrounded, English on one side and Indians on the other. "The *English* gave them two volleys, but the *Indians* did not fire." Jumonville, through his interpreter, called for a cease-fire, then presented the summons for the English to leave the country. Monceau, Contrecoeur reported, "saw all our *Frenchmen* coming up close to M. *de Jumonville*, whilst they were reading the summons, so that they were all in platoons, between the *English* and the *Indians*," at which time Monceau scampered off. He heard no more shooting.[49]

Contrecoeur, who reported this to the marquis Duquesne, seemed at the time more concerned that Jumonville had not shown enough sense about security. "The misfortune is," he said, "that our people were surprized; the *English* had incircled them, and came upon them unseen." Jumonville had not posted sentries.

Another account came from John Shaw, one of Washington's privates, a twenty-year-old Irishman who was not at the glen but learned all he could from others who were. By August charges of a massacre of the French party began bothering several colonial governors. The governor of South Carolina launched an investigation, and on August 21 he had Shaw sworn in and deposed. His was the most complete contemporary account. He said that Washington's party "found them encamped between two hills, being early in the morning some of them were asleep and some eating, but haveing heard a noise they were immediately in great confusion and betook themselves to their arms . . . and one of them fired a gun upon which Col Washington gave the word for all his men to fire."

Several of the French went down wounded, the rest ran to the rear and into the Indians, and "when they saw them imediately fled back to the English and delivered up their arms desireing quarter which was accordingly promised them," Shaw said. The Indians came up a while later, and "the Half King took his tomahawk and split the head of the French captain haveing first asked if he was an Englishman and haveing been told he was a French man. He then took out his brains and washed his hands with them and then scalped him." Shaw admitted that he had only heard about this, but he "never heard it contradicted." He had "seen the bones of the Frenchmen who were killed in number about 13 or 14 and the head of one stuck upon a stick for none of them were buried."[50]

Shaw's account supports Washington's contention that the French—at least one of them—fired first. Otherwise he covers much that the Virginian left out of his journal and official report. There is, for instance, the detail about Tanaghrisson identifying Jumonville before tomahawking him. Contrecoeur's last informant from the scene was Denis Kaninguen, a deserter from Washington's (or possibly Tanaghrisson's) corps who rode into Fort Duquesne on June 30 aboard a stolen army horse. The commandant at Presque Isle transcribed Contrecoeur's summary of Kaninguen's statement before forwarding it to Montreal on July 7. His account was full of valuable intelligence about the size of Washington's force, the shortage of provisions, and the names of the officers killed or taken prisoner. As for the skirmish, he said the English fired first. While the two sides considered the summons for the English to leave, "a savage, came up to him [Jumonville] and had said, 'Tu n'es pas encore mort, mon père' [Thou are not dead yet, my father], and struck several hatchet blows with which he killed him."[51]

Washington had no idea that Tanaghrisson had deliberately held his men's fire. Slaughtering the wounded was the opening move in the sachem's plan to start a war on the Ohio. As soon as the action was over, Tanaghrisson sent a runner to Fort Duquesne to tell Contrecoeur that the English had attacked with malice aforethought. As the commandant reported to Governor Duquesne, the runner added "that M. *de Jumonville* was killed by a musket-shot in the head, whilst they were reading the summons; and that the *English* would afterwards have killed all our men, had not the *Indians* who were present, by rushing between them and the *English*, prevented their design." Monceau's report that the Indians had not fired supported this story.[52]

Tanaghrisson had lost influence among the Ohio nations since Ward's surrender of the Forks, and he had only about eighty Mingo followers, mostly women and children. He had developed a convoluted plan to restore his status. Telling Contrecoeur that the Virginians had massacred his men would provoke French retaliation and in turn spark a war. Tanaghrisson would join the English, and with their backing reestablish himself as a power on the Ohio, or at least resume being an Iroquois half-king there.[53]

Washington knew nothing about Tanaghrisson's machinations, let alone that he had played the young Virginian as a pawn. He was more concerned about justifying what had happened so it would not soil his reputation. He filled his journal with adolescent arguments about how Jumonville and his men were not an embassy but a party of spies. When the prisoners told him "*that they had been sent with a summons to order me to depart,*" he snidely claimed that it was a "plausible pretence to discover our camp, and to obtain the knowledge of our forces and our situation!" Everything about their behavior was incriminating, especially their taking shelter from the rain in the glen and wigwams. Nothing could be sneakier than that.[54]

Washington was both arguing with himself and preparing to meet future accusations that he had acted without honor. This was also material for his report to the lieutenant governor, which he sent on May 29. His description of the action at the glen was stingy on details but lavish about his prisoners, who "pretend they were coming on an embassy, but the absurdity of this pretext is too glaring. . . . These enterprising men were purposely choose out to get intelligence. . . . This with several other reasons, induc'd all the officers to believe firmly that they were sent as spys."[55]

Washington was in over his head but not mature enough to know it. He had lost control at the glen, and his boyish anxiety about how the news would affect his reputation caused him to blame the other side. He was wrong: Jumonville's party was protected by the Right of Embassy fully as much as he had been the previous fall. His actions, or his failure to control his men, could not be justified as a lawful act of war, because the British and French sovereigns had not declared war. Grotius would have called the skirmish "private war," because

Washington had committed an act of war, but privately. The two nations had accused each other of invading their territories, but that did not create a state of war. Now the French could justifiably claim that the unprovoked attack on an emissary constituted a legitimate cause for war.[56]

Washington compounded his error when his prisoners approached him on May 29 and asked him whether he viewed them "as the attendants of an embassador, or as prisoners of war." He told them they were prisoners because they were spies. But legally there could be no prisoners of war without a war.[57]

It was probably expecting too much of someone so green in the world to do better than Washington did under the circumstances. Both the British and French governments had told their colonial governors to use military force to back up their competing territorial claims. Washington was caught up in a conjunction of official arrogance and greed, fear and misunderstanding, mistakes and random circumstances. The interests of the governors of New France and Virginia, of the Iroquois League, of the Ohio nations, of the Mingo Half-King, and of the Ohio Company had collided over his head in a smoky hollow.

Still Washington kept up his drumbeat of self-justifying letters. Dinwiddie took a clue from him, reporting to London briefly that "this little skirmish was by the Half-King and the Indians. We were auxiliaries to them, as my orders to the commander of our forces was to be on the defensive." Washington himself had become more chipper by May 31, when he wrote his brother Jack, who was back home in Virginia, that he expected to be attacked but "shall be prepared for them." As for the action at the glen, Washington told Jack, "I heard the bullets whistle, and, believe me, there is something charming in the sound." This was published in London in August, and the puerile boast caused King George to say, "He would not say so, if he had been used to hear many."[58]

Unaware that he had made himself a target of ridicule, at Great Meadows Washington sent his prisoners off under escort on May 30. He also began "to raise a fort with small pallisadoes, fearing that when the *French* should hear news of that defeat, we might be attacked by considerable forces." He wrote Colonel Fry asking for reinforcements with an outburst of boyish bluster. "If there does not come a sufficient reenforcement," he declared, "we must either quit our ground and retreat to you, or fight very unequal numbers, which I will do before I will give up one inch of what we have gained." Fry would not see this boast, because near Wills Creek he fell from his horse, cracked his head, and died on May 31. The command devolved on Washington.[59]

He was going to need more than bravado to meet what was coming at him. "Sweetheart" Bonin was at Fort Duquesne when the news came in about the glen. "The defeat of what was a sort of embassy," he recorded, "obliged the commander Contrecoeur to inform Governor General Duquesne about it. The latter wrote to the minister of marine, who denounced it to the English ambassador as assassination. It resulted in arousing much feeling in this country between the French and the English." Then word arrived from Quebec that the king of England had ordered his colonial governors to attack Canada "on all sides." Bonin neatly summarized the history when he said that what had begun a couple years earlier as "only traders' quarrels, later became territorial disputes, and finally open war." In the middle stood George Washington.[60]

FIVE

JOIN YOUR FRENCH FATHER AND HELP HIM CRUSH THE ASSASSINS

(1754)

> [War] is a cloud of uncertainties, haste, rapid movements, congestion on the roads, strange terrain, lack of ammunition and supplies at the right place at the right moment, failures of communications, terrific tests of endurance, and misunderstandings in direct proportion to the inexperience of the officers and the aggressive action of the enemy.
>
> —GEORGE C. MARSHALL

After the action at the glen, the French ceased evicting English traders and resumed sending them to Canada. These were civilians. The forty Virginians who surrendered at the Forks were nominally soldiers, but the French had let them go home. The officers and men taken by Washington at the glen were also soldiers, but he denied that status and imprisoned them as spies. What the French realized, and the Virginians did not, was that military conflict outside a declared state of war was an "illegal war" in international law. The keeping of prisoners in such a conflict was also illegal, so they were entitled to immediate release. Yet both the English and the Canadians began taking captives and hostages, outside the purview of the Law of War, because most were colonial civilians or Indians.

Eighteenth-century officers taken in declared war expected early release. Military prisoners taken in an "illegal war" were a delicate question, but custom and law dictated that they receive the same treatment as if a war existed. Washington's failure to protect wounded prisoners—his claim that they hit the ground dead was false—and his confinement of *troupes de la marine* defied both custom and law. That led to widespread mistreatment of military prisoners, in Europe and especially in America.

The situation so troubled conscientious officials that delegations from Britain and France met at Écluse (Sluis) in the Netherlands in 1759 and formalized new procedures even as their declared war continued. The parties agreed that "all prisoners" must be released within fifteen days of capture, by exchange (release of prisoners of equal rank on both sides), parole (prisoners released but they could not fight until exchanged), or ransom.

The Convention of Écluse answered Washington's failure to follow military tradition and the Law of War. It came too late, however, to govern his own treatment if the French got their hands on him after the action at the glen.[1]

The English Have Murdered My Children

Dinwiddie, Washington, and other Virginia leaders had blundered their way into an illegal war because they had talked themselves into believing that the French intended to expand their dominion in North America and drive the English off the continent. The government in London accepted this view, but nothing could be further from the truth. New France had been a drain on the treasury since its founding, because of the expense of running a vast empire at a great distance. "Canada is useful only to provide me with furs!" the king's mistress, madame de Pompadour, famously proclaimed. The furs were fashionable, but the trade with the Indians to get them cost more than they were worth.

The government in Versailles focused on Europe, where its ambitions lay. The cost of running colonies, especially New France, was a serious distraction. That had grown worse with Duquesne's fort program of 1753 and increasing graft by the likes of Bigot, the intendant. At about the time of Jumonville's death, Duquesne received a flat complaint from home. Unless the "excessive costs of the upkeep of the colonies" were reduced, the minister warned, the French government would abandon them. It was entirely possible that New France would retire from the Ohio Country, even that France would leave New France. Washington's attack on a diplomatic party, and the death or capture of its members, changed the situation.[2]

Duquesne agreed to support a campaign of *revanche* ("vengeance") against the Virginians, because Washington's insult to the king's flag required redress. There was also a personal consideration: Jumonville had left behind some very capable older brothers, veterans of frontier service in the *troupes de la marine*. The large Villiers family's roots reached far back into the history of New France. One brother was Louis Coulon de Villiers, forty-four, recently commandant of Fort Chartres on the Mississippi. He was on his way up the Ohio from the *pays des Illinois* with 300 Indian allies, a band of Indian hostages held as security against their nations' attacking Chartres while he was gone, and several boatloads of provisions, when he heard about the death of his brother, "which was regarded as a murder," according to a French soldier.[3]

Fort Duquesne's garrison had already been reinforced to 1,400 men, but in deference to Versailles, Duquesne had told its commandant, Contrecoeur, to exact his vengeance on the cheap: The first plan called for only 100 troops to chastise Washington. Coulon arrived on June 26 and demanded and received command of a much larger expedition. He was a battle-scarred veteran of several campaigns, but more than anything he was an aggrieved brother. He talked Contrecoeur into sending a mixed force of Canadian militia, *compagnies franches*, and fighters from several Indian nations.

Washington did not know it, but Virginia had lost the real struggle in North America, which was not over land but over the sentiments of the Indian nations. His command looked weak, while the French in Ohio grew stronger; strength made better allies than weakness. There were hundreds of fighting men and elders from many nations at Fort Duquesne, and Contrecoeur called them together for a grand harangue late on June 26. "The English have murdered my children," he began; "my heart is sick; tomorrow I shall send my French soldiers to take revenge. And now, men of the Sault St. Louis, men of the Lake of Two Mountains, Hurons, Abenakis, Iroquois of La Présentation, Nipissings, and Ottawas"—he named nations from all over the *pays d'en haut* and from as far away as the Atlantic Coast—"I invite you all by this belt of wampum to join your French father and help him to crush the assassins. Take this hatchet, and with it two barrels of wine for a feast."

The nations named accepted both. Then Contrecoeur turned to the wavering Delawares. "By these four strings of wampum I invite you," he implored, "to follow the example of your brethren." They also agreed to take up the hatchet, but without much enthusiasm.[4]

Coulon would head out with about 800 Frenchmen and at least 400 Indians, although many Indians came and went during the march. The commissaries arranged logistics on June 27, while Contrecoeur, Coulon, and other senior officers held a council of war. They drew up a paper saying that it was *convenable* ("appropriate") to march against the English with a large force, "to avenge ourselves and chastise them for having violated the most sacred laws of civilized nations," meaning Washington's attack on an emissary. The Virginians' conduct justified the French in disregarding the peace treaty of 1748. Yet, after punishing the English and forcing them to withdraw, they should be told that the French still looked on them as friends, pursuant to the king's orders. The officers further agreed that should the English have already withdrawn across the mountains, they should be "followed to their settlements to destroy them and treat them as enemies, till that nation should give ample satisfaction and completely change its conduct."[5]

The point of this diatribe may have been to justify the campaign to history, or at least to superiors in New France and Versailles. It verged on an unauthorized declaration of war to the knife and was quite a contrast to Contrecoeur's usual commonsense approach to tactical and strategic problems. At the least, the document reflected the personal outrage the officers felt at the death of Jumonville and their determination to set things right as a matter of national honor. This was reflected in Coulon's statement to the assembled Indians, when he "told of his resolution to avenge his brother's death," according to "Sweetheart" Bonin.[6]

The expedition heard Catholic Mass on the morning of June 28 and set out up the Monongahela, part of the corps going overland, part by water. According to Bonin, Coulon decided to have scouts "ahead of us continually, and march by short stages." The party reached the Ohio Company storehouse at Red Stone Creek on June 30, left behind a guard for the canoes, and began cutting through the forest. The going was so rough that the chaplain said he could not go on; he absolved all of their sins and went back to Red Stone. "We saw human footprints during the march, which made us fear we had been discovered," Bonin remembered. "This caused us to redouble our precautions, not however fearing a surprise, because we still had scouts ahead of us." The corps reached Gist's on July 2 and found that Washington had had a camp there but abandoned it. The men huddled miserably, drenched all night by ceaseless rain. At dawn the march continued through a gorge in Laurel Hill, the rain still pouring down. A captured English deserter said that Washington was at Great Meadows, not far ahead. Deploying the Indians in front, Coulon formed his troops and advanced to confront the *Anglais*.[7]

I Thought It Necessary to March

Washington had no idea of the power that would bear down on him, so by early June he had decided to resume the advance on Fort Duquesne. He did not try to develop good intelligence about the other side, instead waiting for Indians to bring in news, however reliable. The young commander was beguiled by praise from prominent Virginians, including Charles Carter, a member of the military committee. "I heartily congratulate you and all the brave gentlen. that were of the company" that had defeated Jumonville, he said. Fellow Mason Daniel Campbell expressed his pleasure "with the fruits of your victory over the French." The sight of the prisoners passing through the colony "gave me & your other friends such satisfaction as is only felt by those who have hearts full of mutual affection & friendship."[8]

Flattery only increased Washington's appetite for more, which he expected after he drove the French from the Ohio Country. Before he could do that, he had to receive promised reinforcements and supplies, and secure his base at Great Meadows. The latter he did by ordering his men to clear brush and trees out to about sixty yards, which left his base within musket range of the wooded hills all around. The main defense was Fort Necessity, a circular stockade of timber deals (slabs) split from felled trees, about seven feet high and fifty feet in diameter. It enclosed a small hut for ammunition and supplies, but otherwise it was too small for his command. He surrounded the fort with shallow trenches, work that he had begun earlier. Washington had never built a fort before, nor had he ever faced armed assault, and it showed. He bragged to Dinwiddie that his work could withstand "the attack of 500 men." Tanaghrisson later dismissed it as "that little thing upon the meadow."[9]

The Half-King led about 100 Mingo followers, mostly women and children, into Great Meadows on June 1, followed over the next days by a few Delaware families. Feeding them strained an already impossible supply situation. Provisions had not come up from Wills Creek in any decent quantity for a month, and on June 6 the last of the flour ran out. Soldiers and Indians alike were reduced to eating fresh but tough beef from a dwindling herd; Washington predicted that even that would soon be gone. He begged Dinwiddie and Commissary Carlyle for relief, but all he got was soothing words.

"Very sorry that its not in our power to supply you faster & better than we doe," Carlyle wrote in a typical message on June 17; "its not for want of will but for two reasons first a scarcity of cash & secondly we are deceived by those that we depend upon." His typical excuse was that a contractor had absconded with the goods. Carlyle's promises to provide food and pay were echoed by Dinwiddie. Still the men went unfed, unpaid, and short of ammunition and tools.[10]

Dinwiddie balmed Washington's anxieties with one more promise: that he would ensure that a greater supply of rum was provided to the troops. Carlyle had a subtler distraction, forwarding a letter from his lovely wife, Sally. She tried to turn Washington's head, promising that "you have now a noblier prospect that of preserveing your country from the insults of an enimy." On his return from the campaign, "who knows but fortune may have, reserved for you sum unknown she, that may recompence you for all the tryals past."[11]

Washington was not in an amorous mood, however. Christopher Gist came into camp on June 6, declaring that a pack train with 50,000 pounds of flour should arrive by midmonth. He also reported that Colonel Fry, Washington's commander, had died on May 31. Gist told Washington to expect more reinforcements from the Indian nations, and that he had met a French deserter who claimed that there were only 500 men at the Forks, of whom half wanted to desert to the Virginia corps. Washington did not consider how he would feed such additional manpower, however imaginary; wishful thinking had taken over his outlook.[12]

He cheered up even more on the 9th, when the first reinforcements since he had left Wills Creek trooped into camp. They were the remaining companies of what was now called the Virginia Regiment, about 180 untrained men under captains Robert Stobo and Andrew Lewis and Lieutenant George Mercer, led by Major George

Muse. They brought with them some supplies, but not enough, and nine 2–pounder swivel guns with mounts. These could be loaded with iron shot, but more commonly with iron scrap or pebbles, turning them into large shotguns. They were useless against a fortification, however, so for Washington's planned attack on Fort Duquesne they were just excess baggage.

The new arrivals also delivered a string of messages from Dinwiddie, one of them appointing Washington to command the regiment with the rank of colonel; Muse became lieutenant colonel, and Adam Stephen major. The lieutenant governor reminded Washington, however, that in March he had appointed North Carolina colonel James Innes to command of all colonial forces in the expedition, which he predicted would be "very agreeable to you and the other officers." He hoped Innes would reach Winchester soon and take command shortly thereafter.[13]

The newly arrived Virginia troops said that the South Carolina independent company was not far behind. Knowing that its captain would not submit to his command, Washington apparently decided to avoid him. A false alarm on the night of the 10th caused him to send out Indian scouts to find out what the French were up to. One party returned on June 12, reporting that ninety men were near the Youghiogheny River, aiming to attack him. "Upon this advice," he recorded, "I thought it necessary to march with the major part of the regiment." He trooped out with 130 soldiers and thirty Indians, and half a mile out they met another party of scouts. They advised that the ninety-man patrol was just nine French deserters, so he sent a detail to bag them.

The deserters told him what he wanted to hear "and confirmed us in our opinion" that Jumonville had been sent to spy on the English. They also claimed that French soldiers at the Forks "were only waiting for a favourable oppertunity to come and join us," that Contrecoeur expected reinforcements of 400 men, that the fort was completed, that it had only eight small guns, and that the French knew Washington's strength and location. The Delawares and Shawnees "had taken up the hatchet against us," Washington recorded, "whereupon, I resolved to invite those two nations to come to a council" by sending runners with wampum.[14]

Washington was gullible enough to believe everything he heard, especially that much of the garrison at Fort Duquesne was ready to go over the hill. He got the deserters to write a letter to comrades at the fort urging them to come to him. The message was, not surprisingly, intercepted. Contrecoeur sent a copy to Duquesne, who expressed utter contempt for the Virginia colonel. "You see how treacherous he is," the governor told Contrecoeur, "having expected he could, in trusting our nine vile deserters, make your garrison revolt, by which means they flattered themselves they could take the fort." In his opinion, Washington was not only dishonorable, but stupid.[15]

Captain James Mackay and his South Carolina independents marched into the Meadows late on June 14. The mere appearance of these spit-and-polish redcoats raised the question of relative rank that annoyed Washington and his officers. Dinwiddie had tried to get Mackay to serve under Fry, and then under Washington, but the captain tap-danced around the issue. He reminded the Virginia colonel that his own commission was royal, and that the governor had no power to grant commissions superior to his. His company set up camp separately from the Virginians; Washington declined to inspect it, and Mackay refused to accept the other corps's "paroles" (officers' passwords) and countersigns. He was polite and respectful but adamant that his command was separate. His company would not do road work unless given the pay due to regulars, which was far more than the Virginians got for their labor.[16]

Mackay's independents may have been snobs, but they were good soldiers. Not so the two independent companies from New York. They showed up in Norfolk on June 16 looking like drafted rag pickers, their physical condition poor, their behavior worse, and they had no arms or equipment. Dinwiddie sent them upriver for the commissary to dress and outfit, but they never got into the war. Neither did Innes's North Carolinians, most of whom stayed home, nor southern Indians the governor had tried to recruit, nor the final thirty men allotted to the regiment. The entire campaign to drive the French out of Ohio, assembled at Great Meadows, now numbered around 400 Englishmen. The Virginians' training had been no more than a few militia-style drills, officers and noncoms teaching basic movements out of tactical manuals. They could shoot, after a fashion, but they were not soldiers. They were common laborers building a road.[17]

Washington decided to advance on Fort Duquesne, leaving the independent company behind to guard the stores. On June 15, he reported, his 300 men started clearing the roads. The next day, "Set out for *Red-Stone-Creek*, and were extremely perplexed, our waggons breaking very often." And so it went, the inexperienced Washington unable to anticipate that the worst might happen. He knew firsthand the trackless wilderness he was trying to cut through, but he never considered how hard that would be. Wagons broke down, horses dropped, and progress slowed to a crawl. The little army collapsed in exhaustion on the 18th.[18]

Washington's decision to advance cannot be attributed to inexperience alone. There was also his youthful ambition, because he wanted to win more glory before Innes superseded him. He had complained bitterly about Mackay's refusal to accept him as a superior, and Dinwiddie spent the month of June sending him repetitive letters explaining how his instructions to Innes would overcome all problems. Innes was a veteran of the 1741 campaign against Cartagena, and he held an old royal commission, so Mackay must obey him. Dinwiddie insisted that Innes carried instructions for every part of the campaign, even clearing roads, so Washington feared he would not have much command authority left. Finally, the governor counseled the young man not to advance farther until Innes joined him, softening that with: "but be always assured that I have a true regard for yr. merit & good conduct." By the time Washington received this it was too late.[19]

He Would by No Means Take Advice from Indians

He stalled at Gist's trading post, just a few miles out of the Meadows, because eight Mingos confronted him, declaring that they wanted to attack the French but they needed a show of force from the English. For some reason he did not explain, Washington concluded "that their intentions towards us were evil." He postponed a full exchange of speeches until Tanaghrisson and George Croghan arrived, and the Mingos sent him wampum and apologized for demanding an early council.[20]

The Half-King arrived that afternoon, and through his good offices about forty delegates from the Six Nations, Delawares, Shawnees, and Mingos assembled so Washington could "give them audience" and record it all in his journal. The speaker for the Iroquois directed his speech to the governor of Virginia, saying that the nations had been "informed you threaten to destroy entirely all your Brethren the Indians, who will not join you on the roads," so they feared an English attack. "We would desire to know from your mouth, if there be any truth in that information," the speaker demanded. He apologized for asking that question—Indian diplomacy revolved around politeness—but warned that the Indians would have to answer to the French when they got home.

Washington replied for the governor, delivering an intemperate tirade about the "treacherous" French, who had spread these lies about the English to serve their own purpose, which was to expel the Indian nations from their lands. The English, "your real friends," were "too generous to think of using" the Indians that way. Instead, they had "sent *an army to maintain your rights*; to put you in the possession of your lands," and to drive out the French. The English fought for the safety of Indian wives and children, and since this was the only motive for their conduct, they could not "reasonably doubt of being joined by the remaining part of your forces, to oppose the common enemy." Then he added a threat: "Those that will not join us, shall be answerable, for whatever may be the consequences." He promised that presents were on the way, and he gave over a belt of wampum as token of his honesty.

The council went on for three days, but Washington had already failed as a diplomat. The nations needed only to compare his small, hungry army with the strength of the French to see which was the power to reckon with. Furthermore, they knew that no additional troops were on the way. With the English unable to feed themselves, the promises of lavish presents were empty; gift-giving was an ancient, honored tradition among the nations, showing respect between communities. European goods presented as gifts—above those traded for furs—had over the last century become essential to Indian economies. And last, blustering threats violated traditions of courtesy and negotiation. They cut off discussion and meant nothing if not backed by credible force. Washington had presented himself as arrogant and suspicious, not a friendly ally.

This was reflected in the speech of the Delaware representative, who said it appeared that the English suspected his people of going over to the French. Washington protested, but to no avail. The Delaware reaffirmed his people's loyalty and presented a wampum belt to the colonel. The speaker then addressed the representatives of the Six Nations, reminding the Iroquois that they had warned of a pending war between the French and English, and had advised the Delawares to behave reasonably and remain loyal to the Six Nations as well as the English. This was accompanied by another belt, as was the speaker's address to the Shawnees, reminding them that the Delawares had granted them refuge in their lands.

Washington praised the Delaware speaker's "open and generous conduct on this occasion," calling his people "dearer to us than ever." He promised to fight for their rightful lands, not mentioning that they had lost much of their territory in Pennsylvania to English swindlers. He sealed the international friendship by presenting more wampum belts, urging all nations to stand by the Covenant Chain of agreements between the Six Nations and the English. And so the oratory continued, until the council ran out of collective breath on June 21.

Washington decided that some of the Indians were French spies, because they had claimed that 1,600 French and 700 Indians would reinforce Fort Duquesne. He talked Tanaghrisson into sending three men to spy on the Forks, and the Delaware sachem Shingas into sending a party toward the Monongahela, "to bring us news, in case any *French should come.*" He failed to talk Shingas and his Delawares into moving to his camp with their families. Shingas promised that his men would assist Washington and asked that he prepare "a great warbelt, to invite all those warriors who would receive it, to act independantly from their king and [Iroquois] council." He advised again that he would help "to make the affair succeed," but he dared not "do it openly."

That notwithstanding, the Delawares, the Half-King, "and all other *Indians*" returned to the Great Meadows, despite Washington's attempts to dissuade them. The colonel, not understanding that their positive words were their way of making a graceful exit, continued optimistic, because "though we had lost them, I still had spies of our own people, to prevent being surprised." He sent messengers to the Meadows twice to persuade Tanaghrisson and his people to rejoin the army but failed. To suspicious Indians still at Gist's, he announced that he would cease working on the road but would go across country to the Forks, and that he was waiting only for "the reinforcement which was coming to us, our artillery, and our waggons to accompany us there." As soon as they were gone, he "set about marking out and clearing a road towards *Red-Stone.*"

If Washington believed that this lie would go undetected, his attitude toward Indians bordered on contempt. When Duquesne received the colonel's journal in September and read about the council, he concluded that the Virginian was incompetent. "The hypocrisy of the Englishman is unmasked," he crowed. "That of the Five [sic] Nations is no less exposed, but after all, the Englishman is their dupe, because after so many little promises they abandoned him at the moment when he had the most need of them. On the other hand, you will see the Englishman, wishing to make them believe that he would march only at the solicitation of the Five Nations. The blunderer, thinking that with this strong assistance he could not fail to defeat us." The governor of New France was correct. When Washington lost the support of the Indians he had already lost his war.[21]

How had he alienated his potential allies so completely? Pennsylvania Indian agent Conrad Weiser recorded later that "the Half-King complained very much of the behavior of Colonel Washington to him (though in a very moderate way, saying the colonel was a good-natured man, but had not experience), saying that he took upon him to command the Indians as his slaves." The Virginian, the Mingo believed, expected the Indians to scout and attack the enemy by themselves. More insulting, "he would by no means take advice from Indians; that he lay at one place from one full moon to the other and made no fortifications at all, but that little thing upon the meadow, where he thought the French would come up to him in an open field." Had Washington taken Tanaghrisson's advice to build a stronger fort he would "certainly have beat the French off." The Indians left him "because Colonel Washington would never listen to them, but was always driving them on to fight by his directions."[22]

Tanaghrisson was gravely disappointed in Washington. He was also mournful on his own account, because after the council at Gist's he realized that he would never restore his stature among the Ohio nations, who increasingly leaned toward the French and against the English. Given French power in Ohio, if they joined the English they would have to abandon their homes and move east as refugees. The English had never been reliable allies, and the nations would not support their attempt to get control of the Ohio Country so their settlers could take over Indian lands. The Half-King led his family and remaining followers to Croghan's trading post Aughwick (now Shirleysburg, Pennsylvania), to sit out the war. He died of a mysterious ailment—some said of witchcraft—on October 4.[23]

Washington, meanwhile, resumed trying to cut a road and advance his army to Red Stone Creek. All his flour and bacon were gone by June 23, leaving nothing to eat but some steers and milk cows with their calves. The few Indians still with the command asked sarcastically whether Washington intended to starve both them and his fellow Virginians. Lacking enough food to take the whole corps to Red Stone, on the 27th he sent three officers and sixty-five men ahead to clear the road and build a fort until he came forward with provisions. He retired to Gist's with the balance of his force, which was leaking deserters steadily. He did not know it, but an optimistic letter was on the way from Dinwiddie, who said he had directed presents "to be sent out, to be given among the Indians as Colo. Innes may think proper with your advice." He had also "given orders to keep you duely supplied with provisions, & am in hopes you will have a good number of our friendly Inds to your assistance."[24]

There were not many "friendly" Indians left, but one came into camp on the 28th to report that he and others had passed by Fort Duquesne two days earlier and learned that 800 French and 400 Indians were marching against the Virginians. Washington recalled his advance party and sent word back to Mackay to bring his company forward, while he put men to fortifying Gist's post and setting up the swivel guns. The colonel called a council of his officers, who unanimously resolved that it was absolutely necessary to return to the Meadows and wait there until enough provisions arrived "to serve us for some months." The reasons included the report of the large body of French and Indians advancing, confirmed by captured French deserters. Also, the officers knew that two of their own men had deserted to the French and "acquainted the enemy of our starving condition and our numbers & situation." The French would not have to fight the outnumbered Virginians, merely intercept supply convoys and starve them, and anyway could bypass Gist's and get behind them. Finally, "the Indians declar'd that they would leave us, unless we returnd to the meadows."[25]

Unwilling to admit failure and driven by his ambition to triumph before Colonel Innes showed up, Washington had stuck his head into a noose. Now he faced a perilous retreat. There were too few horses, because he had sent most back for provisions. All that remained were two teams, a few odd nags, and officers' mounts, and these and the men must haul back the nine swivel guns, ammunition, and essential baggage. Adam Stephen later said that the retreat was over "the roughest and most hilly of any on the Allegheny Mountains." There was nothing to eat but some parched corn and scrawny cows, poor nourishment for men trying to lug heavy cargo over the wretched road. Mackay's men, who had come up from Great Meadows in time to go back with Washington, refused to help in the labor. Washington's Virginians wondered, If this was not proper work for soldiers, why should they do it themselves? Stephen recalled, "They became as backward as the regulars," and it was all the officers could do to keep the men at work.

Work it was, pulling wagons and loading their backs. Wagons and horses continued to break down, and the corps left a trail of abandoned goods as it labored toward Great Meadows. It reached Fort Necessity on July 1 and collapsed on the ground, too exhausted to go farther, while the last Indian allies disappeared. The Virginians and the independents did what they could to improve their poor defenses, and a scout came in with an alarm: The French were not far away. They had found Washington's litter trail.[26]

Voulez-Vous Parler?

It began to rain again the night of July 2, and the disordered English huddled with too few tents. By dawn the prairie was a swamp, the trenches filled with water. Washington ordered a roll call early on July 3, during a pause in the downpour. Of his nominal 400 men, including deserters unaccounted for, over 100 were not fit for duty. Those present and fit totaled 284, "fit" meaning starving scarecrows.[27]

Coulon's Canadians and Indians had also spent a miserable night, but shortly after they left their sodden camp on the morning of the 3rd they reached what would become known as Jumonville Glen. Scavengers had made off with most of the remains, but four corpses, "whose scalps had been taken, were still there," recalled "Sweetheart" Bonin. "They were buried and general prayers were said, after which Commander de Villiers addressed the savages upon the spot where his brother had been assassinated, about the vengeance he hoped to have with their help. They promised to back him up." The corps marched until late morning, when scouts reported the English camp ahead.[28]

At daybreak on July 3, while Coulon was at the glen, a single shot
had broken the quiet at Great Meadows and a sentry called for the officer of the guard. Washington and Mackay ordered their men to get
under arms. The rain resumed, and before long the space within the
entrenchments was a lake. The men stood unsheltered for nearly five
hours until nine o'clock, when scouts reported that a large number of
French and Indians were four miles off. The mud was deep, and the
water continued to rise.

Another shot two hours later announced the arrival of the attacking force. Coulon later admitted, "As we had no knowledge of the
place, we presented our flank to the fort, when they began to fire upon
us, and almost at the same time, I perceived the *English* on the right,
in order of battle, and coming at us." Bonin said that "half a hundred
armed men came out to engage us, probably not expecting to find us
so numerous. We advanced in three columns to the right. All the savages went to the left, shouting the war cry." Washington deployed his
men in line, the independent company on his right. The contrast between the redcoats and the ragamuffin Virginians caused some minor
confusion in Coulon's command, and he approached the English as
closely as he could "without uselessly exposing the lives of the king's
subjects." Washington's decision to form a regular line of battle was
foolish. His men lacked the steely discipline to fight in the European
style, and they would have stampeded at the first French volley.[29]

But Coulon was not about to advance directly into the English.
The *troupes de la marine* had their own wilderness tactics, adopted
from the Indians. He deployed his men on two wooded hills, one
sixty yards and the other a hundred yards from the stockade, shel-
tered by trees, crossing fire on the English works. They had scarcely
reached their positions when "the fort's cannon began to fire on us
with grapeshot (they were small cannons)," Bonin remembered. He
referred to the little swivel guns, which Adam Stephen commanded,
his gunners tearing down some of the palisades to give them a field
of fire. "We were in the woods, each behind a tree," Bonin continued. "As we had no cannon, we could only return fire with musket
shots. We nevertheless, reached the fort [with our shots]." The rain
suppressed the heavy gunsmoke produced by black powder, so the
shooting was good.[30]

Washington had pulled his men back to the entrenchments and
ordered them to return fire. He recalled that the enemy "from every

little rising—tree-stump—stone—and bush kept up a constant gald-
ing fire upon us; which was returned in the best manner we could
till late in the afternn when their fell the most tremendous rain that
can be conceived." It overflowed the trenches and by sundown had
drowned all the powder in the men's cartridge boxes and even that
stored in the hut inside the stockade. The French and Indians, under
cover and their ammunition dry, poured hell onto Fort Necessity.
Musketballs smacked into timbers, splashed into flooded ground, and
thunked sickeningly into human beings. Washington walked through
the storm of lead untouched, wondering what to do.[31]

The popping of the French and Indian musketry competed with
the roar of the rain, the screams of the wounded, and the gurgles of
the dying. For a while the besiegers turned their attention from men to
animals, and soon every cow, calf, ox, dog, and even chicken was dead.
By nightfall a third of Washington's command was down, and although
his men had learned to keep their heads low, there was only one case
of outright cowardice: Lieutenant Colonel George Muse hid in the hut
throughout the action. "We took particular care to secure our posts,"
Coulon recorded, "to keep the *English* fast up in their fort all night."

Washington was trapped, and he had not a clue how to get out.
His lack of control became obvious at nightfall when his desperate
troops broke into the rum supply. It was no sooner dark, Stephen
complained, "than one-half of our men got drunk." They were in fact
falling-down drunk, owing to their fatigue and empty stomachs. This
engagement, Washington's second action, would likely end in a massacre. Suddenly, at about eight o'clock, the enemy came to his rescue.
"We let the *English* know," Coulon said, "that if they would speak to us,
we would stop firing."[32]

The shooting ceased and a voice called out from the woods, asking, *"Voulez-vous parler?"* ("Do you want to talk?") Washington's situation was desperate, but Coulon had his own troubles. His ammunition
was running low, and he feared that the English might sally and attack
him in the dark. "As we had been wet all day by the rain, as the soldiers were very tired, as the savages said that they would leave us the
next morning, and as there was a report that drums and the firing of
cannon had been heard in the distance," he decided to offer Washington a conference. There was another reason to give the English a
way out: He and his officers agreed that "it was not proper to make
prisoners in a time of peace."[33]

Coulon wanted to send an officer to negotiate, but Washington feared letting a spy into his works. Coulon agreed to receive an English officer. Van Braam went out and returned with the surprising offer that the English could simply march away. Coulon said he had told van Braam that "as we were not at war, we were very willing to save them from the cruelties to which they exposed themselves, on account of the *Indians*." This was a generous offer, but Washington rejected it until his officers declared that the situation was hopeless. He sent the translator out again.[34]

Coulon told van Braam that his only goal had been to avenge the death of his brother, and now he had no reason to continue the fight. That provided the preamble for the articles of capitulation, of which there were seven. First, the English could return home in peace, and the French would try to protect them from the Indians. Second, they could take with them all belongings except artillery and *munitions de guerre* ("munitions of war"). Third, they would receive the honors of war, marching with drums beating and taking one small cannon. Fourth, they must lower the English flag. Fifth, French troops would take possession of the fort and receive the surrender. Sixth, since they lacked transportation the English could leave their baggage under guard and return for it later, but they must not build any fortifications west of the mountains for at least a year. Finally, the English must leave two captains—van Braam and Robert Stobo were named—behind as hostages against the return of the prisoners taken at the glen.[35]

Van Braam returned to Fort Necessity around ten o'clock with two copies of the articles, both in French. According to Adam Stephen, "It rained so heavily that he could not give us a written translation of them; we could scarcely keep the candle light to read them; they were wrote in a bad hand, on wet and blotted paper so that no person could read them but van Bram." With Washington, Mackay, and Stephen hovering around him, van Braam orally translated the document into English.[36]

Washington objected only to giving up his arms and ammunition, and van Braam crossed out *munitions de guerre* on both copies. Washington let Mackay sign first, a subtle way of making the captain his subordinate, then added his own signature as officer commanding. Van Braam slogged back to Coulon. The French commander accepted the change, signed both copies, and sent one back to Washington, who later learned that he had just confessed to the "assassination" of Jumonville. This was Coulon's whole point in the campaign: "We made the *English* consent to sign, that they had assassinated my brother in his own camp," he wrote.[37]

The term *l'assassinat* ("the assassination which has been done on one of our officers") appeared in the preamble, and the perfect tense of *assassiner* ("when they assassinated Sieur de Jumonville") in the final article. In the Romance languages, "assassinate" and "assassination" meant simply "murder," itself a strong word. William Shakespeare borrowed both from the Italian for his 1607 play *Julius Caesar*, and in English the words connoted sneakiness and treachery. Washington, Mackay, and other officers blamed van Braam for this "confession." The translator's native language was Dutch, into which he probably translated the French, and from that to English. He may not have known the English words, certainly not the load they carried. Reports of other officers differed, but he used a term he was familiar with, "death" or "loss" or "killing."

Washington never forgave van Braam, claiming decades later that the Dutchman "willfully, or ignorantly" deceived him, "I do aver, and will to my dying moment." In his defense, van Braam translated in difficult circumstances. In 1760 the Virginia assembly voted him back pay and an additional £500 as a reward for his service.[38]

That issue aside, Washington later explained his reason for capitulating. With no prospect of improving his situation, he said, he "readily acceded" to the terms of capitulation because his command was almost out of food, "and because a full third of our numbers officers as well as privates, were, by this time, killed or wounded." He did not mention van Braam in this account, nor Captain Robert Stobo, who both volunteered to remain as hostages. He was correct about casualties. The Virginians and independents lost thirty killed and seventy wounded, many mortally, out of the fewer than 300 effectives. Coulon lost three dead, one an Indian, and a few slightly wounded.[39]

The sun rose over the mud and humidity of Great Meadows on July 4, blowflies swarming over the dead, mosquitoes around the living. Coulon reported that he sent a detachment to take possession of the fort as the garrison filed off, "and the number of their dead and wounded, moved me to pity, notwithstanding my resentment for their having in such a manner, taken away my brother's life." He wanted to show "how desirous we were to use them as friends." But the defeated men saw few friends because, Virginian Robert Callender said, the Indians with the French were not from northern nations, as the English assumed. What was "most severe upon us" was that "they were all our own Indians, Shawnesses, Delawares and Mingos."[40]

The French stood between the Indians and the English while the officers picked men able to haul powder, provisions, and the wounded. Private baggage stayed behind, including Washington's best uniform, which he sold to van Braam. Many of the wounded were too weak to move, so the colonel left Dr. Craik and eleven able men to guard them and the goods until later retrieved; the Indians plundered the cache once the Virginians were out of sight. They were not the only scavengers. Adam Stephen, wet, caked with mud and powder soot, was organizing the retreat when his servant shouted, "Major, a Frenchman has carried off your clothes!" Stephen spotted his portmanteau on the shoulder of a French soldier, caught the man, took the case, kicked the culprit, and started back to the fort. Two French officers stopped him, saying that striking a soldier violated the terms of the capitulation. When they asked if he was an officer, he opened his valise, took out his "flaming suit of laced regimentals," and pulled it on over the grime. The officers changed the subject.[41]

The exhausted, hungover survivors of Fort Necessity straggled out of the place through the morning, while buzzards circled overhead. The Indians wanted revenge for one of their own killed the day before. Coulon advised the last Virginians to get out while he "entertained the savages." They took the advice, but an hour later the Indians sent a party after them, returning with ten prisoners. Coulon ordered them taken back to Washington and sent six French soldiers with them. Once out of sight the Indians stripped all the prisoners, killed and scalped three of them, and returned to the fort. The soldiers let the nude Englishmen go and followed the Indians back to the Meadows.[42]

Bonin was in the French party that took possession of the fort, which was in "a state of absolute havoc" from the fighting and the drunkenness of the night before. The French demolished what was left of the place and departed for the Forks. On the way they burned all traces of English presence in the Ohio Country, including Gist's trading post and the Ohio Company's storehouse at Red Stone. Contrecoeur forwarded his report to Governor Duquesne, who ordered all Ohio garrisons to go on the defensive, and at the same time reduced their strength to a total of 500 men to reduce the supply burden. He also ordered generous trade with the Indian nations, so they would not return to the English orbit. Finally, because he had accomplished his mission, Duquesne asked the minister of marine for transfer back to the navy. One of his last duties was to greet a delegation of Iroquois who had traveled to Montreal to repair their relations with the French. If the Iroquois went over to the French, the English would lose their major northern allies; Washington's failure was greater than he knew.[43]

One of Washington's losses was his journal, surrendered to Coulon along with other official papers. Duquesne read it in translation, and it did not improve his opinion of the Virginian, calling him "the most impertinent of all men." He told Contrecoeur that Washington "has wit only in the degree that he is cunning with credulous savages. For the rest, he lies very much to justify the assassination of sieur de Jumonville . . . which he had the stupidity to confess in his capitulation." Victory lay ahead for Duquesne's country. "What desertion!" he crowed. "What difficulties in the provinces where Washington has gone through! That makes me believe that we shall always fight an army as poorly assembled as they are poor warriors."[44]

Washington did not think about his reputation among the French. He was worried about how the news of his capitulation would be received in Virginia. It took five days for his little army to cover the fifty miles to Wills Creek, which it reached on July 9. There he sent his first report to Dinwiddie, asking for surgeons to help with amputations on wounded who still stood a chance of surviving. Men were deserting and continued to do so over the next two months, in groups as large as sixteen. Those who stayed were too weak to run off, and Washington complained to William Fairfax that they were "almost naked." He had 293 officers and men on the morning of July 5, but by the time he reached Wills Creek only 165 remained. His only consolation was an encouraging letter from Fairfax, who said that the history of Marlboro's campaigns showed "many wise retreats performed that were not called flights."[45]

I Wish Washington Had Acted
with Prudence and Circumspection

Flight or no, the young colonel was both humiliated and depressed. "Mr. Washington," Mackay said, "was very sad company." His spirits were not raised by mail waiting at Wills Creek, because the ineptitude that had characterized Virginia's support for his campaign continued. William Fairfax told him the New York independent companies at Alexandria were "not compleat," and further that Colonel Innes would not leave Winchester without them. Innes himself promised, "You may depend I will make all the heast [haste] in my power to join you if you should be obliged to retire you must demolish your works." This answered Washington's earlier call for reinforcements.[46]

Leaving their destitute corps at Wills Creek, Washington and Mackay went on to Winchester to meet Innes for the first time. He let them go on to Williamsburg, which they reached on July 17. The lieutenant governor's reception was cool but polite. Dinwiddie was dodging any responsibility for the catastrophe at Great Meadows. "The late action with the French, gave me much concern," he told his superiors in London. "My orders to the commanding officer were by no means to attack the enemy till all the forces were joined."[47]

Washington was the toast of Williamsburg, where Virginians treated his campaign as a triumph. The *Virginia Gazette* of July 19 heaped praise on Washington for the defeat of Jumonville. As for the capitulation, "Thus have a few brave men been exposed, to be butchered, by the negligence" of other colonial governments that had not supported the campaign. That would be Dinwiddie's line to London the next several weeks.[48]

The King's Council awarded Washington 300 pistoles to distribute among his and Mackay's men, "as a reward for their bravery in the recent engagement with the French." When the Burgesses assembled in August, they also applauded. "I have the pleasure," Speaker John Robinson told Washington, "to acquaint you that the House of Burgesses have taken particular notice of the bravery of yourself, and the rest of the officers and soldiers under your command, in the gallant defence of your country, and have ordered me to return their thanks for it."[49]

Washington's greatest worry, that he would lose the favor of Virginia's important men, was relieved. Important men elsewhere were another matter. In other colonies and in Europe, he was regarded as disgraceful and incompetent. He had failed with the Indians, with the French, and as a commander. London pamphleteer John Huske called the articles of capitulation "the most infamous a British subject ever put his hand to." Governor Horatio Sharpe of Maryland wrote that the disaster at Great Meadows was caused by a reckless advance.

Thomas Penn of Pennsylvania called Washington's conduct "impru-
dent." Lord Calvert of Maryland derided his "unmilitary skill."

These judgments were reinforced when the French government
published and distributed a translation of Washington's journal,
which was translated back into English and printed in London and
the colonies. The enraged colonel had Mackay generate a letter-
writing campaign to refute the criticism, deflecting blame onto van
Braam. Horatio Sharpe at least bought that, telling Washington "that
the blame with respect to the terms of capitulation does not lye at
your door."[50]

Washington had developed a pattern of claiming victory while
passing any fault onto others: Jumonville was responsible for his own
death because he was a spy, van Braam for Fort Necessity because
he made a translation error. The truth, however, had consequences,
and outside Virginia these were laid on Washington's shoulders. The
Board of Trade, supervisor of British colonies, had called a "congress"
at Albany, June 19 to July 11, to unify the colonies in dealing with
the Indians. The latter were not won over because Washington's campaign had destroyed what little influence the English had in Ohio.
Iroquois leaders complained about being treated as pawns. This
generated plots and counterplots among colonial delegations. Pennsylvania delegate Benjamin Franklin's plan for a pancolonial confederation foundered.[51]

Sir William Johnson, Britain's superintendent of Indian affairs for
the north, was frustrated by the outcome. "I wish Washington had
acted with prudence and circumspection requisite in an officer of
rank," he complained to a friend, "and the trust at the same time
reposed in him, but I can't help saying he was very wrong in many re-
spects and I doubt his being too ambitious of acquiring all the honor
or as much as he could before the rest joined him."[52]

General Lord Albemarle, nominal governor of Virginia and ambassador to France, told the duke of Newcastle, "*Washington* and many
such may have courage and resolution, but they have no knowledge
or experience in our profession. Consequently, there can be no dependence on them." His solution was to send officers to "discipline
the militia and to lead them on as this nation; we may then (and not
before) drive the French back to their settlements." Washington's alleged incompetence helped shape British military attitudes toward
colonials, already negative, from then on.[53]

Albemarle's letter reached London while the government was being bombarded by proposals from Dinwiddie. While Albemarle suggested sending regular officers to train colonial troops, Dinwiddie wanted regular regiments to take over the campaign against the French. He warned Lord Granville, president of the king's Privy Council, that the French aimed to conquer the continent and that "the obstinacy of this stubborn generation"—he meant the colonists—left the country open "to the merciless rage of a rapacious enemy." When the governor of South Carolina questioned English claims to the Ohio, Dinwiddie roared back, charging that his colleague's letters and arguments "would have been more proper from a French officer than from one of His Majesty's governors."[54]

Dinwiddie's letters to other governors earned him no support for a renewed march to the Forks. There was an unspoken but noticed subtext to his words: Not just Virginia had been driven out of Ohio, but so had the Ohio Company. He countered with fantasies that the French planned to foment slave rebellions. He claimed that regular troops in America could be supported if Parliament levied a poll tax on all provincials. "Without some such thing," he told Granville, "these obstinate people will do nothing." Regarding another march to the Forks, he told his London partners, "It's of great consequence to the nation and these colonies, that I think no time is to be lost."[55]

On July 20, Dinwiddie ordered Colonel Innes to go to Wills Creek, the Ohio Company's last post, to build a fort big enough to hold six months' provisions. "I think it's not prudent to march out to the Ohio," Dinwiddie told the colonel, "till you have a sufficient force to attack the enemy, and that you be properly provided with everything for that purpose." The new fort was in Maryland, but it was a Virginia project, named Fort Cumberland, for the duke of Cumberland, favorite son of King George. Innes remained at Winchester, in no hurry to go to Wills.[56]

Washington and Mackay left Williamsburg late in July to return to their commands. Mackay went to Wills, where his surviving independents and the useless independents from New York sat. Washington went to Alexandria, where his Virginians had limped for resupply. They were demoralized, almost naked, and in a fighting mood only about not being paid. They had rioted when they passed through Winchester, where Innes failed to control them; he was as ineffective with his own North Carolina troops, who went home disgusted. Other

Virginians deserted, taking their arms with them. Washington fairly begged Dinwiddie to send money to pay and feed his men.[57]

He soon received some money, and something else: orders to invade Ohio again, and to do it immediately.

Our Prospect Is Gloomy

Dinwiddie assembled the Council at the end of July to decide what to do. He told Washington that "considering the present state" of Virginia's forces and a belief that the French would be strongly reinforced next spring, "It was resolv'd that the forces should immediately march over the Allegany Mountains, either to dispossess the French of their fort, or build a fort in a proper place that may be fix'd on by a council of war." Washington would not command the expedition. "Colo. Innes has my orders for the executing the above affair." Washington should complete his regiment to 300 men, and the lieutenant governor had "no doubt" that he would be able to enlist all the men he needed "very soon" and march them to Wills Creek. Repeatedly Dinwiddie told him to hurry.[58]

This order was ludicrous. The only troops who had not deserted were either too weak to do so or they had nowhere to go. The survivors of Fort Necessity told others about their privations, including lack of pay; this was not likely to encourage enlistments. Worse came out of Williamsburg on August 3, when Dinwiddie sent Washington £600, "which is all can be got." He was sure that when the assembly next met, the Burgesses would appropriate more. His sympathy for the complaints of unpaid men was limited, as he told Washington, "I am sorry yr regimt. have behav'd so very refractory" about what was due them. The governor expected "to hear yr. regimt. is compleated & will soon march for Wills's Creek." As for desertion, "It's strange the officers shou'd have allow'd them to desert with their guns . . . it appears to me the want of proper command." That was downright insulting. The letter ended with badgering: "I sent you orders to recruit your regimt. with all possible diligence . . . I repeat my orders now, & I am in hopes you will meet with little difficulty in complying therewith."[59]

It must have taken all of Washington's willpower to control his temper. Dinwiddie really believed that the shattered corps could

take Fort Duquesne before winter. He overestimated how many men
were available, and he underestimated their suffering. Desertion continued, and on August 15 a group of twenty-five went over the hill
at Alexandria, although in their weak condition they were quickly
rounded up and jailed. Washington's numbers were down to about
150 ragged men by the end of the month. Innes as usual was no help.
Still at Winchester, on August 11 he promised to advance to Wills
soon and build a fort there. He did not mention that the last of his
North Carolinians had abandoned him.[60]

To recruit men, Washington called on the county militia lieutenants. In doing this he tried to scuttle the governor's loony project by
way of a personal letter to William Fairfax. He told his patron that
there were too few men and not enough supplies to march on the
Forks and that the coming weather would be deadly. Carrying out
Dinwiddie's plans would be "morally impossible," so he predicted disaster. He asked Fairfax to intervene and get the campaign canceled.[61]

Meanwhile, news from Robert Stobo, hostage at Fort Duquesne,
supported Dinwiddie's case. He wrote two letters late in July and
smuggled them out with the help of an Indian. He described the fort
as undermanned, and the Indians not friendly to the French. "Strike
this fall as soon as possible," he urged, claiming that the place could
be taken with just a hundred Indian allies—as if Washington had any
of those.[62]

This was fantasy. Mackay at Wills knew that there was no hope
of putting an expedition together. He told Washington on August
27 that his men were out of provisions, and "We have been almost
drownded here being threatened wt. a second deluge," the rains
spreading "great sickness among my people," and making the rivers
too high for Innes and his men to cross. He begged Washington to
remember his "fellow suffers" when he raised supplies for the Virginia
Regiment and remind the commissary "that we have no tents or any
other necessarys fitt to take the field wt."[63]

Dinwiddie killed his own project by offending the French and the
Burgesses, both on August 22. He was willing to abide by the terms of
the capitulation, and that day he sent the prisoners taken at the glen
to Winchester. Washington objected to releasing them, especially the
commissary called la Force. When Dinwiddie read Stobo's letter declaring how highly the French esteemed their commissary, at the end
of August the governor marched the prisoners back to Williamsburg.

He sent negotiators to the French to try to exchange all but la Force for Stobo and van Braam, but the other side rejected the proposal.

As for the assembly, the Burgesses refused to spend more money on western campaigns and raised yet another stink over the pistole fee. Dinwiddie prorogued the assembly on September 5. As Fairfax told Washington, "Instead of augmenting our forces, the governor perhaps will have some difficulty to get means for the pay and maintenance of the remaining few you now have. . . . In short our prospect is gloomy." Dinwiddie ordered Washington to take what men he had to Wills Creek and put the Ohio Company store in defensible condition. Not wanting to serve directly under Colonel Innes, who had finally reached the place, the colonel found reasons not to go. Instead, he told Dinwiddie that he would try hard to carry out his orders, but he did not think men could be recruited without money.[64]

Washington sat tight at Alexandria, watching the last of his corps dissolve. Innes agreed on September 8 not to order him to Wills until he completed his regiment. Dinwiddie finally admitted defeat in a letter to Washington on the 11th, outlining his complaints about the Burgesses, who refused to authorize enough men to attack Fort Duquesne. "This late disappointment from the Assembly," he lamented, "has entirely defeated the operations I had proposed."[65]

The campaign ended on a constructive note. Innes sent a detail to Great Meadows to retrieve tools left there, and it "erected a puntion [puncheon, split timber] fort which when compleated must of course be of good service," Innes predicted. He had heard that Maryland Governor Horatio Sharpe would command the next campaign against the Forks, and he started work on Fort Cumberland at Wills. In an attempt to copy French patterns, in the fall of 1754 Innes erected a small square enclosure with storehouses and adjunct works surrounding barracks, and a hornwork projecting from the main enclosure. It was better than the English usually built, but it would not have withstood a determined attack.[66]

You Must Entertain a Very Contemptible Opinion of My Weakness

Innes was correct about a new campaign under Sharpe's command. Its origins lay in the duke of Newcastle's hearing about Fort Necessity, followed by Dinwiddie's official report in mid-September. Now head of the government, Newcastle declared that Britain dared not "suspend, or delay, taking the proper measures, to defend ourselves, or recover our lost possessions." He thought a swift counterstrike could drive the French back without igniting a declared war. He began looking for a commander in chief for North America, even approaching the duke of Cumberland, whom he despised.[67]

That did not work out, but in the fall of 1754 his government sent £10,000 along with a new governor of North Carolina, and orders placing Sharpe in command of the campaign against Fort Duquesne. This raised anew the question of relative rank between provincial officers and those with royal commissions, and Washington asked Innes for his opinion. He sympathized, but it was not his question to decide. In any event, Innes complained that he was wearing out from the burden of command. Washington stewed about his future in Alexandria for the next month.[68]

Hearing that something was afoot, however, he went to Williamsburg, arriving there on October 21 to find the assembly in session. Sharpe and new North Carolina governor Arthur Dobbs were also in town, huddled with Dinwiddie, while the Burgesses voted £20,000, added to the £10,000 Dobbs had carried from London. Orders from the ministry made Sharpe commander in chief of all colonial forces in his part of the continent. The ineffective Innes was reduced to "camp master general" at Wills Creek.[69]

The three governors had hatched their plan of campaign without consulting Washington, probably because he had opposed Dinwiddie's last plan. Nobody wanted to turn him loose with another independent command. As if that was not disappointment enough, Dinwiddie told the young colonel that his regiment would be broken up into its companies, meaning that he would be demoted to captain. The governor claimed that this was on orders from London, but in fact it was his own doing. He told Lord Halifax that his aim was "so that from our forces there will be no other distinguished officer above a captain." Washington resigned his commission in a huff on October 23.[70]

Sharpe had his doubts about Washington's abilities, but he also recognized that the proud young man knew more about the Ohio Country than any other officer. He wanted him in the army, and on November 4 his second in command, Colonel William Fitzhugh, wrote Washington a flattering letter trying to get him to reconsider. The general, he said, "has a very great regard for you, and will by every circumstance in his power make you happy."[71]

If this plea stood any chance of working, that vanished when Washington learned that the king had resolved the question of relative rank between provincial officers and those with royal commissions. The king's officers outranked those commissioned by colonial governors, even "though the commissions of the said provincial officers of the like rank, should be of elder date."[72]

Sharpe might have, under that order, offered Washington a commission equal to one from the king. Before he had a chance, the former Virginia colonel thanked Fitzhugh for his kind offer. He had many reasons for turning it down, one of them being relative rank. More important, he thought the disparity "between the present offer of a company, and my former rank," was too great to provide him "any real satisfaction or enjoyment in a corps, where I once did, or thought I had a right to, command." Moreover, "If you think me capable of holding a commission that has neither rank nor emolument annexed to it, you must entertain a very contemptible opinion of my weakness, and believe me to be more empty than the commission itself."[73]

Washington's temper and pride had gotten the better of him, and he had burned his only bridge. A soldier no more, he was also homeless, since his mother refused to release his inheritance at Ferry Farm. His brother Lawrence's last surviving child died that fall, and her mother had remarried and now lived with her second husband. Mount Vernon sat empty. He rented the plantation, its house, and eighteen resident slaves for 15,000 pounds of tobacco a year on December 17. By the end of the year he had bought more slaves, made arrangements for future crops and livestock, and begun buying furniture for the house. He mostly spent the winter, however, socializing with the Fairfaxes at Belvoir and the Carlyles in Alexandria. Always in the back of his mind was a confident hope that he would again don a uniform. Sharpe's campaign had been canceled, but there was always next spring.[74]

Six

There Has Been Vile Management in Regard to Horses

(1755)

When a man journeys into a far country, he must be prepared to forget many of the things he has learned, and to acquire such customs as are inherent with existence in the new land.

—Jack London

The drunken rampage at Fort Necessity was not unusual, because "spirits" were an essential item of army supply. Eighteenth-century soldiers consumed quantities of alcohol that would amaze modern civilians. The only thing that would surprise modern soldiers is that in the old days the liquor was issued, rather than bootleg. Typical regular army rations in Europe, copied in the colonies, provided a gill (four ounces) of spirits or a quart of beer a day for each enlisted man, and extra if he was assigned to labor. He also got a pint of vinegar.

The hard liquor in America was usually rum, an abundant byproduct of the trade in slaves and sugar, or sometimes the new American whiskey. The liquor was usually diluted with water, sometimes with hard cider, the latter making what was called "stonewall." The beer could be either the thick malt brew of the day or spruce beer, made with green tips of spruce boughs. It tasted like turpentine, but soldiers could get used to anything. Besides, spruce beer was known to prevent scurvy.

Troops in New England enjoyed hot buttered rum, while Virginians favored flip, a spiced rum mixed with sugar and beaten eggs. Other delights included apple jack, Royal Navy grog, gin horror, and makeshift punches. Officers, French and English alike, treated themselves to brandies and wines by the keg.

There were several reasons for the heavy consumption of alcohol. One was morale: Regular soldiers had come to expect it for over a century, and in America the eighteenth century was a heavy-drinking period for civilians as well as soldiers. Militia musters were often no more than drunken revels with muskets. In addition, water supplies were notoriously unreliable and could flatten an army with the "soldiers' disease," as dysentery was called. Alcoholic drinks were also believed to have medicinal value. An extra ration of liquor was a popular reward for good performance or extra duty. And last, liquor was commonly issued before battle, simply because it was easier to send men into a fight if they had a buzz on.[1]

A More Favourable Oppertunity Cannot Be Wished

Relations between Britain and France by the end of 1754 were driven by bad faith all around. King George's government expected to gain imperially by provoking a rupture, while that of King Louis sought to profit in Europe by postponing one. Both planned to send regular troops to America for the first time, taking the pending war away from their colonials. On the English side, this suited plans formulated by Dinwiddie and other governors, because the first item in their program was regiments from Britain. The rest involved cooperation between the colonies and London in the supply of men and provisions, winning over the Indians, and stockpiling stores for a campaign.[2]

In Virginia, this was an exercise in futility, especially because without Washington recruiting dried up; the former colonel had picked capable recruiting officers and driven them to succeed until the money ran out. Dinwiddie set a target of 2,000 new men in October 1754, lowered his goal to 800 by February 1755, and finally talked about drafting men from the militia. He renewed his ambition to lead an army in the field, and he asked for authority to fill in blank commissions issued by the king; London never sent those papers. He

wanted to make up manpower shortfalls by enlisting Indians, but neither they nor other governors were enthusiastic.

Logistics were no better. Horatio Sharpe had visited Fort Cumberland at Wills Creek in November and found a company of Maryland
troops and a few New York independents shivering in wretched conditions, short of food and everything else. The fort started by Colonel
Innes was unfinished and vulnerable, so he ordered a reconstruction.
He wanted to transfer provisions there, and late in 1754 he ordered
a new road built from Winchester. But farmers refused to hire out
horses, and wagons were so scarce that the Virginia government tried
and failed to build its own. Still, by February Dinwiddie claimed that
he had piled up eight months' rations for 3,000 men at Fort Cumberland. This was all paid for with the £20,000 in paper money that the
Burgesses had appropriated, Dinwiddie roaring that other colonies
were not doing their part.[3]

The lieutenant governor had badgered the ministry about the
need for regular troops, warning the Board of Trade that without
two regiments from Britain, the English would be unable to "defeat
the unjust invasion of the French." The ministry advised him in December that just such a contingent would be sent to America. It also
planned to raise two royal regiments in New England, commanded by
Governor William Shirley of Massachusetts and Sir William Pepperell,
the first American baronet.[4]

Evidence of this new commitment arrived in Virginia on January 9, in the person of Sir John St. Clair, a Scottish baronet, and former major of the 22nd Regiment of Foot, now deputy quartermaster
general of all forces in America. Lieutenant Colonel St. Clair was a
logistical expert, an often abrasive, can-do officer who favorably impressed Dinwiddie. He got right to work, contracting for packhorses,
establishing a hospital at Hampton at the mouth of the James River,
and going to Winchester to supervise transport of supplies to Fort
Cumberland. The road between the two places, he groused, was the
worst he had ever traveled. At Cumberland, he reviewed the New York
independents and discharged more than forty as unfit.[5]

St. Clair prepared the way for Edward Braddock, appointed commander in chief of His Majesty's forces in North America and given
a major general's rank for the occasion. He landed at Hampton on
February 19 and was in Williamsburg by the 23rd. "I am mighty glad,"
Dinwiddie said, that the general had arrived. "He is, I think, a very

fine officer, and a sensible, considerate gentleman. He and I live in great harmony." This was noteworthy, because neither man made many friends.[6]

Braddock was a squat, gray-haired, corpulent man of sixty who consumed good food and drink in plenty. He was abrasive and bad-tempered, as foul-mouthed as any of his soldiers, constantly in debt from gambling, but his loyalty and honesty were never questioned. As colonel of the Coldstream Guards, he had had freedom to curry favor at court. He had no experience in battle, or even in the field, although he may have commanded the garrison at Gibraltar for a time. He had a reputation as a skilled administrator and a tough disciplinarian, and he was a favorite of the duke of Cumberland, who promoted his appointment. He got the American assignment mostly because important men thought he was politically reliable.[7]

Few people liked him, but he inspired a kind of grudging admiration. Horace Walpole, chronicler of the follies of George II's court, said of him, "Desperate in his fortune, brutal in his behavior, obstinate in his sentiments, he was still intrepid and capable." Benjamin Franklin observed that the general was a valiant man, but he "had too much self-confidence; too high an opinion of the validity of regular troops; too mean a one of both Americans and Indians."[8]

Braddock proved at the end of his life that he was as brave as a lion, but his bluster masked a tender heart. He really did not want the American command, but he accepted it dutifully. Before he sailed from Britain, he visited his sometime lover, the actress George Ann Bellamy. "Before we parted," she wrote in her memoirs, "the general told me that he should never see me more; for he was going with a handful of men to conquer whole nations; and to do this they must cut their way through unknown woods." He told her sadly, "Dear Pop, we are sent like sacrifices to the altar."[9]

That premonition did not stop Braddock from fulfilling his duty. At Williamsburg he ordered St. Clair to issue contracts for 200 hired wagons and 2,500 horses, to be ready to move when his two regular regiments, under colonels Sir Peter Halkett and Thomas Dunbar, arrived. When they did a few weeks later, he ordered them upriver to Alexandria, where he stationed five companies, and dispersed the others to Fredericksburg, Winchester, and Fort Cumberland. Supply transports were sent up the Rappahannock to Fredericksburg, and county officers were ordered to provide wagons and horses. Braddock was empowered to take command over all civil and military personnel in the colonies, and he promulgated the king's orders giving regular officers precedence over provincials. On February 26 he ordered the British articles of war read to all troops raised or to be raised for his expedition. They would take the "oath of allegiance and supremacy, and in consequence of these articles, they are to obey, from time to time, any orders they shall receive from me, or any of their superior officers."[10]

When Washington learned of Braddock's arrival, he made discreet approaches to the general through his influential friends, skirting around Dinwiddie to get a place in the new expedition. The question of relative rank gave him pause, as did his debt load at Mount Vernon. If he marched off to war again it could bankrupt him, unless he found a capable manager for his estate while he was gone. There was another option, however, and that was to serve as a volunteer, which could give him free time to manage his affairs. This was an old practice in the British army, where young men of the upper classes signed on as cadets or aides, seeking access to regular commissions from which they could retire at half-pay for life. Washington hoped to become a regular officer on merit, but he was barking up the wrong tree. Regular commissions were almost always purchased, making officership the preserve of titled, rich gentlemen. This system guarded England against another Oliver Cromwell, who had used his army to become Lord Protector (military dictator) a century earlier. Officers who bought their posts were men with a stake in the existing social order.[11]

In hoping to earn a regular commission on the cheap, and a high one at that, Washington set himself up for disappointment. Braddock's presence was partly the government's response to the failure of the colonies to mount effective forces against the French—a fault displayed by Washington's disastrous record in 1754. The new commander in chief depended on the colonial governors to raise and support armed forces, and he had a viceroy's powers over them. The aim was to raise new colonial troops, but only as auxiliaries to the regulars. Braddock's two regiments were undermanned and over-officered, and they needed to be brought up to strength.

There were also British recruiting officers assigned to the colonies, to raise the two Royal American regiments and find replacements for them and Braddock's regiments. They proved better at recruiting than the colonials, partly because they offered better pay and rations. They raised troops to the end of the war, especially among indentured servants. They also played dirty tricks to get men into the service and thereby contributed to growing colonial resentment against British high-handedness.[12]

No hand was higher than Braddock's, and he quickly wore out his welcome by sending imperious demands to colonial officials. When the Pennsylvania assembly refused to grant money, he snidely derided "such pusillanimous and improper behaviour" and threatened to quarter troops at that province's expense. Merchants in New England and New York were trading with the French, and he flatly ordered their governors to put a stop to it. He summoned the governors of six colonies to meet him to receive instructions. Braddock's lordly attitude laid the foundation for future resistance to British authority. His viceregal powers did not impress the Americans, who might accept persuasion but would not put up with flat orders to governors and legislatures.[13]

The governors assembled in Alexandria in mid-April. Braddock had brought his plan of campaign from London, where it had been concocted by men who did not know that America was a nearly trackless wilderness devoid of subsistence for the troops. It was a complicated, four-point offensive against New France. Braddock would lead his two regular regiments and colonial auxiliaries against Fort Duquesne. Shirley, with Pepperell his second, would conduct the two new Royal American regular regiments on a campaign to take Niagara. Provincials from New England, New York, and New Jersey under the command of Colonel William Johnson, the Indian agent, would seize Crown Point on Lake Champlain. Lieutenant Colonel Robert Monckton, a regular, would lead other New Englanders to conquer Acadia. The aim of this fantastic enterprise was to drive the French back into Canada without provoking a declaration of war.

The campaign was burdened by provincials annoyed at being subjected to regular commanders, something to which Braddock was supremely indifferent. Moreover, it would take place during a time of peace, reflecting the combined duplicity of lords Newcastle and Cumberland. Their excuse was that the French had invaded British territory, although Acadia and Niagara had long been in French possession. Following Washington's campaign of the year before, it was a recipe for declared war.[14]

Against that background Washington found a place in Braddock's army. "The general having been inform'd that you exprest some desire to make the campaigne," Braddock's aide Robert Orme wrote him on March 2, "but that you declin'd it upon the disagreableness that you thought might arise from the regulation of command, has order'd me to acquaint you that he will be very glad of your company in his family [as British generals called their staffs] by which all inconveniences of that kind will be obviated."[15]

Braddock lacked authority to appoint anyone to a rank higher than brevet (honorary) captain, so Washington was happy to become a volunteer aide, treated with the courtesy due a colonel. He answered Orme with thanks and effusive praise of "the general's great good character." Besides his "laudable desire" to serve king and country, Washington gushed, he wanted "nothing more earnestly than to attain a small degree of knowledge in the military art: and believing a more favourable oppertunity cannot be wished than serving under a gentleman of his Excellencys known ability and experience," he accepted the appointment. However, he asked that he be allowed to first tend to his affairs and not go to Alexandria until the general was there.[16]

Orme and Washington agreed to meet on April 2, but word reached Washington's mother, who stormed into Mount Vernon that morning howling that he was ignoring his duty to wait on her. He missed the appointment and sent Orme his excuses. Unexpected company had arrived, he said, and his mother was "alarm'd with the report of my attending your fortunes." He was "much embarras'd" with his affairs, having nobody to manage them. "Yet, under these disadvantages and circumstances," he was determined to do himself "the honour of accompanying you with this proviso only": that the general would let him return to Mount Vernon during any "period of inaction" or as soon as the campaign was over. He wanted permission to delay joining the army until it got to Wills Creek, "for this the general has kindly promised." He got his wish.[17]

Once that was assured, and his younger brother Jack agreed to run Mount Vernon, Washington wrote to various prominent Virginians—but not Dinwiddie—telling them the news. He asked Carter Burwell, chairman of the Burgesses' military committee, for £50 to compensate him for the loss of his possessions and horses during the last campaign. He added that he was "just ready to embark a 2d. time in the service of my country; to merit whose regard and esteem, is the sole motive that induces me to make this campaigne." He would not profit from this service because he would be an unpaid volunteer; he was "thoroughly convinced" it would "prove very detrimental" to his private affairs. He sent a nearly identical letter to William Bird of the military committee, and another to Virginia treasurer John Robinson, claiming that Burwell had advised him to ask for the £50.[18]

Just twenty-three years old, Washington had a compulsion to brag while he cadged money. He told William Fairfax that he had met five colonial governors in Alexandria and they had all greatly admired him, especially Shirley of Massachusetts. He was about to leave for Wills Creek, where he expected to meet the general "and to stay, I fear too long, as our march must be regulated by the slow movements of the train." From his plantation on Bullskin Creek he sent a note to George William Fairfax's wife, Sally, fairly begging her to write to him, as "a corrispondance with my friends is the greatest satisfaction I expect to enjoy."[19]

Washington was honest when he told Orme that he expected to learn during his time in Braddock's family. When he joined it in May, he borrowed the general's order book and copied every order into his own letterbook. Most covered mundane housekeeping matters, and all began with the day's parole or password. Some were long: A windy order on March 28 covered discipline, issue of rations, reading of orders to the men, duties and positions of company officers, drills and other training, where the women of each regiment should march, mounting of guards, and reports and returns to be presented to the aides-de-camp. Even this had its moments, as when commanding officers of regiments were "directed by his excelly to inform their men, not to suffer themselves to be alarmed upon a march by any stragling fires from the Indians in the woods, they being of no consequence." And there was this: "Any soldier by leaving his company, or by words or gestures, espressing fear, shall suffer death."[20]

Some orders were of moment, such as those laying out instructions for the march to Wills Creek. Others were downright curious, especially when they related to the army's women, most of them laundresses. On April 7 the general declared, "A greater number of women having been brought over, than those allowed by the government, sufficient for washing, with a view that the hospitals might be served, and complaint being made, that a concert is entered into, not to serve without exorbitant wages, a return will be called for, of those who shall refuse to serve for six-pence per day, and their provisions; that they may be turned out of camp, and others got in their places."[21]

This was all new to Washington, who had never issued command orders on so many subjects. What was this army of redcoats, and why did it require such detailed governance? How did this style of command shape it as a fighting force?

I See Nothing That Can Obstruct My March

"Redcoats" was a relatively new term. They had been known as "Lobsters" or "Lobster Backs" since about 1740, and "Bloody Backs" on account of the army's use of whips and cat-o'-nine-tails to punish every imaginable offense. Provincials were horrified at the brutality but found themselves subjected to it. Officers including Washington followed the British example. The severity grew out of a belief that the lower orders required strict control. Wellington famously called the men who gave him victory at Waterloo in 1815 "the mere scum of the earth." A half-century earlier a colonial governor in the West Indies had called his nation's army "the refuse of mankind."[22]

The British army was in theory recruited only from volunteers until the beginning of conscription during World War I. In reality, men were rounded up through a number of disreputable practices. Recruiting parties had quotas to fill and they made the rounds of courthouses and jails, offering enlistment as a way to stay out of prison. Recruiters signed up many men who did not meet physical or mental standards, and they found ways of informally "pressing" men into service, especially by getting them drunk, a practice common in the colonies. Acts of Parliament during the 1750s revived practices from earlier imperial conflicts, conscripting "such able-bodied men as do not follow or exercise any lawful calling or employment, or have not some other lawful and sufficient support and maintenance"—in other words, "vagabonds"; Virginia adopted this practice.

There were other ways to fill the ranks. Papists were excluded by law, but many Catholics were drummed into the army anyway. Another method was drafting, the forcible transfer of men from one regiment to another. This depleted the donor units and handed the recipients unassimilated strangers who resented being jerked around. Donor units used a draft call to rid themselves of misfits.[23]

The iron discipline of eighteenth-century European armies did not grow simply out of the social attitudes of the officers and the fractious nature of the men. When gunpowder warfare became general by the seventeenth century, it introduced to the battlefield men carrying explosives on their belts, holding dangerous firearms and, in the early matchlock days, smoldering cords. The tactics for the new weaponry depended on highly coordinated musket volleys and massed bayonet charges. These conditions gave rise to the manual of arms and close-order drill, in the interest of safety and effectiveness. Regular armies were always training, at least in principle. Drill was not only tactically effective, mimicking movements on the battlefield, but it knit the soldiers into tight units instantly obedient to commands, men melded into teams. Once a regiment was trained, it was a finely honed instrument, able to go from marching column into line of battle promptly and take position precisely. The system had no place for individual initiative.[24]

Regimental cohesion benefited if the men had some commonality to begin with. Most British regiments recruited within given regions among men with similar backgrounds. That was not true, however, of the 44th and 48th Regiments of Foot, the regiments Braddock took to America. They were from the Irish Establishment, an autonomous organization funded by the Irish Parliament and administered by the lord lieutenant of Ireland. Because of the ban against Catholics, the men were mostly raised in England, Wales, and Scotland. When they were ordered to America—"banished," they called it—they were understrength and over-officered; together they were short ten sergeants, ten corporals, ten drummers, and 410 privates. Each was granted 216 men drafted from other British regiments, not all of whom were fit. They were still short 185 men each and recruited them in Virginia. Their lack of cohesion would work against them.[25]

The soldiers were as loutish as any in the British army, foul-mouthed, drunken, and riotous, mobbing brothels whenever they were on the loose. Every other word began with *f*, so they sounded like so many clucking chickens. This was not all that scandalized the good citizens of Alexandria. "It was very usual," said one officer, "to meet officers, and soldiers, drunk every hour of the day! The inhabitants were astonished at our excesses." The orderly book of the 44th

Foot filled up with accounts of drunken soldiers reprimanded for using "insolent expressions" that were "far from their sober thoughts and wholy occationed by the effects of liquor." Drunkards were confined until they slept it off, then whipped when sober.[26]

British regulations typically assigned six women to each 100 men as laundresses and hospital nurses, but most high commanders regarded them as nuisances. They were mainly wives of soldiers and noncoms, but a fair number were prostitutes. Braddock subjected them to the same discipline as soldiers, and he ordered frequent examinations for venereal disease. The army attracted whores even in the wilderness.[27]

Sorry as his regulars were, Braddock considered them vastly superior to American provincials, complaining to a friend that the latter's "slothful and languid disposition renders them very unfit for military service." He divided his Virginians between the two regular regiments, making the colonels of the enlarged corps temporary brigadiers. With this mixed force he intended to penetrate a wilderness about which he knew nothing. When Ben Franklin told him at the governors' meeting about the difficult terrain ahead of him, he declared, "I see nothing that can obstruct my march." As for the possibility that Indians would attack him, "These savages may be a formidable enemy to your raw American militia, but upon the king's regular and disciplined troops, sir, it is impossible they would make any impression."

When others at the meeting told him he had sixty to seventy miles of mountains and forests to cross instead of the fifteen miles he expected, he became peevish about what he saw as excuses for delay. He told superiors in London that when he got to Wills Creek, he would send what information or intelligence he could get there, "it being impractical to get any here, the people of this part of the country laying it down for a maxim, never to speak truth upon any account."[28]

Even Braddock had to admit that regular methods required some adjustment to American conditions. The "heat of the country" hammered his men as they moved into the Virginia countryside in April; it was so debilitating that they could not carry their muskets. Nor were their heavy woolen uniforms suitable to the climate. Orders on April 8 put waistbelts, swords, and other heavy items into storage. The next day Braddock told the officers to supply their men with bladders— disks of thin leather—to put into their hats to protect them from the heat of the sun. As his campaign advanced, he became more tolerant of men adapting to the environment. They ceased whitening their accoutrements with pipe clay, abandoned the use of hair powder, let their beards grow, and put on unconventional headgear. One of the officers thought it unavoidable that troops would abandon the "uniformity of the clean, smart, soldier, and substitute, in his stead, the [look of the] slovenly, undisciplined wood-hewer, sand-digger, and hod-carrier."[29]

Accommodating the wilderness continued after the campaign started. One of Braddock's officers declared that "the very fact of the country is enough to strike a damp in the most resolute mind." The uninterrupted "trees, swamps, and thickets" demoralized officers and men alike. "I cannot conceive how war can be made in such a country," he concluded. Another complained, "Whoever goes to the side of the woods, cannot see twenty yards before their faces in calm weather, there are such clouds of muskitoes and black flies." Yet another complained of constant assault by "myriads of musketas," which were so "immensely troublesome" that men put on long linen trousers and makeshift mosquito nets. That "odious insect" the mosquito and its "pupil" the black fly gave no quarter "either by day or night."[30]

Throughout the war redcoats endured conditions they had never faced in the Old World, including appalling heat and humidity in summer and arctic cold and snows in winter. The woods and mountains of America were as different as could be from the plains of Europe. Yet Braddock gave only a slight nod to the circumstances, even after he established headquarters at Frederick, Maryland, on April 21. To begin with, he decided that he would reach the Forks in one great leap, hauling all supplies with him from his seaport base at Alexandria. If he had based himself out of Philadelphia, he would have had a shorter draft for his supplies and much of his march would have been through farm country that could supply provisions. He could have advanced by stages after establishing supply magazines along his route, but he did not.

When it started moving Braddock's procession ultimately stretched nearly six miles long, and it was in trouble from the beginning. When he called for horses, he assumed he would get the purpose-bred draft animals he was used to in Europe. American horses were too small and weak to haul heavy artillery or overloaded wagons, so clearing a road through the wilderness was burdened by the need to reduce grades and fill gullies to help the animals. Washington tried to talk the redcoats into sizing up both enemy and landscape, first by reducing baggage and using pack animals. He attempted, he claimed years later, to impress them "with the necessity of opposing the nature of his defense to the mode of attack which, more than probably, he would experience from the *Canadian* French and their Indians." He should have saved his breath. "But so prepossessed were they in favor of *regularity* and *discipline,* and in such contempt were *these people held,* that the admonition was suggested in vain."[31]

Braddock might not have started his clumsy expedition at all if not for Benjamin Franklin. When the colonies failed to provide enough transport, the general threatened to go home to Britain, but Franklin promised on his own authority that Pennsylvanians would rally to the cause. The doctor plastered his colony with advertisements, vowing that farmers would be paid hard money for their horses and wagons, and if they signed on as drivers "the service will be light and easy." Anyone not volunteering his property would find his loyalty "strongly suspected"; his animals and vehicles might be seized. Within two weeks Franklin had signed up 259 horses and 150 wagons.[32]

This was the army Washington found when he reached Braddock's camp at Frederick on May 5. It was a mixture of regulars half-trained and ill-disciplined, and colonials who did not know what to expect, supported by a train of wagons too light to carry their loads, pulled by horses too small to haul them. All was under the command of an aging, inexperienced, bad-tempered general who believed he could barge his way to Fort Duquesne as he had bulldozed his way through life.

I Am Very Happy in the General's Family

When he reached Frederick, Washington was immediately detailed to Winchester to wait for baggage trains to catch up. The Maryland government had promised to build a road from Frederick to Fort Cumberland, but it did not. Unaware of that, Quartermaster St. Clair had divided the army, one division escorting powder and the artillery via Winchester, the other military and hospital stores through Frederick, both going on to Fort Cumberland at Wills Creek. The northern party had to turn back, recross the Potomac, and take the Winchester road. Washington told William Fairfax that St. Clair had selected an "uncommon, and extraordinary route."[33]

Washington had troubles of his own. He confessed to Lord Fairfax that he had lost three of his horses since leaving home, and he did not have enough money to replace them or meet other contingencies. He begged for a loan, offering to pay interest, "besides many thanks for the favour." He needed horses to fulfill an aide-de-camp's duty as a messenger. Moreover, field and general officers rode horseback to command their troops: Sitting above the thick smoke of battle allowed them to size up a situation, and it let lower officers see them.[34]

Washington went on to Fort Cumberland, which the general and his headquarters reached on May 10. Orders announced, "Mr. Washington is appointed aid de camp to His Excellency Genl. Braddock." His duties were light: writing up the headquarters orderly book and joining all officers at the general's morning levee at ten o'clock. Braddock also gave him blank commissions for ensigns and the power to appoint whomever he thought fit in the Virginia troops. Otherwise, he filled time writing letters. He sent a typically terse one to his mother, addressing her as always as "Dear Madam," and saying, "I am very happy in the general's family, and I am treated with a complaisant freedom which is quite agreeable; so that I have no occasion to doubt the satisfaction I propos'd in making the campaigne." He said much the same to his brother Jack at Mount Vernon, adding that he hoped to please the general "without difficulty," because Braddock did not stand on ceremony. Jack should take every opportunity to report on the state of George's affairs. Washington wrote teasing letters to the two Sallys, Fairfax and Carlyle (wife of the commissary), playfully asking them to write to him while he was on campaign.[35]

"The Gen'l. has appointed me one of his aids de camps, in which character I shall serve this campaign, agreeably enough, as I am thereby freed from all commands but his, and give order's to all, which must be implicitly obey'd," Washington boasted to Jack. This situation aroused his ambition. "I have now a good oppertunity, and shall not neglect it," he said, "of forming an acquaintance, which may be serviceable hereafter, if I can find it worth while pushing my fortune in the military way." If it suited his interest, the young Virginian was not above using his commanding officer.[36]

When it came to intrigue, however, Washington was outclassed in the battles of wills going on in Braddock's headquarters. First was the struggle between royals and provincials, which a British observer claimed set the expedition up for disaster, owing to the general's "domineering temper and the insolent superiority he affected as an Englishman over Americans." His snide attitude toward colonial troops was not likely to win their loyalty, but the most trouble came from the general's ceaseless castigation of colonial officials for not supplying him with provisions and transport.[37]

There were other squabbles among the royal officers, and for a while Washington stood apart. All around him he saw laziness, stupidity, and inefficiency where there should be command and execution. One British officer said that Braddock "withal was very indolent and seemed glad for anybody to take business off his hands, which may be one reason why he was so grossly imposed upon by his favourite, who really directed everything and may justly be said to have commanded the expedition."[38]

The "favourite" was Brevet Captain Robert Orme, a lieutenant of the Coldstream Guards whom Braddock had appointed as his senior aide. He was a dashingly handsome young man, not much older than Washington, slender of build with dark eyes and dark hair, who looked born to wear a uniform. He and the Virginian became lifelong friends, but others split over his influence. Younger officers gravitated toward him, while older ones believed that Colonel Sir Peter Halkett, Braddock's second, was shoved aside by Orme's access to the general.[39]

Braddock was so ineffective that even his private secretary, William Shirley the Younger (son of the governor of Massachusetts), was disillusioned. He tattled to the governor of Pennsylvania that the general was "most judiciously chosen for being disqualified for the service he is employed in in almost every respect. He may be brave for aught I know, and he is honest in pecuniary matters." As King George had said about another general recommended for his honesty, "A little more ability and a little less honesty upon the present occasion, might serve our turn better." Referring to Orme, Shirley sniffed, "It is a joke to suppose that secondary officers can make amends for the defects of the first; the mainspring must be the mover—the others in many cases can do no more than follow and correct a little its motions."

Shirley did not think much of the others. Some were "insolent and ignorant, others capable," he groused, "but rather aiming at showing their own abilities than making a proper use of them." He expressed "a very great love" for his friend Orme, and thought it "uncommonly fortunate" that Braddock was under the influence of so honest and capable a man, but he wished for the sake of the cause that Orme had more experience. The secretary was "greatly disgusted," he declared, at an expedition "so ill-concerted originally in England, so improperly conducted since in America."[40]

Washington spent considerable time with Orme and Shirley, and he heard such sentiments often. For the time being, however, he kept his own counsel. The whole situation was new to him, and he knew from his own short experience that he was not able to pass judgment on a general, let alone one to whom he owed his position. Still, the attitude of the other young officers influenced him, and he felt the first inklings that maybe this redcoat army was not the elite corps it was cracked up to be.

However deficient Braddock was as a general, he was worse as a diplomat. There were about 100 Indians at Fort Cumberland when Washington arrived, including several sachems. The redcoats enticed the women into camp and seduced them with liquor or money. The general issued a series of general orders first prohibiting soldiers and sutlers from selling liquor to the Indians, then promising the "severest punishment," and finally raising the threat to "900 lashes, without a court martial." Braddock lost credibility by the time of his first meeting with the chiefs on May 12. He presented wampum and boasted that Indian allies would be treated well, but it was not an effective performance, especially since promised gifts had not arrived.[41]

He tried again on the 18th, after Pennsylvanian George Croghan brought in several bands to help with the campaign. Braddock alienated them with his arrogance and such stupidities as ordering them to send their women away; the men followed their wives out of camp. Then Tanaghrisson's successor as Mingo Half-King, Scarouady, Ohio Delaware war chief Shingas, and a few other sachems showed up with their followers. They would not ally with the English without assurances that the latter would not occupy their lands after the French were driven out. Shingas complained that "Genl Braddock said no savage should inherit the land."

The Ohio leaders returned home furious; only Scarouady and seven other Mingo men remained. "He looked upon us as dogs," one sachem complained to Croghan about Braddock, "and would never hear anything that we said to him." The general's behavior so inflamed the Ohio Indians that some of them went to Fort Duquesne to join the French. This was all compounded by Braddock's refusal to learn about Indian politics. He did not know that Sir William Johnson was about to reopen negotiations with the Six Nations to restore their broken relations with Britain, and he expected 400 Cherokee and Catawba men Dinwiddie had promised but failed to recruit for the expedition. Those nations were implacable enemies of the Iroquois whom Johnson wanted to court. In any case, Braddock was too pigheaded to appreciate the fine points of Indian-white relations, let alone relations among the various nations.[42]

He did not do any better with American farmers. The weather had become warmer and wetter by mid-May, and some of the provisions spoiled in storage. The men were running out of everything, especially fresh meat. Braddock established a public market to get farmers to deliver produce or forage to Fort Cumberland. He advanced some gold from the army chest, but there were not enough farmers or productivity to meet the need. So the general lashed out at his own men with a typically draconian order. "Any soldier or follower of the army," he roared, "who shall stop any one bringing in provisions or forage to the camp, shall immediately suffer death." That did not solve the real problem, which was that the army was almost out of money because the price of everything was so high. Accordingly, on May 15 Braddock handed Washington his first order: to go to Hampton to draw £4,000 from the army's paymaster, Colonel John Hunter, and tell Hunter to get another £10,000 up to Fort Cumberland within two months. If the whole amount was not available, Washington should return with what he could get.[43]

This was supposed to be a quick trip—Braddock told Washington to spend no more than two days at Hampton. He made it as far as Winchester the first day and sent a message to Hunter asking him to forward the money to Williamsburg. "I must beg your utmost diligence in this affair," he told the paymaster, "as I have order's not to wait," because the whole army would halt at Wills Creek until he returned, "at immense expence." Then he detoured to Mount Vernon, where he spent a day getting horses.[44]

Washington saw no need to hurry. A week after he left the army he was still on the road to Williamsburg, and he reported his lack of progress to Orme. His message to Hunter had been answered by Dinwiddie, who said the paymaster had gone north to draw funds and was not expected back for two weeks. Washington predicted that his journey would prove "abortive." Then he whined that he was "fatigued and a good deal disorder'd by constant riding," so he would "proceed more slowly back," unless he was "fortunate enough" to receive the money, in which case he would hurry back "with the utmost dispatch."

The next day he wrote from Williamsburg, saying that Hunter's assistant hoped to round up the money with help from Dinwiddie and some of his friends, so he might return to the army soon. While Hunter's agent hunted for the cash, Washington went shopping for toothbrushes, gloves, stockings, and sundries. Money in hand, he left for Wills Creek.[45]

In Washington's absence, Braddock exploded in another of his routine uproars over the logistical dereliction of the colonies. Dinwiddie especially enraged him. The general complained to the governor of Pennsylvania on May 24 about "the folly of Mr. Dinwiddie and the roguery of the Assembly, and unless the road of communication from your province is opened and some contracts made . . . I must inevitably be starved." The Virginia commissary, Carlyle, had "behaved in such a manner that if he had been a French commis[sary] he could not have acted more for their interest. In short . . . I have been deceived and met with nothing but lies and villainy."[46]

As usual, the general took his frustrations out on his men, meting out brutal punishments for this or that. On May 14 he approved a death sentence for desertion, and 1,000 lashes each to three men who had stolen a keg of beer. On the 18th he struck out at surplus women hanging around the army, a particular gripe with him; on the 21st he fixed the liquor ration per the standing regulations, threatening to confine any sutler who sold extra spirits. Gambling invited 300 lashes, and on the 26th the general approved punishments between 200 and 1,000 lashes for theft, desertion, and accidentally shooting another soldier. "If any soldier is seen drunk in camp," the order ended, "he is to be sent immediately to the quarter guard of the regiment he belongs to, and the next morning, to receive two hundred lashes, without a court martial."[47]

The army was falling apart while Washington dawdled. He reached Winchester on May 28, but his cavalry escort had gone back to Cumberland and he had to wait for a militia escort. While he was at it, he asked his brother to find out whether William Fairfax planned to run for his seat in the Burgesses again. If Fairfax did not, Washington would be "glad to stand a poll" if he thought his chances "tolerably good." He ran for office the following December and came in last out of four candidates.[48]

Washington reached Fort Cumberland with the money on May 30, escorted by a small militia party. The camp had descended into drunken debauchery, and the soldiers were losing their heads over the Indian women still nearby. Braddock sent patrols into the woods to catch men seducing the women, and he kept upping the punishment for offenses real or imagined. The brutal discipline offended the few Indian men still in camp, who could not understand this English savagery against fellow countrymen.

The general remained in high dudgeon over the failure of Virginia to supply him, ruffling Washington's feathers at last. Braddock had "lost all degree of patience," he complained to William Fairfax. Instead of blaming nonperforming individuals, the general blamed the whole colony "and looks upon the country, I believe, as void of both honour and honesty." They had "frequent disputes on this head, which are maintained with warmth on both sides, especially on his."[49]

With all the turmoil in camp and at headquarters, the campaign against the Forks went nowhere. Washington told his friends and relatives that he expected no immediate progress, and when the army finally moved out its greatest obstacles would be the forested mountains. The French, he predicted, would withdraw troops from Ohio to meet Shirley's campaign against Niagara. Still, Braddock tried to get ready. He prepared a diagram of how the army would be organized on the march and distributed it to all officers. He obsessively oversaw everything, down to organizing medical examinations for the army's women "to see who was clean and proper," according to a soldier.[50]

On May 27, Braddock increased his camp security, gave special orders about the care of arms and ammunition, and sent detachments to scout the way ahead. The next day he began sending out details in rotation to clear the road, forwarded more scouts, and told the whole army to be ready to march at any time. He also authorized extra pay for soldiers clearing the roads, but since there was nowhere for them to spend the money, he promised to hand it over next fall, in winter quarters.[51]

By the time Washington returned to Fort Cumberland at the end of May, Braddock's entire force was on hand. It included the two royal regiments of 700 men each, three independent companies, one company of volunteers from North Carolina, another from Maryland, and nine from Virginia. Sixty regulars conducted the artillery train, and thirty Royal Navy sailors went along to move the heavy guns with block and tackle. A regular ensign had drilled the Virginians, but Orme said of them, "their languid, spiritless and unsoldierlike appearance, considered with the lowness and ignorance of most of their officers, gave little hope of their future good behaviour."[52]

Braddock was almost ready to drive the French from the Ohio Country.

They Were Halting to Level Every Mold Hill

The campaign began with a dramatic false start. Late in May Braddock sent 500 men forward to partly clear the road and set up a supply depot at Little Meadows. Other parties had spent three days filling gullies, clearing brush, and reducing grades to aid the heavy vehicles. The heaviest were the artillery, including four 12-pounder naval guns mounted on wheeled carriages, six 6-pounder field guns, four 8-inch howitzers, and fifteen Coehorn mortars; each 12-pounder weighed over a ton. Braddock, ignoring even the steep ridge immediately to the west of Fort Cumberland, thought he could go to the Forks in a straight line. He sent the first part of his army out that way on June 1, and Orme was appalled at what they ran into. The advance set out at daybreak, and it was night before the whole baggage train had gotten over the ridge about two miles from the camp. The ascent and descent were almost perpendicular rock, Orme said; three wagons were "entirely destroyed" and many more "extremely shattered."

Braddock went out to take a look and admitted to Washington that the terrain "would occasion great trouble and retard me considerably." He could think of no solution other than to put more men to work with more shovels. But on June 2 a lieutenant went out on his own and discovered a way around the ridge, without steep grades; the failure to find this earlier reflected utter incompetence in the command. Braddock stopped work on the original alignment and ordered a new road to be cut on the lieutenant's route.[53]

The army was stalled at Fort Cumberland until June 6, when it marched out with "the knight [St. Clair] swearing in the van, the genl cursing & bullying in the center & their whores bringing up the rear," according to an officer. Braddock sent the regiments out in succession, the provincials and independents bringing up the rear with the artillery park. Other orders repetitiously limited the number of women going along and prescribed the death penalty for stealing or wasting provisions.[54]

Desertion was a growing problem among the provincial troops, theft among the regulars. Anyone caught stealing, Braddock ordered on the 11th, "shall be immediately hanged." But heavy rain and a spreading epidemic were more serious hazards, and there was nothing the general could do about either. One officer and several soldiers had already died, Washington told Jack on June 7, and many others were sick "with a kind of bloody flux" from dysentery. He was more upbeat in his letters to his mother and the two Sallys, so not very informative. He told George William Fairfax that the army had started out with too few horses and was now losing them. He advised Commissary Carlyle of reports that hundreds of Indians were going to the Ohio to reinforce the French, so he doubted that the army would take possession of Fort Duquesne "so quietly as was imagin'd."[55]

When the rain stopped, the biting insects came out. The men wielded axes, picks, shovels, and foul language, trying to make a road where nature had not intended. One by one or in groups, they ran away or dropped from bloody diarrhea, exhaustion, or work accidents. Colonel Thomas Dunbar and the rear division could not leave Cumberland until the 10th because the way ahead was clogged with forward units stacked up by the slow progress of road-building. The artillery train made only two miles a day, and horses continued to break down. Braddock blamed the provincials for his troubles, and Washington defended his fellow Americans. Virginians, the general advised his superiors in London, were "very indifferent men," who showed a "want of honesty and inclination to forward the service," and the promises of any colonials were "not to be depended upon." Braddock blamed Dinwiddie personally for the fact that no Indians had come forward to help out.[56]

The general's attitude stirred up his quarrelsome officers, and Colonel Sir Peter Halkett ceased hiding his hatred for Orme, who later told Washington that he saw himself "a slave, constantly engaged in keeping peace." Braddock decided that he could stop desertion if he made the men believe they were in dangerous country. He already had flankers out crashing through the understory on either side of his column. Now he outlawed campfires, ordered muskets kept always loaded, noncoms to keep bayonets fixed, and forbade anyone from erecting "bowers" as shelter from the wretched weather. Nobody could fire a weapon within a mile of camp, "but in case of an alarm, or their being attacked." And, "upon any halt, tho' ever so small," the companies were to "form two deep, and face outwards." There were no Indians waiting to scalp stragglers, however, at least not yet, so desertion continued. Braddock moved the tool tumbrels to the head of the column, but that did not speed the road along. After a pause, he ordered a march for the 13th, then countermanded it, and on the 14th ordered the men to sleep with their arms and await an order to advance.[57]

Braddock's methods were getting his army nowhere fast. On June 9 he called a council of war to consider the problem, with Washington keeping the record. The group agreed that the chief difficulty retarding the march was too many wagons to haul. The answer was to reduce the number of wagons and increase the pack loads for horses. Braddock told the officers to send back personal baggage and donate their spare horses to carry provisions, "which was accordingly done with great cheerfulness and zeal."[58]

There was not much "cheerfulness" among Braddock's officers. Moreover, the change did not speed the army's progress, so Braddock called another council for the 17th. The general, knowing that Washington had been in this country before, called him aside and asked his opinion about how to proceed. The Virginian advised pressing on, because he believed the garrison at Fort Duquesne was weak but bound to grow stronger. He proposed going ahead with a light detachment and "artillery and such other things as were absolutely necessary," leaving the heaviest stuff behind "to follow by slow and regular marches." Braddock presented this to the council as his own idea, and the members agreed that he should set out with a light striking force.[59]

The council dissolved into a series of quarrels, the senior officers berating Orme. Colonel Dunbar complained about being exposed "to the ridicule of that young man in his excellencie's hearing," according to a witness. Nothing reflected Braddock's weakness as a commander more than his failure to keep his own officers off each other's throats when they were supposed to be planning how to face the enemy. He decided to march on, but with an army divided in every way.[60]

Braddock sent St. Clair and 400 men ahead to clear the road, increased the number of horses in teams, ordered thirty-five days' provisions loaded on pack animals, and limited the wagons in his striking force to no more than thirty. His manpower totaled about 1,300 picked men, regulars and provincials, under Halkett, later joined by supply escorts who raised the force to 1,459 by early July. Although Washington had advised taking only the most essential artillery, Braddock hauled along four 12-pounders, four howitzers, and two 6-pounders, and the men carried 100 cartridges each. The general led the party out on the 19th. Dunbar lagged behind with 800 men, seventy-two wagons, the rest of the artillery and baggage, and not enough horses.[61]

Washington wrote that the decision to send a fast striking force ahead was a "prospect that convey'd the most infinite delight" to him His delight turned into dismay when he saw that "instead of pushing on with vigour, without regarding a little rough road, they were halting to level every mold [sic] hill, and to erect bridges over every brook," so the command made only twelve miles in four days. There was worse than that, however, because Washington's health had been shaky for several days. As he marched out with Braddock, he was "seiz'd" with violent fevers and headaches. Braddock's aide Roger Morris told Washington to ride in a wagon because he could not sit a horse, but the jolting proved too much. Morris said that the general intended to halt for a rest in a few days, and they would leave him behind under guard until Dunbar's rear division came up. He should follow the advice of Dunbar's surgeon.

Braddock showed real concern for the young man's distress and later sent back Doctor James's Powders, a patent medicine. Washington called it "the most excellent medicine in the world," which gave him "immediate ease." When the general ordered him to stay behind, he promised to call Washington forward before he reached the French fort. "This promise, and the doct'rs threats that if I persever'd it wou'd endanger my life, determin'd my halting."[62]

So the Virginian suffered on a cot, while reports came back from Braddock about "frequent alarms, and several men scalp'd." Dunbar reached his camp on June 22, still in a bad temper over his argument with Orme at the council of war. His mood was not improved by the fact that Braddock had shortchanged him on horses and wagons but ordered him to keep within a one-day march of the striking force. The shortage of transport made that impossible, so Dunbar fell farther and farther behind, dividing the army into separate units that could not support each other.

Washington did not like Dunbar at all. After he had been with his corps for six days, he proclaimed that it was "in a miserable condition for want of horses," wagons being forwarded alternately. The Virginian predicted that "shortly he will not be able to stir at all," telling his brother that "there has been vile management in regard to horses." He stayed with the slow procession as far as the Youghiogheny, which it reached on June 26. The surgeon advised him to rest there, but he wanted to rejoin Braddock, sending a note to Orme saying that his fever had let up. He felt well enough to fire his nurse on the 30th.[63]

Washington knew that action was looming, and he itched to be part of it. A messenger came in on July 1 with orders for beef and flour to be sent up. The aide briefed the officers on Braddock's progress up to June 30. The column had passed the Youghiogheny on the 24th and went through a place where the French had inscribed obscene messages on trees stripped of bark. The forward column got to three miles beyond Great Meadows the next day, but that morning three deserters were found dead and scalped. Braddock posted a reward for Indian scalps, but this did not boost morale among his troops, who griped that their numbers were too small for the work they did, not to mention having little food and nothing to drink but water. The striking force hacked through the woods at under five miles a day.[64]

The supply train went up on July 3, and Washington rode along with it. "I had a letter yesterday from Orme," he told Jack, "that they have sent out partys to scour the country thereabouts and have reason to believe that the French are greatly alarm'd at their approach." He caught up with Braddock on July 8, two miles from the Monongahela and about twelve miles from Fort Duquesne. He received a hearty welcome and learned that harassment of the column had been increasing, stragglers and deserters turning up dead and scalped despite the flankers, who had skirmished with a small party of Indians. He also learned that there had been another council of war that turned into a shouting match on the 3rd. St. Clair had proposed halting until Dunbar closed up, but this was rejected because it would consume too much food and give the French time to marshal their forces. St. Clair said later that his plan, and another one to invest Fort Duquesne with a light force on the night of the 8th, were "rejected with great indignation." He wanted to be recalled, "finding I could be of little use, being never listened to."

In any event, Braddock's guides had scouted the terrain across the Monongahela, and he issued orders to cross the river and move on Fort Duquesne the morning of the 9th. Washington went to bed, sure that the following night he would sleep at the Forks of the Ohio.[65]

SEVEN

I EXPECTED NOTHING BUT DEATH FOR EVER ONE OF US

(1755)

> Imagine that the earth takes up arms to defend itself against invasion, that the hills, the streams, the gorges, the grottos are death-dealing machines which come out to meet the regular troops.
>
> —BENITO PÉREZ GALDÓS

Skill with weapons has been highly prized since the first ape-man picked up a stick and brained another ape-man with it. When styles of war evolved with new weapons and close-order tactics, as in the ancient Mediterranean, it became essential for soldiers to practice their art together so as not to hurt themselves more than the enemy. Gunpowder complicated things further, so from the sixteenth century on, troops slapped wood and iron and marched and countermarched to the choreography of drillmasters.

Tactics in the mid-eighteenth century reflected the fact that the smoothbore musket was not only limited in range but inaccurate; the excitement and stress of combat just made things worse. Relatively few soldiers fell to enemy fire, and many more were a danger to themselves and their fellows. Marshal Gouvion Saint-Cyr studied the problem after the Napoleonic Wars and concluded that a quarter of French infantry casualties were men in the front ranks accidentally shot by men in the rear.[1]

Linear formations and coordinated volleys aimed to shock the other side with muzzle blasts rather than inflict casualties. They worked best in open, level terrain against enemies similarly armed and arrayed, and maneuver rather than fire was often the key to victory. Until the 1770s, the British deployed their regiments—subdivided into battalions, companies, and platoons—in three elbow-to-elbow ranks, each one behind being stepped slightly to the right of the one ahead. Every soldier must handle and fire his weapon at the same time as every other in his platoon, and this required ceaseless practice in formation.

The weapons drill, known as the "manual exercise" or "manual of arms," specified every movement in minute detail. "The Position of a Soldier under Arms," how to stand at attention with a musket, took a full page to describe. To load and discharge a "firelock" (flintlock musket) required no less than twelve commands that set off eighteen distinct motions. The command "Fire!" involved only one motion, but it illustrated the precision necessary to eighteenth-century warfare: "Pull the tricker [trigger] briskly, and immediately after bring up the right foot, come to the priming position, with the lock opposite to the right breast, the muzzle the height of the hat, keeping it firm and steady, and at the same time seize the cock with the fore-finger and thumb of the right hand, the back of the hand turned up." Some motions were altered slightly for the front, center, and rear ranks.[2]

British regulars were schooled in these movements until, in theory, they were synchronized automatons responding to commands from their officers. They had not been trained what to do if the commands ceased coming. American provincials had received only the most basic drill on the parade ground, and they remained individuals rather than cogs in a military machine.

Entire Ranks Fell; All the Officers Perished

As Braddock approached Fort Duquesne, Contrecoeur sent parties of Canadians and Indians to harass the British, he reported to Governor Vaudreuil. However, "their troops marched constantly on guard, always in a line of battle, so that all of the efforts of the detachments were to no avail." On July 7 scouts sighted Braddock's corps eight leagues (about twenty-five miles) out. Contrecoeur immediately sent another detachment, "which the same day reported to me that they were not more than six leagues away, and that they marched in three columns." His works at Fort Duquesne were complete but too small to hold more than about 200 of the 1,600 regulars, militia, and Indians there at the time. He could not let the English invest the place because the Indians would leave rather than defend ground.[3]

The commandant organized a party to engage the enemy, sending everyone he could spare from the fort, 250 Frenchmen and 650 Indians, or about 900 men in all. "M. de Beaujeu, a captain, commanded them," Contrecoeur reported. "There were also two other captains, MM. Dumas and Lignerie [sic], as well as several subalterns." Captain Daniel-Hyacinthe-Marie Liénard de Beaujeu, forty-four years old, had commanded troops in France as well as America. Captain Jean-Daniel Dumas, thirty-four, had had many successful assignments, as had the third captain, François-Marie le marchand de Lignery, fifty-two, a prosperous merchant and militia officer.[4]

Beaujeu went out on the 8th and found a place to ambush the English as they crossed the Monongahela. Returning to the fort, he tried to recruit the Indians. They objected, "Father, you want to die and sacrifice us. The English are more than four thousand, and we are only eight hundred, yet you wish to attack them. Certainly you must see that you are making no sense." They needed time to talk about it and promised an answer the next morning. As Beaujeu prepared to leave with his regulars and militia at dawn, he asked the Indians what they had decided. They declared that they would not march with him, to which he replied, "I am determined to confront the enemy. What—would you let your father go alone? I am certain to defeat them!"

That plea worked, and together with 36 officers, 72 *troupes de la marine*, and 146 militia, Beaujeu led 637 Indians stripped and painted for war. There were a few Mingos and Delawares, more Shawnees, but most were northerners: Ottawas, Mississaugas, Wyandots. One of their leaders was Charles Langlade, scourge of Pickawillany. Some officers wore shirts, others stripped like the Indians, their only badges of rank the silver gorgets hanging from their necks. This hefty party was well armed but dragged along no unnecessary baggage, so it moved fast. It had to, because the negotiations with the Indians delayed the start until nine o'clock.[5]

The day before, Braddock's spies—George Croghan and the Half-King Scarouady with seven Mingos—had scouted out the terrain across the Monongahela. They recommended crossing the river, going a couple of miles down the left side, then crossing back to the right bank over a shallow ford, from which there was a direct route to the Forks. Braddock ordered Lieutenant Colonel Thomas Gage with 300 infantry and two 6-pounders to lead off before dawn, in a column of three. They followed Croghan and Scarouady, who were tailed by a small guide party of foot soldiers and six horsemen, who blazed the path. Gage would take position beyond the second ford to cover the crossing of the rest of the corps.

Behind him Captain Horatio Gates led the New York independent company to protect St. Clair's 250 unarmed pioneers, who would widen the road with tools from their tumbrels. The main body followed an hour after St. Clair, at about five o'clock. Washington, "tho' very weak and low," strapped pillows on his saddle—his afflictions included hemorrhoids—and went out with Braddock and the family. Behind the general were about 500 infantry in columns of two on both sides of a long line of wagons, artillery, the camp women, and a herd of cattle. The rear was guarded by about a hundred provincials under Adam Stephen, while parties of flankers ranged on either side.[6]

Gage got across the river about eight in the morning and sent a note back to Braddock. The water was low and the crossing was easy, but a ridge lay ahead, steep enough that St. Clair's crews did not finish clearing the way until early afternoon. There was also an unexpected development. All the way from Fort Cumberland, the towering, thick-canopied forest had been choked by undergrowth so dense that no one could see more than ten yards, according to St. Clair. But a quarter-mile beyond the river, he said, the troops "came into an open wood free from underwood with some gradual riseings, this wood was so open that carriages could have been drove in any part of it." The army had entered a hunting ground, burned annually to improve game shooting.[7]

It was also good for shooting redcoats, but Braddock saw no reason to heighten the alert. "The general now thinking the dangerous passes were over," a British officer recalled, "did not suffer the advanced party to proceed any farther than just the distance of a few yards from the main body; it was proposed to strengthen the flanks, but rejected." One provincial officer said, "The British gentlemen, were so confident they would never be attacked and would have laid any odds that they never should [be] until they came before the fort." The men were hungry, but otherwise the march had taken on the air of a holiday outing, birds sing-

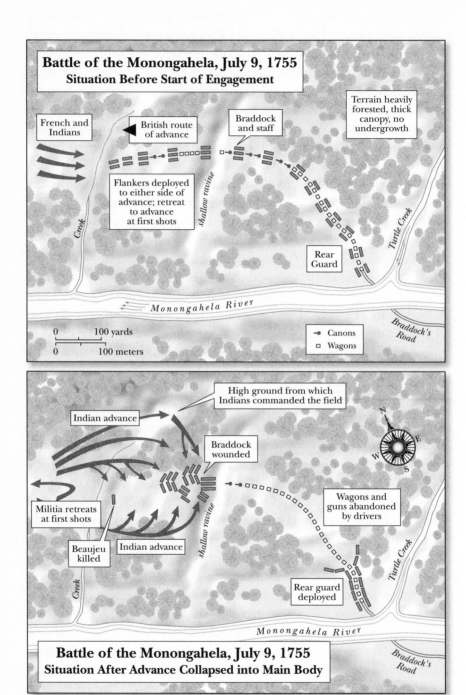

Battle of the Monongahela, July 9, 1755
Situation Before Start of Engagement

French and Indians

British route of advance

Braddock and staff

Terrain heavily forested, thick canopy, no undergrowth

Flankers deployed to either side of advance; retreat to advance at first shots

shallow ravine

Creek

Turtle Creek

Rear Guard

Monongahela River

0   100 yards
0   100 meters

Braddock's Road

→ Canons
▫ Wagons

High ground from which Indians commanded the field

Indian advance

Braddock wounded

Militia retreats at first shots

shallow ravine

Wagons and guns abandoned by drivers

Beaujeu killed

Indian advance

Creek

Turtle Creek

Rear guard deployed

Monongahela River

Braddock's Road

Battle of the Monongahela, July 9, 1755
Situation After Advance Collapsed into Main Body

ing and squirrels barking. "So we began our march again," said one of Gage's men, drums "beating the grannadiers march all the way, never seasing. There never was an army in the world in more spirits than we where, thinking of reaching Fort de Cain the day following." The frolic ended suddenly, however, when one of the guides "in the front of me above ten yards spyed the Indiens lay'd down before us. He immediately discharged his piece, turned round his horse [and] cried, the Indiens was upon us." Birds streaked screeching into the sky, terrified by the sharp noise.[8]

The two opposing corps had blundered into each other on the narrow, dark trail because neither had scouted far enough ahead. The French had overestimated the size of the English force, and Beaujeu "expected to meet the English at some distance, and hoped by some surprise or check, to retard their march," according to a Canadian officer. Beaujeu aimed to set up his ambush at the river and was not on guard when his advance ran into the English guide party. They in turn underestimated the French opposition, thanks to Croghan's early report that there were about 300 of them, led by three French officers "with hats in their hands and with which they gave a signal for the firing." He had seen only half the force and did not know that another 300 Indians had taken a different route and rejoined the main party once the action began.[9]

Officers at Fort Duquesne heard a "blast of great guns & musquetry" that made them "apprehend our detachment had joined in with the English army nearer than they imagined, & that they were ingaged." Back in the British column, at about 2:30 Braddock and Washington heard a volley, then scattered but heavy fire, then another volley, and another, followed by the thump of cannons. Braddock and the family immediately spurred forward but made slow going in the confusion ahead.[10]

The two advances were about 200 yards apart and equally startled. Beaujeu, according to his deputy Dumas, "attacked the enemy with much daring, but with his troops in total disorder." He ordered his Canadians to fire a volley at the English, but they were too far off. At that point, Dumas claimed, "one hundred militiamen—one-half of our French forces—shamefully turned tail, shouting 'Every man for himself!' This retreat encouraged the enemy to resound with cries of 'Long live the king!' and they advanced quickly toward us." Gage rushed his infantry forward, deployed them in ranks across the track, and fired three quick volleys. The range was still too great, except that a ball from the third volley killed Beaujeu. Then Gage got his guns into action on his left. This terrified the Indians, who fled, Dumas reported. They had heard artillery salutes before but had never faced the concussion of a 6-pounder muzzle blast.[11]

The French and Indians were disordered and leaderless, and Gage had a chance to win the battle. His position was commanded by a small rise on his left and a higher one on the right, with clear fields of fire. If he seized the high ground, he could dominate the battlefield. Instead, he hesitated. The other side, in contrast, recovered fast. The trail was paralleled, especially on Gage's right, by a series of gullies, and the Indians used them to move down the length of Gage's formation, firing from behind trees. On the left, also from behind trees, they concentrated on the gun crews and nearly wiped them out within minutes. Gage's men fell back, officers on horseback going down. They were terrified by the war whoops of the Indians and by the shock of surprise. "Our troops keeping in regular close order," recalled Sergeant Duncan Cameron, the Indians could not miss, yet at first they shot too high. Gage wheeled his ranks from right to left to fire into the hidden enemy, and back again, abandoned then retrieved the cannons, and lost them again. When the Indians in the trees found their aim, before Braddock reached the scene, wrote Lieutenant William Dunbar, "most of our advanced party were laid sprawling on the ground."[12]

The Indians deployed in a "half moon" formation, creeping behind cover down both sides, increasing the volume of fire into the English flanks. One French officer called it "a great slaughter." Dumas claimed, "The enemy was attacked on all sides, but fought with unyielding stubbornness. Entire ranks fell; all the officers perished." The racket of musketry, the shouts of the Indians, and the screams of wounded horses and men overwhelmed the senses, the woods filled with thick, stinking smoke, and blood pooled on the ground. "They continaly made us retreat," said one of Gage's men, "they haveing always a large marke to shoute at and we having only to shoute at them behind trees or laid on their bellies. We was drawn up in large bodies together a ready mark. They need not have taken sight at us for they always had a large mark, but if we saw of them five or six at one time [it] was a great sight and they either on their bellies or behind trees or runing from one tree to another almost by the ground."[13]

The French regulars and the few militia who had not run away held Gage's command in the front while the Indians moved down the flanks. One French officer observed that the Indian "mode of fighting" was very different from that of the Europeans, which was "worthless in this region." The Anglos "formed a line of battle, and made a front, which allowed those behind the trees to knock over one or two with each shot." English officers confirmed this, Dunbar claiming that the privates were so panicked that they "threw their fire away in the most confused manner, some in the air, others in the ground, & a great many destroyed their own men & officers."[14]

The unarmed laborers had run toward the rear of the column at the first shots, carrying the New Yorkers along. Braddock had ordered the main body forward to relieve Gage, but it collided with the fugitives, mixing units and spreading more confusion. Gage was isolated, and his officers made tempting targets; within the first ten minutes, fifteen out of eighteen were dead or wounded. That erased the last traces of discipline and control, and Gage's corps stumbled back into the main body. One survivor said that "the men dropped like leaves in *Autumn*, all was confusion." Another called the troops "panick struck," owing to tales they had heard of Indians scalping the fallen, and the officers lost all control. "The whole detachment was frequently divided into several parties, and then they were sure to fire on one another." Men who advanced into the trees were shot by their fellows from behind. Soldiers bunched up twenty or thirty deep, and "during all this time the enemy kept continually firing, and every shot" found a mark in the teeming mass of redcoats. Braddock sent up orders to fire by platoons to straighten out the tangle, "which was impossible to be effected."[15]

The uncontrolled firing by Gage's troops quickly expended the ammunition in their cartridge boxes. The first shots had driven in his flankers and the guides, which completed the confusion. When Braddock and his staff came up, Gage advised charging the hill on the right with bayonets, but it was already too late for that. Gage later claimed that not one platoon could be "prevailed upon to stir from its line of march, and a visible terror and confusion appeared among the men." St. Clair's work party and Braddock's main body were in the same disorder, and "the whole army was very soon mixed together, twelve or fourteen deep, firing away at nothing but trees, and killing many of our own men and officers." Braddock ordered the regimental colors "advanced in different places, to separate the men of the two regiments," according to his aide Orme, but it was no use. Orme, Morris, and Washington galloped here and there delivering orders that could not be carried out, drawing their own share of fire.[16]

Survivors of the battle focused their accounts on the opening phase, the sudden attack and rapid disintegration of the advance, followed by that of the rest of the army. "What could bravery accomplish against such an attack, as sudden as it was unexpected?" one of them asked. "The yell of the Indians is fresh on my ear, and the terrific sound will haunt me until the hour of my dissolution. I cannot describe the horrors of that scene; no pen could do it, or no painter delineate it so as to convey to you with any accuracy our unhappy situation." Unfortunately, the battle had only just begun, and Washington and others had serious work ahead.[17]

The Enemy Pursued Us, Butchering as They Came

Braddock and his aides reached the head of the column and found hell in a very small place: redcoats in a confused mass covering an area less than 250 yards front to rear, about 100 feet wide. The privates of the two redcoat regiments were "entirely at a loss in the woods," Adam Stephen wrote. The British troops were "thunderstruck to feel the effect of a heavy fire, & see no enemy." Yet they tried to do what they were trained to do, bash the enemy with platoon fire. "If any got a shott at one [Indian] the fire imediately ran through the whole line though they saw nothing but trees," a British officer said. Washington and several others thought most redcoat casualties came from their own fire.[18]

They held to their training so tightly that several witness accounts observed that they began retreats and even headlong flight to the rear by turning "right about" (about face). They delayed running off, however, because they were terrified by tales they had heard about how Indians treated captives. "If it was not for their barbaras usage which we knew they would treat us," said an enlisted redcoat, "we should never have fought them as long as we did, but having only death before us made the men fight almost longer than they was able. . . . I expected nothing but death for ever one of us, for they had us surrounded all but a little in the rear."[19]

The ones in the rear who were not so hard pressed were the first to take flight, about the time Braddock reached the front of the column. As soon as the flanking infantry followed the general forward, an officer complained, the wagoneers, "who imagined things would turn out badly," took the gears from their horses and "galloped intirely away, so that if fortune had turned in our favour, we had not one horse left to draw the train along." About fifty or so women who had been with the train and helped drive the cattle were lost during the battle, some of them captured, most dead.[20]

The Virginians performed better than the regulars. One redcoat remembered that about 200 of them plunged into the woods and fought from behind trees "and I belive they did the moast execution of any." A British officer saw a Virginia lieutenant lead 170 men "to where the enemy was hid and routed them: But O unhappy! our infatuateds [regulars] seeing a smoke, fired and killed him with several of his men." Another Virginia company "attacked the enemy before the retreat was beat," but was cut off and slaughtered. Washington remembered another such sally by his countrymen, "but this, *unhappily* from the unusual appearance of the movement being mistaken for cowardice and a running away," a regular officer ordered the men back to the road. Washington proposed to Braddock that he lead his Virginians to take the hill on the right, but he was turned down until the last moment, when it was too late.[21]

This exchange happened in a place dangerous for horses and the men who rode them. Braddock's aides Orme and Morris went down wounded. Braddock himself had five horses shot from under him, and Washington two, the screams of the wounded animals cutting through the general uproar. Both had their coats "intirely shot to tatters with musket balls," according to an officer, and Orme said Washington behaved "the whole time with the greatest courage and resolution." Braddock's escort, Robert Stewart's Virginia Light Horse, lost twenty-five of its twenty-nine horses. Washington said later that he had a strange sense of "the miraculous care of Providence that protected me beyond all human expectation."[22]

Braddock attracted enemy attention to himself and those around him, contributing to the loss of officers. Stubbornly holding to the gunpowder age's definition of bravery—steadfastness under fire—he sat his horse waiting for the French and Indians to give way, because irregulars always gave way before regulars. Instead, his own men were falling back, despite his stalwart example.

His luck ran out about three or four hours after the first shots of the battle, when he ordered Washington to charge the hill with the Virginians. This was the general's last order. A ball hit him from behind and knocked him out of the saddle. Washington, who was the last staff officer still upright, assembled a detail to carry Braddock off the field on the general's own sash, put him into a small cart, and took him over the river. There he ran into Gage, commander of the advance, now unaccountably in the army's rear. Washington returned to the front to see what he could do, but word of the general's wounding had spread through the ranks. The men were mostly out of ammunition anyway, and according to one officer, "they as if by beat of drum, turned to the right about, and made a most precipitate retreat, every one trying who should be the first. The enemy pursued us, butchering as they came."[23]

Washington recalled that he and a few other officers tried to stop the stampede, "with as much success as if we had attempted to have stopped the wild bears of the mountains. . . . They broke and ran as sheep pursued by dogs." Orme said the "officers used all possible endeavours to stop the men," many of whom "threw away their arms and ammunition, and even their cloaths, to escape the faster." Croghan, however, noticed that some of the officers led the panicked mob over the river, out of their own heads with terror. "The unfortunate General Braddock," he said, "was intirely deserted in the waggons with only his servants and a person or two more, & it was some time before they got a party of men to guard him."[24]

"The Indians seeing us masters of the field of battle," said a French officer, "stopped to scalp, we French then halted by parts return'd to carry off the wounded, the remainder with some Indians pursued the English as far as the river." They did not cross it, however, so the Battle of the Monongahela—which Americans would call Braddock's Defeat—was over. The ordeal of Braddock's army, however, was far from ended.[25]

All the Wounded That Could Not Walk
Fell in the Enemys Hands

The battle generated charges that the British regulars either applied the wrong tactics or were simply cowards. "The folly & consequence of opposing compact bodies to the sparse manner of Indian fighting, in woods," Washington observed decades later, "was now so clearly verified." Platoon fire against targets scattered behind cover was a waste of lead. Yet the redcoats fought stoutly, if ineptly, until the very end, when the retreat turned into a rout. Ineptitude grew out of the quick loss of officers, and hence of control, compounded by the fact that the two Irish regiments were anything but well-disciplined fighting machines. They lacked the coherence and long training together needed to make them efficient fighters, but they were not a mob of cowards.[26]

Braddock was criticized for dividing his command, leaving part behind with Dunbar. Sending the whole army into the meat grinder across the Monongahela would not have changed the outcome and might have made it worse. Orme thought dividing both army and supplies prevented a greater loss. "It was extremely happy the general had made this disposition," the aide claimed, because if the army had lost the supplies with Dunbar along with the others, "we must have starved or fallen into the enemy's hands, and the addition of numbers could not have served us as the panic was so general."[27]

That panic turned a chaotic battle into a debacle that cost Braddock 977 officers and men dead or wounded, two-thirds of his force; losses on the other side were about fifty. Many of the wounded would have survived if not left behind when the troops stampeded. "The flight was precipitated and confused, many were killed and scalped by the Indians in repassing the Monongahela," a survivor remembered. Another said, "All the wounded that could not walk fell in the enemys hands."[28]

Duncan Cameron, a sergeant in Gage's corps, saw this firsthand. Wounded early on and stunned for a while, he crawled into the woods. "As soon as the remains of our army had recross'd the river," he related, the Indians "began immediately to scalp the dead and wounded; this I heard and saw, though escap'd being seen." He hid in a hollow tree until after dark, watching "these ravenous hell-hounds" who were "yelping and screaming like so many devils."[29]

This style of warfare appalled Europeans, who did not see savagery in their own military and civil punishments, the brandings and whippings and burnings at the stake over religious disputes. Once the troops had crossed the river, however, the Indians broke off pursuit. "On the other side of the river most of us halted to consider what to do," one redcoat remembered, "but the men being so terrified desired to go on . . . expecting every moment to have our retreat cut off." Nobody followed them, however.[30]

Many men raced down the road toward Dunbar's rear division, leaving behind a trail of weapons and accoutrements, but not all of them did. About a quarter of a mile on the other side of the river, Orme recorded, officers "prevailed upon near one hundred of them to take post upon a very advantageous spot." Lieutenant Colonel Ralph Burton—the senior surviving officer under Braddock, Colonel

Peter Halkett having gone down early—posted some "small parties and centinels. We intended to have kept possession of that ground, 'till we could have been reinforced." Braddock sent Washington out to halt those who had led the stampede across the river. He found Gage with about eighty men around him. When he reported back to Braddock, the officers decided to retreat because there were not enough men to hold their position.[31]

The survivors stumbled off in the dark, "in the utmost horror and distress, most of us wounded, without a bit of any thing to eat & nothing to cover us," said a lieutenant. They still expected to be cut off and surrounded, but that was not how Indians fought. Unlike whites, they had no desire to destroy opposing forces; they fought for captives, plunder, and trophies.[32]

Neither French nor English understood Indian ways, and they were horrified at what happened. "The whole army of the enemy fell to plundering &c.," Cameron observed from his hiding place. "Though I must do the *French* commandant this justice, that as soon as possible he could, he put a stop to the *Indians* scalping those that were not yet quite dead, and ordered those wounded to be taken care of." The "commandant" (Dumas) himself wrote, "The pillage was horrible, on the part of both the French and the Indians." He did what he could for the wounded and retrieved Beaujeu's body, while the Indians found two hogsheads of rum in the British supply train and got so drunk they could not carry off all their plunder.[33]

This behavior did not accord with French ideas of how fighting men should conduct themselves. Contrecoeur avoided mentioning the pillage in his official report, saying that Dumas did not pursue the retreating British "because a large party of Canadians had unfortunately behaved like children and had fled at the first fire." Washington had no idea what was going on at the battlefield, but years later he said, "Happy was it" that the Anglos left "such a quantity of valuable and enticing baggage on the field as to occasion a scramble and contention in the seizure & distribution of it." If there had been a pursuit the rest of the command would have been wiped out. French and English alike condemned Indians for not conducting themselves as a European army would.[34]

Experienced French officers were no better at controlling their Indian allies than the inexperienced Washington had been at Jumonville Glen. Dumas assigned a detachment to guard the captured artillery and stores, and he sent to Fort Duquesne for relief for the wounded and bateaux to ship the English goods. By land and water, over the next two days French dead and wounded, British cannons, eighty head of cattle, small arms, powder, and other military stores arrived at the fort. Hundreds of English bodies remained behind, feasts for blowflies, buzzards, and wolves.

The triumphant Indians reached the Forks on the night of July 9, "with many horses loaded with spoils of the English consisting of furniture [horse furnishings], cloaths, utensils, gold, silver &c.," according to a Canadian who saw them come in. They also had "but 20 prisoners whereof seven women or girls," along with "an infinite number of scalps." To prevent the French from seizing their haul, the Indians distracted them by declaring that the British were marching to recover their cannons. Contrecoeur sent a detachment out because capturing the artillery was the best guarantee against an attack on the fort.[35]

James Smith, a Pennsylvania trader held prisoner at Fort Duquesne, watched the victors arrive with "soldier's caps, British canteens, bayonets," and scores of bloody scalps, whooping their "scalp hallos" while the garrison saluted with muskets and cannons. He saw "about a dozen prisoners, stripped naked, with their hands tied behind their backs, and their faces and parts of the bodies blackened— these prisoners they burned to death." The next morning, the Indians from Detroit and Michilimackinac went home, despite Contrecoeur's attempts to stop them. They left "with their horses & a great booty," said a Canadian. "These Indians," Contrecoeur advised the governor, "have done very well. It is necessary to recompense them."[36]

The departure of the northern Indians left Fort Duquesne vulnerable. If the English had resumed their advance, at least after Dunbar brought up the rear division, they might well have taken the place. That would not happen, however, because the bleeding, dispirited redcoats and provincials were headed in the opposite direction.

Once the decision to retreat was made, Braddock ordered Washington to go back to Dunbar to get supplies, transportation, and medical care sent up, and to cover the retreat of the striking force. Washington had not eaten since the day before, still suffered from the malady and hemorrhoids that had plagued him throughout the campaign, and shook with the emotional and physical aftereffects of battle. These conditions, he said later, left him "in a manner wholly unfit for the execution of the duty," but he obeyed. He was not a real officer, just a volunteer, but with Orme and Morris down he was the only one who could speak in the general's name.

The sun had gone down, and he set out on a forty-mile trek with two guides. The first stretch went through the battle's human wreckage. "The shocking scenes which presented themselves in this nights march are not to be described," he remembered. "The dead—the dying—the groans—lamentation—and crys along the road of the wounded for help . . . were enough to pierce a heart of adamant. The gloom & horror of which was not a little encreased by the impervious darkness occasioned by the close shade of thick woods." It was so dark that his guides could not tell whether they were in or out of the track "but by groping on the ground with their hands."[37]

He reached Dunbar's camp, about seven miles northwest of Great Meadows, at midmorning on July 10. Word of the calamity had preceded him, and the place was in a panic. Stragglers began coming in around noon, and Dunbar ordered the drummers to beat "to arms," which only raised fears among soldiers and teamsters that the French were about to attack. Some ran off down the road, but the numbers of men arriving demonstrated that there was still a force between them and the enemy. Dunbar sent wagons and supplies forward under guard that midafternoon.

Washington collapsed into bed after delivering Braddock's message. When he got up on the morning of the 11th, he found that virtually all discipline had disappeared in the face of wild rumors. Dunbar cracked down on the restless redcoats, and that afternoon he sent two more wagons and two companies of infantry to Braddock. The general and most wounded came in that evening, Braddock reeling in the saddle because the men refused to carry him. Wounded and bleeding, the old soldier ordered that the horses present should haul the two cannons and the wounded in wagons. Everything else would be destroyed: ammunition, food, wagons, everything.

Dunbar later expressed amazement that a man in Braddock's condition could give orders of this "magnitude and importance," but he did not protest or disobey them. Nearly 150 wagons were burned, powder casks smashed in a spring, the Coehorn mortars broken or buried and their shells exploded. Provisions were scattered on the ground or dumped in the water. This caused outrage in London. "Fearful of an unpursuing foe," said an official review, "all the ammunition, and so much of the provisions were destroyed for accelerating their flight, that Dunbar was actually obliged to send for thirty horse loads of the latter before he reached Fort Cumberland."[38]

Even as the defeated army staggered eastward, civilians expected it to return in triumph. Overconfident Philadelphians had launched a campaign to raise funds for a victory celebration. Benjamin Franklin refused to contribute, because "the events of war are subject to great uncertainty." Braddock's losses left the doctor exposed by his loan guarantees for horses and wagons. Lawsuits piled up until a new commander in chief ordered that the farmers be paid from army funds.[39]

Rumors of the disaster reached Fort Cumberland on July 11, and Colonel Innes sent a panicky note out in all directions; William Fairfax in turn sent copies all over Virginia, including one to Dinwiddie. "Sir:" Innes began, "I have this moment receiv'd the most melancholly news of the defeat of our troops. . . . In short the account I have receiv'd is so very bad that as please God I intend to make a stand here. Its highly necessary to raise the militia everywhere to defend the frontier." He claimed erroneously that Braddock and most officers were dead, but the general still breathed.[40]

Braddock in fact continued issuing orders from his cot, aiming to get his army out of the green hell it had been in for the last month. He wanted to resume the retreat on the 12th, but destroying supplies and equipment took too much time, and the wounded continued to straggle into camp. He finally ordered movement on the 13th, leaving a rear guard behind to finish the destruction. Occasionally he reflected on the battle. "Who would have thought it?" he asked at one point. "We shall better know how to deal with them another time." He summoned Washington and gave him the red sash on which he had been carried from the field, as well as a brace of pistols.[41]

The general died at nine o'clock that night, and the next day Washington supervised the burial arrangements, for want of another uninjured staff officer. As a major general, Braddock was entitled to escort by two battalions of infantry and three squadrons of cavalry, with a salute of three rounds by seven cannons. That was out of the question. Instead, Washington ordered burial in the roadway, "with the honors of war," and then had the army trudge over the grave to keep the Indians from finding it. Despite their differences and occasional arguments, Washington had a great deal of fondness for the irascible old redcoat, who had shown him unusual warmth in return.

The Virginian retained his affection thirty years later. "Thus died a man, whose good & bad qualities were intimately blended," he said. "He was brave even to a fault and in regular service would have done honor to his profession—his attachments were warm—his enmities were strong—and having no disguise about him, both appeared in full force. He was generous & disinterested—but plain and blunt in his manner even to rudeness." With Braddock's death, Washington would never again receive guidance from an older patron, as he had from his brother Lawrence, from William Fairfax, and from the general. He was twenty-three years old.[42]

I Now Exist and Appear in the Land of the Living

Washington had a retreat to finish. At Orme's request, he wrote to Innes at Fort Cumberland on July 15, asking that he provide housing and food for wounded officers, make arrangements to dispose of Braddock's personal property, and send fresh horses. He hoped to reach the fort that evening. "I doubt not," he concluded, "but you have had an acot. of the poor genl.'s death by some of the affrighted waggoners, who ran off without taking leave."[43]

It was possible to tally losses after all the survivors had limped into Wills Creek. The final total of casualties was 63 officers and 914 men killed or wounded, out of 1,459 engaged; 387 wounded reached Fort Cumberland. The battle almost destroyed three Virginia companies, half their twelve officers dead. Washington thought that there were not more than thirty men left of those companies.[44]

The British officers blamed the enlisted men for the calamity on the Monongahela. Sergeant Cameron complained that "there was court-marshall, upon court-marshall, and the most cruel whippings succeeded them as ever I beheld . . . some were whipp'd for good reason, some for little, but, in general, they were too severe." The officers declared this to be necessary. "Subordination, and strict discipline," said one, "cannot (from the general depravity of the soldiery) be properly supported, without having recourse to the severest punishments." Even a surgeon who attended whippings and was sickened by them, especially when wounded men were flogged, said the severity was "absolutely necessary, for the proper behaviour, and subordination of the privates." More likely, the officers took out their own frustrations over the defeat on their defenseless soldiers.[45]

Dunbar decided to lead his regulars to Philadelphia to go into winter quarters. Washington objected that this would leave the west defenseless, with too few colonial troops to guard passes and the militia ineffective. The British colonel pointed out that with the artillery lost and the regulars weakened by death, wounds, and sickness, it was impossible to do anything more that year. There was nothing the Virginian could do about the decision, because his appointment expired along with Braddock. He decided to report all to his friends, family, and Lieutenant Governor Dinwiddie.[46]

His first message was an unusually long and detailed letter to his mother on July 18. First he described the march from Fort Cumberland to the Monongahela, saying that the only casualties were occasional stragglers waylaid by Indians. After crossing the river, the army was attacked "by a body of French and Indns. whose number, (I am certain) did not exceed 300 men," an underestimate he would hold to all his life. Most of Braddock's troops were "English soldiers, who were struct with such a panick, that they behav'd with more cowardice than it is possible to conceive." Their officers, on the other hand, "behav'd gallantly in order to encourage their men, for which they suffer'd greatly," sixty of them going down. The Virginia troops, by contrast, "shew'd a good deal of bravery, and were near all kill'd."

After giving a roll call of the dead, Washington again condemned the redcoats: "In short the dastardly behaviour of those they call regular's, expos'd all others that were inclin'd to do their duty to almost certain death." He compared their rout to sheep chased by dogs, "and it was impossible to rally them." As for himself, he luckily escaped without a wound, "tho' I had four bullets through my coat, and two horses shot under me." The loss of the general's other aides "render'd the duty hard upon me, as I was the only person then left to distribute the genl's. orders which I was scarcely able to do, as I was not half recover'd from a violent illness." He said he was still in "feeble" condition, and he would stay at Wills Creek to recover before heading home.[47]

Washington made the letter to his mother the basis for his official report to Dinwiddie, also dated July 18. Much of the language was the same, as were the estimate of enemy strength and the "dastardly behaviour" of the redcoats. "The Virginian companies behav'd like men and died like soldiers." He kept beating up on the regulars, again likened to sheep "before the hounds," and as uncontrollable as "the wild bears of the mountains." He heaped more praise on himself for coming through the battle unscratched despite the rounds through his coat and his horses. He said two-thirds of the casualties "received their shott from our own cowardly English soldier's."

He told Dinwiddie something he did not relate to his mother, that he feared the consequences of the defeat for Virginia's western settlers. "Colonel Dunbar intended "so soon as his men are recruited [recuperated] at this place, to continue his march to Phila. into winter quarters: so that there will be no men left here unless it is the poor remains of the Virginia troops, who survive and will be too small to guard our frontiers."[48]

Washington sent his third and last letter of the day to his brother Jack at Mount Vernon. Again he understated the strength of the French and Indians, illustrated his own bravery, and contrasted the cowardice of the regulars with the valor of the Virginians. He showed a spark of humor, however. Because he had heard "a circumstantial acct. of my death and dying speech, I take this early oppertunity of contradicting both, and of assuring you that I now exist and appear in the land of the living by the miraculous care of Providence."[49]

A disaster on the scale of Braddock's invited inquiry and recrimination. No defeat so lopsided struck British arms again until 1879, at Isandhlwana in the opening action of the Zulu War, when about 1,500 infantry with two guns and a corps of volunteers were wiped out by Zulus armed with short spears and hard-charging tactics of assault and envelopment. Braddock's Defeat was unprecedented. Washington therefore wanted the world to know that a large British force had been whipped shamefully by a smaller force owing to cowardice among the regulars, despite the efforts of their gallant officers. The Virginians, in contrast, behaved nobly, and he was the noblest Virginian of them all. Not only should he escape blame, but when Virginia struck back, he wanted to take the lead.[50]

If he was blameless, the whole enterprise was miserably planned and conducted. The colonial governments had promised Braddock more than they could deliver, especially in transportation. Braddock approached the Monongahela with a force superior to what the French and Indians could bring to bear against him, despite an impossibly strung-out supply line. He had worked his men hard all along the way, without rum or enough provisions. He had alienated potential Indian allies and remained ignorant of the terrain, confident of the superiority of British troops and tactics. Arrogance was his undoing when the enemy made the most of the ground and turned a blundered encounter into a devastating assault. "If on a battle field, with no natural advantage," said a Canadian officer, "this even should happen to brave and well disciplined troops, from . . . not being acquainted with the kind of enemy they had to deal with, it is an impressive lesson." The failure, therefore, was in the commander. Braddock "found to his woeful experience what had been frequently told him," observed Adam Stephen, "that formal attacks and platoon firing never would answer against the savages and Canadians."

Horatio Gates of the New York independents heaped blame on Braddock. "A few who were the generals favourites gratefully strive to save his fame by throwing the misfortune of the day on the bad behaviour of the troops," he wrote, "but that was not the case," owing to Braddock's tactical mistakes and his failure to support the advance. The crack about "favourites" was a dig at Orme. It also meant Washington, who complained to Orme, "It is impossible to relate the different accounts that were given of our late unhappy engagement; all of which tend greatly to the disadvantage of the poor deceased genl., who is censured on all hands."[51]

Washington and Orme spent years defending the general who gave them their positions. They need not have worried, because it was not a good idea for British officers to abuse a dead general who had gotten his command through influential friends; Gates was never promoted again. Colonels Dunbar and Gage, who conducted the first inquest into the disaster, danced around the command failures. They said that "the bad behavior was general," because the troops had been overworked during the advance, were demoralized by want of sufficient provisions, and had "nothing to drink but water and that scarce and bad." Moreover, they had heard from provincials that "if they engaged the Indians in the European manner of fighting they would be beat." And last, there were no "Indians or other irregulars to give timely notice of the enemy's approach." Except for the provincials scaring the men about the Indians, these were all failures of leadership. The official line, however, was to blame the colonials.[52]

No one peddled this view more forcefully than Thomas Gage, commander of the advance. He sent a rambling account of the battle to General Lord Albemarle, repeatedly asking that he be promoted to colonel of the 44th Regiment, in place of the dead Peter Halkett. He avoided details about his own behavior, such as how he disappeared from the front of the army and reappeared in its rear at the end of the fight. "I can with truth assure you," he said, "no officers ever behaved better, or men worse." The reason for the bad conduct was "the talk of the country people, ever since our arrival in America—the woodsmen and Indian traders, who were continually telling the soldiers, that if they attempted to fight Indians in a regular manner, they would certainly be defeated." The "country people," Gage would not admit, proved to be right. Fatigue and scant provisions, he said further, were minor contributors to the defeat.[53]

Civilians in England were less charitable to either Braddock or the regulars. *The Gentleman's Magazine* said that the redcoats ran away "shamefully." Americans were inclined to blame Braddock for the disaster, and they called Washington the "hero of the Monongahela" for organizing the retreat. One newspaper opined that he had earned "a high reputation for military skill, integrity and valor; tho' success has not always attended his undertakings." Ben Franklin praised him, and in August a Virginia minister named Samuel Davies preached a sermon to the militia, printed in Philadelphia and London as *Religion and Patriotism the Constituents of a Good Soldier.* Claiming that patriotic spirit and military ardor had emerged in Virginia, Davies added, "As a remarkable instance of this, I may point out to the public that heroic youth, Colonel Washington, whom I cannot but hope Providence has hitherto preserved in so signal a manner for some important service to his country."[54]

I Am So Little Dispirited at What Has Happen'd

Washington's reputation remained safe as he made his way home in late July. He reached Mount Vernon on July 26 and sent word to Belvoir announcing his return and his need for rest before he could visit. William Fairfax sent a note welcoming him back, to which his daughter-in-law Sally added a postscript, signed by all the Fairfax ladies, "thanking heaven for your safe return" but accusing him "of great unkindness in refusing us the pleasure of seeing you this night." If he did not show up in the morning, they would visit him.[55]

While Washington rested, Dinwiddie was in a lather. He told Lord Halifax of the Board of Trade that he expected a slave rebellion after Braddock's Defeat. "These poor creatures imagine the French will give them their freedom." The governor was especially upset by Washington's report that Dunbar planned to leave Fort Cumberland. Refusing to acknowledge the scale of the disaster, he sent Dunbar

r white Americans, as bounties on scalps offered by colonial gov-
ments provided incentive. Nominally, bounties were to be paid
for killing men at war with the English, but the terms were loose
ugh that men were paid for scalps of Indian women and children,
of Frenchmen. Absence of a state of war was immaterial. Parties
ackwoods entrepreneurs ranged through the west seeking grisly
its, and scalp-hunting rangers earned reputations as wild, undis-
ined barbarians. Killing defenseless victims for money became
ermanent part of colonial economies and of the way Americans
ed war in the wilderness.[1]

My Orders Are Only Conditional, and Always Confused

shington recalled that after Dunbar left Fort Cumberland, "the
ntiers were continually harassed." He believed that the Indians
ed as pawns of the French, and like other Virginians he considered
ly military measures, not diplomacy, to deal with the nations. He
d higher authorities that another campaign against the Forks was
ential to protect the Old Dominion. Even the victory of the En-
sh and Mohawks over the French and their Indian allies near Fort
orge in northern New York on September 8 could not distract this
rochial Virginian, who failed to see that northern campaigns could
t Fort Duquesne off from Canada, reducing its alleged threat to his
ovince or the Ohio Company's ambitions.[2]

Washington wanted to lead the next campaign, so he lobbied in-
ential men, who were receptive to the "hero of the Monongahela."
e heard from his contacts in Williamsburg early in August 1755.
ilip Ludwell advised that the House of Burgesses had voted to raise
200 men, and he had told Dinwiddie that Washington had earned
e command. Ludwell urged Washington to get to Williamsburg to
ake his own case.[3]

Charles Lewis of the military committee said that it was "unani-
ously agreed" that Washington would command Virginia's forces
n the next scheme." His neighbor George Mason hoped that Wash-
gton would find the colony's new military program agreeable to
is wishes so he could accept the command "with honour." Probably
ecause of what he had told his brother Augustine about his losses in
ast campaigns, lawmakers made sure that his monetary wishes were

his own estimate of resources available to the colonel, as well as a
campaign plan. "Are you not able, after a proper refreshment of your
men," he asked, "to make a second attempt to recover the loss we
have sustained?" Good weather still remained, he asserted, and he
had called the assembly together for August 5, "when I think I can
promise you a reenforcement of at least 400 men." Governor Shirley
of Massachusetts had succeeded Braddock as commander in chief, so
Dinwiddie sent a similar message to him.[56]

Dinwiddie was out of touch with reality, and as ignorant as he had
been when he sent Washington westward the year before. His campaign
plan reached Fort Cumberland on the same day as Governor Horatio
Sharpe of Maryland. Dunbar and Sharpe called a council of war, which
declined Dinwiddie's proposal. Sharpe wrote that all present "apprehended your meaning in general to be that if the particular modes of
reducing Fort DuQuesne . . . specified [in your proposal] could not be
followed, any other step should be taken whereby the enemy might be
most offended and His Majesty's service best advanced." To that end,
curiously, Dunbar would retreat to Philadelphia.[57]

He began moving out on August 2, the day after the council, taking with him 1,516 officers and men. Dunbar appeared, Dinwiddie
complained, "to have determined to leave our frontiers as defenceless
as possible." The governor accused the redcoats of opening a road for
a French advance into Virginia, leaving only the surviving provincial
troops and the sick and wounded to block the way. He complained to
Sharpe that "the whole conduct of Colonel Dunbars appears to me
monstrous." Indian raiders soon showed up in the frontier counties,
and the governor called out the militia and got the assembly to authorize four companies of rangers.[58]

Washington remained adjutant for the Northern Neck, so on August 2 he ordered his county lieutenants to muster their militia for the
adjutant's inspection. He had just advised the governor and Council
that Dunbar's retreat meant "the frontiers of [Pennsylvania] but *more especially* those of Virginia and Maryland were laid *entirely* open." As soon
as Dunbar left Fort Cumberland, the provincials there began to desert
because, as Dinwiddie put it, they thought "they were left by the regulars to be destroyed by the barbarous enemy." The 200 or so colonials
Dunbar left behind were down to fewer than 100 by early September.[59]

Some new military adventure was in the offing, and Washington
wanted a place in it. His half brother Augustine was a member of the Bur-

gesses, so he sent him an account of the Braddock campaign that echoed his earlier messages from Fort Cumberland. "I can nevertheless assure you, and other's . . . that I am so little dispirited at what has happen'd, that I am always ready and always willing, to offer my country any services that I am capable off; but never upon the terms I have done, having suffer'd much in my private fortune, besides impairing one of the best of constitutions," meaning his health. He was fishing for back pay and a promotion.

Washington thought himself ill-used by Virginia's government. "I was employ'd to go a journey in the winter . . . and what did I get by it?" he asked. "My expenses borne! I then was appointed with trifling pay to conduct an handful of men to the Ohio. What did I get by this?" Detailing the costs of outfitting himself for that campaign, he said he "went out, was soundly beaten, lost them all—came in, and had my commission taken from me." His service under Braddock had also cost him. He had "been upon the loosing order ever since I enter'd the service, which is now near two year's." He wanted another command, but he expected to be paid decently for it.[60]

The assembly was about to meet, and the frontier was aflame. Virginians including Washington assumed that the Indian raids were prompted by the French. Instead, the nations had their own interests at heart. The Shawnees, for example, declared war on the English in Virginia and the Carolinas for their own reasons. Old grievances, including the imprisonment of six Shawnee men in South Carolina since 1753, came to the fore, erupting into open war when Braddock's Defeat made the English appear defenseless.

Over the next several years the Shawnees and their allies raided English frontiers, killing or capturing hundreds of men, women, and children, adopting some and ransoming others back. The Shawnees made up the larger share of raiders into Virginia. To the north, the Delawares spread dismal fear across western Pennsylvania, striking back against a long history of English encroachment on their lands. Those attackers called themselves "Allegheny Indians," meaning they were from the Ohio Country. Soon they attracted allies among Pennsylvania Indians who had formerly been neutral, particularly the eastern Delawares.

A whole new chapter of war had opened in North America. This was not between the French and the English, but between the English and Indian nations who had scores to settle and, after the Battle of the Monongahela, an opportunity to do just that.[61]

EIGHT

WE TOOK SOME P
VIGOROUS MEAS
TO COLLECT A F

(1755–1756)

There is nothing more difficult to take in hand,
to conduct, or more uncertain in its success, th
lead in the introduction of a new order of thing

—NICCOLÒ MACHIAVELLI

The term "ranger" first appeared in English du
century, with two meanings. One identified a wand
a low reputation, a transient thief or vagabond. T
royal officer who patrolled the king's parks and
poaching or other trespass. Sometime later it also
of a scouting party attached to regular troops.

The first American company of rangers was
England in 1675, during a war between English c
ans. A few dozen Englishmen and twice or three ti
of Indian allies went out, in the first company's ord
pursue, fight, surprise, destroy, or subdue" enemy n

The idea spread to Virginia the next year, whe
raised a 125-man mounted company to "range" be
waters of the Piedmont's rivers, without Indian allie
eighty years rangers had more experience in fronti

satisfied. Washington answered Lewis that he was grateful for the compliments he had received but warned: "I am unequal to the task, and do assure you it requires more experience than I am master of."[4]

Washington often turned on his modesty when it furthered his case. He as much as admitted such to Burgess Warner Lewis, who also had urged him to go to Williamsburg. Washington wrote that he had not done so because he believed that he could not get a command "upon such terms" as he would accept. If he accepted, he would insist on several points. He should approve all officer appointments, because he would answer for their performance. He needed a "small military chest" of money to campaign with. Moreover, he believed that without a significant commitment of the colony's resources, the commander of its forces was likely to "loose in his reputation." Offering himself for the post with such conditions would make him "appear too forward," but if the command was offered to him, then he could "make such objection's."[5]

Washington's young ego had been so stoked by the praise heaped on him lately that he almost forced the politicians to beg him to take what he wanted most. His mother fretted that he would march away once more. He did not want to go to the Ohio again, he told her, but if the command was pressed on him with acceptable terms, it would "reflect eternal dishonour upon me to refuse it." She should prefer his absence to his disgrace.[6]

The Burgesses, governor, and Council gave him everything he wanted on August 14, beginning with £300 to him and lesser amounts to lower officers, to reward them for "their gallant behaviour and losses" at the Monongahela. The Burgesses voted £40,000 in paper money, and the governor and Council authorized sixteen companies, to be assembled in one regiment; the first establishment was 1,000 enlisted men, along with the previously authorized 200 rangers in four companies. Dinwiddie told London that Virginia's officers were "greatly dispirited" by their lack of royal commissions to make them equal in rank to regulars. He was "convinced" that if Braddock had survived, "he would have recommended Mr. Washington to the royal favor."[7]

Dinwiddie sent Washington his commission as "colonel of the Virginia Regiment and commander in chief of all forces now raised in the defense of His Majesty's colony," along with a windy set of instructions. The assembly had voted money for frontier defense and for an expedition to drive the French from the Ohio. The lieutenant governor forwarded blank commissions for officers and authority to organize the regiment. Washington should leave six officers at Fort Cumberland and fan the rest out to recruit, and establish his own headquarters at Winchester. His salary would be 30 shillings per day, and he would receive £100 per year for expenses and a 2 percent commission on all official purchases he made. This last was a common gratuity for public officials at the time.

Dinwiddie promised that the men would receive clothing and their full pay with no "stoppages" (deductions) except 2 pence per month for surgical services. Washington should forward weekly returns of company strengths the first of every month. The colonel could also buy goods for the Indians, and he was entrusted with a military chest to spend as "the nature and good of the service requires." He should lay in stores for the next campaign and was empowered to appoint an aide-de-camp, military secretary, and other staff officers. Lastly, "I sincerely desire that you will inculcate morality and virtue among your men, to punish drunkenness and swearing."[8]

Washington had his command, at least on paper, and remarkable independence to act "defensively or offensively." Defense was the immediate concern, because Virginia had a western frontier extending 300 miles from the North Carolina line into present-day western Pennsylvania. Much of the border ran through the Shenandoah Valley, which had a scattering of "plantations," as frontier farms were grandly called. When one was raided, its neighbors fled over the Blue Ridge to the east. The valley had only one town of consequence, Winchester, a collection of about sixty rude log hovels. Sixty miles to the northwest stood Fort Cumberland, guarding the major pass from the west.

To defend this line, Washington must appoint officers, who would in turn raise enlisted men. These regular troops (not part-time militia) must be fed and equipped, armed and trained, disciplined, and paid. He must accomplish all that with no guidance other than what he had learned during his time with Braddock. To raise such a command required a colonel who was a model of efficiency.

First things first. Washington designed a uniform for himself, had a tailor make it, then used it as a model for others. "Every officer of the Virginia Regiment is, as soon as possible, to provide himself with an uniform dress," he ordered on October 5, "which is to be of fine broad cloath: The coat blue, faced and cuffed with scarlet, with a plain silver lace (if to be had), the breeches to be blue; and everyone to provide himself with a silver-laced hat, of a fashionable size." This was his first frustration, because he repeated the order through the fall, until he lost his temper. "Colonel Washington," orders announced, "is a good deal surprized to find that some officers are yet unprovided; and declares, that if they do not immediately procure them, or such thereof as can be had; it will be looked upon as disobedience of orders."[9]

Finding capable officers proved a greater challenge than making them dress properly. There were a few available from the last campaign, most notably Adam Stephen, promoted to lieutenant colonel and placed in command of Fort Cumberland. Captain George Mercer became Washington's aide-de-camp, and he promoted Captain Andrew Lewis to major, putting him in charge of new companies as they arrived at Winchester. Lewis should inspect the men for fitness, prepare daily returns of strength, take roll three times a day, draw "absolute necessaries" from the commissary, and keep discipline according to the British articles of war. The men were to be "regularly practised in shooting at targets," Washington commanded. Finally, captains should put themselves under Lewis's orders as they arrived at Winchester.[10]

Every younger son of a would-be grandee wanted a commission. Washington was bombarded with letters of recommendation, and parents asked him to watch out for their boy once he became an officer. Youngsters arrived at headquarters carrying messages such as the following: "His circumstances are such that nothing but a view of serving his country could induce him to this undertaking." Some of these letters bore signatures of highly influential men. Still, Washington wanted his officers to merit their positions, not gain them through the influence peddling that had made him colonel.[11]

New officers were sent out to recruit, so most of them were far from Washington's sight. The colonel complained to Dinwiddie on October 17 that because he did not know where many officers were or what they were doing, "my orders are only conditional, and always confused." He also needed a commissary of supply at Winchester, or else "things will suffer greatly here." He would not take blame for the government's failure to meet his needs.[12]

Messages to officers typically ended: "This order I expect will be immediately complied with; and that no delays be offered." The colonel was losing patience with dilatory subalterns, most of whom were younger than he. One he ordered "peremptorily" to get a move on. "Your late disobedience of orders has greatly displeased me," Washington growled. The officer's "crime" was "sufficient to break the best officer that ever bore a commission."[13]

Complaints poured in from citizens about some officers. The commander at Fredericksburg had impressed more houses than he needed, so the colonel ordered him to desist and also put a stop to plundering. Another civilian accused Captain Peter Hog of poaching his indentured servant and making her his mistress. Washington complained that he "did not expect such behaviour from an officer." He ordered the captain to compensate the girl's master immediately, "or expect to answer it in a more disagreeable way." Hog bought the girl's indenture from her complaining master.[14]

In early January, Washington approved the finding of a court-martial in the case of an ensign convicted of cheating at cards and suspended him from duty. The young man had "acted inconsistently with the character of a gentleman, and scandalously for an officer." The colonel issued a general order calling the conviction a "timely warning of the effects of misbehaviour" that, he hoped, would be "instrumental in animating the younger officers to a laudable emulation in the service of their country." They should concentrate on their duties, and their first responsibility was professional improvement. "There is Blands and other treatises which will give the wished-for information," he said, a reference to Humphrey Bland's *Treatise of Military Discipline*, the British officer's bible. He then offered some fatherly advice, remarkable for a twenty-three-year-old. He thought it his duty "to give this friendly admonition." Officers should look to their colonel as an example, "to observe the strictest discipline through the whole economy of my behaviour." They could "certainly depend upon having the strictest justice administered to all." He would "make it the most agreeable part of my duty, to study merit, and reward the brave, and deserving." He promised to treat them without partiality or prejudice.[15]

We Are at a Loss for Want of Almost Every Necessity

The first duty of these officers was recruiting, and Washington issued instructions on September 6. Each captain was to raise thirty men, each lieutenant eighteen, and each ensign twelve. They should draw funds for expenses, enlistment bonuses, and the care of recruits. Men signed up must be between sixteen and fifty years of age, over 5 feet 4 inches tall, and in good health. He told every officer that he expected "immediate compliance; and that no excuse shall occasion the least delay."[16]

But not many men wanted to join the regiment, because memories of the Fort Necessity and Braddock campaigns remained strong. One lieutenant's father, fearing that his son would be punished for not carrying out orders, explained that he had tried every place where there was "the least liklyhood" of getting recruits, but with no luck, because men were "determined not to go till they are force'd."[17]

The colonel warned Dinwiddie that recruiting would go slowly. "And to draught them will answer no end," he observed, "unless they are put under better regulations." In one case, a party of reluctant recruits was jailed to prevent escape, but their friends broke them loose. He needed more than one subaltern per company to enforce discipline.[18]

The commander in chief fumed that recruiting officers did not obey orders, but two of them reported that they had reached their rendezvous and found no orders. Those supposed to gather at Alexandria on October 20 were granted until November 15 to fill their quotas, but men still refused to sign up. The recruiting officer at Alexandria said that he had "no hopes." Officers spent their funds but with small results.[19]

Washington gave officers an extension to December 1 to fill their quotas, threatening trial by court-martial if they did not succeed. Intemperate threats were pointless if civilians did not want to become soldiers, so Washington extended the deadlines to December 20, then to the 25th. He asked the assembly to authorize a draft from the militia, but it refused. Still, by November 22 Stephen reported that manpower was up to 330 men, not all fit.[20]

Washington's threats made officers adopt dubious practices. One was recruitment of indentured servants and apprentices, who signed on as a way to get free of their masters; they usually had to be sent home. The colonel urged his officers to recruit in "public places," such as town squares, so they reached into taverns. He rebuked one recruiter for confining and torturing men who refused to sign up. This was not as heinous as cheating at cards, evidently, because he let the man off with a warning.[21]

Washington's demands caused the enlistment of many unfit recruits and the discharge of others because officers had gotten them drunk and tricked them into signing up. Robert Stewart, of the light horse, condemned the "prevalent spirit of opposition, to the service." His "utmost efforts" had been "ineffectual," and some that he did recruit deserted. Washington was so frustrated that he approved Peter Hog's recruitment of "mulatto's and negroes" for his company, remarkable for a slaveowner.[22]

He was ready to throw up his hands by the end of November, railing against "total negligence among the recruiting officers," whose difficulties he refused to concede. Some, he claimed, had been out many weeks partying with their friends. He threatened to assemble all the officers and read them the riot act to improve performance, but that did not happen. The effort continued into 1756, bringing in the few who wanted to serve and were fit to do so. Virginia, Washington had discovered, was gun-shy.[23]

Nor was the province a font of business talent. To supply the men the army needed commissaries, purchasing agents with money to spend or authority to obligate the government to pay for goods. John Carlyle operated at Alexandria, but Washington needed commissaries where his troops were stationed. Charles Dick and Thomas Walker had served the Braddock expedition, but when Dinwiddie extended their contracts in August they objected because the government had not repaid what they had spent. Washington talked Dick into serving until the military committee of the House of Burgesses heard his complaints.[24]

Walker went to Williamsburg in October and came to terms with the committee. He left the capital November 12, but as of the end of the month Stephen reported that he had not reached Fort Cumberland as ordered. Washington declared that "such disobedience of commands" would not go unpunished. He could not punish commissaries, however, because they were civilian agents for the colonial government. They filled his needs as he relayed them, but they were not under his command.[25]

The commissaries' job was nearly impossible because Virginia could not supply the regiment's material needs, in particular clothing and munitions. What they did acquire was often substandard and could not be moved anyway for want of horses and wagons. This was a double problem: The commissaries needed transport to get goods to the troops, and Washington needed it to take the goods along when his troops moved. He gave officers authority to impress horses and wagons, which merely caused their owners to hide them. The colonel issued minutely detailed orders on the handling and safeguarding of all sorts of supplies, but conservation was no answer for failure to deliver. As the year wore into December, men became sick for want of medical supplies. Worse, the governor and Council imposed charges against the men's pay for clothing. An exasperated Washington told his officers that if the men had not gotten uniforms—a misnomer if ever there was one, because instead of blue and red, most were in nondescript garb—their pay should not be stopped for them.[26]

The colonel received an alarm from Fort Cumberland early in October that Indians were raiding the neighborhood. Washington advised Dinwiddie that he would march troops out from Fredericksburg, Alexandria, and Winchester at once, but lack of wagons prevented movement for the next ten days, when the emergency had passed. "We are at a loss for want of almost every necessity," he complained to the lieutenant governor.[27]

Vendors in Maryland and Pennsylvania would not accept Virginia's paper money; recruiting suffered because not even Virginians trusted the currency. In December Washington sent Dinwiddie a laundry list of complaints about shortages of everything, and he asked that the colony's treasurer, House Speaker John Robinson, release the last £10,000 from the August appropriation, in gold and silver. Robinson could scrape up only £4,000, 10s., not all of it hard money.[28]

Of all items of supply, food was the most basic. When he told a commissary to buy 5,000 pounds of flour and ship it to Winchester, Washington "positively ordered" the man to collect as many wagons as he needed. If the citizens refused to provide them, he should ask the nearest officer to order soldiers to bring them in by force. After Indian raids on farms near the Potomac, he ordered detachment commanders to send out parties to harvest the corn at the plantations of people who were "supposed to be killed or taken prisoners by the Indians."[29]

The major challenge was to get a supply of meat, preserved or on the hoof, to Fort Cumberland, to not just tide its garrison over the winter but to lay in stores for a campaign against Fort Duquesne. Commissary Walker had the greatest responsibility for this after he showed up, but he was often the victim of unscrupulous beef suppliers, competition from Pennsylvania buyers, and a shortage of salt for preservation. Cattle imported from North Carolina reached Winchester so weak they could not be driven to Fort Cumberland, according to Walker. Some meat already stored at Cumberland was "quite spoild and more I am afraid in danger." By one means or another, Walker got enough cattle butchered to supply Fort Cumberland and other posts for the season. To supplement the beef, Walker had found sources of hogs, but he ran out of money before Christmas, and could not buy them.[30]

Washington was so busy supervising supply that during the fall of 1755 a complaint crept into messages from several officers: that they heard nothing from him but orders, and their questions were unanswered. That was probably unavoidable, given his administrative burdens. His most important challenge was to see that the men were paid; they were eventually, but never on time. He tried everything he could think of to better their lot. At Dinwiddie's suggestion, men who died should be "continued on the rolls as effective men, twenty-eight days, to pay for their coffins, &c."[31]

Pay was vital to soldiers, and not just for obvious reasons. Until fairly modern times they received only the most basic food, clothing, equipment, and housing. Everything else they paid for out of their own pockets, including such small "necessaries" as needles and thread to keep their buttons on. Except for enlistment bonuses, the men were not paid at all until November 1, when enough money arrived from Williamsburg to pay everybody up to October 1, minus "stoppages." Washington heard from ranger Captain Hog that his "men begin to grumble for their pay and I am utterly at a loss where to apply for it," in the absence of instructions from Washington. He also had no money for food.[32]

By early December the men's pay was two months behind, and Washington sent Paymaster Alexander Boyd enough to pay them for one month, giving special attention to Hog's company. Hog's rangers remained cranky and raised a ruckus about the deductions. Complaints about "stoppages &c.," Washington told Hog, were "groundless and unnecessary; it is the custom of the army," something other soldiers "submit to with chearfullness." Not even he believed that, but he sent funds to pay the rangers for December and January.[33]

Hog's men, like some in other detachments, were building a fort and were entitled to extra pay for their labor. If the carpenters were "kept closely to their work," Washington declared, they should receive one shilling extra per day, but officers should "not throw away the country's money idly."[34]

I See the Growing Insolence of the Soldiers

The Virginia troops were underfed, underpaid, poorly clad, and overworked, so desertion was a wholesale problem. When Washington stopped in Fredericksburg, he learned that local authorities had drafted some "vagabonds" who protested so violently that they were locked in the county jail. Their friends then stormed the building and set them free. This was just a foretaste of what was to come.[35]

By late November officers complained that recruits were deserting as fast as they could be raised, owing to lack of pay. Adam Stephen delayed leaving Winchester for Fort Cumberland because of the "disagreeable service of apprehending deserters—four, out of a gang of 20 banditti, all with arms and ammunition, are apprehended." A few days later his bag held six, and he offered a reward for any taken dead or alive.[36]

At Washington's urging, the assembly made it a crime to harbor deserters. This was a controversial move, because many citizens were sympathetic to refugees from hard life in the army. Soldiers often ran off with their enlistment bonuses, their clothes, and their muskets, which they traded for protection. Washington as usual blamed the officers, who he said did not pursue deserters "with proper resolution, or they might be taken." Given the availability of hiding places in the Old Dominion, this was unfair.[37]

Washington also proposed that Dinwiddie order that the new law be read out in every parish church to acquaint the people with it. Few of them knew that it was a crime to aid deserters, he said. The measure also allowed relief for redcoat deserters who returned voluntarily. There were many men, he claimed, who would "gladly return, if they could be sure of indemnity." These were men drafted earlier into regular regiments from the Virginia Regiment, and the colonel suggested that Dinwiddie pass this advice on to Commander in Chief Shirley.[38]

Short of keeping all the men in chains, there was no way to stop the flow of desertion because the men ran away from conditions they thought intolerable. They went over the hill from nearly all posts every night, and only occasionally did civilians bring them back. Washington tried to solve the problem mostly with brutality. Any soldier who deserted, he declared, "though he return again, shall be hanged without mercy." This was not likely to encourage deserters to come back.[39]

Desertion was part of a larger problem of disciplining a regiment composed of men who were not soldier material. Regular armies kept troops too busy to get into trouble. The construction of barracks, storehouses, and a few small forts did some of that. The other solution was training, which not only inspired fighting efficiency and unit cohesion but also kept the soldiers under watch. Yet only twice in his first five months did Washington speak about training. On December 20 he ordered the officers "to see that the sergeants who understand the manual exercise, do drill the recruits, at least twice a day." This followed the British army's habit of leaving training to sergeants instead of officers. The other order on training appeared on December 28, requiring that the troops be "train'd to their exercise and practis'd to bush fighting." This implied that the regiment would fight like Indians, dispersed behind cover.[40]

Washington occasionally reminded his captains to have sergeants read all pertinent orders to the soldiers every day, "that they may not plead ignorance." Other orders were more like this: "Any soldier who is guilty of any breach of the articles of war, by swearing, getting drunk, or using an obscene language, shall be severely punished, without the benefit of a court martial." That echo of Braddock's draconian style meant the whip, as when Washington sentenced a man to receive 600 lashes for "uttering treasonable expressions."[41]

When militia were called up, their behavior was worse than that of the regulars, so Washington asked for new regulations for the militia and a Mutiny Act for the regiment. As an example of the riotous state of discipline, he said he had recently led a detachment out of Winchester to answer an alarm of an Indian attack just outside town, witnesses reporting that they heard "the shrieks of the unhappy murder'd!" When he reached the scene, he found that the disturbance was owing to "3 drunken soldiers of the light-horse, carousing, firing their pistols, and uttering the most unheard-of imprecations." Another report of an Indian raid was caused by two slaves rounding up cattle.

"These circumstances are related," he continued, "only to shew what a panick prevails among the people." False reports of Indian raids poured in, he claimed, because the regiment's officers did not do their duty patrolling. If the assembly did not give him new legislation to enforce discipline, he must, "with great regret, decline the honour that has been so generously intended me." This was not the last time he threatened to resign, but he was honestly pessimistic. "I see the growing insolence of the soldiers," he complained, and "the indolence and inactivity of the officers." He predicted that "under our present establishment, we shall become a nusance, an insupportable charge to our country, and never answer any one expectation of the Assembly." Undisciplined behavior would not occur if the regiment was "under restraints, that would terrify the soldiers from such practices."[42]

Dinwiddie called the assembly together to pass a Mutiny Act. Washington wanted Virginia to copy an act of Parliament of 1689, providing that mutiny, sedition, or desertion "should be punished with death or such other penalty as a court-martial might judge." Virginia's military establishment did not fall under this law, so the colony must devise its own.[43]

While Washington awaited replies to his requests, he had some units organized enough to send on to Fort Cumberland. He warned officers that there had been "great complaints" from civilians about soldiers pillaging and plundering private houses. If any such "irregularities" happened again, "the person guilty shall receive five hundred lashes, without the benefit of a court martial."[44]

Washington reached Williamsburg in mid-November to promote the new Mutiny Act. He was lionized as a great hero and attended balls, soirees, and open houses held in his honor. He wrote Stephen that the new law was coming and advised him to be "particularly careful in seeing strict order observed among the soldiers, as that is the life of military discipline. We now have it in our power to enforce obedience . . . the men being subject to death, as in military law."[45]

With the new Mutiny Act in hand, Washington had no excuses if discipline did not improve. He found one anyway. The legislation provided that the findings of courts-martial must be approved by the governor before sentence could be executed, which meant delay. This, he complained to Dinwiddie, would be "morally impossible" if the regiment was on the march to the Ohio, causing "great expense, trouble and inconveniency." He had protested this to the Council, and it agreed that the governor should issue signed, blank warrants approving court-martial findings. He asked for "fifty or a hundred."[46]

Dinwiddie gave him what he asked for, but it took time to print the new law and warrants. In their absence, Washington resumed his heavy hand. He gave Sergeant John Campbell a nitpicking order about taking care of wagons to bring recruits to Winchester. If he heard "any just complaint" about Campbell's party, he warned, "you will be punished by a court martial." Sure enough, Campbell displeased the colonel, who tossed him into the guardhouse. Instead of a trial, he released the man after two weeks on the grounds that he had "received a sufficient reprimand for his disorderly behaviour."[47]

That was the pattern until the Mutiny Act and warrants arrived at the end of the year. Washington already had power to confine offenders, so courts-martial could wait. On December 26 he ordered the commissary to hire a smith to make six pairs of handcuffs, so deserters in the guardhouse could be cuffed while subsisting on bread and water. Three days later, he sent officers to see if the handcuffs were too tight, "and if they occasion their hands to swell, the smith must be ordered to alter them."[48]

Washington likely knew from the beginning that disciplinary problems such as drunkenness, theft, and insubordination would arise. Other disorders amazed him. "I am very much surprized to hear the great irregularities which were allowed of in your camp," he complained to ranger captain John Ashby, who sold rum to his men through a hired bartender. Ashby's wife spread "sedition among the men, and is chief of every mutiny. If she is not immediately sent from the camp," Washington thundered, "or I hear any more complaints of such irregular behaviour," he would personally drive her out.[49]

Of all the Virginia troops the rangers were the least disciplined. Instead of the four companies authorized in August, there were three understrength companies under captains Peter Hog, John Ashby, and William Cocke. The rangers were not part of the regiment, but they answered to Washington because he was commander in chief and the only source of money for their support. The rangers were a rough-and-tumble lot of Indian traders, packers, and hunters driven out of the Ohio Country by the French. They occupied the most isolated posts, closest to the frontier in sparsely settled country: Ashby and Cocke on the South Branch of the Potomac, Hog in the southern valley at Fort Dinwiddie on the Jackson River.

Washington did not expect much from them, but Cocke's journal shows almost constant patrolling by his company south of the Potomac, twenty to thirty miles a day, although his men saw little action. Mostly they reached the scene after Indian raiders had already left. On October 2, "Recd. an express that the Indians had killd four families on the creek—went immediately . . . but they had went off before we got there." On October 5, "Recd. an express that the french & Indians had killd several families and besieged" a farm. On the 7th Cocke led seven men escorting three families evacuating the threatened area, then spent the next week guarding inhabitants.[50]

Washington may have read that highly professional report with pleasure, but his joy did not last. The rangers were soon downright mutinous. Ashby's entire company threatened to leave because it had received no pay or clothes. The commander in chief told the captain it was his "express orders" that Ashby's rangers not leave their post "on any pretence whatsoever." He promised to send clothes and money "immediately." A few days later he ordered Ashby and Cocke to relocate to Patterson's Creek on the Potomac twelve miles below Cumberland, to protect the settlers and guard supplies.[51]

The new locations required new forts, so Washington borrowed an engineer from the Maryland independent company to design them and supervise construction. He told Cocke and Ashby to keep the men from abusing citizens and otherwise put them under strict discipline. Their increased isolation increased their disorder, however.[52]

Adam Stephen reported on December 23 that ten of Ashby's men had left their post. He thought it was just "a scheme to go home & keep the holly-days." Cocke also left his post, complaining to Washington at Winchester that his men needed clothes. The colonel sent him back with a copy of the Mutiny Act and orders to warn the men "that if any soldier deserts, although he return himself, he shall be hanged."[53]

Peter Hog's company caused Washington the most grief, but not solely on account of its behavior. When the captain reached Fort Dinwiddie in late September, he found it only partially complete. There were not enough men to build the fort, guard settlers at harvest, and range the countryside. Unless he received reinforcements, he warned, the area would belong to the Indians by winter. Moreover, supplies of everything were short. Washington ordered Hog to do what he had just said was impossible without reinforcements. Hog received more food, although the price of beef depleted his funds. So had hiring a doctor to cure men of "diseases that rendered them useless."[54]

Hog's men were crammed into a wretched log fort, feeding bedbugs and lice, wearing rags and homemade moccasins, going out to patrol the woods as often as they could. These were tough backwoodsmen used to privations, but they believed themselves taken for granted by the government. Hog spent what money he had to buy beef, so he could not pay them. The rangers were becoming mutinous. Hog complained that his men were "uneasy abt. their pay," because while regimental companies had been paid, they had not. The rangers felt like abandoned stepchildren.[55]

They were right, because Washington's main interest was the regiment. The rangers were uncouth and beneath his approval, and besides they were damnably hard to supply at their isolated stations. Hog's men were soon running away. Washington blamed their captain for that, sneering: "You do not take proper means to prevent it." He had ordered provisions and money sent to the rangers, but he had not followed up. He wanted Hog to offer rewards for the capture of deserters, but Hog was broke.[56]

Hog answered Washington's charge that he failed to prevent desertion by relating an account of the capture of two "having been concealed by some lawless fellows who assaulted him [the sergeant in pursuit] but on whom he was amply revenged by cutting off the arm of one! this I hope will remove your fears as to using all the means I can think of to prevent it." All Hog received in reply was a copy of the Mutiny Act and orders "to have the deserters punished accordingly."[57]

Washington's regiment was poorly supplied, but no companies suffered from official neglect more than the rangers. Given the independent character of those men, it is a wonder that any continued in service. Still, they were the units closest to the frontier and so were the colony's first line of defense. They deserved better from their government, and from their commander in chief.

It Is Impertinent, I Own, in Me to Offer My Opinion

Virginia needed defense, because there was a war going on. It was not on a large scale, and most of the action centered around Fort Cumberland, in Maryland, and in lands that Virginia claimed in modern Pennsylvania. When the governor of Pennsylvania offered to share intelligence, Washington accepted, pointing out that defense also required armed force. "We took some pretty vigorous measures to collect a force upon our frontiers, upon the first alarm," he said, "which have kept us peaceable ever since."[58]

The Shawnees waged what Virginians regarded as a war of terror. They attacked isolated farms, killed the men, carried off the girls and women, and burned what they left behind, retaliating for abuses they felt they had suffered over the years, and not because of French incitement. Much of this activity occurred along the Potomac and its tributaries. Adam Stephen complained that his men were constantly watched by the enemy, and they were too few to protect the neighborhood. He believed at first that a major French-Indian invasion was likely. Washington warned the rangers on the South Branch to expect attack, and either to endure siege or retreat no farther than necessary. The attack never came, but the alarm put Winchester into "the greatest hurry and confusion," the colonel told Dinwiddie. He had heard the rangers "were blocked up by the Indians in small fortresses," and he accused them of cowardice, but they were just following his orders.[59]

False alarms vastly outnumbered real Shawnee raids. They were so great a nuisance that Washington published a notice saying that the Indians had gone home. Advising his countrymen "not to be alarmed on every false report they may hear," he promised that in a short time the frontiers would be "so well guarded, that no mischief can be done." That went for naught when some pranksters disguised as Indians terrorized Fairfax County.[60]

Rumors of a French and Indian invasion persisted. Adam Stephen put his feelers out from Fort Cumberland but said he could "hear of no person that has seen this large body." He concluded that it was much ado about nothing. Christopher Gist, in Pennsylvania, dismissed the rumors. He had heard a report, however, that a large French corps was on its way to attack an English expedition to the north.[61]

Washington left what little campaigning there was to Stephen and his captains. He was more interested in winning over Indians who had not sided with the French. On September 19 he had invited his former translator Andrew Montour to join the regiment, and if he brought some of his Indian relations along, so much the better. They would be "better used than they have been," he promised, "and have all the kindness from us they can desire." He received no immediate response but later heard that Montour was headed for Venango with 300 Indians. He sent an effusive letter of congratulations, renewed his invitation, and said he hoped Montour would tell "our brothers" that the colonel was "invested with power to treat them as brethren and allies; which I am sorry to say, has not been of late."[62]

He wanted to sweeten the bad taste Braddock had left in the Indians' mouths, and to help him do that nobody was better qualified than Christopher Gist. Since Braddock's Defeat he had roamed Pennsylvania as a volunteer, recruiting men and providing Washington with intelligence. The colonel had tried to give a company captain's commission to him, but he met opposition from those who wanted officers to be from the gentry. He appointed him captain of a company of scouts instead.[63]

The colonel told Dinwiddie that he would send Gist and Montour out to win the loyalty of the nations. He thought "no means should be neglected, to preserve what few Indians still remain in our interest." Alleged French attempts to alienate the affections of the less than affectionate Cherokees and Catawbas required the "greatest and most immediate attention." The Virginia government had not done enough in Indian relations, and someone of high rank should be Virginia's emissary to the nations. "It is impertinent, I own, in me to offer my opinion in these affairs," he admitted, "but my steady and hearty zeal for the cause . . . would not suffer me to be quite silent."[64]

Without waiting for a go-ahead from Dinwiddie—and still not having heard from Montour—Washington ordered Gist to visit the nations along the Susquehanna River to get them to "assist us in fighting their own battles." The chief scout should also send an Indian runner to "captain" Montour to ask for his help and tell him that if he raised a company of sixty Indians he would earn a captain's commission and pay. Gist should assure the sachems that they would receive provisions, "and that we shall take every oppertunity to testify the love we bear them."[65]

The colonel was optimistic, telling Major Lewis on the South Branch that when the Indians arrived with Montour or Gist, he should supply and encourage them, and the officers were "all desired to take notice of them and treat them kindly." This was sound diplomatic advice, but it was premature. Gist reported from Philadelphia that he had set up meetings with several sachems and would forward "all the intelligence that can possibly be got." There Indian affairs in the north rested until spring.[66]

In the south, Adam Stephen volunteered to go "on embassy" to the Creeks and Cherokees, but Washington had no authority to grant extended leave. He recommended that Dinwiddie send Stephen to those nations. That letter crossed one from the lieutenant governor, relaying a report that the Cherokees had declared war against the French and the Shawnees and had sent a large force to attack the Shawnee towns. Dinwiddie ordered Washington to send four companies to join them, and have Stephen or Lewis take command. That would have insulted the Cherokees, but they had no such expedition out. Meanwhile, Dinwiddie would send commissioners to the Catawbas and Cherokees to urge them to join Virginia's forces in the spring. As in the north, there Indian affairs rested for the time being.[67]

The French and the Indians—the ostensible objects of Washington's command—consumed little of his time and energy during his first five months on the job. He concentrated on raising and organizing his troops, embarking on a nearly ceaseless tour of the several stations—stopping to inspect his properties and scout out promising new real estate when he could—and pouring out a stream of orders. From Winchester he went to Fort Cumberland. Later stops included the South Branch posts, Alexandria, Fredericksburg, Winchester, back to Cumberland, and so around the territory. His orders were a marvel of painstaking detail, everything that a functioning staff might have taken care of for him.[68]

Fort Cumberland caused the greatest headaches. When Washington first visited the post in September, he issued orders to clear the surrounding woods, repair the buildings and defenses, and make arrangements for recruits as they arrived. The garrison had dwindled to under 150 men, Virginians and a Maryland company of thirty under Captain John Dagworthy. "I have reason to believe Capt Dagworthy will look upon himself as commanding officer," Stephen warned Washington.[69]

That he would. He had a captain's commission from the governor of Maryland and claimed an old royal commission as an ensign from the last war. He refused to obey orders from provincial officers and even countermanded those Stephen gave his own men. Washington advised Dinwiddie to abandon Cumberland and build a new fort in Virginia, but the governor and Council believed it was a royal work that Virginia was obliged to maintain. As for the impertinent Dagworthy, his commission had actually lapsed. Washington protested the absurd situation, and Dinwiddie wrote to Commander in Chief William Shirley asking for brevet commissions for Washington and his officers. November passed without a response, and the colonel fumed.[70]

Massachusetts governor Shirley, as the new commander in chief for North America, could straighten the mess out if he wanted to. Command at Fort Cumberland deteriorated into ceaseless squabbling between the short-tempered Stephen and the stuffy Dagworthy. It also raised the old issue of relative rank between royal and provincial officers that rankled Washington and his subordinates. Stephen advised that his officers were "big with jealousy" over their own rights and that of their province. He urged Washington to go to Wills Creek to see what he could do.[71]

Washington refused. Dinwiddie suggested that he might have "obviated the incontinent dispute with Capt. Dagworthy" by asking him if he commanded by virtue of a Maryland commission, because his royal commission had lapsed and he was not on the half-pay list; and the commission of a Virginia colonel was superior to that of a Maryland captain. House Speaker John Robinson was sympathetic. It gave him "great concern to find you meet with so many obstacles in the discharge of your duty," he told Washington. It "astonishd" him to hear that "a petty officer should pretend to command the forces raised by this colony." He hoped His Majesty would straighten out the mess.[72]

Washington told Dinwiddie early in December that he did not expect "any great danger" at Fort Cumberland over the winter and that he would be more useful "riding from place to place, making the proper dispositions." He did not admit that he wanted to avoid confronting Dagworthy. Dinwiddie agreed, so long as training continued. Christmas approached, and still no word arrived from Shirley, but the Dagworthy problem appeared to solve itself. Stephen reported (prematurely, as it turned out) that another officer had bought his ensign's commission and he had purchased a lieutenancy in a regular regiment.[73]

Virginia's officers at their fort in Maryland could relax and enjoy the holiday. "I had the honour to dine at the head of 24 fine gentlemen yesterday," Stephen told Washington. "We had an extreamly good dinner, and after drinking the royal healths in a huff and a huzza at every health we pass'd an hour in singing and taking a cheerful glass. We then amus'd ourselves with acting part of a play, and spending the night in mirth, jollity and dancing, we parted very affectionatly at 12 o'clock, remembering all absent friends." He wished his colonel a happy new year, "and that it may be remarkable for your victorious achievements."[74]

Washington's first achievement of the year occurred on January 9, 1756, when he "activated" the Virginia Regiment. There were enough men to form sixteen companies, ready to march from Winchester to Fort Cumberland. The outfit was still shorthanded, but each company had a captain. Officers commissioned on the condition that they raise their troops were expected to do so "with the greatest punctuality." There followed the usual lecture about officers doing their duty and a promise that the troops would be paid when they reached Wills Creek.[75]

The young colonel had repeatedly condemned his officers over the past five months. He accordingly must have been sure that no one could blame him if the Virginia Regiment failed in its assignment.

NINE

I Am Afraid to Turn to This Hand or to That

(1756)

> The great wish of some is to avenge themselves on some particular enemy, the great wish of others to save their own pocket. . . . Meanwhile each fancies that no harm will come of his neglect . . . and so, by the same notion being entertained by all separately, the common cause imperceptibly decays.
>
> —THUCYDIDES

When Washington received the title "commander in chief" in August 1755, the lieutenant governor lost one of his own functions. To Americans of the present day, the role of commander in chief is first among the duties of the president. A glance at the list of duties of the president in Article II of the Constitution shows it to be just one of many. It is not a role often played, at least not in a formal sense. The first order issued by a president in the capacity of commander in chief of the army and navy appeared in 1889, by Benjamin Harrison. Presidents have usually issued directives as proclamations or executive orders.[1]

When the Constitution made the chief executive commander in chief, it followed the examples of state constitutions adopted after 1776 and even the history of feudal Europe, when kings were nominal heads of their armed forces. This duty of the executive was so incidental that it received little mention in *The Federalist Papers*, the essays that helped persuade the New York convention to ratify the Constitution in 1788. Federalist 49 notes that the commander-in-chief title gives the president less power than was wielded by the British king and some state governors, because the president cannot declare war himself or raise and regulate armies and navies. Federalist 74 declares: "The propriety of this provision is so evident in itself . . . that little need be said to explain or enforce it," because "of all the cares or concerns of government, the direction of war most peculiarly demands those qualities which distinguish the exercise of power by a single hand."

During the 1700s the British designated a senior army or navy officer as commander in chief in a given region; the first assigned in North America was Braddock. In Virginia, Washington's position divided the executive power between the highest civil officer, Dinwiddie, and the top military officer, the colonel. So long as the two of them cooperated, this arrangement could work.

This Sits Heavy on an Active Spirit

As soon as he activated the regiment on January 9, 1756, Washington gave it its first orders. Lieutenant Colonel Adam Stephen was to march the main body to Fort Cumberland, and Captain Thomas Waggoner would take a detail from Cumberland to the South Branch and build two small forts. Washington repeatedly interrupted these operational commands with instructions about keeping money accounts and the like, reflecting the penny-pinching nature of the enterprise. Moreover, the orders to move were countermanded so the corps could chase deserters and round up transport, then reissued, then countermanded again.[2]

Stephen reached Cumberland by January 18. The place was agitated by false alarms of Indian raids every night, but patrols found nothing but tracks. The normally pugnacious Stephen was discouraged. "I'm sorry the face of affairs is so unpromising," he told Washington. The season was advanced and there was no plan of operations. Virginia had only a third of a regiment and little hope of recruiting more. "This sits heavy on an active spirit." Two weeks later he pleaded, "I long to hear from you."[3]

Washington was consumed by details, as he had been since August, and over the same concerns: desertion, supplies, recruiting, and the rest. Officers still caused problems. Despite his claims to impartiality, the colonel indulged Captain Charles Lewis, brother of Andrew Lewis, who had helped get him his colonelcy. The young man had been drunk on duty. Such behavior, he advised, was intolerable in an officer, who must set a good example for his men. "This comes from me as your friend, not as a superior officer."[4]

Washington gave Dinwiddie his first full report on January 14, saying he had issued "all necessary orders for training the men to a proper use of their arms, and the method of Ind'n fighting, and hope in a little time to make them expert." Much of his report was on the shortage of money and supplies, and pleas for more. The colonel who dreamed of commanding troops in the field had become instead their manager, a bureaucrat begging for support from his government. Washington's frustration grew out of the persistent shortage of money in the colonies. Virginia had decided to create a professional regiment rather than rely on the militia, but the appropriation ran out with the enlisted strength only about a third of authorization.

There had never been a strategic decision about what the regiment should do. Dinwiddie and the aristocracy wanted another campaign to drive the French out of Ohio. An alternative would have been to abandon the frontier and guard the passes through the Blue Ridge. Washington, however, favored a forward defense of the existing frontier. The colonel urged Dinwiddie to make a strategic decision for the coming year, by "express commands" to prepare either for taking the field or for frontier defense, "because the steps for these two are very different." He favored defense, because without more men than he expected to get he did not think it possible to campaign in the west. He wanted to build a strong fort in Virginia, giving up Fort Cumberland.[5]

That post's problems still revolved around Maryland captain Dagworthy, who had not gone away after all. Adam Stephen ordered a court of inquiry in the case of a Virginia lieutenant who had refused to turn out his guard unless so ordered by Dagworthy, whom he considered in command. The court found that the officer had only followed orders. Stephen was incensed, and so was Washington.[6]

Dinwiddie was also outraged, partly because Dagworthy claimed that all provisions at Cumberland belonged to Maryland, although Virginia had paid for them. He blamed Stephen for "tamely giving up the command," although that was not the case. He was in a lather because Commander in Chief Shirley had told Governor Sharpe of Maryland, who had commissioned Dagworthy, to take care of the situation. Washington asked permission to visit Shirley in Boston, and the governor approved.[7]

Washington exploited the Dagworthy affair by going behind Dinwiddie's back to other influential politicians. Dagworthy's behavior, and the lack of royal commissions for himself and his field officers, he told several burgesses, hampered Virginia military operations. He got uniformly favorable responses. Washington also heard from Stephen, who curtly answered the charge that he had surrendered command: "I have given up nothing hitherto."[8]

Washington told Stephen on February 1 that he was leaving for Boston, hoping to solve the Dagworthy problem and gain the brevet commissions. "You may depend upon it, I shall leave no stone unturned for this salutary end," he promised. Stephen should keep up discipline and training in the colonel's absence. This was the last the Virginia Regiment would hear from its colonel until April 7.[9]

Washington, his aide Mercer, and two personal servants left Alexandria on February 4. He reached Philadelphia on the 7th or 8th and spent most of a week visiting tailors and hatters to buy the kind of clothing that a Virginia gentleman ought to have.[10]

He reached New York late on the 15th and stayed with Speaker Robinson's brother Beverly, who had married into money and prospered as a merchant. His household included his wife's younger sister Mary Eliza "Polly" Philipse, age twenty-six, herself a wealthy landowner. There were attempts at matchmaking, but Polly was somewhat horse-faced and definitely bossy; Washington was not about to marry another version of his mother. Still, he escorted the ladies to events in the bustling city and spent more money on shoes, clothing, and replacement horses. The party rode out for Boston on February 20, stopping in New London, Connecticut, to stay with Joseph Chew, an old friend of the family. The journey continued on to Newport, Rhode Island, where Washington took a ship to Boston, which he reached on February 27. He stayed in a tavern while he awaited an appointment with Shirley. He was delighted to find that he was a celebrity in the great port city, entertained in wealthy houses with nightly card games, which he mostly won. He bought more hats, suits, silver lace, and gloves.[11]

His luck ran out during his first visit to Shirley's mansion, Province House, a three-story pile of bricks capped by a cupola, the largest and most lavishly appointed residence in British North America. Shirley and his friends cleaned Washington's purse in a card game, and soon other Yankees had his measure; gambling losses added to the money he spent on fancy goods. Shirley was a tall, slope-shouldered man with a broad face divided by an enormous nose, with friendly eyes and the half-smile of a royal courtier. Washington had met him at Braddock's Alexandria conference the year before and pronounced him a "great politician." He proved he was just that by sidestepping the issue of brevet rank for Washington and his field officers. Shirley had authority to grant such ranks, but he knew that his tenure would not last long. Moreover, brevets would expire at the end of the current emergency and so were not a gateway to the regular commission on which Washington had his heart set. The Virginia colonel did get half of what he wanted, however, when Shirley solved the Dagworthy problem: Given that Dagworthy acted under a commission from the governor of Maryland, and that as a provincial captain he was junior to provincial field officers, "it is my orders that Colonel Washington shall take the command."[12]

Maryland Governor Horatio Sharpe, meanwhile, obeyed Shirley's orders to assume command of all provincial forces from Pennsylvania to South Carolina. When that news reached Fort Cumberland, Stephen said that Dagworthy declared himself "counsellor and aid de camp to Govr. Sharpe." Stephen promised Washington, "I will never submit to any regulation but what you approve." In any event, Sharpe eventually sent Dagworthy back to Annapolis.[13]

Stephen was not optimistic about the mission to Boston, because he thought Shirley was an empty suit. On the issue of royal commissions, Stephen advised seeking the Virginia Regiment's admission to the regular establishment.[14]

Washington and his party began retracing their journey on March 2, calling on the governors of New York and Pennsylvania on the way. He had spent too much and lost at gambling, and lodgings in Boston were expensive. He borrowed £91 from Beverly Robinson to get home, but when he fell sick in Philadelphia, he hired a nurse and had to stay four extra days. The party proceeded to Annapolis, where Washington met Sharpe, to whom he had taken a dislike a year earlier. This time, however, he impressed the governor, who admitted that the colonel "really seems a gentleman of merit." Because he had failed to get a commission from Shirley, the young man left Annapolis resolved to resign from the Virginia Regiment. He reached Winchester on April 7. He had commanded the regiment for eight months and had been away from it fully half that time.[15]

I Am Distracted What to Do!

Washington did not resign when he returned because the frontier was aflame. Whereas there had been only isolated killings for some months, in early April he told Dinwiddie, "The enemy have returned in greater numbers, committed several murders not far from Winchester, and even are so daring as to attack our forts in open day." The colonel did not tell the governor that this time the Virginians had started the war, and the Shawnees were striking back. He may not have realized that himself.[16]

The cause was a campaign Dinwiddie had dreamed up in December, when he had heard that the Cherokees had declared war on the Shawnees and were sending a large force against them. Washington put off the governor's orders to join the Cherokee expedition until his regiment was activated in January, and even then he predicted that such a campaign would prove "abortive" because the Shawnees had moved west. Dinwiddie continued to push, sure that the expedition would succeed. So Washington ordered Major Lewis to attack the Shawnee towns on the Great Kanawha River with seven companies, a total of 356 men, which included only a small party of Cherokees. They set out late in February, while Washington was in Boston, to endure six weeks of suffering and starvation, eating their horses and abandoning the campaign without reaching their objective because of flooded rivers. The Virginians returned early in April, starving, ragged, and disease-ridden.[17]

The Shawnees knew that the expedition had been aimed at their towns, and its inept outcome suggested that the Virginians were not much of a threat as soldiers. Washington told the governor, "However absurd it may appear, it is nevertheless certain, that five hundred Indians have it more in their power to annoy the inhabitants, than ten times their number of regulars," and he predicted that a general war was coming.[18]

"We have been much harassd by the Indians," Stephen reported from Fort Cumberland at the end of March. This activity reflected rare French intrusion into the Shawnee-Virginia conflict. Captain Jean-Daniel Dumas, veteran of the Monongahela and now commandant at Fort Duquesne, wanted to learn whether the English were preparing another campaign against his post. On March 23 he sent Ensign Dagreau Donville at the head of a party of fifty "*sauvages*" toward Fort Cumberland with orders to observe the movements of the English, harass convoys, burn magazines, and take prisoners. A patrol out of Cumberland ran into this party, and in the exchange killed Donville and scalped him; the Virginians lost one dead and two wounded. Washington sent the scalp and Donville's captured orders to Dinwiddie, recommending that the Frenchman's killer receive a reward. The Burgesses soon posted a reward of £1 for every enemy Indian killed or captured. Donville's men retaliated against settlers in Fairfax County.[19]

Washington urged early action by the assembly to recruit Indian allies. "Indians are the only match for Indians," he said, "and without these, we shall ever fight upon unequal terms." He sent detachments out to "scour the woods" for the enemy, but they seldom made contact. The Indians were not the only threat; a Virginia ensign got into an argument with a Maryland citizen, who shot him dead.[20]

Dinwiddie reported on April 15 that there were Cherokees in Williamsburg negotiating an alliance, but the Burgesses were so "tedious in their consultations" that he doubted he could get more than forty or fifty to join Washington. Negotiations of another sort took place at Captain John Ashby's fort near the Potomac that same day. He was surrounded by Shawnees who claimed they numbered 400 men and demanded his surrender. Ashby vowed to fight to the death, so the two sides parleyed, the captain brought out rum, everyone took a swig, and the Indians left. Ashby later heard shooting at the neighboring fort, but that post drove off its attackers. "The design of the Indians was only, in my opinion," said Washington, declaring the obvious, "to intimidate him into a surrender."[21]

The 15th was a busy day. Washington heard about a large Shawnee camp with English prisoners, and he sent Captain John Mercer out to locate it and await his arrival with militia he had called out. Only fifteen of them showed up, so Washington stayed at Winchester fuming about the "timidity" and "perverseness" of the inhabitants. The advance party fought a skirmish in which Mercer and several of his men were killed. Washington sent another party out with excessively detailed orders not to be "decoyed into any snares of the enemy." By this time alarms of pending attack had reached even Winchester.[22]

Washington called a council of war on the 21st. He could send the few recruits available at Winchester to the threatened areas, or he and the nine officers present could wait until militia and provisions arrived. The council decided to stand pat, because there were not enough resources to do any good in the field. Washington called up the militia, sent for gunpowder, and advised his outpost commanders to retire to posts nearer Winchester. Another council of war two days later advised abandoning the most exposed forts and concentrating troops at Cumberland and Winchester.[23]

Dinwiddie told Washington on April 23 that the Cherokees and Catawbas had agreed to provide 600 men if Virginia would build forts in each nation's territory as refuges for women and children when the men went off to war. Dinwiddie agreed to that and ordered construction of a fort for the Cherokees; North Carolina promised to build one for the Catawbas but never finished it. The Cherokees in Williamsburg were reluctant to go north until this was done, but the governor talked them into sending sixty men. It was too late, because Washington believed himself besieged in Winchester, where the local people had built a breastwork around the courthouse. "Not an hour, nay scarcely a minute, passes, that does not produce fresh alarms and melancholy accounts," he told Dinwiddie. "So that I am distracted what to do!"[24]

Washington had urged an increase in the authorized strength of his regiment, and Dinwiddie had supported him before the Burgesses, but he complained about "the slowness of the House in raising men." He had done what he could, ordering the militia commanders of ten counties to march half their men to Winchester and sending powder and muskets to Fredericksburg for Commissary Walker to distribute. "Desolation and murder still increase, and no prospects of relief," Washington wailed. Railing against the militia's refusal to answer his appeals, he warned that a large part of the colony was destined to be lost. Washington was becoming thin of skin, fearful of being blamed for the state of things. He ended his letter to the governor, "In order to avoid censure in every part of my conduct, I make it a rule to obey the dictates of your Honour, the Assembly, and a good conscience."[25]

Washington also complained that he had not received clear

instructions from Williamsburg on such matters as how he should supply the militia if it did show up. "The want of due direction in matters of this nature causes great inconvenience," he wrote. He had reports that people around Winchester were holding meetings "to very dishonorable purposes." Believing that their own government would not protect them, they proposed to make a separate peace with the French and Indians. Dinwiddie replied that Washington could issue any supplies the militia needed. As for the surrender talk, he wanted the colonel to round up the malcontents and see that they were punished.[26]

Dinwiddie did his best from a distance, and it paid off when 150 Fairfax militia reached Winchester on May 3; Washington ordered them to march out for the South Branch. The worst was over, however. The Shawnees had taught the Virginians a lesson, so they returned west of the mountains. Reports of raids continued to come in during the next several weeks, but they were mostly hunting parties, and casualties among settlers had ceased. Washington published a proclamation on May 24 declaring that the danger was "pretty much over" and urging people to return to their farms. The last alert came on May 29, when Stephen reported both a mutiny among the militia and a skirmish near Fort Cumberland that claimed six Shawnees and four Virginians.[27]

Washington was convinced that the Indians were pawns of the French, so he made no effort to understand the rhythms of their way of war. In late fall and winter men hunted and ran their trap lines to supply the fur trade. Early spring was the time to raid enemy nations, after which another hunting season opened; hunters also guarded their towns and farms during the growing season. Early fall provided another period for raiding. Washington did not see this pattern when he reported that he could not explain why the raiders had left.[28]

If the Virginians had recognized the seasonal nature of Indian warfare, they could have concentrated their resources and interdicted invasion routes when raids could be expected. During other seasons there were only incidental clashes with hunting parties. Yet the frontier was in a constant uproar because alarms were exaggerated. There was an outbreak in Augusta County in midsummer, and Washington predicted "continual alarms of this kind" until the French were driven from the Ohio. But the action in Augusta was a minor clash with Cherokees retaliating for depredations by whites. Washington toured the area at the end of the summer and claimed he narrowly escaped an ambush.[29]

Attempts to win over allies among the nations were also hampered by the failure to understand their cultures. Washington sent a wampum belt and speech to the sachems of the Tuscaroras in August, "to assure you of our real friendship and love—and to confirm & strengthen that chain of friendship, which has subsisted between us for so many ages past." He either did not know about or ignored the destructive war earlier in the century that had driven the Tuscaroras out of North Carolina at great loss of life and made them the sixth of the Six Nations. They declined to rally to the English side.[30]

Washington remained beguiled by Dinwiddie's promises that he could enlist massive help from the Cherokees and Catawbas, despite the fighting in Augusta. The lieutenant governor was sure that when these allies arrived, Virginia could carry the war into French territory. Dinwiddie could not understand why Cherokees in the hundreds had not arrived to fight alongside Virginians by the end of September, "only that naturally they are lazy & must be humour'd as to their slow marching." Just seven men and three women met Washington in October.[31]

The Indian nations were not lazy, nor were they simple mercenaries. They had their own interests to look after, including subsistence. Washington sent a message late in October to the Catawbas, asking them to tell the Cherokees how disappointed the English were that they did not join their war. They had fallen under the sway of the French, "whose hearts are false, and rotten as an old stump." The Cherokees, he predicted, would have "great cause to be sorry." This kind of talk not only put off the Cherokees, but also the Catawbas he expected to meet with him in November; only eleven of them showed up at Winchester. Washington charged that there were no more because Dinwiddie's government had neglected to send guides for them.[32]

A better approach to Indian affairs was in order. To find out how to win the nations to the English side, in 1754 the Board of Trade, London's supervisor of the colonies, had asked for advice from Edmund Atkin, a prominent Indian trader based in Charleston. He turned in a very long plan in 1755 detailing the potential contribution of the Indians to the imperial struggle in America, the policies of France and Britain, the importance of trade with the Indians, and the "character and disposition of the various Indian nations." He advised taking Indian relations away from the colonial governors and putting them under two superintendents, one north and one south. The board agreed and appointed Atkin superintendent for the south in 1756.[33]

I Am Very Much Afraid We Shall Have Few Men Left

Atkin's services could potentially relieve both Dinwiddie and Washington of Indian diplomacy, at which they were inept, and let them concentrate on the Virginia Regiment. It needed attention, because throughout the year it was short of everything. Pay was a particular problem. As Washington repeatedly warned, low or absent pay produced desertion. In response, the military committee ceased deducting pay for clothing and medical care in August. Dinwiddie told Washington that this measure should give men "spirits & engage them to do their duty." He hoped for the future that the regiment would "not have many desertions."[34]

To save paper the government paid the soldiers in large bills, which meant giving the pay of two or three soldiers to one man. Washington complained that too often that soldier would drink or gamble it away before the others had their share. The only vendors who could handle large bills were tavern keepers, to predictable effect.[35]

The cash shortage and high prices crippled all efforts at supply. Food was so short that men foraged in the woods for "wild sallad," as Washington called it, and many ended up in the hospital, where there was no medicine for them. Sickness spread through the whole regiment by summer, with several companies entirely out of action. The regiment's troop of light horse went without mounts for more than a year.[36]

Clothing was gone before winter. Lack of clothing was another cause of desertion, Washington declared, "and I am very much afraid we shall have few men left" if a shipment did not arrive soon. Blankets would help, but he had none of those either. The men shivered into 1757.[37]

Supply was complicated further when Commissary Walker hinted in September that he would resign. Washington urged his early replacement. He had ordered the assistant commissary at Winchester to lay in a year's stores and reported enough provisions on hand at every post to last until May; hence the regiment would be ready to march in the spring. But he complained, "These orders I have given, not knowing what else would be satisfactory," owing to lack of guidance from Williamsburg.[38]

Washington recommended that John Carlyle and William Ramsey be appointed commissaries, but Dinwiddie refused to approve them. Carlyle had had the position and resigned, while Ramsey was a stranger to both the country and business. Washington ran around the governor to Speaker Robinson with the same recommendation. Robinson assembled the military committee, which agreed that if Walker resigned Carlyle and Ramsey should be appointed. Walker in fact had not formally stated his plans to anybody, and Dinwiddie doubted he would quit, so he declined to appoint anyone else. The regiment ended the year without knowing if it still had its key supply officer.[39]

Discipline remained a serious problem. The governor had given Washington revised powers to call courts-martial early in April 1756, and the colonel complained that the Virginia act against mutiny and desertion was not broad enough. Dinwiddie believed the act did give Washington power to punish most crimes, including cowardice or corresponding with the enemy, "& as to other neglects, you may venture to take it upon yourself by inflicting corporal punishment." The governor added, "The Assembly were greatly inflamed being told that the greatest immoralities & drunkenness have been much countenanced and proper discipline neglected."[40]

Dinwiddie's worries were well founded. The men at Winchester in particular were out of hand, and on May 1 Washington issued a sweeping order covering negligence by noncoms, rioting, fighting, drunkenness, and theft. Men on patrol, citizens complained, committed looting, vandalism, theft of livestock, and general meanness. Washington ordered courts-martial on average every other day, and his punishments were such that Braddock would have approved: lashes by the hundreds and many instances of death by hanging or firing squad. It did not help, as men went over the hill by whole platoons, eighteen in one night alone.[41]

Dinwiddie cheered the colonel on with his brutal punishments. Not even the expiration of Virginia's act for punishing mutiny and desertion in November changed anything, in the lieutenant governor's opinion. Desertion increased suddenly near the end of the year, when recruiting officers for the newly authorized Royal American Regiment enticed men to desert and accept the Royal Americans' enlistment bonuses. Washington asked Dinwiddie to intervene, and the trespasses ceased, at least for the time being.[42]

"Colonel Washington has observed," said orders for July 7, "that the men of his regiment are very profane and reprobate." He threatened that if "such practices" continued, "they shall be severely punished." There followed the usual prescriptions of the cat-o'-nine-tails, as if that would stop "that ill habit." Swearing was about the last pleasure left to his suffering troops. The colonel tried an appeal to pride, ordering the men to "dress their hair, and appear as soldier-like as possible."[43]

Another chance to instill pride arrived on August 14 with word that King George II had declared war against France on May 17. Washington assembled his soldiers on the 15th, marched them into town, and had the declaration read; toasts were drunk, cannons and muskets volleyed three times, and the troops paraded through the streets. He capped that off with a windy announcement calling on all subjects to be loyal to the king. The day before, however, the British cause had suffered a major setback when 1,134 survivors of three regiments and a royal artillery detachment surrendered Oswego to the French and Indians. As with the rest of the war outside Virginia, Washington took no notice.[44]

The colonel agreed with most upper-class Americans of his day that organized religion, however little he participated in it himself, kept the lower classes on good behavior. Accordingly, he ordered Sunday services to be attended by the men. Officers read sermons solicited from preachers in the neighborhood, but the colonel wanted something more. He often asked Dinwiddie to appoint a chaplain, but he did not.[45]

To buttress the understrength Virginia Regiment, the government turned to the militia. This was a triumph of hope over experience. Washington refused to admit that he could not turn civilians into instant soldiers, that their officers were not about to impose his kind of discipline, and that they would not put up with that from him either. When they deserted, it encouraged his own men to leave. "I am sensible," William Fairfax told him in May, "such a medley of undisciplined militia must create your various troubles," but, like Caesar, Washington should expect to suffer "fatigues, murmuring, mutinies, and defections." That fatherly advice was lost on an impatient twenty-four-year-old frustrated that the world did not work the way he thought it should, but he recognized that a better way to raise manpower than calling out militia was essential.[46]

Washington called for volunteers, promising that anyone who joined the regiment "without any expectation of pay" would receive provisions and ammunition during their service. This inspired Attorney General Peyton Randolph to organize the Gentleman Associators, sixty volunteer horsemen from the gentry. Fairfax told Washington to expect them in Winchester by May 25, but they were never heard from again.[47]

Washington recommended conscription, using the militia as a manpower pool rather than calling it up by units. He told Dinwiddie that if there was a draft, he could get better men. He recommended to Speaker Robinson that the assembly impose a quota on every county and draft "active and resolute men." Limiting draftees' required service to eighteen or twenty months, he believed, would reduce their propensity to desert.[48]

Washington's proposal enjoyed support in Williamsburg among the ruling class, who would not themselves or their sons be drafted. In the middle of April Dinwiddie predicted that the Burgesses would increase the regiment to 2,000 men by draft. The colonel offered a plan to form them into one regiment with two battalions of ten companies each, raising the number of privates per company to eighty-seven. He did not point out that in his scheme he would remain the only colonel in Virginia's service.[49]

Washington was young enough to believe that his view of the world was the right one, so everyone else should agree and the lawmakers should make it happen. That has never been the custom among what he called "chimney-corner politicians." The assembly debated raising the regiment to 1,500 men by enlarging the existing companies. This would save money, but it produced a row between Robinson and Dinwiddie that held up sending funds to Washington. The wrangling continued, Dinwiddie pressing for 2,000 men, the House of Burgesses choking on the expense, even during the Shawnee raids of the spring. Landon Carter, a member of the Council, claimed he tried to convince the Burgesses of the danger but, "like stingy creatures," they were "willing to wait for rains to wet the powder and rats to eat the bow strings of the enemy."

A draft was in force by early May, but the legislature permitted anyone who would not serve to buy out for £10. The terms of service would expire on December 1, despite the governor's plea for at least eighteen months. He suspended Washington's two-battalion proposal because of the assembly's limit of 1,500 men.[50]

The new legislation raised many questions. It provided that draftees could not be forced to march out of Virginia with the regiment. Another issue was what to do with drafted pacifists, because to fill their quotas some county officials had selected unpopular Quakers and others. They refused to serve, so Washington had them confined but let them out when they promised to stay in Winchester until the draft expired. Then it turned out that draftees were auxiliaries to the regiment, so they would not expand it to 1,500 men. Dinwiddie suggested recruiting for the regiment among draftees, giving them bonuses if they agreed to serve beyond December. He also advised recruiting from the ranger companies, whom Washington declared "of no use or benefit to the country," because incorporating them into the regiment would help meet the target of 1,500 privates. Appropriations for rangers ran out, Washington furloughed their captains, and by the end of September virtually all the rangers had disappeared.[51]

The draft was a flop, producing only 246 conscripts by June 25, of whom "several" deserted, leaving behind others unfit for duty and the Quakers. "I am really ashamed of the dastardly pusillanimous spirit of the people in general at this time of danger," Dinwiddie roared. Virginia would produce fighting men by the thousands under able generals in the next century, but it was not yet that society.[52]

The governor let Washington proceed with the reorganization, but with only one battalion. He set up seventeen companies, including a headquarters company, of thirty-seven privates each, and assigned their officers. Dinwiddie reduced the number of captains, assigning each field officer a company to command. The search for new recruits took on signs of desperation. Washington wanted to enlist indentured servants, buying them from their masters with money draftees had paid to get out of serving. The governor agreed, so long as he did not recruit convicts. Washington blamed the assembly for the failure of the draft that he had proposed. A campaign against Fort Duquesne, he concluded, was impossible.[53]

The regiment was also plagued by chicanery or incompetence among the officers. On August 5 the colonel's muster rolls of the regiment, including drafts, scouts, and the remaining rangers, totaled 926 men, but the paymaster had issued pay for 1,080. Washington wondered how that news would be received in Williamsburg, and he worried that the discrepancy reflected fraud. At Dinwiddie's urging the assembly ordered each county to draw up a list of all single able-bodied men and offer them a chance to volunteer. If that did not fill the quota, they would draw lots. Fairfax County lined its men up, but none volunteered, and more than sixty failed to show up at all. William Fairfax, the county lieutenant, ordered the absentees arrested and sent to Washington in chains. There was "a great unwillingness in our young men to enlist," Fairfax complained. Washington pressed ahead with his last hope, ordering his officers to sign up servants and see that their masters were paid for their contracts.[54]

The regiment's strength continued to decline. In September Dinwiddie ordered a further reduction in the number of officers after the conscripts left on December 1. Then he suspended recruitment of servants because there was no governing law, and he asked the assembly to provide one. Moreover, the home government ordered the colonies to pay for raising their quotas for the new Royal American Regiment, and the assembly voted £8,000, "but where to get the men I know not," Dinwiddie admitted. The lieutenant governor and Washington both felt that Virginia had become a sideshow in the war, and they resented it.[55]

If Virginia could not defend itself with men, maybe forts would do the job. In March 1756 the assembly had raised £25,000 for frontier defense, including construction of a fort at Winchester. The manpower shortage prevented much progress.[56]

Washington had proposed a major fort at Winchester because its location in the Shenandoah made it a good place for a supply depot. It also supported his argument that Virginia should abandon Fort Cumberland. Dinwiddie was adamant that Cumberland was the king's property and that it was not in his power to order its evacuation. Shirley's replacement as commander in chief in North America, Lord Loudoun, was expected in Williamsburg in the fall, and he could decide. Until then, Fort Cumberland "must be properly supported with men."[57]

Washington habitually went behind Dinwiddie's back to Speaker Robinson and other important figures, and the governor resented it. Robinson passed on the colonel's recommendations on Fort Cumberland to the military committee, which unanimously agreed that the place should be abandoned. But when this decision was presented to Dinwiddie, he became "very warm" and flatly refused. The colonel kept harping on the subject, not wanting to take the blame if Cumberland fell to attack. The place must be fortified with strong works "or else inevitably fall" into the enemy's hands, he warned the governor. "How fatal a stroke! and what noise this will make, the censure of mankind will speedily declare."[58]

Dinwiddie retained his objection to abandoning Cumberland until Loudoun decided, but because Washington felt so strongly about the subject, the colonel should call a council of officers to consider the matter. The governor cautioned that he should be explicit in his arguments, as they must be presented to Lord Loudoun. Washington ordered Adam Stephen, commanding Fort Cumberland, to chair the council.[59]

Before the group could meet, Dinwiddie heard from Loudoun, and he passed part of his message on to Washington. His Lordship did "hope & trust" that the government of Virginia would not give up Fort Cumberland. He approved of the decision to build a post at Winchester, which might be useful in a future campaign. With Loudoun heard from, Dinwiddie changed his tune: He ceased ordering the retention of Fort Cumberland, leaving Washington to justify to Loudoun whatever different course the council might advise.[60]

The council met at the end of October. The officers unanimously concluded that if Virginia, Maryland, and Pennsylvania strengthened and reinforced Fort Cumberland it might be "useful." Otherwise, surplus stores should be sent to Winchester, Washington should enlarge Cumberland's garrison if troops were available, and the final decision should be left to Loudoun. The colonel endorsed the minutes, saying he would prefer to demolish the fort, but he left the final decision to higher authority. Loudoun, meanwhile, had been misinformed that Washington had already abandoned the place. That, the earl warned Dinwiddie, would have "a bad effect as to the Dominion, and will not have a good appearance at home."[61]

Dinwiddie and his Council ordered Washington to strengthen and reinforce Fort Cumberland, taking men from smaller forts and 100 from Winchester. Washington himself should lead the party from Winchester, but he answered that that would leave Winchester defenseless, because there were fewer than 100 men there. He spent the rest of the year offering excuses for not moving to Cumberland. After hearing further from Loudoun, who preferred to abandon all small posts rather than Cumberland, the governor so ordered Washington.[62]

The colonel was "a little at a loss to understand" the point of those orders. If the stockade forts were all abandoned, the eighty-mile route between Winchester and Wills Creek would be "unguarded and exposed," he observed. He complained that the orders had not prescribed how Fort Cumberland was to be strengthened, "*i.e.*, whether it is to be made cannon-proof or not," and moreover had not stated what the budget would be. Fort Cumberland should be kept as defensible as possible until spring, Dinwiddie answered, but not made cannon-proof unless it could be done "at a small expence." He advised Washington not to take offense at Loudoun's comments about a "bad effect," as the earl did not know the facts.[63]

The abandonment of the small forts in favor of Cumberland and Winchester terminated the only fortification policy Virginia had: a "chain of forts" along the frontier. In February 1756, Dinwiddie had proposed to the Board of Trade that Britain build a line of forts from Canada to Florida, to be paid for by a land and poll tax enacted by Parliament. Failing at that, in May he had told Washington that the assembly had decided on a chain of forts and that the first duty of the attorney general's Gentleman Associators would be to help the colonel select locations. The Associators never showed up, so in June the governor advised, "The building the forts in proper places must be left to you, as you know the situation of the country."[64]

This was amateur strategizing at its worst. Virginia would never have enough troops to build and occupy a long line of forts and at the same time patrol the frontier and guard the settlers. Nor would a line of posts deter raiders, who could pass between them. Washington made a show of complying, preparing two standard plans for timber stockades with bastions, and he called a council of officers at Fort Cumberland on July 10. They were less than enthusiastic about turning their regiment into a construction company, but they bowed to the governor's wishes.[65]

Few officers had construction experience, tools were scarce, and alarms, sickness, and bad weather plagued the program. Dinwiddie badgered the frontier militias for advice on where forts should be built in their counties. Most failed to answer, but Augusta County recommended fourteen forts housing 680 men. The program went nowhere, and Washington admitted to his officers that it was "impossible to comply" with the government's plans. Another council of war agreed, saying that the troops would better spend their time guarding settlers.[66]

Washington altered the program on his own authority. Instead of a chain of government forts, troops would help settlers build private forts, guard people at their farm work, escort supplies, and forward intelligence. He told Dinwiddie that the choice was "to neglect the inhabitants and build the forts, or neglect the forts and mind the inhabitants." There were now, he declared, enough small posts. "If I have done amiss, in not adhering to the *letter* of the *law*, I hope your Honour will intimate the same, and give directions how I am to proceed." The governor agreed in principle because Washington was "the only judge from your knowledge of the country."[67]

Washington proposed building three or four large, well-defended works from which patrols could range out; a few large garrisons would be easier to supply. "I believe I might also add," he concluded, "that no person, who regards his character, will undertake a command without the means of preserving it; since his conduct is culpable for all misfortunes, and never right but when successful." Dinwiddie replied that the assembly had called for the chain of forts, so he could not formally abandon the program on his own. He promised to ask the lawmakers for a change in November. The chain of forts had been stillborn, and now it was buried.[68]

I Never Intended Insults to Any

The decision to abandon the small forts included the posts on the South Branch of the Potomac. Some of Washington's best officers were stationed there, and they had done as effective a job as possible defending the settlers. Such officers, in Adam Stephen's opinion, were too few in the regiment. Most, he thought, shirked their duties. "We stand in need of a purgation," he told Washington. He claimed that "the men come on in exercise and bush fighting better than the officers."[69]

Washington spent his first eight months in command often condemning his officers but making little effort to instruct them. Too many were rakehells, as became apparent by April 1756. William Fairfax said there was talk "among the Burgesses that an enquiry is intended relating to the misbehaviour" of some of the officers. Speaker Robinson warned that there had been "terrible reports" about them and advised the colonel to "put a stop to their irregularities." Dinwiddie also complained about "the greatest immoralities and drunkenness," which had been "much countenanced and proper discipline neglected."[70]

Washington took that as an attack on his command competence and fired back a long, tendentious self-defense. He asked others to "witness how much I have, both by threats and persuasive means," tried to prevent gambling, drinking, swearing, and "irregularities of every other kind," while presenting himself as a good example. "How far I have failed in this desirable end, I cannot pretend to say," as if that were a point in his favor. "However, if I continue in the service, I shall take care to act with a little more rigor, than has hitherto been practised."[71]

When William Fairfax warned him that members of the military committee thought his appointment of an aide-de-camp and military secretary should be disallowed, Washington again hinted at resignation. His high-placed friends did not like that. Fairfax said that Washington's "endeavours in the service and defence of your country must redound" to his honor. Dinwiddie assured him that Loudoun would arrive with blank commissions for the Americans; "if so, I doubt not you will be taken care of." That catered to the young man's ambition, but the governor chided him for not sending in his accounts, "for I cannot have my supplies settled without your assistance."[72]

Dinwiddie worried about Washington's resignation talk, but before he addressed him directly he consulted Fairfax. The lieutenant governor, said Fairfax, expressed concern about Washington's "great uneasiness of mind," and he wanted the colonel to know that "his endeavors has been to make your situation easy." Dinwiddie was on Washington's side, Fairfax assured him, but he felt unappreciated. Dinwiddie himself followed up, saying he was "sincerely concern'd & heartily griev'd for your present situation & be assured every thing I can shall be done for your relief & assistance."[73]

Washington's troubles really arose from some of his worst officers, Charles and Landon Carter advised him. They drank too much, talked too much, and sent out letters "charging the country with ingratitude." The colonel changed his tone slightly, complaining that he received too little instruction and information from Williamsburg to guide him. He had "to *guess* at every thing" and was "kept in the dark." Despite this habitual passing the blame for any shortcomings up to the top, Robinson, Fairfax, and other patrons continued to chuck the young man under the chin. Fairfax, however, became annoyed at Washington's growing hostility to Dinwiddie.[74]

The colonel was thin-skinned, owing to youthful anxiety about the burdens of command. But things were looking up. The king had issued a new proclamation on relative rank of regular and provincial officers. The colonial general and field officers remained junior to all holding royal commissions at the same rank, but in North America they rated as "eldest captains," superior to regular captains and subalterns. Meanwhile, Shirley continued to plan a campaign against the Forks under Horatio Sharpe, with Washington second in command.[75]

John Campbell, earl of Loudoun, succeeded Shirley as commander in chief in North America early in the summer, accompanied by his deputy, James Abercromby. Washington asked Dinwiddie to send a letter of recommendation to Loudoun. The governor wrote instead to Abercromby, who was his "particular friend," because that was "much better than writing directly to his lordship, as I know the influence he has with him." It was a gracious letter, calling Washington "a very deserving gentleman." Washington was "a person much beloved here and has gone through many hardships in the service, and I really think he has great merit." If His Lordship promoted Washington in the British establishment, he would exceed all expectations. Lord Fairfax sent his own recommendation directly to Loudoun.[76]

Washington had gone to Williamsburg in May, seeking clarification of his instructions, although Dinwiddie, Robinson, and Fairfax had repeatedly told him to act on his own discretion and they would back him. Dinwiddie was wearing down at age sixty-three, and he talked about retiring and going home. He told the colonel that "as many things may occur that cannot be directed, your own judgement must be your guide." Not even that could relieve Washington's anxiety whenever anyone questioned anything he did. Having "no certain rules for the direction of my conduct," he complained to Robinson, "I am afraid to turn to this hand or to that, lest it be censured."[77]

The military committee reviewed Washington's pay and allowances in August. He had asked for an additional allowance for his "table," meaning entertainment expenses. The members declined to set a figure for that but agreed to pay at the end of the year all reasonable expenses. Washington set himself up for correction, however, because he had taken over the largest house in Winchester and entertained in high style. He took fencing lessons and was often away attending to his private affairs. He received permission to go to Alexandria for meetings to settle his brother Lawrence's estate. He went in September, but the meetings were postponed, so he went again in December.[78]

Affairs blew up over complaints about misbehaving officers that had circulated in Williamsburg since April. An anonymous writer calling himself the "Virginia Centinel" had for some months been publishing essays, Roman-numbered in sequence, in the *Virginia Gazette*. Centinel X appeared on September 3, calling Washington's officers "rank novices, rakes, spend-thrifts, and bankrupts" who abused their soldiers. They "browbeat and discouraged" the militia and presented "an example of all manner of debauchery, vice, and idleness when they lie skulking in forts," while the country was "ravaged in their very neighborhood." The regiment's officers expected the governor to refute this, but when he did not they sent Washington a petition to present on their behalf.[79]

Washington had not yet learned that anonymous charges were not worth a response, and he reacted defensively. Referring to the "unjust remarks," he told Dinwiddie he just wanted "to make the country sensible, how ardently" he had "studied to promote her cause." He wished "very sincerely" that his successor would fill his place "more to their satisfaction in every respect" than he had been able to do. This might have become tedious from an older man, but one after another his patrons reassured him that his reputation was safe from "the vain babbling of worthless, malicious, envious sycophants," as one burgess called the Centinel.[80]

Washington's relations with Dinwiddie deteriorated. He complained repeatedly about his "ambiguous and uncertain" instructions, and was repeatedly told that if he declared what he needed, the government would take care of it. The strain wore on the governor, who complained in October, "I have been much out of order & confined to my room this fortnight, that I write this with pain." When Washington accused him of failing to provide guides to bring enough Indians into camp, Dinwiddie snapped back that "the charge is unmanerly." When the governor rebuked the colonel for not providing enough information to make a decision, Washington snapped back in turn but apologized for his "unmanerly" remarks. "I never intended insults to any," he protested.[81]

In an unguarded moment, Washington confessed to Robinson that he would not resign, but he did hope for a better state of affairs after Loudoun arrived. Robinson again expressed sympathy and support, and Washington remained in command of the Virginia Regiment. He spent the last part of the year at Mount Vernon, however.[82]

TEN

DISCONTENT AND MURMURING WILL ENSUE

(*1757*)

O, what can ail thee, knight-at-arms,
Alone and palely loitering?

—JOHN KEATS

Washington won wide praise for his coolness under fire at the Monongahela. He and the other officers there followed a tradition born two centuries earlier. Since ancient times the measure of a warrior's bravery had been taken in fighting man-to-man with swords and other personal weapons. The supremacy of gunpowder ended all that, the air now filled with an anonymous hail of lead and iron projectiles. Individual aggressiveness, sword in hand, gave way to a passive disdain for danger. The measure of a gentleman became his refusal to flinch under fire.

An early demonstration of this took place during the siege of Oudenaarde, near Brussels, in 1582. Dutch rebels stood fast in their fortified town, surrounded by the trenches of the Hapsburg army commanded by Alexander Farnese, duke of Parma. Cannons thumped and muskets popped on both sides. The weather had been miserably wet and cold, but anon the sun came out and the earth warmed.

Parma ordered his servants to set up a table near the trenches, so he and his officers could dine *al fresco* in the lovely weather. This was too good an opportunity for rebel gunners to pass up.

The party had just sat down to eat when a cannonball obliterated the head of a young staff officer seated next to Parma. Part of the officer's skull took out the eye of another gentleman. Another ball tore through two more guests, their blood and brains spraying all over the table and diners. This ruined the appetites of the survivors, who got up to leave. Parma ordered the attendants to remove the bodies, clear the table, set a new cloth, and replace the lost dishes. He commanded his guests to resume their places, and so the luncheon continued.[1]

Washington had demonstrated his steadiness twice, and he would do so again. Regular officers continued to expose themselves to enemy fire until a generation of them was virtually exterminated in the trenches of World War I.

My Nature Is Open and Honest and Free from Guile!

John Campbell, fourth earl of Loudoun, landed in New York in July 1756. The fifty-one-year-old nobleman brought with him a reputation as a skilled military administrator, with Scottish thrift and efficiency. Americans generally harbored great hopes that he represented a royal commitment to their cause; forts in several colonies were named in his honor, including the post at Winchester.

Youthful portraits of the earl show a short, slender fellow with a long, handsome face, a very high brow above and a lantern jaw below, with a cleft chin. The eyes are kindly, the nose straight, and the mouth on the verge of a smile. By the time he reached America, the eyes were shifty and the mouth was set hard. He had become muscular, with massive arms and shoulders. He was also an aristocratic snob who believed that colonials were wretched soldiers who would not help the British cause. Like Braddock, he carried a viceroy's powers over the provincial governments.[2]

Washington hoped Loudoun would help him achieve his personal and professional objectives. Flattery, he decided, was a ticket to advancement, so he dictated a letter to His Lordship that all his officers signed. "We humbly represent," it began, "that WE were the first troops in action on the continent, on occasion of the present broils." In several engagements and skirmishes they had acquired a knowledge of the enemy, "and of their crafty and cruel practises." The officers were "ready to testify" to their abilities "with the greatest chearfulness and resolution," whenever Loudoun commanded."[3]

This accompanied a long, impassioned letter from Washington, giving a history of Virginia's war since 1753, emphasizing his personal burdens. He blamed every misfortune on Dinwiddie and the assembly. If they had listened to him, the French would have been headed off before they fortified the Forks. He waltzed around the Jumonville affair and Fort Necessity, avowing that the 1754 campaign fell short because Virginia's authorities had not supplied or paid the troops.

Washington went on (and on) about how recruitment and draft acts had been framed to defeat their objectives, over his protests. The lack of an appropriate military code made punishment of malefactors almost impossible. Williamsburg had burdened him with "vagabonds," criminals, inadequate clothing and supplies, neglect of the wounded, and assorted failures that caused mutiny, desertion, and "other irregularities" to "creep into the camp." On the other hand, "I can truly say and confidently assert that no soldiers were ever under better command"—meaning himself. Despite all this, his regiment had "engaged in upwards of twenty skirmishes, and we have had near a hundred men killed and wounded," something no other colony could claim.

Washington repeatedly insisted that Fort Duquesne must be destroyed. The assembly's misguided chain of forts reflected the amateurism of the cheapskates he answered to. On the other hand, if he had been given enough men and resources, he could have made even that a success. If his regiment were supported and set loose, it could invade the Ohio Country, "gaining honour to ourselves or reputation to our regiment." Instead, the assembly had prevented his troops from serving outside Virginia. "I must beg leave to add, my unwearied endeavours are inadequately rewarded," he whined. The orders he received were "full of ambiguity." He was "answerable for consquences and blamed without the privilege of defense." He had "long been satisfied of the impossibility of continuing in this service without loss of honour." He had persevered, however, because he saw a "dawn of hope" when he learned of Loudoun's appointment, knowing the earl's splendid record. "Do not think, my Lord, that I am going to flatter," he gushed, "notwithstanding I have exalted sentiments of your

Lordship's character and respect to your rank, it is not my intention to adulate. My nature is open and honest and free from guile!"

He did offer an excuse for his colony's failures. Virginia had no experience of war, he pointed out, but, guided by Loudoun's ability and experience, Virginia would meet the highest expectations. "I do not know my Lord in what light this short and disinterested relation may be received by your Lordship," but he hoped that "if there be anything in it which appears worthy of redress," Loudoun would "condescend to point out the way it may be obtained." He ended by thumping his own "affectionate zeal" to serve his country.[4]

Washington believed that praising himself and his regiment and blaming everyone else would win the favor of a British aristocrat and regular army general. Despite the examples of his brother Lawrence and William Fairfax, he had not yet learned how to deal with his superiors gracefully. The boy colonel of the 1750s was a long way from becoming the sage general of the 1770s, because he was too wrapped up in himself to see the world and other people objectively.

Rather than send this letter to Loudoun directly, Washington enclosed it with one to the earl's aide, Captain James Cunningham. He claimed that 3,000 men "under good regulation," raised from the three middle colonies, could invade the Ohio Country and drive the French out, if the regulars provided artillery and engineers. He hinted that he would accept command of the expedition if it was offered.

It was all a waste of ink. Cunningham answered for Loudoun, who was too busy: "His Lordship seems very much pleased with the accounts you have given him of the situation of our affairs to the south'ard." This was a brush-off.[5]

When he became commander in chief in North America, Loudoun also became royal governor of the Old Dominion. Like his predecessor Lord Albemarle, he never set foot in the colony. He summoned the governors of North Carolina, Virginia, Maryland, and Pennsylvania to meet him in Philadelphia on February 17, to set the strategy for the war. Washington asked Dinwiddie for leave to attend. The lieutenant governor could see no point in that, but because he was "so earnest to go" he granted leave. The colonel went, and along with the governors arrived to find that Loudoun was insultingly late. At the same time, the English translation of the French documents of the 1754 campaign, including Washington's captured journal, appeared in America. Washington did not respond, to avoid drawing attention to Jumonville Glen and Fort Necessity.[6]

Washington had been accused by British agents of spying for the French. The charge was based on letters intercepted on their way to France in 1756, probably forgeries. Authorities in London and New York put together a picture of an officer in American service who might be having a "treasonable correspondence" with the enemy. The culprit was described as a tall, dark officer, with black hair and a red coat faced with blue, thirty-eight years old, a veteran of frontier service. Except for the uniform, little of that matched Washington, and Loudoun dismissed the whole thing as a fraud.[7]

Washington was sure that his smarmy letter would persuade Loudoun to give him a royal commission. His friend Joseph Chew reinforced his hopes, predicting that the earl would do just that. Loudoun finally showed up on March 15, and for the next week he huddled with the disgruntled governors—barring Washington from the meetings. The government, he said, aimed its next campaign at the north, not the Ohio, and the governors were there to arrange the defense of the southern colonies.

This was not so much a conference as an audience for the earl's orders. The governors should supply 3,800 men over the next year to join with 1,200 of the king's troops. Of these forces, 2,000, including 500 regulars and 200 independents, would go to South Carolina to meet a threatened French attack; Virginia would send 400 men. The British government would provision all troops in South Carolina, but the colonies must cover the cost of getting them there. As for their own defense, the other provinces were on their own. Of the troops remaining in Virginia, its regiment should post 100 at Fort Loudoun at Winchester, 50 at a place between Winchester and Fort Cumberland, and scatter the rest along the western frontier. Maryland would send 300 men to Fort Cumberland, which Virginia would vacate, and 200 to other posts.[8]

Loudoun summoned Washington separately to hear the troop arrangements, waving aside all objections or questions and allowing only discretion on how to distribute troops between Forts Loudoun and Cumberland. The earl dismissed all the problems Washington said he faced and flatly refused to take the Virginia Regiment into the regular establishment. The young colonel was stunned and dismayed, his hopes dashed. He suggested to Dinwiddie that all Americans had just been insulted.[9]

Virginia offered Washington's only chance for continued military service, but he was losing officers. In January Dinwiddie had reported "great clamours" in Williamsburg about the excessive numbers of officers in the regiment, compared to the few men to command. Company officers expected reductions, so they petitioned Washington for leave to quit so they could seek commissions in regular regiments.[10]

Partly to stem these losses, and partly because he would not take Loudoun's "no" for an answer, in April Washington dictated another petition for all his officers to sign, directed to Lieutenant Governor Dinwiddie. They pointed out how for three years as the first colonials in war service they had fought actions, labored hard, faced danger, and even gone without decent winter quarters. Their uncertain future presented "serious and melancholy considerations." The officers wanted to know what was to become of them. They could not conceive that because they were Americans, they "shou'd therefore be deprived of the benefits common to British subjects." They had served in "three bloody campaigns, without royal notice!" They deserved royal commissions. "If it shou'd be said the troops of Virginia are irregulars and ought not to expect more notice than other provincials," commissions from His Majesty would make them "as regular a corps as any upon the continent." Washington forwarded this "remonstrance I received just now" to Dinwiddie. Just what he expected the lieutenant governor to do with it he did not say.[11]

Nothing Ought Ever to Be Promised but What Is Performed

Having gotten that off his chest, Washington returned to managing his regiment. The burden was as great as ever, and 1757 was a reprise of the year before. There was never enough money, and each new appropriation involved a vicious struggle in the House of Burgesses, which would eventually have to back its paper money with future tax receipts. Loudoun's demands increased the load on Virginia. There was no commissary to coordinate purchases, although in January John Carlyle resumed doing that in Alexandria on a voluntary basis, until the government failed to repay what he spent out of his own pocket. Throughout the year the troops suffered for want of clothing, provisions, and other supplies—burdens worsened by scattering them all over the map in small detachments. Pay, as always, was late and short.[12]

Desertion remained the greatest headache. The year began with a mutiny at the reestablished posts on the South Branch, followed by mass escapes. Stephen rounded up all but six, identified the ringleaders, put them in front of a court-martial, and sentenced some to death and others to be "flogged severely." Dinwiddie praised Washington for handling the mutiny so efficiently but suggested that those under sentence of death should be made "sensible of their atrocious crime" and then pardoned. Recruitment was so slow that the regiment could not afford to execute even mutineers.[13]

By spring Washington was ordering the legal maximum 1,000 lashes for every deserter apprehended. The situation worsened in late spring when the assembly instituted a new draft, emphasizing the enlistment of "vagabonds," who then deserted by the score. In July Washington ordered a "*Gallows* near 40 feet high erected (which has terrified the *rest* exceedingly,)" and he planned "to hang two or three on it, as an example to others." He did.[14]

No subject generated more correspondence than desertion. "Your Honour will, I hope excuse my *hanging*, instead of shooting them," the colonel advised Dinwiddie about two deserters on August 3. "It conveyed much more terror to others; and it was for example sake, we did it." Washington had become a hard case at the age of twenty-five, but hanging deserters was ineffective. In September Dinwiddie ordered him to suspend recruiting until he found some way to "reclaim the deserters."[15]

Washington occasionally pardoned offenders, and Dinwiddie praised his mercy, but men continued to go over the hill in mobs. "Lenity emboldens them," the colonel complained, so there were no more pardons in the Virginia Regiment. Colonel John Stanwix, commanding regulars in Pennsylvania, told Washington that desertion was "a crime grown to so enormous a height on this continent" that the only way to stop it would be "to put to death every deserter we take."[16]

In April the assembly enacted a new mutiny law providing authority to punish all types of crimes. Washington had still not received his copy three months later and so was "greatly at a loss how to proceed" against offenders; in August Dinwiddie gave him authority to use his own judgment. Washington tried exhortation, telling his officers at the end of July, "Discipline is the soul of an army. It makes small numbers formidable; procures success to the weak, and esteem to all."[17]

In September an investigation led to the discovery of property embezzled from the regiment by the acting quartermaster at Fort Loudoun. The culprit got away, but search warrants revealed government
property hidden all around Winchester. Receivers of stolen goods
were arrested, but the local justice turned them loose. Winchester
was generally a hell hole, owing to its many "tippling houses." Their
owners enticed soldiers to sell their clothing, arms, and anything they
could steal, in return for liquor.[18]

The obvious way to keep the regiment up to strength was by
recruiting. In January Dinwiddie had suspended enlistment of servants because the treasury had run out of money to pay their masters. Court papers in Baltimore revealed in April that deserters had
been recruited on the promise that their service would not exceed six
months; they were released by the court and not returned to Virginia.
The assembly passed an act on April 21 to raise three new companies of rangers, with a general draft to enlarge the Virginia Regiment
to 1,270 enlisted men. County and city officials were ordered to list
men between the ages of eighteen and fifty and select from them
able-bodied men "found loitering and neglecting to labor for reasonable wages; all who run from their habitations, leaving wives or
children without suitable means for their subsistence, and all other
idle, vagrant, or dissolute persons, wandering abroad without betak-
ing themselves to some lawful employment."[19]

The new law was anything but helpful. The colonel went to Williamsburg at the end of April to complain, first about the fact that
recruiting officers were losing money. He wanted good men recruited
and paid well, not the "vagabonds" the assembly specified, assurances
to officers that they would not be dismissed, and other reforms.[20]

Washington ran into a buzz saw in the assembly, which decided
that the regiment cost too much because it had too many incomplete
companies, and reduced it on May 16 to ten companies of 100 men
each. All but seven captains were to be discharged or voluntarily demoted to lieutenant. Subalterns would number twenty lieutenants
and ten ensigns. The regiment was distributed to various posts, but
Washington was to remain at Winchester supervising work on Fort
Loudoun. A week later the assembly raised the strength back to 1,270
men, along with the three 100–man ranger companies, but neglected
to revise recruiting instructions.[21]

Increasing and reducing the regiment overlapped, because the

Burgesses and the Council were in a power struggle. Rumors that the Burgesses would increase the regiment suggested Washington need not discharge the captains, although some of those who had left he was glad to see gone. Williamsburg was silent about what would really happen, and the colonel knew only that he would have about 420 men left when he sent a corps to South Carolina as Loudoun had ordered.[22]

The men were also scattered among too many small posts, by order of the assembly and the governor. It was not until late June that Washington learned that the assembly was going ahead with the 1,270-man regiment, authorizing enlistment bonuses of £5. The reversion to drafting "vagabonds" prevented any effective enlargement of the force, because county lieutenants forwarded too few men, many deserted before they reached the rendezvous, and those who arrived were often unfit. Williamsburg advised Washington to fill the gaps by calling up militia, but as he told Stanwix in mid-July, "no dependence is to be placed upon them."[23]

Enlisted men were not Washington's only behavioral problem. He shed some of his worst officers during the reorganization, but in the spring his second in command, Adam Stephen, exhibited signs of erratic behavior. Washington talked about him behind his back, and word reached the lieutenant colonel. He was plainly hurt, saying, "Believe me, Sir . . . it gives me the greatest uneasiness to have reason to believe that I do not enjoy the same share of your confidence that I once was happy in. Depend on it, Sir," he concluded, "my constant endeavours shall be to deserve it."[24]

When Dinwiddie complained in May that Stephen had disobeyed orders, the colonel declared that this was "not the only instance in which he has used such liberties." In July Stephen gave the regiment's supply of blankets to Indians without authority, and later in the month he obligated the government for unauthorized construction. Stephen had given "so many strange orders," the colonel groused, "that it will be with great difficulty, if it is even possible, to extricate the officers and myself from the dilemma and trouble they have occasioned." Whether Stephen was on one of the binges that would blot his later career is not now apparent, but he soon straightened himself out.[25]

Stephen had begun the year at Fort Cumberland, where his men obeyed the governor's orders to strengthen the place while Washington badgered Dinwiddie about abandoning the fort. There was joy in Williamsburg at the end of March when word arrived that the fort would be turned over to Maryland. Washington complained that he received no instructions on how to withdraw the troops or where they should be posted, nor what to do about the stores at Wills Creek. Dinwiddie's dispatches had gone astray, so Washington called a council of war to work out the details. Governor Sharpe announced that the unavoidable Captain Dagworthy would take over at Cumberland.[26]

The Fort Cumberland headache was replaced by another at Fort Loudoun. Washington had designed a square, four-bastioned timber, earth, and masonry work covering about half an acre, to mount twenty-four guns, with barracks for 400 men. When completed in October, as planned, it was supposed to withstand anything the French could bring to bear on it, although the French had no intention of invading Virginia. As usual Washington never had enough men, militia refused to help out, and sickness periodically ravaged the work force. Dinwiddie nagged the colonel all through the year, but in the end the fort remained unfinished.[27]

Attempts to win over allies among the Cherokees and Catawbas paralleled the fitful construction at Fort Loudoun. The French ably shored up alliances with nations in the *pays d'en haut* and others in Canada, although the Iroquois and some other nations stood aside. The Virginians, in contrast, continued as clumsy as ever at Indian diplomacy. Dinwiddie kept predicting that large numbers would join Washington at Fort Loudoun. When some did reach Winchester, they usually needed all sorts of supplies.[28]

A better hand at Indian affairs was needed, so Washington recommended that Christopher Gist be appointed Indian agent. But Edmund Atkin, the new Indian affairs superintendent for the south, showed up in the capital on April 9 with his commission and a salary and expense fund from Lord Loudoun. Instead of going to Winchester, he remained in Williamsburg lobbying the legislature, which at his urging raised the bounty for enemy scalps to £10. Now unemployed, Gist hoped to become an assistant to Atkin.[29]

Dinwiddie had assured the Cherokees and Catawbas that Atkin would soon join them at Winchester and supply all their wants. A party of Indians came into Fort Loudoun with four scalps and two prisoners on May 24, and according to Washington they were "much dissatisfied" because there were no presents for them. He called them "the most insolent, most avaricious, and dissatisfied wretches" he had ever dealt with, not understanding that they were free agents who came and went as they pleased.[30]

Washington told Dinwiddie on May 30 that the Indians remained in an uproar because Atkin had not shown up, but the presents for them had, and the colonel asked for orders on how to distribute them, otherwise they would leave "full of resentment." Assuming that Atkin never would do his job, he recommended appointing one person to be in charge of all Indian affairs. He favored Gist, because unless things were straightened out, Virginia would lose all hope of help from Indians. "An Indian will never forget a promise made to him," he advised. "For which reason, nothing ought ever to be *promised* but what is *performed.*"[31]

Atkin finally showed up on June 3 and asked Washington to call a conference with Indian leaders. He planned to visit the Carolinas before the end of the month and appointed Gist to act in his absence. The superintendent did not accomplish much because since his arrival the Indians had been "pleased and displeased oftener than they ought to have been," Washington groused.[32]

It Would Give Pleasure to the Governor to Hear That I Was Involved in Trouble

Besides managing the regiment and trying to win allies, Washington spent the first half of the year looking after the colony's defense. In April he recommended that the law restricting troops to service in Virginia be changed so he could take the offensive. Instead, the assembly's act enlarging the regiment also listed places the lawmakers wanted adorned with small forts. Construction cut into military operations, but Washington kept patrols out to the west. Five soldiers and fifteen Cherokees under Lieutenant James Baker collided with a French patrol in early June. French losses were six killed, two wounded, and four prisoners, and in return they killed a Cherokee chief and wounded his son. In revenge, the Indians killed two of the prisoners, Baker saving one ensign and an enlisted man. This party should be rewarded "for their scalps and services," Washington advised Dinwiddie. Otherwise, "discontent and murmuring will ensue."[33]

Washington told Colonel John Stanwix, his military superior, that the captured ensign declared that the garrison at Fort Duquesne counted 600 French and 200 Indians; "I believe he is a Gasconian," a braggart, Washington said. Baker and his Cherokees reached Winchester with the prisoner on June 19. Washington and Atkin together interviewed the young officer, who said a "large body of Indians was hourly expected" at Fort Duquesne, but the place had no artillery train. That might have arrived with 300 men expected after he left the Forks. Washington talked to the Cherokees, who claimed that the French were bringing howitzers to attack Fort Loudoun. The only route they could follow without cutting a new one would be Braddock's Road, so he discounted the intelligence.[34]

There were unconfirmed reports that French and Indians were thick around Fort Cumberland. Cherokees told Dagworthy that on June 8 they saw a large body of troops march out of Fort Duquesne with wagons and artillery. He concluded that they aimed to attack Fort Cumberland and raised an alarm. Washington ordered out the militia (which ignored him) and advised Dinwiddie that he could not relieve Cumberland. He thought the real object of the expedition was Fort Loudoun, so he called in his outposts. It was a false alarm, and Dagworthy forwarded further information that another party of Cherokees saw nothing near the Forks but a scouting detail headed east.[35]

When Dagworthy's first report reached Colonel Stanwix at Carlisle, he mustered five companies of Royal American redcoats and a few Pennsylvania troops; because there was no direct route to Cumberland, he headed for Winchester. The first party of Cherokees denied that they had told Dagworthy that there was a large force marching on Fort Cumberland. "Capt. Dagworthy might easily have misunderstood these people," Washington advised Stanwix.[36]

Stanwix reversed his march when he received Dagworthy's second report. On June 25, Washington cancelled his militia call-up and concluded that the alleged big French raid had broken up into small parties. There had been some action against settlers in Maryland and along the South Branch, and three children had been captured not far from Winchester, but the excitement was all over by the end of June.[37]

Washington had reported to Colonel Stanwix because since January he had been his commanding officer, appointed by Loudoun to command the 60th Regiment (Royal Americans) and the troops of

Pennsylvania, Maryland, and Virginia. He was a highly experienced regular officer, in the army since 1706. The division of authority between Dinwiddie and Stanwix gave Washington an opportunity to play them against each other, as he already did with the lieutenant governor and Speaker Robinson.[38]

The tussle between Washington and Dinwiddie went forward as the lieutenant governor's health declined. On March 22, he had asked the prime minister for a leave of absence or permission to resign. He told Washington in early April that he was "very much indispos'd," so much so "that I can write no more at present." When he addressed the assembly on April 14, he spoke as if his departure for England was imminent.[39]

Washington saw weakness in his adversary. When Dinwiddie persuaded the military committee in April to drop the two-percent fee paid the colonel for financial accounts he handled, replacing it with an annual £200 for his "table and expenses," Washington pounced. He demanded to know "upon what terms your Honour purposes to continue me, and what may be my certain dependence?" He needed the two-percent commission as compensation for his services and the "extraordinary trouble and confinement I shou'd meet with in the prosecution of such complicated duties" as the service required. He hoped Dinwiddie would not renege on his promises and make his situation "*worse* by taking away the only perquisite I have."[40]

Dinwiddie answered calmly that Washington had been relieved of the burdens of financial accounts, which paymasters would take over, and Indian affairs, which Atkin would assume. Washington calmed down for the moment, and on May 16 he signed a contract ratifying the new state of affairs. Still his resentment grew. In June he complained to Robinson that people owed money by the regiment had "grown very clamorous" and might sue if the next appropriation was insufficient and went to pay the troops instead of civilian vendors. He was convinced that "it would give pleasure to the governor to hear that I was involved in trouble, however undeservedly, such are his dispositions to me."[41]

The governor had praised Washington effusively for his efficient response to the Dagworthy alarm, but the colonel chose to ignore that. He complained that while Dinwiddie had told him to obey Stanwix's orders he had continued to issue contradictory instructions of his own. Stanwix granted Washington discretion to manage his regiment, so the Virginian tried to draw him into an alliance against Dinwiddie. During the pay negotiations, the governor had complained about the number of batmen, servants drawn from the ranks, that Washington and his officers employed, claiming that they exceeded the number in regular regiments. The colonel sent Stanwix a detailed set of questions about the numbers, pay, and subsistence of batmen in the regulars, with more questions about provision of horses for officers.[42]

Washington told Dinwiddie in July that he had heard from Stanwix, who "approved much of the steps I had taken." His commander had answered all his questions except the ones about batmen; Stanwix was too smart to get drawn into a provincial skunk fight. Washington accused Dinwiddie of claiming that he had exceeded his authority by allowing batmen and transport for the officers of the Virginia Regiment. If the lieutenant governor looked to the regulars as precedent, Virginia should pay for batmen and transport for the officers. Dinwiddie answered that the government had paid for those things all along.[43]

There were more important things to worry about, beginning with Loudoun's orders to send 400 men to South Carolina. Dinwiddie kept getting frantic appeals from the governor of that colony, who believed the French were about to invade. He in turn passed on the alarm to Washington and ordered him to send 200 men to Fredericksburg in April to board ship. Dinwiddie expected to raise the other 200 out of the 1,270 projected for the Virginia Regiment, but no more men went south. Dinwiddie left it to Washington to dispose of the remaining troops as he thought proper. He was "very sensible" that Virginia had too few men on its frontiers.[44]

Despite the fragile condition of Virginia's military establishment, Washington urged Stanwix to order an advance on Fort Duquesne because spy reports said its garrison was very small. This was "too precious an opportunity to be lost." In response, Stanwix ordered him to forward a large part of his arms and ammunition to supply other troops going to South Carolina. Washington did, and Dinwiddie was outraged but could not do anything about it. There were not enough munitions left in Virginia to supply the regiment if it reached full size.[45]

There had been no news from either Britain or Loudoun for two months, Dinwiddie complained at the end of June. Loudoun was at Halifax, Nova Scotia, starting his main project for the year, a campaign against Louisbourg, the fortified port on Cape Breton Island. It was a fiasco. The French reinforced the place, disease ravaged the

English fleet and troops, and in September a storm drove the ships aground. His Lordship was back in New York by the middle of the month, doubts about his competence spreading. Meanwhile, negotiations at Easton among Pennsylvania's Indian commissioners, representatives of the Six Nations, and Teedyuscung, leader of the eastern Delawares, concluded on August 8 with a general peace that took the eastern Delawares out of the war. The stage was set for another conference to separate the western Delawares and other Ohio nations from the French the following year.[46]

Disaster struck the English when Fort William Henry, on Lake George north of Albany, New York, fell to the French on August 9, but the Americans did not know that things were actually looking up. In London, William Pitt had gained power as secretary of state, leader of the House of Commons, and in full control of the war and foreign affairs. Said the supremely self-confident Pitt, "I am sure that I can save this country, and that nobody else can." This amazing patriot dominated his nation for the next four years. The war had gone badly everywhere except India, but now it was in the hands of someone who could plan and make decisions, and would appoint proven fighters to command. Pitt declared his objectives from the outset: to annihilate France's power in America, destroy her navy, cripple her trade and economy, ruin her prospects in India and Africa, and make Britain lord of the seas. "England has long been in labor," said Frederick the Great of Prussia, "and at last she has brought forth a man."[47]

Almost as favorable for the English cause in America were events taking place at Versailles. Madame de Pompadour, Louis XV's mistress and by 1757 the real power in government, ousted the only two ministers—of war and of marine and the colonies—who had shown any ability. She wanted to run the war, and with nothing but yes-men under her she did. One disaster followed another over the next months, the treasury ran into trouble, and she commanded the nation from her boudoir like a Roman empress, prattling on about campaigns and battles that she knew nothing about.[48]

I Have Great Reason to Suspect You of Ingratitude

The American war between Britain and France paused after Fort William Henry and Louisbourg. On the western frontier it was mostly shadow boxing. The terror among the English settlers was real but baseless except for an occasional Shawnee attack on a farmstead. The alleged French invasion of Virginia kept rearing its head, no more real than before. Washington worried that he would be criticized for not relieving Fort Cumberland, and he had Stanwix reconfirm that he had been ordered to make a stand at Fort Loudoun. He passed this on to Dinwiddie so that "the charge of negligence shou'd not lie at my door."[49]

Shawnee raids in the Shenandoah Valley stepped up slightly in September, the early fall raiding season. Washington, who still believed the French were behind whatever hostile Indians did, told Dinwiddie that unless an expedition against Fort Duquesne set off next spring, "this country will not be another year in our possession." He kept thumping this drum, urging Robinson and Stanwix to pressure the lieutenant governor to recommend a campaign against the Forks. Dinwiddie had asked Loudoun for a campaign westward but was always turned down.[50]

That the effect of frontier raiding was more psychological than physical was reflected in Governor General the marquis de Vaudreuil's annual report to Versailles for 1757. Raiding out of Fort Duquesne, he said, had produced "nothing very important," just twenty-seven scalps and twenty-seven prisoners from the three middle colonies. The troops and Indians had been active, but there were too few English to raid. The settlers had retreated "to the city or into the forest." But Fort Duquesne was transferring men north, and the Shawnees and Delawares limited raids for reasons of their own.[51]

Washington's outlook was not brightened by the loss of 200 men to South Carolina, where instead of fighting French invaders they were stuck in Charleston. His aide George Mercer declared in August that it was a grubby place, and its merchants were squeezing the troops for money. The officer in charge, Colonel Henry Bouquet, was an admirable man who did not look down his nose at colonials. "In short we are looked upon in quite another light by all the officers than we were by Genl. Braddock," Mercer reported. Stephen, commanding the Virginians, credited their fair treatment to their superiority to other American troops. By November, the troops had gone without pay for four months, because Williamsburg had sent no money. Morale was low among the Virginians, said Mercer, because they saw "every soldier (except themselves) paid weekly." The men had had no mail and were homesick, but Bouquet said the earliest they could leave would be next spring.[52]

Washington spent July completing and organizing the regiment according to the new establishment, accusing Dinwiddie of failing to help. "Irregularity and confusion will continually prevail among us," he charged on the 12th, "till the companies are formed, and the proper officers appointed to each," which could not happen "unless your Honour will take the trouble upon yourself, or invest me with power and blank commissions to do it." Those took time to print, and Dinwiddie gave the colonel authority to arrange everything according to his judgment. "I hope I have omitted nothing essential," he said on the 18th, "indeed I am not in health for writing long letters." The regiment was complete at the end of the month, eight companies of eighty rank and file each, with four officers, four sergeants, and two drummers. Washington issued blanket orders to the officers covering nearly everything and sent detachments to places specified by the assembly.[53]

The lawmakers had decreed where they wanted units stationed, but Washington changed locations when the situation called for it. The isolation of the scattered commands aggravated the problems of counting heads, managing supplies, and communications generally. Washington told Dinwiddie late in August that there was good news and bad news: that late drafts in July had raised the companies to eighty-six privates each, but it was impossible to report just what the actual strength of any of them was because desertion drained the regiment as fast as the draft could fill it.[54]

The colonel and the lieutenant governor were in open warfare by August. Dinwiddie's failing health worsened early in the summer when he came down with malaria, and he may have had a mild stroke later in the season. He was bending under the weight of office and could be crabby. Washington, on the other hand, grew increasingly impertinent. Dinwiddie complained on August 13 about receiving incomplete accounts, which he called "a loose way of writing, and it's your duty to be more particular to me." Washington shot back that his "best endeavours lose their reward" when his conduct did "not appear to you in a favourable point of light." The matter at hand involved Indian affairs, and Washington reminded the governor that he had been instructed "in very express terms" not to deal with that subject.[55]

Relations between the two were toxic by September, when Dinwiddie again objected to Washington's sending in incomplete returns. The colonel replied that the regiment's scattered deployment, uncertain recruitment, and continuing desertion made that impossible. He claimed he was the victim of anonymous charges that he had exaggerated the Indian danger to get more appropriations and a larger regiment. "It is evident, from a variety of circumstances, and especially from the change in your Honour's conduct towards me," he whined, that some malicious villain was at work to "impress you with so ill an opinion of my honor and honesty." Dinwiddie replied that Washington should ignore idle rumors.[56]

Everything added to the strain between them. William Fairfax urged Washington to give his middle son William Henry a commission as a lieutenant, and the colonel stalled. The elder Fairfax went to the governor, who reminded Washington that he had the blank commissions and the power to appoint. "I esteem him greatly on account of his father," he replied, but appointing him over ensigns with seniority would invite charges "that my friendship and partiality to the family were the causes of it." Washington dodged what he viewed as unseemly pressure by arming William Henry with letters of introduction and sending him north to see Loudoun. Young Fairfax joined the 44th Regiment at New York as a volunteer and later purchased a commission.[57]

Another bone of contention appeared in September when, because of Washington's claims that the frontier was undefended, Dinwiddie reversed his earlier orders not to recruit rangers. It was not in the governor's power to do more than recommend that Washington quickly execute his orders to raise a company of rangers, "to effect which I pray you to exert yourself." Washington doubted he could raise even 100 rangers and added, "I am quite at a loss how to act, as you did not inform me upon what terms they are to be levied and supported, what bounty money to allow, what pay to engage the officers and men, how clothed and supported, what the officers' pay and what kind of commissions they are to have."

That was insubordinate, because laws and regulations governed those subjects. Washington charged that Dinwiddie had accused him of ingratitude, "a crime I detest." If "instances of my ungrateful behaviour had been particularized, I would have answered to them." They continued battling back and forth over rangers. Dinwiddie wanted

Captain Peter Hog to command them, but Washington called him "the most unfit person in the world." He recommended Robert Rutherford instead, and Dinwiddie agreed but added an insulting list of demands that Washington supervise Rutherford's expenditures. It so happened that nobody wanted to join the rangers because they might be absorbed into the regiment, as had happened the year before.[58]

Indian affairs provided other sources of conflict. The colonel repeatedly complained about not being reimbursed for goods supplied to the Indians, while Dinwiddie declared himself "much fatigued" by Indian affairs in general. Atkin, the Indian superintendent, added his own fuel to the fire. He held a commission from London, so he could not be gotten rid of, but Washington and Dinwiddie cooperated for once by appointing Christopher Gist a captain in charge of Indian financial accounts.

In July Atkin accused ten Cherokees in Winchester of being spies and asked Washington to arrest them. The colonel warned of the consequences but complied. Other Cherokees declared that Virginia had made war on them, the evidence being their friends in the Fort Loudoun guardhouse. Washington and Stanwix both sent runners to wherever Cherokees had gathered, to explain away what had happened. Washington did not bother to inform Dinwiddie, however, who heard about it from others. The prisoners were released, but the damage had been done. By September there were no more Indians at Winchester.[59]

Stanwix's energetic diplomacy averted a crisis. He was so successful that in September Sir William Johnson, superintendent of Indian affairs for the north, entertained a delegation of Cherokees at his home near Albany, hoping to lay a foundation for an alliance among the Six Nations, the English, and the southern nations. He sent them home with messages to other nations and to the colonial governors, who provided escorts and supplies for them on their way. "You did very right in furnishing the Cherokees from Pensylvaa. with horses &c.," Dinwiddie complimented Washington.[60]

Their exchanges were seldom that friendly. When Dinwiddie told Washington to manage the Indian financial accounts, the colonel exploded. That duty, he pointed out, had been handed to Gist by the governor himself. "It cannot reasonably be supposed that I, who am stripped of the help I once was allowed"—meaning his aide-de-camp—"can turn my hands and my thoughts to such a multiplicity of business." He worked so hard "that very little recreation falls to my lot." Dinwiddie returned the responsibility to Gist.[61]

Washington complained ceaselessly about the "mismanagement" of Indian affairs. Cherokees who visited him in October were outraged that there were no supplies for them. The colonel supplied them out of regimental stores. Virginia was losing "our interest of that people," he warned. This neglect was not his fault, but the government's for failing to provide what the Indians needed to travel and wage war. Gist wanted to help, but he had no goods, money, or even an interpreter. Atkin, thankfully, was out of the territory. Dinwiddie forwarded more presents and approved issuing what was needed out of regimental stores.[62]

Nothing poisoned Washington's relations with Dinwiddie more than the time he spent on his private affairs rather than the regiment's, even as he complained about suffering from "bloody flux," meaning diarrhea from dysentery. He arranged for crops, purchases of slaves, and other management of his estates, and he bought a partnership in a mine. That was a bad investment, and Washington repeatedly lent money to the mining company. He also badgered the governor for permission to take leave for the final settlement of his brother Lawrence's estate. Getting no response, he asked Stanwix, who told him to use his own judgment.

When Washington heard that the lieutenant governor would be going home in November, he asked for leave to go to Williamsburg to settle his accounts. Dinwiddie said no, because he had been "frequently indulged with leave of absence." Washington objected, "It was not to enjoy a party of pleasure I wanted leave of absence; I have been indulged with few of those, winter or summer!" He complained to Robinson about Dinwiddie's denying him leave.[63]

Washington's last mentor, William Fairfax, died on September 3, a man loved by all and revered by the young colonel. Sorrow over that may have contributed to his gloomy outlook, along with his dysentery, and attending the funeral late in the month became a difficult trip. His health deteriorated along with the governor's, whose pending departure Washington's friends did not mourn. Robinson said that nobody knew who would replace Dinwiddie. "God grant it may be somebody better acquainted with the unhappy business we have in hand." He urged Washington to persevere, as he had through "the discouragements and slights you have too often met with."[64]

Dinwiddie's constant wrangles with upstart colonials would have worn an iron man down. Washington took their disagreements personally. He wrote his last letter to the governor on November 5 and in return received Dinwiddie's last to him, written on the 14th. "My conduct to you from the beginning was always friendly," the sick old man avowed, "but you know I have great reason to suspect you of ingratitude. . . . I wish my successor may show you as much friendship as I've done." He sailed for England in January 1758.[65]

If Washington had any regrets about his relations with Dinwiddie, he never got a chance to express them. His "bloody flux" worsened, "attended with bad fevers," then on November 7 he was "seiz'd with stitches & violent pleuretick pains," as Captain Robert Stewart informed Dinwiddie. The doctors bled him, their treatment for everything in that day, and he got worse. They advised "immediately changing his air," meaning he should go home. He refused without getting permission from the governor, but he was too weak to write. He surrendered his command to Stewart and left for Mount Vernon on the 9th, asking his successor to inform his superiors. Dinwiddie was troubled by the news. Washington's "violent complaint" gave him "great concern," he told Stewart; "it was unknown to me or he shou'd have had leave of absence sooner, & I am very glad he did not delay following the doctrs. advice, to try a change of air, I sincerely wish him a speedy recovery." On the 25th, hearing that Washington was no better since getting home, his physician Dr. James Craik warned him that he needed a long rest away from public affairs.[66]

If Washington regained his health enough to return to his regiment, he would find his prospects brightened, as Pitt had overhauled Britain's strategy in the war. He would keep England off the continent by subsidizing his German allies. The British Isles would be defended by a reformed territorial militia, freeing up redcoats for action in India, Africa, the West Indies, and North America. Pitt also fired Loudoun for incompetence. Major General James Abercromby, his deputy, replaced him as commander in chief, with personal command of a campaign against Fort Ticonderoga. Major General Jeffrey Amherst was to attack Louisbourg, and Colonel John Forbes of the 17th Foot, promoted to brigadier, would lead an expedition against Fort Duquesne.

Pitt reversed everything Braddock and Loudoun had represented, because he wanted the colonies to join in a common effort. The commander in chief in North America no longer had viceregal authority, and the governors took orders only from London. If the provinces raised men the home office would supply them equally with regular regiments, and the king promised compensation for whatever the colonies spent on their own. The nicest touch was that all provincial officers would rank the same as regulars. Colonel Washington would be junior only to regulars of the same or higher grades, and no longer "senior captain."[67]

It was not everything he had wanted—provincial officers would not be inducted into the regulars, and the royal regiments raised in America were officered by Britons. Still, being respected as an equal was worth something in its own right.

ELEVEN

ALL IS LOST BY HEAVENS! OUR ENTERPRISE RUIN'D!

(1758)

Sing, goddess, the wrath of Peleus' son Achilles, a destroying
wrath which brought upon the Achaeans myriad woes.

—HOMER

Pitt's overhaul of Britain's war unleashed armies and navies on a
scale not seen for centuries. A tightening naval blockade cut seriously
into New France's imports of food and of goods to trade with the
Indians by the end of 1757. The campaigns of 1758 sent against New
France almost 50,000 troops along with bateaumen, wagoneers, and
other support, a figure equal to two-thirds the French population of
Canada. The marquis de Montcalm, who had commanded the army
in New France since 1756, faced the flood of redcoats and English
provincials with only 6,800 regulars, 2,000 *troupes de la marine*, and
less than 16,000 militia. He was also losing support among the Indians, partly because a series of smallpox epidemics in 1757 persuaded
many that having the French nearby was not healthy. The far western
nations had risen up against the French.

The state of Canadian food supplies was desperate following two
bad harvests in a row. The arrival of a relief convoy on May 22 pre-

vented actual starvation, but people in Quebec had literally been eating grass. Diverting food and farmhands to the coming military campaign meant that most Canadians would be hungry all the time. Worse, by early 1758 Versailles had written New France off, concentrating its resources in Europe and the West Indies.[1]

Pitt sent a circular to the colonial governors at the end of 1757, asking full cooperation from their assemblies in the projected campaigns. The only cost to them would be levying, clothing, and paying the men; everything else would be supplied by the king. Major General James Abercromby, Loudoun's successor as commander in chief, asked for a total of 6,000 troops from Virginia, Maryland, and Pennsylvania to march against the Forks along with the regulars. The assemblies responded enthusiastically.[2]

The expedition against Fort Duquesne was commanded by Brigadier John Forbes, age fifty, who took his post at Carlisle, Pennsylvania, on March 21, 1758. Born into Scottish nobility, he had attended medical school before joining the army, and he served in the War of the Austrian Succession and the Scottish campaigns of 1745–1746. He earned a distinguished reputation as a quartermaster and had been Loudoun's adjutant during the Louisbourg campaign. He was patient, cheerful, cordial with officers and men alike, but throughout 1758 he suffered from a combination of dysentery and what was probably stomach cancer. A logistical genius, he was cautious about advancing before everything was arranged, but he worked like a mule to that end.

His deputy was Colonel Henry Bouquet, thirty-nine, who despite his age had vast experience to his credit, most recently the expedition to South Carolina. Born in Switzerland, he entered the Dutch army as a cadet in 1736, then served in the Sardinian army during the War of the Austrian Succession. In 1748 the Prince of Orange appointed him captain-commandant of the new Swiss Guards, with the rank of lieutenant colonel. He transferred to the British army's new Royal American Regiment in 1755. He was a successful recruiter, portly and unimpressive in appearance, but friendly and open to all. A practical scholar, when he arrived in Pennsylvania he studied Indian tactics and later developed light-infantry doctrine for Britain.

If there would be cooperation between redcoats and the local governments, Forbes and Bouquet were likely to achieve it if the other side went along. But as Bouquet warned, civil government in America was "almost negligible."[3]

Mention Me in Favourable Terms to General Forbes

Washington convalesced at Mount Vernon for more than three months. The Fairfax ladies brought wine, jellies, and other delicacies, but mostly he suffered alone except for his slave attendants. Friends advised him to follow the doctors' advice and rest. He was impatient as ever, however. On January 30 he asked John Blair, president of the King's Council and acting lieutenant governor, for permission to visit Williamsburg to settle his accounts. Blair approved.[4]

Washington set out the first of February, but his fever and pains forced him back to Mount Vernon. He felt ready to travel again on March 4, to visit a Williamsburg physician recommended by friends. The new doctor gave him his powders and he recovered rapidly, enough to set out for Fort Loudoun in early April.[5]

He was not entirely off duty in his sickbed. In January Blair had told him that he had reports that about 800 Indians were on their way to Fort Loudoun to join the English cause. Blair doubted the numbers, but Dinwiddie had stated before he left that there were plenty of goods for Christopher Gist to distribute. Gist reported that stores on hand were about a third of what Dinwiddie had declared. In April Blair forwarded £1,500 worth of additional Indian goods and paid out £500 to discharge debts on such supplies.[6]

Washington received notice at the end of January that a prominent citizen of Prince William County had complained he was abused by Virginia soldiers. The man made so much noise that several officers challenged him to a duel, but he dodged them, and the controversy died down without the colonel's intervention. Nor could he do much about Fort Loudoun, where construction continued under the supervision of Lieutenant Charles Smith, although stonework fell behind because the mason was sick.[7]

In early March a cashiered officer named Major John Smith presented Washington and Colonel Stanwix a plan for invading Ohio, based on his alleged experience as an escaped prisoner of the French. He proposed to bypass Fort Duquesne and aim straight at Detroit. "Surely," Washington sneered to Stanwix, "he intended to provide them with wings to facilitate their passage over so mountainous and extensive a country." Stanwix heartily agreed.[8]

Washington was well enough after his miracle cure to think about his personal future. On the way home from Williamsburg, on March

16, he stopped at White House, an estate on the Pamunkey River and home to an acquaintance, the richest widow in Virginia, Martha Dandridge Custis, just a year older than he was. She owned three plantations totaling 18,000 acres, worked by over 200 slaves, and was worth at least £30,000. Widowed eight months, Martha controlled her entire dower because her husband had died without leaving a will. She was five feet tall, pretty, pleasingly plump, with tiny hands and feet, a noble brow and equally noble Roman nose, and large eyes beneath wide eyebrows. She had a warm, relaxed personality charming to men.

Washington gave her servants hefty tips and entertained her two children. Martha needed a new husband for financial and legal protection. Washington's comparative lack of a fortune was not important because she had enough for both of them. She asked him to come back a week later, and he did—after she had checked him out with friends. He may have proposed marriage then; in April he ordered fine suits from London, and in May a ring for her from Philadelphia. She ordered a trousseau, including "one genteel suite of cloathes for my self to be grave but not to be extravagant." Washington called again in June and they set their wedding for after the end of the current campaign.[9]

Even before the engagement was sealed, Washington set out to make Mount Vernon an elegant seat for his new family. Serving as his own architect, he ordered materials, hired a superintendent, built a brick kiln, and imported furniture and trim from London. Throughout the year the colonel spent an amazing amount of his time on personal business.[10]

Such distractions aside, the colonel returned to Fort Loudoun on April 5 and took up his duties. Two days later the assembly voted to increase Virginia's forces to 2,000 men in two regiments, along with three ranger companies. Each recruit would receive an enlistment bounty of £10, the term of service to expire on December 1. The restrictions against serving outside the colony were repealed. Washington remained head of what was now called the 1st Virginia Regiment, and he also commanded both regiments with the unofficial rank of brigadier. The colonel of the 2nd Virginia was William Byrd III, twenty-nine-year-old scion of one of Virginia's oldest families. He had successfully negotiated with the southern Indians, lived in England for a few years, and had a good record as a volunteer in the Louisbourg campaign.[11]

Washington's letters to the acting governor, Blair, were generally shorter than those he had written to Dinwiddie, and his adolescent hostility was gone. Real harmony prevailed over the next several weeks. The change was evident from the outset, although Washington asked "impatiently" (as he put it) on April 9 for Blair's instructions on assembling the new military establishment. For the moment, the best the acting governor could advise was to be ready to move "on short notice."[12]

Meanwhile, about 400 Indian allies who had reached Fort Loudoun had to be dealt with. Washington badgered Blair, Colonel Stanwix, and Forbes's quartermaster general, Sir John St. Clair, about the need to have supplies on hand for them and an early campaign to keep them from going home. At about the same time, troops responding to a citizens' alarm shot and killed two civilians whose "dress, disguise and behavior" made them appear to be enemy Indians. Given that frontiersmen and Indians dressed pretty much alike, the case raises the question of how many mistaken identities occurred.[13]

Washington learned that Stanwix had been promoted to brigadier and ordered to take post between the Mohawk River and Lake Ontario, where he built a work later called Fort Stanwix. The Virginian congratulated him and asked him "to mention me in favourable terms to General Forbes"—not for "military preferment" but as someone "distinguished in some measure from the *common run* of provincial officers."[14]

Washington wrote to several officers, asking in almost identical language that they commend him to Forbes. The earliest response showed that at least his advice on Indian allies had been heeded. St. Clair told him that Forbes had ordered him to forward coats and light arms to equip the Indians. He also sent Gist £300 Virginia currency to buy anything else the allies needed. Washington should tell the Indians that "nothing in our power shall be wanting to accommodate them," the quartermaster concluded. Washington was delighted by that, writing to "express the great pleasure" he felt, he told St. Clair, at learning that General Forbes was "so heartily disposed to please the Indians."[15]

Once he had settled in, Washington concentrated on raising and organizing his command, beginning with a council of war to consider how to carry out the assembly's orders that militia garrison the forts when the regiments marched out. The group kicked that problem back to the governor and Council, because orders from Washington would likely provoke what the officers called a "general mutiny" of militia. When his former aide George Mercer, now lieutenant colonel of the 2nd Virginia, proposed that some officers be transferred from the 1st to the 2nd, Blair asked Washington's opinion. The colonel said that none of his officers would accept transfer. But he was losing officers to various causes; one of them had embezzled his own men's pay.[16]

There remained the problem of recruiting privates for the two regiments, rangers aside. The 1st Virginia needed at least 150 men to fill out its companies, and the 2nd the full 1,000. Blair advised waiting until the assembly had appropriated the enlistment bonuses, but the colonel ordered officers out anyway. Response, not surprisingly, was slow until Washington received recruitment money on April 30.[17]

Recruitment proceeded rapidly compared to the past, and desertion took a sudden drop. The reason for both was that the enlistment bonus and limited term of service brought in better men than the "vagabonds" of previous years. There was another factor that Washington did not seem to realize, and that was loyalty. His regiment had a solid cadre of officers and men who had been in the service for a considerable time. If anyone wanted to desert, he had long since done so. The 1st Virginia Regiment was a solid, experienced, and capable body of soldiers.

Militias were another matter. Blair heeded the council of war and the advice of his own Council, and on May 4 he laid down the law to county lieutenants. Because the forts must be garrisoned by the militia in the absence of the regiment, he declared, "I do therefore by virtue of the power and authority with which I am invested as commander in chief hereby require and command you to raise and send one hundred men of your militia," along with officers, to a fort specified, and remain there until the return of the regiment. Washington was delighted to pass the militia problem to the governor, but not so much when he realized that Blair had reclaimed the title of commander in chief.[18]

Lack of money retarded the stocking of supplies for the campaign, but Washington foretold his future approach to uniforms when he ordered cloth from Philadelphia to make Indian leggings for 1,000 men. He ordered for his own use pack saddles, tack, a leather stationery case, boots, a trunk, and half a dozen china cups and saucers for his "table." He would campaign in style.[19]

As important to Washington as getting his regiment ready was earning the favor of his new superior, Forbes. It was "very acceptable news" to Forbes and his staff to hear that Washington was well enough to join the campaign, St. Clair told him on April 20. Forbes commended the colonel to Blair, and this offered an opportunity to turn on the flattery, with more grace than he had shown to Loudoun the year before. Washington thanked the general for his kind words, promising that he would continue to merit the general's approval. The Virginia colonel praised Forbes's "experience, abilities, and good character," and he predicted "a glorious campaign."

There followed more repetitious advice about supplying the Indians, which Washington offered to St. Clair whenever he had ink on his pen. He also apologized for his regiment's "shabby appearance," for want of clothes and tents. Blair ordered him formally late in April to place himself under the British officer's command, which set off more effusive flattery to St. Clair. He would think himself "quite happy," he gushed, to maintain "the good opinion" the general and his aides entertained of him. He wanted no other reward for his services "than the satisfaction arising from a consciousness of doing my duty, and from the esteem of my friends."[20]

His regiment was understrength, scattered, and undersupplied, but Washington responded quickly whenever his new superiors needed anything. St. Clair sent an engineer to repair roads near the Potomac and asked for 200 troops to provide labor and protection; he got them. The Virginian sent St. Clair a long letter asking all sorts of questions about transportation, ending: "I am sorry to give you so much trouble at a time when I am sensible you are greatly hurried." The provincial colonel, the hidden text read, was both eager and obedient.[21]

It Is but Poor Encouragement for the Exertion of My Zeal

This eager officer had just over a month to get his troops ready to join Forbes's expedition. There was much recruitment yet to do, but that was difficult because Williamsburg was slow to forward money. What had been sent ran out, and in early May Washington diverted funds from other accounts. His officers formally supported him on grounds of necessity, but it left him liable if the governor and Council did not approve. "If I am to suffer," the colonel complained to Speaker Robinson, "I can only say that it is but poor encouragement for the exertion of my zeal." Blair summoned the Council to straighten everything out. By the last week in May the 1st Virginia was nearly at full strength; the officers of the 2nd had raised 600 men.[22]

Those men needed officers, and the many vacancies in the two regiments meant that Washington faced constant pressure to appoint the favorites of prominent men, sometimes over officers with greater experience and rank. The colonel resisted all such entreaties. "Faith these are discouraging circumstances," his neighbor George Mason said of the pressures Washington faced.[23]

Washington had an additional problem mobilizing his forces in the spring of 1758 because he was suspended between two powers, the king's and the province's, with considerable confusion about who should pay for what. St. Clair, ordering him to assemble all troops at Fort Loudoun, promised to meet with the governors of Maryland and Virginia "to regulate many things." The meeting did not take place, and if it had it would have been complicated by the Marylander's proposal to Forbes that Virginia pay Maryland troops.[24]

Forbes had established Philadelphia as his receiving port, not Alexandria and Fredericksburg as Braddock had done. Goods shipped there at the king's expense included arms and ammunition, tents, foodstuffs, and other supplies, but the provinces were expected to pay, feed, and clothe their own troops. St. Clair performed the labors of Hercules getting war materiel distributed to the various provincial stations, much of it intended for Indians allied with Virginia. Clothing and tentage remained Washington's biggest challenges.[25]

Washington's control over outposts, militia, and rangers was weak. Blair's orders calling out the militia, Washington thought, would "be sufficient," because he doubted that the enemy would invade the province after Forbes marched out. There would be small raiding parties, but no number of militia could deter them. Direction of Captain Robert Rutherford's ranger company was also dubious, and citizens complained that it did nothing. Rutherford said he had too few men.[26]

Indians, allied and otherwise, were even farther from Washington's control. Forbes's brigade major, Francis Halkett, heard in early May that a party of Catawbas had reached Winchester from the Ohio with scalps and prisoners, and he wanted them sent to Philadelphia for examination. Nothing of the sort had happened, and the colonel complained that neither the Catawbas nor the Cherokees had produced any prisoners so far that year. A party had brought in two scalps from home, passing them off as fresh; thirty Cherokees stormed off in a huff when Washington refused to pay for counterfeits.

Halkett and St. Clair repeatedly told Washington to keep the Indians busy and well supplied, and they forwarded regular shipments of goods for them. But there were exaggerated reports from Augusta and Bedford counties of Shawnee raids that killed fifty or sixty citizens and an officer and eighteen rangers. There was actually more pillaging than killing, and militia officers claimed this was the work of Cherokees going between Carolina and Winchester. The colonel warned Halkett that some of the Cherokees planned to visit Pennsylvania and Maryland seeking presents and were likely to stir up trouble; they did, at both Carlisle and Philadelphia. Washington complained that Indians often went home when they pleased, showing his indifference to their interests. He also failed to understand that the Cherokees and Catawbas had a long history of alternating peace and war with the English, with no incentive to form a lasting alliance.[27]

Halkett told Washington on May 4 that efforts were under way to assemble a conference of Ohio Indians, eastern Delawares, and British and Pennsylvania officials, aiming for a treaty of some sort. He did not reveal that a major rethinking of English-Indian relations was underway. Alone among British generals, Forbes saw the strategic importance of the nations, although he made no more efforts than the others to understand their points of view. He urged Pennsylvania's governor to keep promises made to Teedyuscung in 1757 to settle the eastern Delawares in the Wyoming Valley, because they were the only channel of communication to the western Delawares and other Ohio nations. In May Forbes moved to negotiate "a treaty on foot" between the Shawnees, the Delawares, and the people of Pennsylvania, to deprive the French of their American allies. This diplomacy would take as much of his effort as the military campaign, but Washington paid it no mind.[28]

St. Clair visited Fort Loudoun and on May 24 relayed Washington's first marching orders. He should assemble his whole regiment at Winchester except for two companies on the South Branch, until those were relieved by militia. Both Virginia regiments should make ready to march on short notice, assembling provisions for eight days.

Forty men from the 1st Virginia were assigned to Robert Stewart's light horse troop, replaced by transfers from the 2nd. Washington should ask President Blair for instructions on how to complete his regiments.[29]

He arrived in Williamsburg on the 28th and gave Blair a twelve-point presentation asking for early action by Virginia's government to meet Forbes's call. In contrast to his angry exchanges with Dinwiddie, he phrased everything as requests for guidance. He began by describing the shortage of arms, tents, and other essential field equipment. Officers should receive transport, forage, and batmen, rebuking Dinwiddie's alleged refusal to offer these. Clothing stocks could not last the campaign, and the government should lay in a supply for winter. When the Indian leggings he had ordered arrived, should the men have their pay stopped for them? "As they have not received the clothing they are entitled to, they may think this latter rather hard." Political appointments of officers over others more qualified should cease. On another touchy issue, Forbes had ordered that the 1st Virginia should be completed immediately, leaving it to Williamsburg to figure out how.

The colonel asked for signed, blank commissions to fill officer vacancies. Should work on Fort Loudoun continue? He thought it should, but he wanted to know who would do it. He recommended that Charles Smith, who had managed the project for two years, should continue. Ammunition taken on campaign should be replaced and properly stored. Finally, Rutherford's rangers should remain where they were, and more militia should be called out. Washington wound up this long plea by urging that the government not delay getting its troops ready to march. Any hesitation, he warned, would cause the Indians to go home and invite desertion by idle recruits.[30]

Washington returned to Fort Loudoun on June 14 to find orders from St. Clair waiting for him. He was to march out with five companies of the 1st Virginia and a company of artificers (craftsmen) from the 2nd that very day. Byrd would lead out what companies of the 2nd were ready on the 26th, the rest to follow under Lieutenant Colonel Mercer when assembled. Two companies of the 2nd would replace those of the 1st at posts on the South Branch until militia took over. The commissary should lay in provisions for 1,800 men for six weeks at Fort Cumberland. Washington told St. Clair that he was short of muskets, bayonets, cartridge boxes, and blankets, and so could not comply. On the 15th, he announced to his officers that he would lead the first units out on June 23, and he told the commander on the South Branch to leave even if the militia had not shown up. The Prince William militia came into Winchester on the 19th, 73 men without arms instead of the requested 100 equipped, but Washington ordered them to the South Branch.[31]

Dinwiddie's replacement as lieutenant governor, Francis Fauquier, had arrived while Washington was in Williamsburg. He waited until he was back at Fort Loudoun to congratulate his new superior on his appointment and apologize for not calling on him because his business "was of too urgent a nature to admit of delays." He added that he needed more funds and blank commissions. This was a lame excuse for his discourtesy, but Fauquier did not seem to notice, sending the blanks and £2,000.[32]

St. Clair hoped that by now Washington had solved his problems, but if he was still short of anything, "let me know it." The army's stocks could at least fill Washington's need for bayonets. Meanwhile, he should send an officer and eight or ten of the light horse to Carlisle for escort duty.[33]

Washington told Forbes on June 19 that a march through the wilderness to Fort Duquesne would not be possible without "a considerable body" of Indians, who were "the only troops fit to cope with Indians in such grounds." Success in the woods, he continued, would not come from unwieldy numbers, but from guarding the van and flanks with bush fighters—an implicit criticism of the Braddock expedition, which he did not want to see repeated. Washington urged an early rather than a late campaign, to keep the Indians along and deny the French a chance to alienate them. He ended by apologizing for his presumption.

Brigade Major Halkett replied that the general agreed with Washington's thinking, and the colonel's experience with Indians justified his advising the general. Forbes, he said, had confidence in Washington's "way of thinking," and he invited the Virginian's continued advice. That boded well for the future.[34]

Washington and St. Clair spent a week firing letters past each other, trying to sort out supplies and equipment. Still short of many things, by June 24 Washington was ready to lead his troops out. He left Smith in charge at Fort Loudoun, and to put an end to citizen complaints about the rangers, he told Rutherford to send twenty of his "worst rangers" to work on Fort Loudoun.[35]

Virginia's little army was on the march by the 26th, trickling into Fort Cumberland in late June and early July to become part of an expedition that included 1,200 British troops, mostly Scottish Highlanders, 350 Royal Americans, 2,700 provincials from Pennsylvania, 1,600 from Virginia, 200 or so Marylanders guarding Fort Frederick, and two companies of North Carolinians. Counting teamsters, the force numbered between 6,000 and 7,000 at any time, but it never was together in one place. The Highlanders were the most interesting part of this array. The royal army wanted to not only acquire aggressive fighters for the current war, but it was seeking a way to channel the energies of the revolt-prone clans a decade after the Rising of '45. These fighting Scots later proved to be sometimes too aggressive.[36]

Washington had hoped to lead a unified command of Virginians as part of this expedition, but instead his men again were scattered. Adam Stephen went north to Raystown, which he reached with his corps and 500 Pennsylvanians on June 24. The wagons were "overloaded & all broke on the road," Stephen said. Colonel Bouquet was there, and he ordered Washington to start clearing a proper road to Raystown from Fort Cumberland at once, giving the men an extra gill of rum per day for roadwork, the same as the regulars. Bouquet followed this on July 1 with orders to build another road eastward to Frederick, toward a party cutting its way westward.[37]

Despite these orders, the Virginia officers thought that Forbes would follow Braddock's Road to Fort Duquesne and assumed Cumberland would be the army's base, a regular officer advised Bouquet. Another told Bouquet that the belief was general that Forbes would not cut a new road westward to the Forks. As it happened, the great battle of the Forbes expedition was not over the French fort but over how to get there.[38]

I Shall Believe It When I Am an Eye Witness to It

Washington reached Fort Cumberland on July 2, and the next day he sent Bouquet his excuse for taking so long: The road was wretched. He would not put any of his men to work on the Raystown road until Colonel Byrd joined him with the 2nd Virginia. Besides, there were not enough tools on hand to improve the rough road northward.[39]

Fort Cumberland put Washington at the center of Forbes's supply network; goods were coming up from Virginia and in from Maryland, to be stored or passed on to the growing supply depot at Raystown. Managing this traffic took considerable time, although under Fauquier's direction Virginia provided goods and money more regularly than before, and when there were shortages St. Clair's efficient operation shifted stuff between posts. Nobody went seriously hungry or without rum in this campaign.[40]

Sickness and road-building injuries were major concerns. Byrd led eight companies of the 2nd Virginia into Fort Cumberland on July 7 but left a quarter of his men behind owing to disease. Stephen complained from Raystown a week later that he was overloaded with hospital cases, but he lacked even a surgeon's mate to treat them. Smallpox broke out there early in August, forcing him to build a quarantine hospital outside the camp. Then sickness spread back to Fort Cumberland, and Bouquet advised Washington to move his troops to someplace less "sickly" than the present camp.[41]

The old issue of relative rank arose again when Washington learned that Horatio Sharpe, who was a lieutenant colonel in the regular army as well as governor of Maryland, would arrive at Fort Cumberland. He asked Bouquet whether he must surrender command to Sharpe. Governors, he learned, had no command of troops when joined with regular troops, and Washington outranked Sharpe.[42]

Fauquier had relieved Washington of responsibility for supervising commissaries working in Virginia and for Fort Loudoun, and the militia sent to the forts were under the governor's direct command. Loudoun, however, claimed the colonel's attention throughout the summer. It had turned into a great hospital by early July, filled with men from Byrd's regiment and other patients sent down from Fort Cumberland. Rutherford's rangers presented their usual behavioral problems, generating complaints from citizens that they were not ranging, until most of them fell sick. When they recovered, Smith sent those who did not desert out on patrols. Medical expenses left too little money to continue construction, so Fort Loudoun vegetated.[43]

Although Washington continued to believe that allied Indians were the keys to the campaign's success, he objected when they behaved according to their own customs. Some regrettable incidents persuaded Bouquet to order that all friendly Indians should wear yellow cloth badges when they left camp, so they would not be taken for enemies and fired upon by white people.[44]

They could be difficult allies to Anglos who refused to see the world their way. Catawbas at Bouquet's camp behaved in "the most shamefull" manner and abandoned him. He asked Washington to get Fauquier to send an emissary to their nation, to win them back. The lieutenant governor refused, on the grounds that Indians could never be useful to the English. The Cherokees were "rascalls," in Bouquet's view, who absconded with army property. "I think it would be easier to make Indians of our white men, than to cox that damned tanny race." Other Cherokees refused to leave home for the army until summer's heat had passed.[45]

Forced to adapt to their allies' customs, the Anglos used Indians to fight Indians, as Washington advised. French-allied Indians prowled around Forbes's units all summer. The governor general of New France, Vaudreuil, recruited nations from the Great Lakes to help out; his greatest worry was that the slow progress of the English would cause the Indian allies to get tired of waiting. When Anglo stragglers or cattle guards turned up dead and scalped, Washington or Bouquet sent out mixed parties of troops and Indians to find the culprits. They seldom did, except when they ran into an ambush.[46]

Two sides could play at that game. Indians were the only match for Indians in their own country, so parties of Indians with a few white soldiers ranged westward from Fort Cumberland and Raystown. Forbes wanted to "harrass the ennemies at home," so Bouquet asked Washington's advice on sending a large mixed force to attack Indian settlements on the Ohio, which would force them to defend their families and "leave to the French their own quarrels to fight." The Virginian objected, because big parties were too easily detected and risked losing men or wearing them out.[47]

That made sense to the British commanders, who reverted to ordering out small parties. They did not do much damage, because Indians were also good at dodging other Indians. They could bring back intelligence, however, and several parties penetrated as far as Fort Duquesne during July and August, reporting that the place looked weak, with few French or Indians around, and no defensive work going on. The most successful of these patrols was a party of whites and Cherokees under Lieutenant Colbey Chew, son of Washington's old friend Joseph Chew. In August they followed old trading paths through "very bushy and thick" country, up and down ridges, to a rise overlooking the French fort. The Cherokees stopped to paint themselves and say their prayers. Their chief took certain charms from an otter-skin bag and tied them around the necks of his men. He tied the bag itself around Chew's neck and gave his sergeant a packet of paint, telling Chew that these things would deflect musket-balls. The sachem "shook hands with us, and told us to go and fight like men." There was no fight, however, and the party returned with a detailed description of the French position, a report Bouquet called "full and very satisfactory."[48]

Despite Washington's disapproval of Indian behavior, he learned to use them more effectively than any other officer in the expedition, and his grudging admiration for their wilderness talents led him to copy their appearance. He told Bouquet on July 3 that if left to his own incli-nations, he would "not only order the men to adopt the Indian dress, but cause the officers to do it also," and he would set the example him-self. He hesitated only because he did not know if the general would approve. It was "unbecoming dress" for an officer, he admitted, but "convenience rather than shew," he thought, "shou'd be consulted." Besides, it would reduce the need for transport.[49]

By "Indian dress" he meant costume common to whites as well as Indians in the west: moccasins, leggings, breechclout, and a hunting shirt, a knee-length smock of linen, wool, or linsey-woolsey, drab and durable. Forbes was delighted. "In this country we must learn the art of war from enemy Indians," the general said. Within weeks all Vir-ginia troops were dressed Indian style, and when Bouquet first saw them he told Washington, "Their dress should be our pattern in this expedition." The Virginian was gratified that, in this at least, royal of-ficers could learn from provincials.[50]

Washington had one more matter to take care of, running for the House of Burgesses from Frederick County. Having lost his first at-tempt, this time he mobilized supporters, including some of his own officers. His fans wanted him to campaign in person and Bouquet granted him leave, but he decided that leaving his post would not look good. When the votes were counted on July 24, Washington was the winner, mostly because his 391 voters consumed twenty-eight gal-lons of rum, fifty gallons of rum punch, thirty-four gallons of wine, forty-six gallons of beer, and two gallons of cider royal, a quart and a half per vote, not counting a dinner he provided for his campaigners. Buying votes with alcohol was normal in that day, and Washington had gone all out.[51]

As congratulations poured down on him, Washington considered how to get to Fort Duquesne. Braddock's Road was obvious to him, but not to his superiors. The American landscape was new to them, but they had devised a wilderness-campaigning doctrine. It was a challenge. Forbes warned William Pitt that between Carlisle and Fort Duquesne stretched an immense forest and mountain ranges "impenetrable almost to any thing humane save the Indians." He soon was cursing the "hellish woods."[52]

Forbes chose to avoid Braddock's major mistake, dragging all his supplies and overhead with the army. Instead, he would advance a series of fortified supply depots. He did not pick his route of march at the outset, although respectable people in Philadelphia recommended going west through Pennsylvania. That way offered somewhat easier terrain than Braddock's, was about the same distance, and went through country with more settlers who could supply food and forage. St. Clair strongly advocated a direct route, and in June he ordered the clearing of a road from Lancaster through Carlisle, York, and Fort Frederick, to Fort Cumberland. The British commanders recognized that there was competition between Virginia and Pennsylvania over which province would be the gateway to the Ohio, but they relied on their own military judgment. Moreover, Forbes's chief aim was to separate the Ohio Indians from the French, which required time, so he was not in a great hurry. He was not obliged to explain that to Washington or anybody else, and he expected his orders to be followed.[53]

A way north from Fort Cumberland to Raystown (now Bedford) had been blazed, but it needed to be improved into a wagon road. When Bouquet ordered Washington to march his entire command to Raystown early in July, he objected, proposing to send a road crew ahead and stay at Fort Cumberland with the rest. He also claimed that the Indians refused to follow any route but Braddock's, which was familiar to them. Bouquet revised his orders. Washington should send 200 men to Raystown, and a road-building party should follow them. Lieutenant Colonel Mercer started opening the road northward while Maryland troops finished the one from Fort Frederick. Opening a way to Raystown alarmed Virginians who wanted to follow Braddock's Road.[54]

Forbes had met a delegation of Cherokees at Philadelphia early in June. Then he dispatched a Moravian named Christian Frederick

Post and his Delaware friend Pisquetomen to get the Ohio nations to send representatives to Easton for a conference. They were an odd pair, Post an inexperienced negotiator but a thoroughly honest and friendly man, Pisquetomen famous for his English profanity and his record in war. Behind them loomed Forbes's army, more formidable than Braddock's. The Ohio nations were sick of war, short of food, ravaged by diseases, and no longer abundantly supplied by the French.[55]

With the Delaware leader Teedyuscung and Pennsylvania agents as intermediaries, Forbes pressed ahead with attracting the nations to his support. His cousin, former South Carolina governor James Glen, brought the Cherokees back to the campaign, although Forbes later alienated them and they left again. Events in other theaters strengthened the British cause. The Anglos were repulsed from Fort Carillon (Ticonderoga) with terrible loss on July 8, 1758, but regrouped to advance against Fort Frontenac at the northeast end of Lake Ontario. Louisbourg fell to the Anglos on July 27, and the eastern Delawares declared war on the French.[56]

Forbes's overtures to the Ohio nations required a credible show of force. His advance post at Raystown was impressive, the main work 400 feet square, with earthen walls surrounded by a ditch, bastions on each face, and buildings housing 1,500 men in mid-July and room for 2,500 more. Said an admiring James Glen, "such wonders does the admirable Bouquet work in the wilderness." In contrast, a spy party returned from Fort Duquesne and reported few Indians there, but many Frenchmen digging trenches outside the fort.[57]

The show of strength depended on good roads to move up supplies and artillery. Mercer and his 300 men made slow going out of Fort Cumberland, just six miles in five days, because Washington had ordered a road thirty feet wide. He received permission to scout out Braddock's Road, and he turned that into a reconstruction project as soon as tools were available. Repeatedly he told Bouquet that the old road needed only small repairs that could be made as fast as the army could march. By July 21 Bouquet saw what the Virginians were up to. "I must work with circumspection in order to reply to their clamors," he advised Forbes, because if anything went wrong "they would not hesitate to attribute it to the choice of the road."

The real issue was competition between Virginia and Pennsylvania to become gateway to the west, via either Braddock's Road out of Fort Cumberland or a new one cutting westward across Pennsylvania. Washington had denounced the other colony's ambitions to his friends in Williamsburg and received support in return. He charged ahead repairing Braddock's Road, although Forbes had not yet decided on a route to Fort Duquesne. Washington learned that a light corps would go ahead of the army, and he asked to lead it with the 1st Virginia because his men were "as well acquainted with all the passes and difficulties, as any troops that will be employ'd." Then he reversed himself, asking that Virginia troops at Raystown be sent back to him so he could advance down Braddock's Road.[58]

Bouquet told Washington on July 24 that Forbes had decided to follow a route west from Raystown to the Forks. The Virginian made a show of obedience, saying he would "most chearfully" follow any route the general ordered. However, he had a number of objections to building a new road and nothing but praise for Braddock's. He asked for a meeting to discuss it, as if Forbes had not already made his decision. Bouquet scheduled a meeting for July 29 and told Washington to withdraw his parties from Braddock's Road.[59]

The Virginia colonel meanwhile aired his complaints to his countrymen, including his officers. The response was outrage at the British command. Washington and Byrd both told the lieutenant governor that building a new road would delay reaching Fort Duquesne. Fauquier replied that Forbes should understand that Virginia's investment of men and money had been based on a decisive effort during 1758.[60]

Bouquet complained to Forbes that when he asked Washington how he would overcome the problems that Braddock's route presented, he could not get a straight answer. The Virginians were so set on having their way that they disregarded "all that does not support their ideas, never seeing the difficulties." Washington sent Bouquet a long, tedious letter going into great detail about why Braddock's was better than a new road. His only interest was the success of the campaign, he claimed, so his case for Braddock's Road did not reflect "any private interest or sinister views."[61]

This was disingenuous because as a Virginian he saw his province's interests threatened by a new road out of Pennsylvania. He also misinterpreted Forbes's continued absence from the army, which was owing to sickness and dealing with the Indians. He concluded that Bouquet dominated the general, and he wrote insubordinately to Francis Halkett, Forbes's brigade major. "If Colo. Bouquet succeeds in this point with the General, all is lost!" he wailed. "All is lost by heavens! Our enterprise ruin'd!" he added, hinting that Halkett should intervene. Still refusing to accept the decision as final, Washington went at Bouquet again, predicting disaster if the army followed a new road.[62]

Washington's deceitful letter to Halkett was a big mistake, because as Forbes told Bouquet, it "accidentally fell into my hands." The general was "now at the bottom of their scheme against this new road, a scheme that I think was a shame for any officer to be connected with." Forbes no longer trusted Washington or Byrd. He was especially upset because they had plotted against his decision before he made it. He reported to the commander in chief, Abercromby, that he had told them that "their judging and determining my actions and intentions before I had communicated my opinion to them was so premature" and "so ridiculous" that he "could by no means suffer it."[63]

Ever diplomatic, Bouquet had his staff mollify Washington. Abraham Bosomworth, his Indian liaison, confirmed that all troops would move to Raystown, then make a new road to the Forks. He knew that would not be agreeable to the Virginians, "but we must submit." The route was "superior to Braddock's." Bouquet ordered Washington on August 10 to forward troops over the mountains to the most advanced post at Loyalhanna (later Fort Ligonier). "We find happily less difficulty in opening the road than we imagined," he announced. The choice of roads had not slowed the expedition. Washington snidely told Commissary Walker that the redcoats "flatter themselves with getting a better [road] than Genl. Braddocks; they may do so, and I shall believe it when I am an eye witness to it."[64]

Washington hypocritically congratulated St. Clair "upon the discovery of a *good road* which I hear you have made." He told Bouquet, "I wish with all my soul you may continue to find little difficulty in opening your road." If there were difficulties in road-making, the campaign would accomplish little else. He told friends in Virginia, meanwhile, that the new road was a boon to Pennsylvania at Virginia's expense. In response, they agreed that the new road was too difficult and that disaster loomed.[65]

"I went Saturday to the top of the Allegheny Hill," Bouquet wrote on August 21, "where I had the satisfaction to see a very good road." Loyalhanna was fixed as the advanced post where stores would be stockpiled and scouts would go out. Bouquet summoned almost all

troops not required to guard rear depots, while Virginians continued
to complain about the harm done them by redcoats in league with
Pennsylvanians. "It has long been the luckless fate of Virginia," John
Kirkpatrick agreed with Washington from Alexandria, "to fall a victim
to the views of crafty neighbours." It was a metronome, such sentiments alternating with Bouquet's chipper reports.[66]

The road was open to Loyalhanna by the end of August. Washington chafed at sitting at Fort Cumberland with the 2nd Virginia while
most of his troops had gone ahead. Bouquet ordered him to advance
by Braddock's Road to a post where he could communicate with Loyalhanna. Forbes, meanwhile, had recovered enough to come forward
on a litter and was expected at Raystown any day. Washington was fortunate to take part in the campaign's last stage despite his behavior.[67]

He would never admit that Forbes's methodical advance had been
successful. Fort Frontenac fell to the Anglos on August 17, and Fort
Duquesne was isolated, the French position weakened, thus support-
ing the strategic goal of winning over the Ohio nations. The steady
advance of the army made Christian Post's diplomatic mission easier,
and he returned with a message that the Ohio nations would attend
a peace conference. "After many intrigues," Forbes told Bouquet on
August 18, he hoped he had finally achieved "a general convention of
the Indians." Bosomworth told Washington on the 23rd that a conference was scheduled for Easton in September, "which will make an excellent diversion." Washington never acknowledged this dimension
of the war because he saw Indians as either undependable pawns or
blood enemies.[68]

With the army closing on Loyalhanna and delegations from many
nations headed for Easton, the stage was set for the conquest of Fort
Duquesne. Would Washington admit that?

Nothing but a Miracle Can Procure Success

He would not. Instead, he wrote long, screechy letters to Virginia's
leaders. "That appearance of glory once in view, that hope, that laudable ambition of serving our country and meriting its applause is now
no more!" he roared. He even called Forbes and Bouquet names, "evil
geni" being one. "Can G—l F—s have orders for this? Impossible: Will
then our injur'd country pass by such abuses? I hope not." Virginia

should send a delegation to England to tell the king how "grossly" his honor and public money had been "prostituted." Forbes had summoned Washington and Byrd to meet him at Raystown on September 15. Unless the Virginians could persuade him to switch roads, they avowed, the expedition would bog down. Otherwise, "nothing but a miracle can procure success," Washington predicted.[69]

If Washington hoped to stir up a hornet's nest, he got what he wanted. Fauquier had not called the assembly since his arrival, but he now summoned it for September 12. Speaker Robinson laid Washington's letters before the Burgesses, who "from the long delay . . . and the partiality they imagined shewn to Pensylvania, were not in a very good humor." Expecting no attack on Fort Duquesne that year, they voted to withdraw Virginia's forces to its borders as of December 1, later extended to January 1. Forbes must take the French post soon or without Virginia's help.[70]

Washington obeyed orders, but always with some objection or another. He declared that he was ready to advance, except that he wanted his wagons replaced with packhorses, he needed provision for the sick at Fort Cumberland, and he questioned the wisdom of dividing the army in two. Forbes had his guard up. Bouquet should consult Washington but not follow his advice, "as his behaviour about the roads was no ways like a soldier." Bouquet repeated the order to advance and explained that the army lacked enough gear for packhorses. Morale among Virginians at Raystown collapsed. Christopher Gist complained that his advice carried no weight with those in command there. The situation had become Virginia against all.[71]

It boiled over at Loyalhanna, where Adam Stephen supervised construction. Quartermaster General St. Clair, who had alienated both Forbes and Bouquet with his infamously bad temper, was there in early September. He argued with Stephen, who objected to Virginians' working without help from other provincials, and St. Clair called the Virginians "mutineers." They in turn rallied in defense of their lieutenant colonel when St. Clair placed Stephen under arrest. Stephen's energy had impressed Bouquet and Forbes. The general ordered St. Clair to explain his behavior, and Bouquet released Stephen from arrest. St. Clair was sent to Philadelphia to hire wagons.[72]

Continued delays and Forbes's absence caused their own morale problems. Fort Cumberland repeatedly ran short of provisions and had to be supplied from Raystown. Colonel Byrd was sick and his recovery uncertain. Reports about the road west from Loyalhanna, from British and provincial officers alike, alternated between positive and negative. The Virginians grew ever more sure that the campaign was stalled. Washington reached Raystown on September 12 to meet with Forbes, who rode in on a litter three days later. The first issue was supplies, with the Virginians objecting to theirs coming out of Pennsylvania. The general groused to Bouquet that he did not care where the army's provisions came from, so long as the troops got them.[73]

While Washington awaited his meeting with Forbes, he was diverted by a letter from Sally Fairfax. This was a rare treat, since she had scarcely written since 1755. She offered news from the neighborhood and teased him about getting Mount Vernon ready for his betrothed, Martha. He answered on September 12 with some teasing of his own, and in eighteenth-century style the two of them pretended hidden meanings behind their words. She answered promptly without saying much, and he turned to news from where he was. This exchange had no meaning beyond the flirtation popular among gentry at the time. He was going to marry Martha, and he showed no hesitation or doubt.[74]

Another diversion was provided by Major James Grant of the 77th Highlanders. Small parties of Indians prowled around Loyalhanna, killing and scalping a few deserters. Bouquet skirted the place with patrols, but Grant wanted more. He said that if he could withdraw enough men from road-building and lead them to Fort Duquesne, he would end the nuisance. Forgetting that Forbes wanted to conquer that place without a fight, Bouquet let Grant march out on September 9 with 300 Highlanders, 100 Royal Americans, 175 men of the 1st Virginia, 200 Pennsylvanians and Marylanders, and a few Indians. The corps got to within sight of the French works on the night of the 13th and burned down a nearby log house. The troops hunkered down until daybreak, when Grant sent Virginia major Andrew Lewis and part of his command two miles back to guard the baggage train. Seeing the Anglos divide their force, the French sallied against Lewis's Virginians. British officers later accused Lewis of deserting Grant, but that was not true. An unknown number of men died in the French attack, and at least seven officers, including Grant and Lewis, and thirty-two men were taken prisoner. Virginia captain Thomas Bullitt prevented utter catastrophe with a stubborn rear-guard action. Bouquet declared that the loss would have been greater "had not Captain

Bullet of the Virginians, with 100 men, sustained the combat with all their power."[75]

Washington met with Forbes on the 16th. Byrd had recovered enough to attend, and Stephen came from Loyalhanna to tell them that a road from there to the Forks was impracticable. Washington passed this on to Forbes, who concluded that the Virginians would be happy if their predictions of disaster came true. Forbes told them, he advised Bouquet, "that, whatever they thought," the selection of the road had "proceeded from the best intelligence that could be got" without favoring one province or the other. He added that he had told Washington and Byrd that they were "the only people I had met with who had showed their weakness in their attachment to the province they belong to, by declaring so publicly in favor of one road without their knowing anything of the other." Pennsylvanians had been silent. It was a stinging rebuke; Washington showed contrition, and Forbes integrated him back into the royal command by reassigning him and his men from Braddock's Road to Loyalhanna.[76]

Supply bottlenecks eased in late September, negotiations at Easton dragged on without an end in sight, Cherokees retaliated for murders of their men in southern Virginia, the nights became frosty, and venereal disease spread through Forbes' army. It was time to move on to the Forks, and the general assembled his colonels on October 5. Washington submitted a plan for a line of march through wooded country, a textbook exercise that suggested how he would have conducted Braddock's campaign, but it accorded with Forbes's and Bouquet's tactics. When the army marched out of Loyalhanna, it more or less followed the Virginian's scheme.[77]

The army was scheduled to move out on October 14, but the French struck first. Officers at Loyalhanna heard firing southwest of camp on the 12th and deployed small detachments against what was assumed to be raiders. The Anglos ran into a considerable body of Canadians and Indians, so the commander in Bouquet's absence sent out 500 men who were driven back into the earthworks. The enemy peppered the place with musketry for about two hours but did not attack. The snipers withdrew, returned that night, were driven off, and disappeared. They had killed two officers and killed or captured about sixty others.[78]

The army's vanguard moved out on the 14th, while Washington hurried back to Fort Cumberland to lead the balance of his Virginians to Loyalhanna. He resumed griping that he had been right about the roads all along. It was not likely that things would have gone better on Braddock's Road, however, because incessant rains turned the ground into soup, the horses started failing, and advancing provisions became difficult. "I am in the greatest distress," Forbes wrote Pitt on the 20th. Unless the weather broke, he would be trapped. On the other hand, his engineers had found a passable way around the worst part of Laurel Ridge, the last major barrier to the Forks.[79]

Forbes sent the Moravian envoy Post to Easton to implore Pennsylvania's negotiators to get all sides to drop "foolish trifles" and agree to something with the nations "to strengthen ourselves and diminish our ennemys influence with them." Post got there on the 20th to find more than 500 Indians from thirteen nations in attendance. The Six Nations had each sent representatives, demanding dominance over their former tributary nations in Ohio. The Ohioans wanted their territories guaranteed to them, and Pennsylvania restored lands west of the Alleghenies taken from them earlier. The principle of Iroquois hegemony in Ohio was restored, but not its substance, and a general treaty was concluded on the 26th. Post and others raced to the Ohio to spread the word.[80]

That would take time, and Forbes did not want to fight any nation before it abandoned the French. He must soon choose, he advised Pitt on October 27, to risk everything and march to the Forks, retreat across the mountains if the Virginians left him, or dig in where he was until spring. He resumed his advance on the 30th, dropping Washington's plan of march and sending the Virginian ahead to supervise road-clearing. The colonel complained, as always, to Fauquier about the "indescribably bad" road, which he predicted would end the expedition for the year. This renewed calls in Williamsburg to withdraw Virginia from the campaign, until the governor heard contradictory advice from Byrd. Fauquier called the assembly on November 10 to keep the Virginians in the field. This was the only step he could take, he claimed, to prevent the ruin of the expedition and save Virginia from censure for "being the sole cause of the miscarriage of the whole."[81]

Most of the army was still at Loyalhanna on November 12, when outposts warned that the enemy was approaching in force. Forbes sent Lieutenant Colonel George Mercer with 500 men of the 2nd Virginia to locate the opposition, and in a small skirmish they captured a white man and two Indians seated at a campfire. The shooting was heard at camp, and Forbes let Washington lead another 500 Virginians out to Mercer's relief. The two corps collided in the underbrush after dark. They both fired, and above the screams of the wounded Mercer and Washington heard familiar voices—each other's. This blunder killed one officer and thirteen enlisted men and wounded twenty-six. Washington was so ashamed of what happened that he did not mention the incident for thirty years. The only contemporary report was Forbes's to Commander in Chief Abercromby that "unfortunately our parties fired upon each other in the dark." The only Virginian to leave an original account was Thomas Bullitt, who blamed Washington for the calamity and said he did nothing to stop it. When Washington related his own version in the 1780s, he blamed Mercer and made himself the hero who ran "between two fires, knocking up" muskets with his sword and stopped the shooting. He said he "never was in more imminent danger."[82]

Mercer's white prisoner was a British subject who had served in the French garrison at the Forks. Forbes's officers told him he could be executed for bearing arms against his king or rewarded for a verifiable report on the French situation. He said Fort Duquesne was nearly empty because most French troops had gone north, and the northern Indians had gone home. The two Indian captives supported the story. Forbes, who had been ready to halt the advance, sent 2,500 of his fittest men ahead with the lightest possible baggage to cut a hasty road. This striking force was in three "brigades" under Bouquet, Lieutenant Colonel Archibald Montgomery of the 77th, and Washington, each of whom received the courtesy title of "brigadier."

They set out on the 14th. Washington, still in charge of construction, reached the road crew the next day. For the next week he plodded ahead, complaining of shortages of tools and other supplies, and of course the difficult road. He continued, griping all the way, until November 24, when an Indian reported smoke rising from Fort Duquesne. Another scout confirmed that the garrison had set the place ablaze and left. Washington sent scouts forward and followed in the morning.[83]

He found the outworks wrecked, the rest charcoal. Thirty naked chimneys stood around the site. One magazine had exploded, and another was cleaned out except for some worthless junk. Indians said the French had loaded their guns and baggage on boats and floated downstream toward Illinois. The irony of Fort Duquesne's "conquest" by an army marching on a road that he had predicted would lead to disaster was lost on Washington. Taking the fort was "a matter of great surprise to the whole army," he told Fauquier. Forbes planned to stay a few days, settle affairs with the Indians, then except for a garrison return all troops to their colonies. Washington asked the governor to forward food and clothing to the Virginians on the road to Winchester.[84]

He changed his tune about Forbes in this report, calling him "very assiduous" and a man of "great merit" despite being "infirm and worn down." The general wanted to garrison the Forks with 600 men from the three middle colonies, but supply shortages reduced that to 200. Washington objected to leaving any Virginians until Forbes flatly ordered him to. He begged the governor to send supplies and especially winter clothing, and reinforcements next spring. He also advised negotiating a general peace treaty with the Ohio nations, although Forbes had accomplished just that.[85]

Forbes led a party to Braddock's battlefield, where the skulls of more than 450 men were gathered and buried; scavengers had made off with the rest. He was within weeks of his own death. Bouquet gave the general entire credit for success, owing to his methodical campaign and his refusal to yield to the Virginians on Braddock's Road. Following it "would have been our destruction," by leading to a premature action before the French had lost the support of the Ohio nations.[86]

Washington reached Winchester on December 8, the troops with him hungry, ragged, and ailing, to find no provisions or pay for them. There was not even a surgeon on hand until James Craik arrived on the 20th, having left many sick behind at Raystown and Fort Cumberland. Fort Loudoun lacked medicines or decent hospital facilities.

Washington was back at Mount Vernon by the 20th, claiming ill health. Everyone knew he would quit for good this time, and he made it official at the end of the year. His Virginia Regiment continued to exist until 1762 but mostly on paper.[87]

I DO NOT THINK MYSELF EQUAL TO THE COMMAND

(1759–1799)

Ah, me, the times I've knocked at my sepulchral door, yet never found it open! Why have I so often escaped a sword thrust, why do the storm clouds thicken, yet never overwhelm my unlucky head?

—OVID

On the last day of 1758, twenty-seven officers of the 1st Virginia signed a letter to George Washington and sent Robert Stewart to deliver it in person. It expressed their "great concern, at the disagreeable news" of their colonel's determination to resign. "The happiness we have enjoy'd, and the honour we have acquir'd, together with the mutual regard that has always subsisted between you and your officers, have implanted so sensible an affection in the minds of us all, that we cannot be silent on this critical occasion." From their "earliest infancy" he had taken them in hand, trained them in discipline, showed "steady adherance to impartial justice," rewarded merit, and presented a shining example. "Judge then, how sensible we must be affected with the loss of such an excellent commander, such a sincere friend, and so affable a companion." They marveled how rare it was to find "those amiable qualifications blended together in one man? How great the loss of such a man?"[1]

The colonel answered this "most obliging and affectionate address" on January 10. "That I have for some years," he began, "been able to conduct myself so much to your satisfaction, affords the greatest pleasure I am capable of feeling." Their tribute and his service with them "I must esteem an honor that will constitute the greatest happiness of my life, and afford in my latest hours the most pleasing reflections." He was leaving the corps but promised to support its interests. "I always thought it, as it really was, the greatest honor of my life to command gentlemen, who made me happy in their company & easy by their conduct." Then he showed rare emotion. "But this brings on reflections that fill me with grief & I must strive to forget them; in thanking you, Gentlemen, with uncommon sincerity & true affection for the honor you have done me—for if I have acquired any reputation, it is from you I derive it." He thanked them "for the love and regard you have all along shewn me. It is in this I am rewarded. It is herein I glory."[2]

Everyone Will Applaud Your Prudence

Washington spent his adolescence in military service. In the long history of western civilization there was nothing unusual about that. What was remarkable was that he started out as a colonel in command at the age of twenty-two. He came from a society without a military tradition. He was not trained as a cadet with experienced officers over him to guide and educate, nor were there battle-wise sergeants under him to keep him out of trouble. Utterly unprepared, when he took command he was on his own.

It might be objected that adolescence is a modern concept, born with the invention of the "teenager" in the middle of the twentieth century. That was probably true for the mass of people over the centuries. Yet the word has been in the language since before the fifteenth century, and it has always applied to youngsters of the well-fed classes. Washington had a period of deferred maturity in which to learn and grow and wallow in his own selfhood. Few people at such a young age are fit for independent military commands.

The boy colonel's performance during the French and Indian War reflected his youth and inexperience, and weak guidance from Virginia's government. He eagerly took on the assignment, wrapped up in boyish dreams about glory and honor, but that was to be expected at his age. His failures over five years—and there were many—were owing to the elders who gave him a responsibility he was not prepared to carry. Lieutenant Governor Dinwiddie should have known better, and the absence of anyone else at hand to take on that burden was no excuse.

Virginia was no more ready to conduct military campaigns than its colonel, and no more able to predict the social and economic demands of war. The leaders of this peaceable agricultural colony believed that if they simply sent a small body of untrained men westward, the veteran soldiers of New France would run away. Nor did the province's elders understand that the country really belonged to the Indian nations, and they would not suffer invasion without a fight. Virginia blundered into a war, and Washington and his men—undersupplied, underpaid, understrength—suffered for the ignorance and arrogance of their leaders. The butcher's bill piled up, as Virginia's war became a world war.

Washington's adolescent outlook explained his tendency to shade the truth and pass responsibility for failure on to others. Two cases especially illustrate his youthful insecurity and self-focus. The first was the campaign of 1754, when his inadequate army was out on a limb and could not drive the French from the Forks. An older, wiser man would have called the whole thing off. Washington feared that he would be accused of failure if he gave up, threatening the "honor" that obsessed him. The result was the disaster at Fort Necessity.

The other matter was his relations with Dinwiddie, which went from partnership in 1754 to open hostility by 1757. Washington felt very alone in his command, tormented by his government's inadequate material support. Again he feared taking the blame for failure, and he badgered the governor for instructions, refusing to accept repeated advice to use his own judgment and his civilian superiors would back him up. As his anxieties grew, his letters to the governor became nasty and accusatory—adolescent fury that any parent would recognize. Dinwiddie was old enough to be Washington's grandfather, and so he should have known how to handle an insecure youngster. But his health was failing, and he had his own frustrations with the assembly and the loss of his Ohio Company investments. Speaker John Robinson, in particular, did not help matters by taking Washington's side in an otherwise avoidable conflict. Dinwiddie was not an enemy, but Washington thought he was. The uncertain young colonel needed a Dutch uncle, but with the sickness and death of William Fairfax, no one was around to fill that role.

Washington's experience—what he should have learned—offered a mixed record by the time he left the regiment. He had assumed responsibility but dodged accountability. He learned to deal effectively with his subordinate officers but antagonized his civil and military superiors. He established a commendable record of fairness and justice to officers under him, but he failed to praise those who did well. He imposed brutal, retaliatory discipline to fight drunkenness and desertion, but without success. In recruiting, he discovered more about how and where he could not get good men than how and where he could. He learned a lot about planning and logistics, but he bogged down in details. His army was always short of everything, but that taught him how to make the best of what he had. He emerged from the war with some understanding that waging one requires a sound economy.

One of Washington's most admirable traits was his ability to learn. This became apparent in the larger army of the Revolution. Although he paid little attention to scenes of conflict outside those involving Virginia during the French war, he recognized that Britain's greatest failure was inadequate intelligence. In 1775 he constructed his own intelligence apparatus. As president, he established very respectable foreign intelligence operations. No presidential successor showed his appreciation of the need for both military and foreign intelligence until the twentieth century.[3]

He also transferred his personal experience of the 1750s to the Continental Army of the 1770s, with mixed results. He tried to reinstitute his brutal style of discipline, but neither the troops nor Congress would let him go to the extremes he wanted. It took him time to learn that born "gentlemen" were not automatically officer material, but commoners could be. Some of his worst commanders—Charles Lee, Horatio Gates—were gentlemen with military records, while some of his best officers—like Nathanael Greene and Henry Knox—were not. Remembering the criticism of his frequent absences in the 1750s, during the Revolution he did not leave the army without permission from Congress—he was away from Mount Vernon for six and a half years. On the other hand, he continued his high living and lavish entertaining at public expense.[4]

George Washington as a Young Surveyor, by John Gadsby Chapman, 1841. The artist effectively emphasizes his subject's youthfulness, in the Romantic style of the nineteenth century.

1

2

Lawrence Washington, ca. 1740. George's half-brother, he was also his hero, mentor, and the son-in-law of George's most important patron, William Fairfax. George inherited Mount Vernon from Lawrence.

3

Robert Dinwiddie, ca. 1760–65, copy of the original at the National Portrait Gallery, London. His relationship with Washington while lieutenant governor of Virginia, 1751–58, started as patronage and ended in mutual recrimination.

Washington on His Mission to the Ohio in 1753, engraving after Alonzo Chappell, from John Frederick Schroeder, *Life and Times of Washington* (1857). The figure accompanying Washington is his guide and protector, Christopher Gist. Washington and his party trekked through a frozen wilderness to deliver an ultimatum ordering the French to leave the Ohio Country, claimed by Virginia.

5

Washington Presenting Dinwiddie's Letter to Jacques Legardeur, by Augustus Heaton, ca. 1890. Delivering the letter ordering the French to leave the Ohio was the aim of Washington's wilderness adventure in 1753. It was not the end of his ordeal, because he still had to return to Williamsburg with the French officer's reply.

6

Iroquois (probably Seneca) sachem, ca. 1860, photographer unknown. Tanaghrisson and other sachems may have appeared to Washington much like this, because their descendants held on to their costume traditions into the twentieth century, especially the beaded cap or turban with feathers and horsehair. This man holds a staff of office and wears a beaded baldric over a buckskin jacket.

7

Jumonville Glen, October 2009, looking from the site of the French camp, scene of the massacre of the French prisoners, toward the rock ledge where Washington and his men stood. In 1754 the forest trees were fewer but much larger, the canopy thicker. Small growth would have been cut for firewood and shelter.

8

Modern reconstruction of Fort Necessity, scene of Washington's bloody defeat and humiliating surrender in July 1754, as it appeared in October 2009. Note the commanding heights all around.

9

Facsimile of the Capitulation of Fort Necessity, on display at Fort Necessity National Battlefield, October 2009. By signing this document, Washington confessed unknowingly to the "assassination" of Jumonville. The effects of the rain on legibility are apparent.

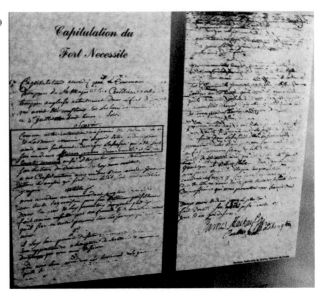

Edward Braddock, medallion on his grave monument. The first British commander in chief in North America led his army to disaster on the Monongahela, July 1755, a calamity often called "Braddock's Defeat." There are no portraits from life. Like all others, this depiction is based on a nineteenth-century engraving that appears to be an alteration of an earlier portrait of Benedict Arnold in his Continental Army uniform.

A surviving stretch of Braddock's Road, the path his army opened from Wills Creek toward Fort Duquesne in 1755, protected by the National Park Service, October 2009. Washington wanted to reopen this route in the campaign against Fort Duquesne in 1758, but his superiors disagreed.

12

British regimental uniforms, documentary prints by David Morier, 1751. These heavy, elaborate outfits were not adapted to campaigning in the American wilderness. The 48th Regiment (right) was one of the two that Braddock took to America.

13

Captain Daniel-Hyacinth-Marie Liénard de Beajeu, engraving, nineteenth century. He commanded the attack on Braddock's corps at the Monongahela, July 1755, but died in the opening exchange of fire.

14

Grenadiers under Fire at the Monongahela, by Howard Pyle, from *Scribner's Magazine* (1893). The compacting of formations, which spelled disaster, is well represented.

15

Battle of the Monongahela, souvenir print, mid or late nineteenth century. This gives a good view of the action from the Indian side, but the costumes resemble those of Plains Indians a century after the battle. The contrast between the close-order formations of the redcoats and the open order of the Indians firing from cover, however, is spot on.

Braddock Wounded, print after P. Philippoteaux, late nineteenth century. The figure on horseback probably represents Washington, who emerged intact from the battle as the "Hero of the Monongahela."

Indian (probably Shawnee) scalping a redcoat, print of an eighteenth-century painting by an unknown artist, possibly a British soldier. The fear of meeting such a fate paralyzed many of Braddock's regulars.

Washington's Plan for Fort Loudoun, 1756, copy of his original in the Library of Congress. It was intended as a supply base and strongpoint against a possible French invasion of the Shenandoah Valley. Construction was started but never finished.

Evacuation of Fort Duquesne, the French strongpoint at the Forks of the Ohio, 1754–58, print after W. P. Snyder, late nineteenth century. The French shipped out their equipment and destroyed the place before Washington reached it, achieving the aim of the Forbes campaign without a battle, despite Washington's prediction that the expedition would end in disaster for the British.

The Marriage of George Washington to Martha Dandridge Custis, the richest widow in Virginia, by Junius Brutus Stearns, 1849, copy of the original at the Virginia Museum of Fine Arts, Richmond.

A Virginia Colonel, by
Charles Willson Peale,
1772. Frequently copied by
Peale and others since, the
original is at Washington and
Lee University, Lexington,
Virginia. Washington loved
uniforms and designed them
throughout his life; this, for
the Virginia Regiment, was
his first.

Mount Vernon, lithograph by F. Collins after C. H. Wells, mid-nineteenth century. Washington's
home from 1754 until his death in 1799, it eventually became possibly the best-known private
residence in North America, and so it remains.

Washington's most significant change from the 1750s was his conviction that the American military was subordinate to the civil power, which in return must deal with the army through its commander and not interfere politically. This was revealed in the "Conway Cabal" of 1777, a failed attempt to politicize the army command; and in the "Newburgh Addresses" of 1783, when some of his officers threatened to march on the capital to force Congress to pay them. Washington advised the Continental Congress, but he never defied it as he had Dinwiddie, and he always accepted its decisions. The subordination of the military to the civil power became a founding principle of the United States.

Washington profited from his adolescent missteps when he stopped another young officer from flying off the handle. Early in 1778, the Board of War sent the twenty-year-old marquis de Lafayette to Albany to command an "incursion" into Canada. The troops, supplies, and money for the campaign were wholly inadequate, and the lakes he must cross were about to thaw. The boy general got it into his head that he was being set up for failure and ridicule, and he exploded in adolescent rage. "The world has theyr eyes fixed upon me!" he wailed, and sent intemperate letters to the president of Congress, Washington, and others, not wanting to take the blame for a debacle.

Washington surely heard an echo of his own self-focus during the Fort Necessity campaign. He wrote Lafayette to "dispel those fears respecting your reputation, which are excited only by an uncommon degree of sensibility." Rather than suffering censure, the young fellow should understand that the mere fact that he had "received so manifest a proof of the good opinion and confidence of Congress as an important detached command" would resound to his favor. Moreover, the general was "persuaded that everyone will applaud your prudence in renouncing a project, in pursuing which you would vainly have attempted physical impossibilities." Washington had matured into a wise counselor as well as an able supreme commander.[5]

He thought he had put war behind him in 1758, because Virginia was safe. Any progress made without his contribution was on account of luck. "The scale of fortune in America," he said of the fall of Quebec in 1759, "is turned greatly in our favor, and success is become the boon companion of our fortunate generals." He already understood another lesson he would transfer from the French war to the Revolution. A commander should focus on strategic goals, because victory or defeat in battle did not always determine strategic success. So he kept the Continental Army, however weak and ill supported, however often defeated, in the field until the other side gave up.[6]

It is not easy to sort through Washington's record in the Revolutionary War to specify just what lessons he applied from his first war, because he continued to learn from his mistakes—and in the later war's first three years he made many of them, which caused him to rethink his earlier experience. At the outset, he retained his low opinion of redcoats as soldiers, at the same time he underestimated the level of training required to forge a modern regular army. Both tendencies drew him into stand-up battles against the British that his troops could not sustain. One defeat followed another through 1776, until he hit on indirect tactics at the end of the year that brought him victories at Trenton and Princeton. But he reverted to attempting to challenge the enemy on equal terms, only to get beaten again at Brandywine and Germantown. As for training, he left that to sergeants until Steuben imposed uniform tactics on Washington's veteran but awkward army, requiring officers to train their own men. The result was an American regular army equal to the British, as demonstrated at Barren Hill and Monmouth in 1778. He and the British mutually avoided further head-on battles, however, until Yorktown in 1781.

More positively, Washington had learned in the 1750s how to sustain an army with inadequate support from an impoverished government, and by 1775 he understood that begging his civilian superiors for supplies was not personally demeaning, just part of the commander's job. He learned by early 1777 that he must appeal to the loyalty of his private soldiers to keep them from deserting or leaving when their enlistments expired. No longer a distant tyrant but still a hard man, the Washington of the 1770s was more popular with his enlisted men than he had been in his first war. That he was always in front of the action did not hurt his reputation, and when musketballs filled the air he continued a charmed life under fire. He had discovered that leadership (a term that did not exist in his day, although its principles did) involved more than giving commands and ordering punishments.

It seems apparent in hindsight that Washington did not take advantage of all the educational opportunities the redcoats had offered him in the 1750s on planning, logistics, and command principles. One point is clear, however. He never acknowledged his insubordination during the Forbes expedition, but it is evident from his behavior in the Revolution that he recognized that a commander must have obedience from those under him or he could not lead his army. He was utterly intolerant of insubordination in his second war, to the extent that he was often too demanding of his juniors. This cost him some of his best officers, Alexander Hamilton's storming off his staff being an outstanding example. And although he continued holding frequent councils of war, his soldierly belief that a commander's decision was absolute and final gave him problems in political life, where nothing was ever final: Witness his difficulties as president with his best cabinet officers, Hamilton and Thomas Jefferson, who definitely had minds of their own.

So the boy colonel of 1759 was not yet fully formed as a military leader, and there were years to come before he was prepared to command the much larger army of the Revolution. Even then he remained a work in progress, learning the hard way until he got it right. He finally knew he had achieved that in 1781, when he watched the British and Hessians march out of Yorktown and ground their arms in the only surrender he ever dictated.

Long before that, in 1759 Washington took up the life he had wanted all along as a Virginia grandee. He and Martha married at White House on January 6. It was a lavish affair, and important people from all over the Tidewater were there. She wore a deep yellow brocade overdress with silver lace at the neck and sleeves, the skirt open in front to show a petticoat of white silk with silver interweavings. She adorned her dark hair with pearls and covered her tiny shoes with purple satin trimmed in silver. He wore his new blue suit.

Martha was a prize catch, but so was George. She had full responsibility for her great estate because her first husband had died intestate, and managing it was an enormous burden. Her bridegroom was a proven manager, ready for the responsibilities he married along with her. They suited each other, affectionately as well as practically. After he died, she burned their personal letters, but all evidence shows that they learned to love each other deeply. That was normal in that day, when love followed rather than preceded most marriages. Theirs lasted forty years.[7]

Washington attended his first session of the Burgesses in February 1759, renting quarters for his new family in Williamsburg. Never an outspoken member, he was the house military expert, and he used his influence to keep the Virginia Regiment in being. Legislation

reauthorized 1,000 men in the regiment, and Lieutenant Governor
Fauquier appointed William Byrd its colonel and Adam Stephen its
lieutenant colonel. The assembly authorized Virginia troops to serve
outside the province, but no farther than the Forks; they were specifi-
cally kept out of any invasion of Canada. Men remained at the Forks
from the previous campaign, and the lawmakers sent more to help
build Fort Pitt, Fort Duquesne's replacement, under the direction of
a royal engineer. Pennsylvania also sent troops to keep Virginia from
gaining a permanent hold on the Ohio, so the old rivalry over the
gateway to the west continued. Building Fort Pitt violated the Treaty
of Easton, which had promised to keep the English out of the lands
of the Indian nations.[8]

Virginians feared a new French invasion of the Ohio, but the
French fell farther back into Canada until Montreal and all of New
France surrendered in September 1760. Things were peaceful on
the colonial frontiers until the Cherokees declared war on the Carolina colonies just as the French left the scene. Washington was more
interested in the possibilities of western real estate. Dinwiddie had
promised land bounties to veterans in 1754, and the former colonel
crusaded to get warrants issued, then bought them from other veterans at a sharp discount. With the Ohio Company all but defunct, he
joined other western land companies and claimed 20,000 acres on
the Great Kanawha River. He explored the possibility of opening the
upper Potomac as a link to the Ohio.

These ambitions were frustrated by events. The Cherokee war became general in 1763, when Commander in Chief Jeffrey Amherst
reduced presents to the Indians in a misguided attempt to cut costs.
Many nations rose up, some in a confederacy led by the Ottawa war
chief Pontiac. All British outposts but Detroit and Fort Pitt fell until
Henry Bouquet rescued the latter in 1764. The king issued a proclamation forbidding English settlement west of the Appalachians,
renewing the promises at Easton. "I can never look upon that proclamation in any other light," Washington declared, "than as a temporary expedient to quiet the minds of the Indians." The proclamation
prevented whites from gaining legal title to western lands.[9]

Washington's occasional travels west took him to the scenes of
his earlier actions. In 1770 he bought Great Meadows from the Pennsylvania government for 30 pistoles (about £25). The purchase was
not nostalgic: He expected the meadow to provide hay for traffic on

Braddock's Road, assuming that his land schemes would draw settlers to his claims on the Great Kanawha and other lands in the Ohio
Country. He tried and failed several times to find a tenant to harvest
the hay. The traffic did not develop, partly because a new route west
opened up to the south at Cumberland Gap, mostly because the Indian nations fiercely defended their homelands.[10]

For What Wise Purposes Does Providence Permit This?

If nostalgia played no part in Washington's purchase of Great Meadows, over the rest of his life his memories from the 1750s grew fonder.
In 1772 he had his portrait painted for the first time, and Charles
Willson Peale executed the work at Mount Vernon. "A Virginia Colonel" shows him in his blue-and-red regimentals, with the background
the woods and mountains of his old campaigns. There is a folded
paper labeled "order of march" in his pocket, along with an officer's
gorget at the throat, a sword at the waist, and a musket slung over
his back. Over the coat is a faded red sash of heavy silk mesh. This
was Braddock's, and it is still at Mount Vernon showing the general's
bloodstains.[11]

Another personal legacy of the campaigns of the 1750s was Washington's lifelong interest in designing uniforms. In November 1774,
with relations between the colonies and Britain tense, he agreed to become the field commander of five Virginia "independent companies
of volunteers." They never assembled, but he designed a blue-and-
buff uniform for himself and had a tailor make one. It became the
standard for officers of the Continental Army. In 1794, as president,
he organized a militia campaign against the so-called Whiskey Rebellion near the old battlefields of western Pennsylvania. He considered
donning his uniform to lead the expedition but stayed in the rear and
let others do that; back pain from a fall contributed to his decision.
Finally, in 1799 Congress appointed him "general of the armies of the
United States" with the rank of lieutenant general and command of
a "provisional army" to defend against a French invasion. He never
took the field, but one of his last deeds was to design and order a
uniform for that position.[12]

On July 20, 1776, with another war underway, Washington wrote
to Adam Stephen, who had been his lieutenant colonel in the 1750s.

Not mentioning the Declaration of Independence or other events swirling around him, he said he did not "let the anniversary of the 3d or 9th of this inst [month] pass off without a grateful remembrance of the escape we had at the Meadows and on the Banks of Monongahela." His nostalgia for his early campaigns continued to grow. In the 1780s his Continental Army aide David Humphreys prepared a biography of his general and sent a draft for Washington's review. That produced his only extended autobiographical writing, probably written near the end of 1787. Except for a few corrections about Mount Vernon, the remarks were all about the war of the 1750s.[13]

War did not make Washington a religious man. He was a Deist, believing that a Supreme Power may have created the universe, but there was no point in trying to get its attention; he quoted Scripture, but he did not pray. He referred increasingly to "Providence" as the years went by, which suggests that emerging intact from hails of lead at Fort Necessity, the Monongahela, Monmouth, and other battles gave him a mystical outlook. Preachers claimed that Providence had saved him for an important purpose, but he never admitted to believing that. Still, he told Stephen in 1776 that he hoped that "the same Provedence that protected us upon those occasions will, I hope, continue his mercies."

Providence was not something to be worshiped or appeased but rather the overriding mystery of the universe, a vague explanation for how chance rules the affairs of men. When Lafayette told him in 1786 about his tour of European battlefields with the aging Frederick the Great of Prussia, Washington said that viewing those scenes could not "have failed to excite this thought, here have fallen thousands of gallant spirits to satisfy the ambition of, or to support their sovereigns perhaps in acts of oppression or injustice! melancholy reflection! For what wise purposes does Providence permit this? Is it as a scourge for mankind, or is it to prevent them from becoming too populous?"[14]

The horrors of battle made him not only philosophical but also a pacifist. Responding to rumors of war in Europe in 1788, he told the comte de Chastellux, an old friend from the Revolution, that it was "more consonant to all the principles of reason and religion (natural and revealed) to replenish the earth with inhabitants rather than to depopulate it by killing those already in existence." It was time, he continued, "for the age of knight-errantry and mad-heroism to be at an end." Recalling his own outlook in 1754, he said, "Your young military men, who want to reap the harvest of laurels, don't care (I suppose) how many seeds of war are sown; but for the sake of humanity it is devoutly to be wished, that the manly employment of agriculture and the humanizing benefits of commerce, would supersede the waste of war and the rage of conquest." He wished fervently that swords could be turned into plowshares, spears into pruning hooks, "and, as the Scripture expresses it, 'the nations learn war no more.' "[15]

That was his desire after two wars. His experience of the first one affected his approach to the second. He wore his uniform to the Continental Congress in 1775, served on the military committee, and let himself be treated as the body's military expert. He even suggested the title of the supreme commander of the Continental forces: commander in chief, a title he had held before acting governors Blair and Fauquier took it back. It was no surprise that Congress unanimously offered him the position on June 16. He had prepared a written statement, which he read to the body.

He thanked the delegates for the "high honor" of his appointment, although he felt "great distress from a consciousness that my abilities and military experience may not be equal to the extensive and important trust." If Congress insisted, he would accept the post and "exert every power I possess" in order to succeed. Thanking the members for "this distinguished testimony of their approbation," he added a caution. "But, lest some unlucky event should happen, unfavourable to my reputation, I beg it may be remembered, by every gentleman in this room, that I, this day, declare with the utmost sincerity, I do not think myself equal to the command I am honoured with."[16]

This expression of modesty thrilled the world. This was no bloody-minded rebel screaming for the heads of his enemies but an honest farmer forced to take up arms to defend his country. As much as the Declaration of Independence a year later, Washington's reluctant acceptance of command ratified the sincere purposes of American resistance to British occupation. He was correct that he was not prepared for this new responsibility, but he learned, often from his own errors. Still, there was an echo of the boy colonel of the 1750s, obsessed with personal honor and trying in advance to avoid blame for whatever might go wrong. He entered this new war, however, as a man, and emerged from it a great man. If the Washington of the 1750s had wanted honor above all, the Washington of two decades later knew that he must earn it. And so he did.

BRADDOCK'S GRAVE

(October 13, 1913)

Sent off to eastern mountains,
To war unending and no return,
I'm finally back home again,
And the rain drizzles on and on.

— *The Book of Songs*

The day was crisp, the leaves beginning their colorful turn on the trees surrounding the opening in the forest of western Pennsylvania. The people who gathered beside the trace of Braddock's Road where it ran through the woods and across the meadow were as somber as a funeral assembly. The women wore fur wraps and laced bonnets, the men dark suits and homburgs. Only the scarlet tunics of the British army officers stood out in the crowd of preachers and citizens and history buffs.

They were there to pay tribute to Edward Braddock, a man not often hailed as an American hero. His remains had been discovered in 1804 by a county crew repairing the road that bore the dead general's name; all that was left were his bones and British military buttons. The bones of his right hand were sent to the Peale Museum in Philadelphia, the rest reburied on a low rise next to the road. Over the years there were markers and fences, but mostly neglect, although the location was never again lost.

Its significance was recognized around the 150th anniversary of the general's death, and a movement arose among patriotic and historical societies in western Pennsylvania to commemorate the departed. Interested parties formed a committee to raise funds for a monument, and the officers of Braddock's regiment, the Coldstream Guards, lent their support. Years of planning and spending had now paid off. After the invocations and speeches and remarks, the tarp covering the monument came off. It was a handsome stone stela, mounted on a stepped pedestal and capped by a peaked crown with a geometric frieze. On one side, beneath a medallion bearing the crest of the Coldstream Guards, was a bronze plaque with this legend:

HERE LIETH THE REMAINS OF MAJOR GENERAL EDWARD BRAD-
DOCK WHO IN COMMAND OF THE 44TH AND 48TH REGIMENTS
OF ENGLISH REGULARS WAS MORTALLY WOUNDED IN AN ENGAGE-
MENT WITH THE FRENCH AND INDIANS UNDER THE COMMAND OF
CAPTAIN M. DE BEAUJEU AT THE BATTLE OF THE MONONGAHELA
WITHIN TEN MILES OF FORT DUQUESNE, NOW PITTSBURG, JULY
9, 1755. HE WAS BORNE BACK WITH THE RETREATING ARMY TO
THE OLD ORCHARD CAMP ABOUT ONE FOURTH OF A MILE WEST OF
THIS PARK WHERE HE DIED JULY 13, 1755. LIEUTENANT COLONEL
GEORGE WASHINGTON READ THE BURIAL SERVICE AT THE GRAVE.

There was polite applause, a few more benedictions and remarks, and the crowd dispersed to its buggies. Braddock's monument stood secure behind a wrought-iron fence, and it is still there. To be sure, there was a grammatical error in the first line ("lieth" should have been "lie"), and no mention that Americans had also taken part in that fight on the Monongahela. The text on the plaque did not admit that the English side lost, other than by implication in "the retreating army." The common name "Braddock's Defeat" was not heard that day, and the plaque did not use the phrase. On the other hand, mentioning Beaujeu (but without saying he also died, on the winning side) was a gracious touch.

Americans have always wanted their history sanitized, battles evoking glory but not blood, defeat unthinkable, so there was nothing untoward in the delicate way Braddock's death was described. The general had long been an American scapegoat. Now, a century and a half after the Treaty of Paris ended that mostly forgotten conflict, Braddock had received the honor that Washington always maintained was his due. He was at long last forgiven. The ceremony granting him a monumental tribute was the last act of the Seven Years War, the French and Indian War, George Washington's first war.

CHRONOLOGY

1697   War of the League of Augsburg (King William's War) ends after eight years

1713   April 11: Treaty of Utrecht ends nine-year War of the Spanish Succession (Queen Anne's War), declares the Iroquois to be the subjects of the British crown

1732   February 22 (February 11, Old Style): Washington born

1734   French establish fort at Crown Point on Lake Champlain

1741   March–April: British defeat at Cartagena, Lawrence Washington's military adventure

1743   January: Lawrence Washington returns home
        April 12: Washington's father dies; Washington inherits land and slaves

1744   Treaty of Lancaster and Iroquois land cessions

1745   Fairfax land claims acknowledged by Virginia Council

1748   Washington becomes public surveyor
        October 18: Treaty of Aix-la-Chapelle ends four-year War of the Austrian Succession (King George's War); French-English boundaries in North America to be fixed later by a joint boundary commission meeting in Paris

1749   March 15: Ohio Company formed
        Summer: Céleron's expedition into Ohio Valley
        July 20: Washington appointed surveyor of Culpeper County

1750   August 31: North American boundary commission first meets in Paris

1751   Washington accompanies brother Lawrence to West Indies, contracts smallpox

1752   June 21: French and Indian allies attack British-allied Indians at Pickawillany
        July 1: Duquesne arrives as governor of New France

July 26: Lawrence Washington dies; Washington executor of estate and residuary heir to Mount Vernon, which becomes his in 1761

November: Washington joins the Freemasons

1753   February: Washington begins lobbying to gain appointment as adjutant of Virginia militia; receives commission in November

Spring: Marin moves into Ohio Valley with large French force, begins building line of forts from Lake Erie toward the Forks of the Ohio

Fall: Washington carries Dinwiddie's ultimatum to the French forts

December 11: Washington arrives at Fort Le Boeuf, delivers ultimatum; leaves December 14

1754   February: Washington reaches Williamsburg and delivers report; is rewarded with appointment as lieutenant colonel of Virginia militia

April: Washington leads small force into territory claimed by the French near the Ohio

April 16: French begin building Fort Duquesne at Forks of the Ohio

May 28: Jumonville massacre, Washington sends prisoners to Williamsburg

June: Coulon de Villiers goes looking for Washington with strong force of French and Indians, aiming to avenge his brother Jumonville's death

June 28: Learning of French force coming at him, Washington orders retreat to Great Meadows, completes defensive works, Fort Necessity

July 3: Coulon de Villiers attacks Fort Necessity; Washington surrenders that night

July 4: Capitulation completed, Washington retreats toward Virginia; French and Indian War begins

July 11: Albany Congress adjourns, having failed to develop common defense against French

September 15: Braddock appointed commander in chief of English forces in America

October 23: Washington resigns commission in dispute with Dinwiddie

1755   February 20: Braddock arrives in Virginia, begins organizing expedition to Fort Duquesne

March 2: Washington offered volunteer position as aide to Braddock, honorary rank of colonel

June: Vaudreuil arrives as governor of New France

June 6: Braddock expedition begins its slow march westward, building Braddock's Road

June 9: English fleet intercepts and captures French ships

July 9: Battle of the Monongahela (Braddock's Defeat)

July 13: Braddock dies, is buried in Braddock's Road

August 14: Washington appointed colonel and commander in chief of Virginia forces

September 8: Battles at Lake George

1756   January 9: Virginia Regiment declared activated
        March–April: Washington goes to Boston to meet Shirley
        May 12: Montcalm arrives at Quebec
        May 18: Great Britain declares war on France; Seven Years War begins
        June 9: France declares war on Great Britain; war soon spreads around
        the oceans, in India, and in America
        July 23: Lord Loudoun arrives at New York as new commander in
        chief
        August 14: British forts at Oswego surrender to French
        August 29: War spreads to mainland Europe when Prussia invades
        Saxony
        November: William Pitt enters the British government
1757   March 17: French attack on Fort William Henry defeated
        April 6: Pitt leaves government
        June 29: Pitt returns in Pitt-Newcastle ministry
        August 5: Loudoun abandons Louisbourg campaign
        August 9: Fort William Henry surrenders to French under Montcalm
        December 1: James Abercromby replaces Loudoun as commander in
        chief in America
1758   Forbes-Bouquet expedition against Fort Duquesne; Washington be-
        gins major construction on house at Mount Vernon
        April: Amherst replaces Abercromby as commander in chief of British
        forces in North America
        June 1: Forbes meets with Cherokees at Philadelphia
        July 8: British repulsed at Fort Carillon (Ticonderoga)
        July 24: Washington elected to House of Burgesses from Frederick
        County
        July 27: French surrender Louisbourg to British under Amherst
        August 27: Bradstreet takes Fort Frontenac
        September 14: French and Indians maul James Grant's corps near
        Fort Duquesne
        October 12: Lignery attacks Forbes's units at Loyalhanna
        October 26: Treaty of Easton concluded
        November 12: Virginians under Washington and Mercer mistakenly
        fire on each other
        November 25: Forbes-Bouquet expedition occupies Fort Duquesne,
        abandoned and wrecked by French the previous day
        December: Virginia regiments return to Winchester, disintegrating
        from cold, hunger, disease, and lack of money
        December 31: Washington's resignation takes effect
1759   January 6: Washington marries Martha Dandridge Custis
        February: Washington takes seat in House of Burgesses for first time
        June 26: Wolfe lands troops near Quebec, begins siege
        July 25: British capture Fort Niagara
        July 26: French abandon Ticonderoga

September 13: Battle on the Plains of Abraham; Montcalm and Wolfe both mortally wounded

September 17–18: French surrender Quebec, British take possession

1760   February 16: Cherokees attack Fort Prince George

April 28: Battle of Sainte-Foy (Sillery Woods, Second Battle of Quebec); French try but fail to retake Quebec

May 15: British fleet arrives and secures Quebec

August 7: Cherokees attack Fort Loudoun (South Carolina), which surrenders next day

September 8: Montreal and all of New France surrender to Amherst

September 16: Sir William Johnson makes peace with the Iroquois at Montreal

October 25: King George II of Great Britain dies, is succeeded by George III

1761   August 15: French and Spanish kings sign the Bourbon Family compact; Spain enters war as French ally in November

September 23: Cherokee-Carolina war ends with peace treaty

October 4: William Pitt resigns; resignation accepted next day

1762   Conference of delegates from Britain, the colonies, and the Delawares and Iroquois at Easton, Pennsylvania, ending much of the war between whites and Indians

All year: French and Spanish lose many possessions in West Indies

June 24: St. John's, Newfoundland, taken by French, retaken by British September 18; last major French-British action on North American mainland

1763   February 10: Treaty of Paris ends Seven Years War, French lose all claims in North America, Spain gains Louisiana and the Floridas, Britain gains Canada; French and Spanish possessions in West Indies restored

May 7: Pontiac's War breaks out with attack on British fort at Detroit, followed by capture of several military posts; war continues into 1764 until final defeat of Indians

October 7: George III issues Proclamation of 1763

November 17: Thomas Gage succeeds Amherst as commander in chief in North America; retains post until driven out of Boston by Washington in 1776

1766   Pontiac and William Johnson meet at Oswego, formally ending the war

1769   April 20: Pontiac assassinated at Cahokia

December: Washington buys 235 acres including Great Meadows and site of Fort Necessity

1770   With relations between Britain and her colonists deteriorating over the previous decade, Washington joins radicals in Virginia House of Burgesses adopting a nonimportation agreement

1772   Washington poses at Mount Vernon for his first portrait, by C. W. Peale

1774   Fall–winter: Washington accepts command of proposed independent companies of several Virginia counties, designs the blue-and-buff uniform

1775   June 15: Congress elects Washington commander in chief of Continental forces resisting British; commissioned June 17

1781   October 19: Washington accepts surrender of Cornwallis at Yorktown, Virginia

1783   December 23: Washington resigns as commander in chief, returns to Mount Vernon

1784   Washington embarks on an extensive exploration westward that lays the foundation for the Potowmack Company, his scheme to restore Virginia as a gateway to the west; sends crews of slaves to begin dredging for a canal on the upper Potomac

1787   Summer: Washington presides over Constitutional Convention, Philadelphia

1789   April 30: Washington sworn in for first of two terms as president of the United States

1794   Fall: Whiskey Rebellion, western Pennsylvania

1797   March 4: Washington retires from the presidency

1799   Washington appointed commander of provisional army; designs a uniform

        December 14: Washington dies at Mount Vernon

1804   Workmen on Braddock's Road discover the general's remains, rebury them with a marker beside the road

1913   October 13: Braddock's grave monument dedicated

NOTES

Complete data on works cited in the chapter Notes are presented in the Bibliography. Names of months are given standard three-letter abbreviations in the Notes.

ABBREVIATIONS USED IN NOTES

adc	aide-de-camp
AS	Adam Stephen
d.	penny/pence
EB	Edward Braddock
FGW	Fitzpatrick, *Writings of George Washington*
Freeman	Freeman, *George Washington* (7 volumes)
GO	General Order(s)
GW	George Washington
GWD	Jackson and Twohig, *Diaries of George Washington*
GWP	George Washington Papers at the Library of Congress
	L (with number): Letterbook
	S (with number): Series
JAW	John Augustine Washington
JR	John Robinson
MBW	Mary Ball Washington
n.	note
nd	no date given
np	no place given
npub	no publisher given
RD	Robert Dinwiddie
s.	shilling

SGW   Sparks, *Writings of George Washington*
WF   William Fairfax

PROLOGUE

1.   This account of the Pickawillany attack follows Longueuil to Minister of Marine, APR 18, Duquesne to Minister, OCT 25, 1752, and the Journal of William Trent, who visited the scene a few days after the fight, in Parkman, *Montcalm*, 49–50; Gipson, *Zones*, 186–224; White, *Middle Ground*, 229–31; and Anderson, *Crucible*, 28–30. Both original and secondary sources conflict on some details. The origins and significance of the event are discussed below.

CHAPTER ONE

1.   The chief history of the Cartagena campaign is Harding, *Amphibious Warfare*, Wentworth quoted 70. Summaries are in Freeman, 1:65–70, and Lengel, *General George Washington*, 3–6, Lawrence Washington to Augustine Washington, MAY 30, 1741, quoted 6. "Old Grog" acquired his nickname when he regularized the grog (daily rum) ration in the Royal Navy, a custom that endured until near the end of the twentieth century. Clary, *Adopted Son*, 459 n.4.

2.   Biographies of GW are beyond counting. The most comprehensive are the seven volumes of Freeman and the four of Flexner. Recent entries into the field include Ellis, *His Excellency*, Burns and Dunn, *George Washington*, and Ferling, *Ascent*. A nice summary of his early years is Langguth, *Patriots*, 290–95. GW's birthday was FEB 11 until 1752, when Britain adopted the modern calendar.

3.   Gus's friend and GW both quoted Wiencek, *Imperfect God*, 31.

4.   Flexner, *GW Forge*, 11–14; ibid., 31.

5.   Freeman 1:57–58, 76–78; Flexner, *GW Forge*, 13.

6.   Freeman 1:70–72.

7.   Ibid., 1:73–75. Augustine's will and others surviving of the Washington family from 1697 on, including GW's half brother Lawrence's (1752), are in GWP S4.

8.   Flexner, *GW Forge*, 19–20; Clary, *Adopted Son*, 32; cousin quoted Wiencek, *Imperfect God*, 32. Flexner effectively demolishes the tendency of GW's earlier biographers to portray Mary as the saintly mother of the plaster idol they offered as their version of GW. As his fame increased, so did her jealousy, and her claims of neglect inspired a bill in the Virginia legislature to support her, although GW had amply provided for her. As Flexner observes, "[H]istory does not always draw noble men from

noble mothers, preferring sometimes to temper her future heroes in the furnaces of domestic infelicity."

9. Freeman, 1:102–07.

10. Ibid., 1:76–78.

11. The sketches of the Fairfaxes follow Rasmussen and Tilton, *George Washington*, 20–28, and the editorial notes in GWD 1:1–4. See also Flexner, *GW Forge*, 26–33, and Fleming, *Intimate*, 6–7.

12. Quoted Flexner, *GW Forge*, 26, and Clary, *Adopted Son*, 34.

13. Clary, *Adopted Son*, 34.

14. On GW's reading during this period, see Brookhiser, *Founding Father*, 122–25; Ferling, *Ascent*, 1–12; Wiencek, *Imperfect God*, 35–37; Clary, *Adopted Son*, 33; Longmore, *Invention*, 8–9; Wall, "George Washington"; Spaulding, "Military Studies."

15. GW's holograph "Rules of Civility" is in GWP S1. Virtually every biographer has played up this influence on his life. See for instance Flexner, *GW Forge*, 21–23; Clary, *Adopted Son*, 33; and Wiencek, *Imperfect God*, 35–37. See also Moore, *George Washington's Rules*.

16. "Forms of Writing," GWP S1. See also Wiencek, *Imperfect God*, 29–30, one of the few biographies to have recognized this exercise.

17. I follow Longmore, *Invention*, 2–6, for this review of the Virginia aristocracy.

18. Clary, *Adopted Son*, 33; horse story quoted Wiencek, *Imperfect God*, 32–33. My reference to Alexander is to Plutarch's tale of how he tamed Bucephalus.

19. Freeman, 1:229.

20. Jennings, *Ambiguous Empire*, 355–60; Merrell, *Into Woods*, 219, 230–82; Freeman, 1:186–89, 447–513.

21. McCleskey, "Rich Land"; Dorothy Twohig, "The Making of George Washington," in Hofstra, *George Washington and Backcountry*, 6–8.

22. Freeman, 1:197–98; GWD 1:4–5. The technical aspects of surveying are beyond the reach of this study. For more detail, see Philander D. Chase, "A Stake in the West: George Washington as Backcountry Surveyor and Landholder," in Hofstra, *George Washington and Backcountry*, 162–63, and more generally on techniques, Danson, *Drawing the Line*, especially 67–99.

23. Freeman, 1:202–23; Clary, *Adopted Son*, 35; GWD 1:4–5; Chase, "Stake in the West," preceding note. GW's "Journal of My Journey over the Mountains" is in GWD 1:6–23, and all GW quotations relating to this trip are from that source.

24. Freeman, 1:232–34, 237–39, 242–44; Ferling, *Ascent*, 14. Some of GW's surveying and military drawings survive in GWP.

25. Petition of John Hanbury, JAN 11, 1749, in Mulkearn, *George Mercer Papers*, 246–48; Minutes of Privy Council, MAR 16, 1749, quoted GWD 1:121; Bailey, *Ohio Company*. The original members of the company

were John, Capel, and Osgood Hanbury, Quaker merchants of London; and Thomas Cresap, William Thornton, John Carlyle, National Chapman, Richard Lee, Thomas Lee, George William Fairfax, and Lawrence and Augustine Washington. Eminent figures who joined later included Robert Dinwiddie, Robert Carter, George Mason, and Philip Ludwell Lee, listed in GWD 1:120 n.4.

26. Lee quoted Freeman, 1:236–37; Flexner, *GW Forge*, 47–48.
27. Freeman, 1:170–72.
28. Biographies include Alden, *Robert Dinwiddie*, and Koentz, *Robert Dinwiddie*. See also GWD 1:118 n. 2, and Freeman 1:170–72.
29. Greene, "Case of the Pistole Fee." This is summarized also in Freeman 1:171. A pistole was originally a Spanish 2-*escudo* gold piece, but by the eighteenth century the term referred in English to any of a number of small gold coins of several European nations, with about the same low value.
30. Freeman, 1:237–39.
31. Freeman 1:23–31, who idealizes GW, concludes that he was smitten but that it went no further than that. Flexner, *GW Forge*, 39–41, inclined to be more objective and critical, believes that there was love between the two, but the relationship was "no more than playful," at least at first. My own judgment on this is supported by the latest inquiry, Fleming, *Intimate*, 6–15. See also Fleming, "George Washington in Love." On GW and Peggy Arnold, see Clary, *Adopted Son*, 278–81.
32. Freeman, 1:231, 241–43, 247–58, 146–66; Flexner, *GW Forge*, 46–47, 50–51; Ford, *Writings* 14:423–27. Lawrence's will is in GWP S4.
33. Roberts, *George Washington Master Mason*; Ridley, *Freemasons*, 94; Brockett, *Lodge of Washington*.
34. GWD 1:118 n.2; Freeman, 1:266–70; Spaulding, "Military Studies."
35. Gipson, *Zones*, 222–24 (quotation); Freeman, 1:272–73, referring to the Council minutes of OCT 27, 1753.
36. Mercer to a friend, nd 1760, quoted Wiencek, *Imperfect God*, 65–66.

CHAPTER TWO

1. Quoted Freeman, 1:280.
2. The standard description of North American plant communities is Barbour and Billings, *North American Terrestrial Vegetation*. Peyton quoted Strach, "Preliminary Documentary Review," no page number. Gist's journals are reproduced in Gist, *Christopher Gist's Journals*, and in Darlington, *Christopher Gist's Journals*. His explorations are described below.
3. The pioneering study of Indian use of fire to manage landscapes was Stewart's *Forgotten Fires* in the 1950s, since updated. Other useful works include Vale, *Fire, Native Peoples, and the Natural Landscape*; Krech, *Ecological Indian*; Harkin, *Native Americans and the Environment*;

Silver, *New Face*; Arno and Allison, *Flames in Our Forest*; and Pyne, *Fire in America*.

4. Hodge, *Handbook*; King, *Thunderbird and Lightning*; Johnson and Hook, *Encyclopedia*.
5. Calloway, *Shawnees*, 7–8.
6. Grenier, *First Way*, 21–26.
7. On the origins of French-Indian relations, see Fischer, *Champlain's Dream*.
8. Richter, *Ordeal*, 30–38; Eid, "National War"; Parker, *Military Revolution*, 118; Morgan, *Boone*, 237–41. Daniel Boone was captured and adopted as an adult by a Shawnee band. On the English trade in Indian slaves during the colonial period, see Manegold, *Ten Hill Farm*.
9. Gallay, *Indian Slave Trade*; Dowd, *War Under Heaven*; and Grenier, *First Way*, 11–12.
10. Gipson, *Zones*, 153–85; White, *Middle Ground*, 1–49; McConnell, *Country Between*, 1–24.
11. Richter, *Ordeal*, 134–42.
12. McConnell, *Country Between*, 20–24; Anderson and Cayton, *Dominion*, 118–19.
13. Lancaster conference and treaty in Franklin, *Indian Treaties*, 41–79; Mulkearn, *George Mercer Papers*, 400–03; Quebec meetings in Kent, *French Invasion*, 1–24.
14. Johnson to Clinton, APR 28, 1749, quoted Parkman, *Montcalm*, 37–38.
15. Thomas Pownall to Earl of Halifax, JUL 23, 1754, in McAnear, "Personal Accounts," 742; Merrell, *Into American Woods*, 57–58.
16. RD to Hamilton, MAY 21, and Hamilton to RD, MAY nd, 1753, both quoted Parkman, *Montcalm*, 24.
17. White, *Middle Ground*, 122; Anderson and Cayton, *Dominion*, 119–20. Biographies of Croghan include Volwiler, *George Croghan*, and Wainwright, *George Croghan*.
18. Mulkearn, *George Mercer Papers*, 172–73; Gist, *Christopher Gist's Journals*, 32–79.
19. This account of Gist's adventures follows Parkman, *Montcalm*, 31–33.
20. Ibid., 21–30, 44–45; Freeman, 1:270–72.
21. Parkman, *Montcalm*, 45–46; Freeman, 1:270–72.
22. Comte de Raymond to Jonquière, SEP 4, 1749, Ward, *Breaking Backcountry*, 23–24.
23. Ministry to Jonquière, MAY 1749, and Orders of the King and Ministers to Jonquière, APR 15 and nd, 1750, all quoted Parkman, *Montcalm*, 46.
24. Clinton, Jonquière, and Johnson quoted ibid., 46–47.
25. Orders of the King, nd, 1750 and JUN 6, 1751, and Jonquière to Minister, OCT 19, 1751, quoted ibid., 47.
26. Jonquière, Raymond, and Minister quoted ibid., 47–49.
27. Dinwiddie to Lords of Trade, OCT 6, 1752, quoted ibid., 35.
28. Bailey, *Ohio Company*, 132–38; "Treaty of Loggs' Town"; minutes of

councils with Indians in Mulkearn, *George Mercer Papers*, 273–84; Anderson, *Crucible*, 26–28.

29. Longueuil to Minister, APR 21, 1752, quoted Parkman, *Montcalm*, 48–49.

30. White, *Middle Ground*, 218–26; Anderson, *Crucible*, 28–31.

31, Parkman, *Montcalm*, 50; Dahlinger, "Marquis Duquesne."

32. Quoted Anderson, *Crucible*, 31–32.

33. Duquesne to Minister, OCT 25, 1752, quoted Parkman, *Montcalm*, 50; Tasse, "Memoir."

34. Orders of the King and Ministers, nd, 1753, and Duquesne to Minister, SEP 29, 1754, quoted Parkman, *Montcalm*, 51.

35. Kent, *French Invasion*, 24–26.

36. These summaries follow Leckie, *Wars*, 1:39–40, and Parkman, *Montcalm*, 5–20.

37. Weigley, *History*, 3–12; Hill, *Minute Man*, ch. 1; Boorstin, *Colonial Experience*, passim; Boucher, "Colonial Militia"; Ekirch, "Idea"; Ferling, "Soldiers for Virginia."

38. Chartrand, *French Soldier*, 5–36; Kennett, *French Armies.*

Chapter Three

1. This discussion follows Robinson, *American Forts*, 10–31; Chartrand, *Forts of New France*; Kent, *French Invasion*; Anderson and Cayton, *Dominion*, 120–22. For a history of European fortifications in general, with an excellent account of Vauban's contributions, see Hughes, *Military Architecture.*

2. Clary, *Fortress America*, 2–3; Robinson, *American Forts*, 35–39. On fort construction and vermin, see Clary, *These Relics*, passim, and especially ch. 19.

3. Jennings and others, *History Iroquois Diplomacy*, 250–51; Anderson, *Crucible*, 11–32; Richter, *Ordeal*, 1–50; Daniel K. Richter, "Ordeals of the Longhouse: The Five Nations in Early American History," in Richter and Merrell, *Beyond Covenant*, 11–27; Wallace, *Death and Rebirth*, 21–107; Richter, *Looking East*, 167–69; Crane, *Southern Frontier*, 158–61. The Great League of Peace and Power, the Five Nations, had been around for 300 years and became the Six Nations in the 1720s, after the Tuscaroras were driven out of North Carolina by English colonists, migrated north, and joined the others.

4. Duquesne to Minister, OCT 27, and William Johnson to George Clinton, APR 20, 1753, both quoted Parkman, *Montcalm*, 51–52.

5. Lieutenant Holland to George Clinton, MAY 15, Duquesne to Minister, NOV 2, 1753, and an officer's reports of sexual influence in the command, ibid., 51–52, 76.

6. Dinwiddie to Glen, MAY nd, 1753, quoted GWD 1:125.

7. Dinwiddie to Hamilton, MAY 22, 1753, quoted ibid., 1:126.
8. Chartrand, *Forts of New France*, 44–45; Parkman, *Montcalm*, 75–76.
9. Bonin, *Memoir*, 53.
10. Chartrand, *Forts of New France*, 45.
11. Ibid., 45–47; Anderson, *Crucible*, 32. The comte de Machault was minister of the marine.
12. Anderson, *Crucible*, 32; Duquesne to Marin, AUG 27, 1753, quoted Parkman, *Montcalm*, 76.
13. Parkman, *Montcalm*, 76–77, Duquesne to Minister, OCT 31, 1753, quoted 76.
14. "*Conseil tenu par des Tsonnontouans venus de la Belle-Riviére*," "*Parole des Chaouanons*," both SEP 3, 1753, and Marin to Joncaire, nd, 1753, in Grenier, *Papiers Contrecoeur*, 53–62, 588–59; Duquesne to Minister, OCT 31, 1753, quoted Parkman, *Montcalm* 76. The French commonly called the Ohio "Belle Rivière" (Beautiful River).
15. Weigley, *History*, 5–12; Morton, "Origins of American Military Policy."
16. Flexner, *GW Forge*, 52–53; Spaulding, "Military Studies"; Nelson to GW, FEB 22, 1753, GWP S4; GWD 1:118–19.
17. Richter, *Looking East*, 155, 164 (Wraxall quotation).
18. Browning, *Duke of Newcastle*, 82–88; Clayton, "Duke of Newcastle"; Anderson, *Crucible*, 33–35.
19. Instructions to governors and cabinet minutes, AUG 21, 1751, quoted Clayton, "Duke of Newcastle," 584.
20. William Trent to RD, AUG 11, and RD to Board of Trade, JUN 16, 1753, quoted GWD 1:123, 126.
21. Anderson, *Crucible*, 38–40.
22. Holderness to the governors, AUG 28, 1753, quoted Clayton, "Duke of Newcastle," 584; Holderness to RD, AUG 28, 1753, quoted Bailey, *Ohio Company*, 202–03, 486n.
23. Koontz, *Robert Dinwiddie*, 201–35; Alden, *Robert Dinwiddie*, 26–37; RD to Holderness, NOV 17, 1753, quoted GWD 1:126.
24. Quoted Clary, *Adopted Son*, 37.
25. Freeman, 1:274–76; Journal of the Council, OCT 27, 1753, quoted GWD 1:127.
26. Freeman, 1:274–76; Anderson, *Crucible*, 41; GW to JR, MAY 30, 1757, quoted GWD 1:130 n.23.
27. Freeman, 1:280; GW in Anderson, *George Washington Remembers*, 16–17.
28. RD to GW, OCT 30, 1753, GWD 1:127–28.
29. RD, GW's passport, OCT 30, 1753, ibid., 1:129.
30. RD to French Commander, OCT 30, 1753, ibid., 1:127 n.17, and in Stevens and Kent, *Wilderness Chronicles*, 76–77.
31. On van Braam, see Koontz, *Robert Dinwiddie*, 243 n.29, and Eccles, *Canadian Frontier*, 205 n.15. GW's journal is GWD 1:118–61. Gist's is in Darlington, *Christopher Gist's Journals*, 80–87. Quotations and details are from those sources unless otherwise indicated.

32. The case involved trader John Trotter and his employee James McLaughlin, captured AUG 15, 1753. GWD 1:138 n.41.

33. The English had called the French "frog-eaters" and "frogs" (from their alleged dietary preferences), and the French had called the English "*rosbifs*" (from their habit of eating meat roasted instead of boiled) and "*les goddams*" (for their commonest word, at least as the French heard it), since the Hundred Years' War. During World War I American troops became known in France as "*les sombiches*," for their favorite word. Clary, *Adopted Son*, 459 n.11.

34. Besides GWD, see Peyser, *Jacques Legardeur*, 201–04, on his view of GW.

35. The translator, whom GW called "Monsier Reparti," was Louis le Gardeur de Repentigny. He had been at Fort Le Boeuf when Marin died and commanded there until relieved by Legardeur, when he took command at Presque Isle. Grenier, *Papiers Contrecoeur*, 74n; GWD 1:148 n.54.

36. Legardeur to Dinwiddie, DEC 15, 1753, Kent, *French Invasion*, 75–76. There is a more literal, hence awkward, translation in Peyser, *Jacques Legardeur*, 205–06.

37. Grenier, *Papiers Contrecoeur*, 98–99; Bonin, *Memoir*, 84–85.

38. Brock, *Official Records*, 1:73–74; GWD 1:160 n.68.

39. GW, *Journal of Major George Washington*. See also GWD 1:160–61, n.68.

40. Burgesses quoted GWD 1:161 n.68; Freeman, 1:327–28.

CHAPTER FOUR

1. Grotius, "Right of Embassy," *Law of War and Peace* 2:XVIII. The modern Law of War, which draws on Grotius, began with conventions at Paris in 1856, and later at other places, and now is codified in the United Nations Charter, the record of the Nuremburg and Tokyo war-crimes trials, and subsequent conventions and treaties. See also Winthrop, *Military Law* 2:773–900.

2. Freeman, 1:328–29; Brock, *Official Records*, 1:61–71, 73–79.

3. RD to Trent, JAN 26, 1754, Brock, *Official Records*, 1:55–57; Gipson, *Zones*, 299–302; GWD 1:162 n.2

4. RD to WF, JAN nd, 1754, quoted Freeman, 1:329.

5. Ibid., 1:329; RD to GW, JAN 21, 1754, quoted GWD 1:162–63, editorial note.

6. Freeman, 1:330–32; Brock, *Official Records*, 1:59, 82.

7. Greene, "Case of the Pistole Fee"; the act is in Hening, *Statutes at Large* 6:418; Freeman, 1:332–33; Gipson, *Zones*, 299–302.

8. GW to Lord Loudoun, JAN 20, 1757, quoted GWD 1:163 n.6; RD to John Hanbury, MAR 12, 1754, quoted Parkman, *Montcalm*, 82. GW's long letter to Loudoun is discussed below.

9. Gipson, *Zones*, 302–04; Anderson, *Crucible*, 46–47.

10. RD to James De Lancy, MAR 1, 1754, Brock, *Official Records* 1:83–85; RD to Sharpe, MAR 1, 1754, quoted Freeman, 1:339.

11. RD to Hanbury, MAR 12 and MAY 10, 1754, quoted Parkman, *Montcalm*, 82; Freeman, 1:338.

12. GW to Corbin, quoted GWD 1:164; the letter is in FGW 1:34–35.

13. RD to Sharpe, MAR 1, 1754, quoted Freeman, 1:339; Flexner, *GW Forge*, 81; quotations in Freeman, 1:334–35, 340–41.

14. GW to RD, MAR 9, 1754, quoted GWD 1:174 n.19.

15. Freeman, 1:336–37, 343–45; Glen to RD, JUN 1, 1754, quoted GWD 1:181 n.34.

16. RD to GW, MAR 15, 1754, quoted GWD 1:166, editorial note.

17. Freeman, 1:341–42; GWD 1:174; Alberts, *Charming Field*, 3.

18. GWD 1:174–75. The Swede was Carolus Gustavus de Spiltdorf, commissioned an ensign July 1754 and killed in action July 1755. Biographical summaries in GWD 1:174 n.20, 175 n.22, 23.

19. GWD 1:176, n.25; Freeman, 1:345–46. AS was one of GW's division commanders during the Revolution. Drunk at the Battle of Germantown, he ordered his division to fire on Anthony Wayne's brigade; he was cashiered in November 1777. Ward, *Major General Adam Stephen.*

20. Freeman, 1:346–47. GW did not record this in GWD, and the only evidence is in his account books, showing the reward paid to the informant. Whipping was the usual punishment for every sort of misdemeanor, and GW soon made a regular practice of it.

21. Kent, *Contrecoeur's Copy*, 12. This does not appear in the printed version of GWD.

22. GWD 1:177–78; Freeman, 1:349–50.

23. Contrecoeur's account is in Grenier, *Papiers Contrecoeur*, 117–19, Ward's in Gist, *Christopher Gist's Journals*, 275–78, quotation at 278. "Jolicoeur" offered his own account in Bonin, *Memoir*, 90–91. See also Gipson, *Zones*, 307–10 and n.113; Jennings, *Empire of Fortune*, 64–65; and Anderson, *Crucible*, 48–49.

24. Robinson, *American Forts*, 31–33; Gipson, *Zones*, 307–10.

25. GWD 1:177–78.

26. Ibid., 1:183.

27. Ibid., 178–80, 182–83, including GW to RD, APR 25, and to Horatio Sharpe, APR 27, 1754.

28. GW to RD, APR 25 and May 18, 1754, in ibid., 1:182 and n.35; Brock, *Official Records*, 1:155–56.

29. Kent, *Contrecoeur's Copy*, 18–20.

30. Quoted GWD 1:180 n.32.

31. Kent, *Contrecoeur's Copy*, 18–20; GWD 1:187–88; Croghan to James Hamilton, MAY 14, 1754, quoted Wainwright, *George Croghan*, 61.

32. GWD 1:185; Freeman, 1:366–67.

33. GWD 1:187. Innes, a Scot and an old friend of RD, had considerable regular-army campaign experience and was commander of all North Carolina

forces. After Joshua Fry's death (below), RD appointed Innes to overall command of the combined colonial forces in the Ohio campaign; he never got there. He died in 1759. Brock, *Official Records*, 1:194–95.

34. GWD 1:188; RD to GW, MAY 4, 1754, in Brock, *Official Records*, 1:148–49. RD also said Trent would be tried for leaving his post at the Forks.

35. Harden, "James Mackay," presents this dispute from the regulars' side. GW's position is discussed below. Mackay and his men did not catch up with GW until June, when the issue of relative rank arose at once.

36. GW to RD, MAY 18, 1754, quoted GWD 1:189 n.44; Freeman, 1:360–62. The original petition is lost, but RD refuted it point by point in his reply MAY 25, 1754.

37. RD to GW, MAY 25, 1754, quoted ibid. See also Gipson, *Years of Defeat*, 22–30; Jennings, *Empire of Fortune*, 65–70; and Anderson, *Crucible*, 50.

38. GWD 1:189–90.

39. GWD 1:189–91; GW to Fry, MAY 23, 1754, FGW 1:52–53.

40. Contrecoeur to Duquesne, JUN 2, 1754, in *Memorial Containing a Summary View*, 67–68; Grenier, *Papiers Contrecoeur*, 130–31, 204 n.3. The cadets were identified only as Boucherville and Dusablé.

41. GWD 1:192.

42. GWD 1:192, GW to RD quoted n.52. National Park Service studies of Great Meadows and its ecology include Harrington, *New Light*, Strach, "Preliminary Documentary Review," and Thomas and DeLaura, *Fort Necessity Historic Resource Study*. The first two are available on-line at nps. gov. After reaching Great Meadows, GW heard from William Fairfax who, with RD and other members of the Council, was at Winchester hoping to meet with the chiefs of several nations, to keep them on the English side, or at least neutral. He asked GW to send the Half-King, and he forwarded the request. The group waited sixteen days, but no chiefs showed up. GWD 1:193; RD to Sir Thomas Robins, JUN 18, 1754, Brock, *Official Records*, 1:201–05.

43. Anderson, *George Washington Remembers*, 17; GWD 1:192–93, GW to RD, MAY 27, 1754, quoted n.55

44. Lewis, *For King and Country*, 68–70; Anderson, *Crucible*, 52–53, 754 n.4; GWD 1:193–95, GW to RD, MAY 27, 1754, n.56.

45. GWD 1:194–95.

46. AS's version of the events, which claimed falsely that the Virginians won the ensuing action with a bayonet charge, was published in at least three colonial newspapers in July, August, and September 1754, aiming to refute charges that what happened had been a massacre of the French party. It is reproduced or quoted in, among other sources, Hall, *Gen. Braddock's Defeat*, 18–19; Freeman, 1:372–74; and Anderson, *Crucible*, 754–55 n.6. It is generally contrary to the facts.

47. GWD 1:195.

48. Thirty years later GW described that day very tersely. Before Mackay reached him, he said, "the French sent a detachment to reconnoitre

our camp to obtain intelligence of our strength & position; notice of which being given by the scouts. G. W. marched at the head of a party, attacked, killed 9 or 10; & captured 20 odd." Anderson, *George Washington Remembers*, 17.

49.   Contrecoeur to Duquesne, JUN 2, 1754, *Memorial Containing a Summary View*, 69; the French original and other documents are printed in Grenier, *Papiers Contrecoeur*. See also Robitaille, *Washington et Jumonville*, and Faÿ, *George Washington*, 73–75. Monceau's veracity is supported by the fact that GW's Indian allies had seen him after he got away. One of them came into Great Meadows from the Forks on JUN 5 and reported having "met a *Frenchman* who had made his escape in the time of M. *de Jumonville's* action, he was without either shoes or stockings, and scarce able to walk; however we let him pass, not knowing we had fallen upon them." GWD 1:199

50.   "Affidavit of John Shaw," AUG 21, 1754, in McDowell, *Colonial Records*, 4–5.

51.   "Journal de Joseph-Gaspard Caussegros de Léry," 372–73. Slightly different English translations of this are in Stevens and Kent, *Journal of Chaussegros de Léry*, 27–28, and Anderson, *Crucible*, 57–58.

52.   Contrecoeur to Duquesne, JUN 2, 1754, *Memorial Containing a Summary View*, 69.

53.   Anderson, *Crucible*, 56–57, and McConnell, *Country Between*, 110, advance similar cases, although they disagree on just how desperate Tanaghrisson was to regain his status.

54.   GWD 1:197–99.

55.   GW to RD, MAY 29, 1754, in ibid., 1:195 n.59.

56.   Grotius, *Law of War and Peace*, 1:III.

57.   GWD 1:198–99.

58.   RD quoted Flexner, *GW Forge*, 91; GW to JAW, MAY 31, 1754, FGW 1:70; king quoted Walpole, *Memoirs*, 1:400. Walpole from then on ridiculed GW, calling him a *fanfaron* (braggart), and saying that he soon "learned to blush for his rodomontade." Walpole to Sir Horace Mann, OCT 6,1754, quoted Longmore, *Invention*.

59.   GWD 1:165 n.8, 199; GW to Fry, MAY 29, 1754, quoted Freeman, 1:379; Brock, *Official Records*, 1:88–90.

60.   Bonin, *Memoir*, 97.

CHAPTER FIVE

1.   Grotius, *Law of War and Peace*, 3:VII, XIV; Savory, "Convention of Écluse"; Steele, "Hostage-Taking 1754"; Steele, "When Worlds Collide."

2.   Minister to Duquesne, MAR 3, 1754, quoted Freeman 1:414n.

3.   Bonin, *Memoir*, 98.

4.   Coulon's journal, quoted Parkman, *Montcalm*, 89–90.

5. Ibid., 90.
6. Bonin, *Memoir*, 98–99.
7. Ibid.; Parkman, *Montcalm*, 90–91.
8. Carter to GW, JUN 5, and Campbell to GW, JUN 28, 1754, GWP S4.
9. GWD 1:199; GW to RD, JUN 3, 1754, GWP S2 L1; Tanaghrisson quoted Jennings, *Empire of Fortune*, 67. On Fort Necessity, see Alberts, *Charming Field*, 21, and Harrington, *New Light*.
10. Carlyle to GW, JUN 17 and 28, and RD to GW, JUN 27, 1754, GWP S4, are typical of these exchanges. See also GWD 1:199, and Freeman 1:380–81, 387.
11. Sarah F. Carlyle to GW, JUN 17, 1754, GWP S4.
12. GWD 1:200; RD to GW, JUN 4, 1754, Brock, *Official Records*, 1:193–94, confirming Fry's death; Anderson, *Crucible*, 60.
13. GWD 1:200; RD to GW, JUN 1, 2, and 4, 1754, GWP S4; Freeman 1:381–84.
14. GWD 1:200–01.
15. Ibid., 201 and n.68. The deserters' letter has disappeared; Duquesne's to Contrecoeur, SEP 8, 1754, is in Grenier, *Papiers Contrecoeur*, 249–53.
16. Freeman, 1:38–90; Flexner, *GW Forge*, 95.
17. Freeman, 1:419; John Carlyle to GW, JUN 17, 1754, GWP S4.
18. GWD 1:201–02; Freeman, 1:390–93; Wainwright, *George Croghan*, 62–63; Anderson, *Crucible*, 60–61; Gipson, *Years of Defeat*, 32–33.
19. RD to GW, JUN 25 and 27, 1754, GWP S4, repeating several earlier letters.
20. All quotations from the Council of JUN 18–21 are from GWD 1:202–09, unless otherwise indicated. GW did not understand the subtleties of Indian diplomacy, but he kept a faithful record.
21. Duquesne to Contrecoeur, SEP 8, 1754, Grenier, *Papiers Contrecoeur*, 249–53.
22. Quoted Flexner, *GW Forge*, 100–01.
23. Tanaghrisson's people returned to Fort Duquesne and made peace with the French after his death. His successor as Half-King, the Oneida Scarouady, had been at Jumonville Glen and so stayed a refugee in Pennsylvania until 1756. Duequesne to Minister of Marine, NOV 3, 1754, in Stevens and Kent, *Wilderness Chronicles*, 84; McConnell, *Country Between*, 110–11; Jennings, *Iroquois Diplomacy*, 250–52.
24. Freeman 1:394–96; GWD 1:209–10; RD to GW, JUN 25, 1754, GWP S4.
25. Minutes of Council of War, JUN 28,1754, GWP S4.
26. Freeman 1:396–99, AS quoted 400; Anderson, *Crucible*, 62; Clary, *Adopted Son*, 40–41; Bonin, *Memoir*, 99–100.
27. Gipson, *Years of Defeat*, 35; Freeman 1:403.
28. Bonin, *Memoir*, 100.
29. "Journal of M. de Villiers," Grenier, *Papiers Contrecoeur*, 196–202; Freeman 1:403–04; Bonin, *Memoir*, 100–01.
30. Bonin, *Memoir*, 100–01; Freeman 1:409.

31. Anderson, *George Washington Remembers*, 17; Freeman 1:404–05; Clary, *Adopted Son*, 40–41.

32. AS in *Maryland Gazette*, AUG 29, 1754, quoted Gipson, *Years of Defeat*, 39; Ward, *Major General Adam Stephen*, 10–11; Freeman 1:413; Alberts, *Charming Field*, 31–32; "Journal of M. de Villiers."

33. "Journal of M. de Villiers."

34. Ibid.; Freeman 1:406–08.

35. The capitulation is copied in many sources, including Alberts, *Charming Field*, 61–62.

36. AS in *Maryland Gazette*, AUG 29, 1754, quoted ibid, 35.

37. "Journal of M. de Villiers."

38. GW to Jared Sparks, nd, Sparks, *Writings*, 2:463–65, copied in GWD 1:169–71; Freeman 1:413, 546–49.

39. Anderson, *George Washington Remembers*, 17–18; English casualties counted in Gipson, *Years of Defeat*, 41 n.60; French losses in Varin to Bigot, JUL 24, 1754, in Stevens and Kent, *Wilderness Chronicles*, 81.

40. "Journal of M. de Villiers"; Callender quoted Gipson, *Years of Defeat*, 41.

41. Freeman 1:409–11.

42. Bonin, *Memoir*, 103–04.

43. Ibid., 102–03; Eccles, *Canadian Frontier*, 164–67; Anderson, *Crucible*, 65; Stanley, *New France*, 57.

44. Duquesne to Contrecoeur, SEP 8, 1754, Grenier, *Papiers Contrecoeur*, 249–53.

45. GW to WF, AUG 11, 1754, GWP S2 L1; Leach, *Arms for Empire*, 342; Titus, *Old Dominion*, 55–57; RD to Lords of Trade, JUL 24, 1754, cited Freeman 1:412; Anderson, *George Washington Remembers*, 18; WF to GW, JUL 10, 1754, GWP S4.

46. Mackay quoted Alberts, *Charming Field*, 43–44; WF to GW, JUL 5 and 10, and Innes to GW, JUL 5, 1754, GWP S4.

47. Quoted Flexner, *GW Forge*, 110.

48. Quoted Freeman 1:423.

49. Council Minutes, JUL 18,1754, quoted ibid., 1:424; JR to GW, SEP 15, 1754, GWP S4.

50. Flexner, *GW Forge*, 106–07; Huske, Sharpe, Penn, and Calvert quoted Longmore, *Invention*, 23–24; Mackay to GW, SEP 28, and Sharpe to GW, OCT 1, 1754, GWP S4. The publication history of GW's journal is explained in detail in GWD 1:165–74.

51. Parkman, *Montcalm*, 101–03; Anderson, *Crucible*, 77–85; McAnear, "Personal Accounts."

52. Johnson to Goldsbrow Banyar, JUL 29, 1754, quoted Freeman 1:415.

53. Albemarle to Newcastle, SEP 11, 1754, quoted ibid., 1:423–24.

54. RD to various recipients, JUL 1754, quoted Parkman, *Montcalm*, 103–04.

55. RD to John and Capel Hanbury, JUL 23, to Albemarle, to Lords of Trade, to Lord Granville, to James Ambercromby, and to the Hanburys,

all JUL 24, and to Horatio Sharpe, JUL 31, 1754, all quoted Freeman 1:416–22.

56. RD to Innes, JUL 20, 1754, quoted ibid., 1:422; Innes to GW, SEP 27, 1754, GWP S4.

57. Freeman 1:424–25.

58. RD to GW, AUG 1, 1754, GWP S4.

59. RD to GW, AUG 3, 1754, GWP S4.

60. Freeman 1:425–28; Innes to GW, AUG 11, 1754, GWP S4.

61. GW to WF, AUG 11, 1754, GWP S2 L1.

62. Stobo to English Commander at Wills Creek, JUL 28 and 29, 1754, quoted Freeman 1:425n.

63. Mackay to GW, AUG 27, 1754, GWP S4.

64. Freeman 1:430–35; Savory, "Convention of Écluse"; WF to GW, SEP 5, 1754, GWP S4; GW to RD, SEP nd, 1754, GWP S2 L1.

65. Innes to GW, SEP 8, and RD to GW, SEP 11, 1754, GWP S4.

66. Innes to GW, SEP 27, 1754, GWP S4; Robinson, *American Forts*, 35–39.

67. Newcastle to Lord Albemarle, SEP 5, 1754, quoted Anderson, *Crucible*, 67.

68. Innes to GW, SEP 27, 1754, GWP S4; Freeman 1:436–37.

69. GW to Speaker of the House of Burgesses, OCT 23, 1754, GWP S2 L1; Freeman 1:436–37.

70. Freeman 1:440–41; RD to Halifax, OCT 25, 1754, in n.75 to GW to William Fitzhugh, NOV 15, 1754, GWP S2 L1.

71. Anderson, *Washington Remembers*, 18; Fitzhugh to GW, NOV 4, 1754, GWP S4.

72. George II of England, Orders on Rank of Officers, NOV 12, 1754, GWP S4.

73. GW to Fitzhugh, NOV 15, 1754, GWP S2 L1.

74. Indenture between George Washington and George Lee and his wife, DEC 17, 1754, photostat at Mount Vernon, in Flexner, *GW Forge*, 114; Freeman 2:1–5.

CHAPTER SIX

1. Beverage, *Cups*, 3–8, 67–72; Clary, *Adopted Son*, 479 n.50.

2. Parkman, *Montcalm*, 107–08; Freeman 2:6.

3. Freeman 2:6–9.

4. RD to Lords of Trade, NOV 16, 1754, and *Maryland Gazette,* JAN 2 and 9, 1755, printing dispatches from London OCT 8 and 12, 1754, all in ibid., 2:9–10.

5. Hildeburn, "Sir John St. Clair."

6. RD to Arthur Dobbs, FEB 28, 1755, quoted Parkman, *Montcalm*, 110.

7. Anderson, *Crucible*, 86; Parkman, *Montcalm*, 110–12. Biographies include McCardell, *Ill-Starred General*, and Sargent, *History of Expedition*.

8. Walpole quoted Parkman, *Montcalm*, 112; Franklin quoted Clary, *Adopted Son*, 43.

9. Quoted Parkman, *Montcalm*, 112.

10. EB, GO, FEB 26 and 28, 1755, GWP S2 L1.

11. Brumwell, *Redcoats*, 93–95; Freeman 2:12–14; Weigley, *History*, 20–21.

12. Weigley, *History*, 16–18.

13. Anderson, *Crucible*, 86–87; Rogers, *Empire and Liberty*, 76–80.

14. Anderson, *Crucible*, 88–90; Parkman, *Montcalm*, 114.

15. Orme to GW, MAR 2, 1755, GWP S4. The etymology of "family" as the retinue of a general officer is traced in Clary, *Adopted Son*, 466 n.27.

16. GW to Orme, MAR 15, 1755, GWP S2 L1.

17. GW to Orme, APR 2, 1755, GWP S2 L1; Flexner, *GW Forge*, 116–17.

18. GW to Bird, Burwell, and Robinson, all APR 20, 1755, GWP S2 L1.

19. GW to WF, APR 23, and to Sarah Cary Fairfax, APR 30, 1755, GWP S2 L1.

20. EB, GO, MAR 28, 1755, GWP S2 L1.

21. EB, GO, APR 7, 8, and 9, 1755, GWP S2 L1.

22. Quoted Brumwell, *Redcoats*, 69; see also 100–01. Flogging was abolished in 1881.

23. Ibid., 57–58, 63–67.

24. Weigley, *History*, 19–20.

25. Houlding, *Fit for Service*, 48–51.

26. Kopperman, "Cheapest Pay"; officer and orderly book quoted Brumwell, *Redcoats*, 105.

27. Kopperman, "British Command and Wives"; Brumwell, *Redcoats*, 122–23.

28. EB quoted Parkman, *Montcalm*,118; Freeman 2:19–21; Franklin, *Autobiography*, 148–52; Isaacson, *Benjamin Franklin*, 166–67; EB to Robert Napier, APR 19, 1755, quoted Freeman 2:26.

29. Halkett's orderly book and John Knox, both quoted Brumwell, 145–47.

30. All quoted ibid., 141, 150.

31. EB, GO, APR 21, 1755, GWP S2 L1; Anderson, *George Washington Remembers*, 18–19. See also Parkman, *Montcalm*, 110–112; Freeman 2:26; Clary, *Adopted Son*, 43–44.

32. Isaacson, *Benjamin Franklin*, 167.

33. GW to WF, MAY 5, 1755, GWP S2 L1.

34. GW to Thomas Fairfax, MAY 6, 1755, GWP S2 L1.

35. EB, GO, MAY 10, GW to MBW and to JAW, both MAY 6, to Sarah Fairfax Carlyle and to Sarah Cary Fairfax, both MAY 14, 1755, all GWP S2 L1.

36. GW to JAW, MAY 14, 1755, GWP S2 L1.

37. Quoted Freeman 2:92n.

38. Anonymous letter, JUL 25, 1755, quoted ibid., 2:37.

39. Ibid; Anderson, *George Washington Remembers*, 48–51.

40. Shirley to Robert Hunter Morris, MAY 23, 1755, quoted Parkman,

Montcalm, 110–11. Shirley was the son of the governor of Massachusetts.

41. EB, GO, May 11, 16, 21, and 23, 1755, GWP S2 L1; Freeman 2:38.
42. EB, GO, May 18, 1755, GWP S2 L1; Anderson, *Crucible*, 95–96, including Shingas' account; sachem's complaint quoted Parkman, *Montcalm*, 119.
43. EB, GO, MAY 12, 1755, GWP S2 L1; EB to GW, MAY 15, 1755, GWP S4; Freeman 2:38–39.
44. GW, Memorandum, MAY 15, and to John Hunter, MAY 16, 1755, GWP S2 L1.
45. GW to Orme, MAY 22 and 23, 1755, GWP S2 L1; Freeman 2:41–42.
46. EB to Robert Hunter Morris, MAY 24, 1755, quoted Freeman 2:44–45.
47. EB, GO, MAY 14, 18, 21, 25, and 26, 1755, GWP S2 L1.
48. GW to JAW, MAY 28, 1755, GWP S2 L1.
49. GW to WF, JUN 7, 1755, GWP S2 L1.
50. GW to JAW and to John Carlyle, both MAY 14, 1755, GWP S2 L1; diagram of march in GWP S4; "Journal of Captain Robert Cholmley's Batman," in Hamilton, *Braddock's Defeat*, 15–16.
51. EB, GO, May 27 and 28, 1755, GWP S2 L1.
52. Quoted Freeman 2:44.
53. GW to John Carlyle, JUN 7, 1755, GWP S2 L1; Orme quoted Freeman 2:47; EB quoted Ellis, *His Excellency*, 20. See also Nichols, "Organization of Braddock's Army," and Russell, "Redcoats."
54. John Rutherford to Richard Peters, received AUG 13, 1755, quoted Anderson, *Crucible*, 96; EB, GO, JUN 6–8, 1755, GWP S2 L1.
55. EB, GO, JUN 11, and GW to JAW, to John Carlyle, to George William Fairfax, to MBW, to Sarah Fairfax Carlyle, and to Sarah Cary Fairfax, all JUN 7, 1755, GWP S2 L1.
56. EB to Robert Napier, JUN 8 (quotation), and to Sir Thomas Robinson, JUN 15, 1755, quoted Freeman 2:48–50. EB's criticism of Virginia and Virginians caused enormous resentment. WF to GW, JUN 28, 1755, GWP S4.
57. Orme to GW, NOV 10, 1755, quoted Freeman 2:49; EB, GO, JUN 10–14, GWP S2 L1.
58. GW, Memorandum, May [June] 30, 1755, GWP S2 L1
59. GW to JAW, JUN 14 and 28, and EB, GO, JUN 17, 1755, GWP S2 L1.
60. Account of "British B," in Kopperman, *Braddock*, 167.
61. Ibid.; Freeman 2:53–54; GW to JAW, JUN 28, 1755, GWP S2 L1.
62. Roger Morris to GW, JUN 19, 1755, GWP S4; GW to JAW, JUN 28, 1755, GWP S2 L1. GW's white servant John Alton came down with the same affliction, and GW hired a nurse to tend to him.
63. GW to JAW, JUN 28, and to Orme, JUN 30, 1755, GWP S2 L1; Freeman 2:55–58.
64. Freeman 2:59.
65. GW to JAW, JUN 28, postscript JUL 2, 1755, GWP S2 L1; St. Clair to

Robert Napier, JUL 22, 1755, in Kopperman, *Braddock*, 223; Freeman 2:60–63. On the flankers, see Russell, "Redcoats."

CHAPTER SEVEN

1. Keegan and Holmes, *Soldiers*, 66.
2. Bland, *Treatise; The Manual Exercise* (quoted).
3. Contrecoeur to Vaudreuil, JUL 14, 1755, Kopperman, *Braddock*, 249, see also 19–30; Gipson, *Years of Defeat*, 90–92; Anderson, *Crucible*, 97–99.
4. Contrecoeur to Vaudreuil, JUL 14, Dumas to Minister of Marine, JUL 24, 1756, and statement of "French C," Kopperman, *Braddock*, 249–50, 251, 257. On the two leading captains, see Shea, "Beaujeu," MacLeod, "Beaujeu," and Audet, *Jean Daniel Dumas*. Dumas' letter was an attempt to make himself the hero of the action, because he had been seriously criticized in the year since.
5. Kopperman, *Braddock*, 19–30, account of the meeting with the Indians at 255–56; Gipson, *Years of Defeat*, 90–92; Anderson, *Crucible*, 97–99.
6. Freeman 2:54, 62–63; GW, note added in 1785 to 1755 letterbook, GWP S2 L1; Kopperman, *Braddock*, 31–49 (order of march); Anderson, *Crucible*, 97. Scarouady's son had been shot to death on JUL 6 by a soldier who mistook him for an enemy, and the Half-King "was hardly able to support his loss," according to one of the officers. "Journal of a British Officer," JUL 6, 1755, Hamilton, *Braddock's Defeat*, 48.
7. Cholmley's Batman, Robert Orme's journal, JUL 9, and St. Clair to Robert Napier, JUL 22, 1755, Kopperman, *Braddock*, 181, 213, 224; Freeman 2:65–67.
8. "British A," and Cholmley's Batman, Kopperman, *Braddock*, 163, 181–82; provincial officer quoted Freeman 2:64.
9. François Pouchot, Charles Swain to Richard Peters (Croghan's report), AUG 5, 1755, and Godefroy (300 Indians), Kopperman, *Braddock*, 184, 259, 262.
10. Journal of M. Roucher, JUL 9, 1755, and "British A," ibid., 164, 268; Freeman 2:68–69.
11. François Pouchot, Dumas to Minister of Marine, JUL 24, 1756, "French A," confirming Dumas' account of the first Indian reaction, and "British A," Kopperman, *Braddock*, 164, 251, 253–54, 263; Eid, "A Kind of Running Fight."
12. Duncan Cameron, Dunbar to unknown, JUL 20, 1755, and "British A," Kopperman, *Braddock*, 164, 178, 187.
13. Journal of M. Roucher, JUL 9, 1755, Dumas to Minister of Marine, JUL 24, 1756, and Cholmley's batman, ibid., 182, 251–52, 268.
14. "French B," and Dunbar to unknown, JUL 20, 1755, ibid., 187, 256.
15. Anderson, *Crucible*, 99–100; "British A" and British D," ibid., 164, 176.
16. Lieutenant William Dunbar to unknown, JUL 20, Commissary James

Furnis to Board of Ordnance, JUL 23, Gage to Lord Albemarle, JUL 24, Chaplain Philip Hughes to unknown, JUL 23, and Orme's journal, JUL 9, 1755, Kopperman, *Braddock,* 187–92, 203, 214.

17. Matthew Leslie to a respectable merchant of Philadelphia, JUL 30, 1755, ibid., 204–05.

18. AS to John Hunter, JUL 18, 1755, ibid., 226; "Journal of a British Officer," Hamilton, *Braddock's Defeat,* 50.

19. Cholmley's batman, Kopperman, *Braddock,,* 183.

20. "British A," ibid., 165; Morgan, *Boone,* 43–45. Contrecoeur later reported twenty women captives brought to Fort Duquesne. Anderson, *Crucible,* 760n.

21. Cholmley's batman, and letter from a British officer in the *Whitehall Evening Post,* OCT 9–11, 1755, Kopperman, *Braddock,* 55, 182; Anderson, *George Washington Remembers,* 19–20.

22. Cholmley's batman, "British A," "British B," and Stewart to a friend, JUL 19, 1755, Kopperman, *Braddock,* 165, 171, 182, 229; Orme to Robert Hunter Morris, JUL 18, 1755, quoted Longmore, *Invention,* 29; GW quoted Flexner, *GW Forge,* 129.

23. Harry Gordon to unknown (last order), JUL 23, 1755, and "British A" (turned right about), Kopperman, *Braddock,* 165, 197–201; Anderson, *George Washington Remembers,* 20.

24. GW to RD, JUL 18, 1755, GWP S2 L1; Robert Orme's journal, JUL 9, and Charles Swaine to Richard Peters (repeating Croghan), AUG 5, 1755, Kopperman, *Braddock,* 185, 215.

25. Journal of M. Roucher, JUL 9, 1755, Kopperman, *Braddock,* 268–69.

26. Anderson, *George Washington Remembers,* 21.

27. Orme to Augustine Keppel, JUL 18, 1755, quoted Freeman 2:102.

28. "British B" and Cholmley's batman, Kopperman, *Braddock,* 171, 183.

29. Ibid., 178–79.

30. "British A," ibid., 165.

31. Orme's journal, JUL 9, 1755, ibid., 215–16; Anderson, *George Washington Remembers,* 20. Croghan claimed that Braddock was suicidal and tried to grab his pistols but failed. Nobody else remembered that. Charles Swaine to Richard Peters, AUG 5, 1755, ibid., 185.

32. Dunbar to unkown, JUL 20, 1755, Kopperman, *Braddock,* 188; Richter, "War and Culture"; Anderson, *Crucible,* 103–04.

33. Cameron, Dumas to Minister of Marine, JUL 24, 1756, and François Pouchot, Kopperman, *Braddock,* 179, 252, 263–64.

34. Contrecoeur to Vaudreuil, JUL 14, 1755, ibid., 250; Anderson, *George Washington Remembers,* 21.

35. Journal of M. Rouchet, JUL 9–11, 1755, Kopperman, *Braddock,* 269–71.

36. Smith quoted Freeman, 2:78; Journal of M. Rouchet, JUL 10, and Contrecoeur to Vaudreuil, JUL 14, 1755, ibid., 250, 270.

37. Anderson, *George Washington Remembers,* 20–21.

38. Commissary James Furnis to Board of Ordnance, JUL 23, 1755, Kop-

perman, *Braddock*, 190; Freeman 2:80–81; "Review of the Military Operations in North America," attached as note to GW to RD, JUL 18, 1755, GWP S2 L1.

39.   Isaacson, *Benjamin Franklin*, 168.

40.   James Innes to all to whom it may concern, JUL 11, 1755, GWP S4.

41.   EB quoted Freeman 2:81–83; Anderson, *George Washington Remembers*, 55. The pistols and sash remain at Mount Vernon.

42.   Freeman 2:83; Anderson, *George Washington Remembers*, 21.

43.   GW to James Innes, JUL 15, 1755, GWP S2 L1.

44.   GW to RD, JUL 18, 1755, GWP S2 L1; Freeman 2:86.

45.   All quoted Brumwell, *Redcoats*, 101.

46.   Freeman 2:86–87.

47.   GW to MBW, JUL 18, 1755, GWP S2 L1.

48.   GW to RD, JUL 18, 1755, GWP S2 L1.

49.   GW to JAW, JUL 18, 1755, GWP S2 L1.

50.   Clary, *Adopted Son*, 459 n.20.

51.   François Pouchot, and Gates to Robert Monckton, SEP 5, 1755, Kopperman, *Braddock,*, 195–96, 264; AS quoted Freeman 2:91n; GW to Orme, JUL 28, 1755, GWP S2 L1.

52.   Dunbar and Gage, "Inquiry as to the Behaviour of the Troops at Monongahela, NOV 21, 1755, quoted Freeman 2:92; *Review of the Military Operations in North America*, quoted FGW n.41 to GW to RD, JUL 18, 1755, GWP S2 L1. Examples of the defense of EB are Orme to GW, AUG 25 and NOV 10, 1755, and MAR 2, 1756, and Joseph Ball to GW, SEP 5, 1755, GWP S4.

53.   Gage to Lord Albemarle, JUL 24, 1755, Kopperman, *Braddock*, 193–94.

54.   *Gentleman's Magazine* quoted FGW n.41 to GW to RD, JUL 18, 1755, GWP S2 L1; newspaper quoted Ellis, *His Excellency*, 23; Flexner, *GW Forge*, 134; Davies quoted Jared Sparks in n.45 to GW to JAW, JUL 18, 1755, GWP S2 L1.

55.   WF to GW, and postscript signed by Sally Fairfax, Ann Spearing, and Elizabeth Dent, JUL 26, 1755, GWP S4.

56.   RD to Halifax, JUL 23, 1755, quoted FGW n.41 to GW to RD, JUL 18, 1755, GWP S2 L1; RD to Dunbar, JUL 26, and to Shirley, JUL 29, 1755, quoted Freeman 2:104, 104n.

57.   Sharpe to RD, AUG 2, 1755, quoted Freeman 2:105.

58.   Quoted ibid., 2:105–06.

59.   GW to Militia Officers, and to Collin Campbell, AUG 2, 1755, GWP S2 L1; Anderson, *George Washington Remembers*, 21; RD to Henry Fox, AUG 20, 1755, quoted Freeman 2:110.

60.   GW to Augustine Washington, AUG 2, 1755, GWP S2 L1.

61.   Calloway, *Shawnees*, 27–28; Steele, "Shawnee Origins"; Merrell, *Into American Woods*, 227–30; and for the full story, Ward, *Breaking Backcountry*.

CHAPTER EIGHT

1. Grenier, *First Way*, 33–34. See also Ross, *War on the Run.*
2. Anderson, *George Washington Remembers*, 22.
3. Philip Ludwell to GW, AUG 8, 1755, GWP S4.
4. Charles Lewis to GW, AUG 9, and George Mason to GW, AUG 21, 1755, GWP S4; GW to Charles Lewis, AUG 14, 1755, GWP S2 L1.
5. GW to Warner Lewis, AUG 14, 1755, GWP S2 L1.
6. GW to MBW, AUG 15, 1755, GWP S2 L1.
7. RD to Sir Thomas Robinson, SEP 6, 1755, n.56 to GW to Warner Lewis, AUG 14, 1755, GWP S2 L1.
8. RD to GW, Commission, Instructions for Colonel George Washington, Commander in Chief of the Virginia Regiment, and "Memo.," all AUG 14, 1755, GWP S4.
9. GW, Memorandum, OCT 5, 1755, GWP S2 L1, and GO, DEC 31, 1755, GWP S2 L3.
10. GW to Andrew Lewis, to Robert Spotswood, and to others, SEP 6, 1755, GWP S2 L1.
11. Examples include William Brockenbrough to GW, SEP 19, John Tayloe to John Champe, SEP 27, John Champe (quoted) to GW, OCT 30, William Byrd to GW, DEC 12, and Robert Duncanson to GW, DEC 30, 1755, GWP S4.
12. GW to RD, OCT 17, 1755, GWP S2 L1.
13. GW to William Fleming, to Peter Hog, and to David Bell, all OCT 28, 1755, GWP S2 L1.
14. GW to George Frazier, NOV 18, GWP S2 L1, and to Peter Hog, DEC 27, 1755, GWP S2 L3; and Hog to GW, JAN 27, 1756, GWP S4.
15. GW, GO, JAN 8, 1756, GWP S2 L3. GW got his own copy of Bland in APR 1756.
16. GW, Recruiting Instructions, SEP 3, and letters to captains and to Andrew Lewis, SEP 6, and Instructions for AS and letters to his captains, SEP 11, 1755, GWP S2 L1.
17. GW to Joshua Lewis and to others, SEP 19, GWP S2 L1; William Brockenbrough (quoted) to GW, SEP 29, and Gist to GW, OCT 15, 1755, GWP S4.
18. GW to RD and to JR, SEP 11, 1755, GWP S2 L1.
19. GW to John Hall, to John King, to William Peachy, to Robert Spotswood, OCT 16, and to Calendar, OCT 20, 1755, GWP S2 L1; Carlyle to GW, OCT 17, and Thomas Bullitt to GW, OCT 18, 1755, GWP S4.
20. GW to AS, OCT 20 and NOV 18, GO, OCT 28, to John Mercer, NOV 1, to Ensigns Dangerfield and Dean, and to Captain Savage, NOV 8, to Captains McKenzie and Cocke, NOV 11, 1755, GWP S2 L1; Robert Stewart to GW, NOV 21, AS to GW, NOV 22, and Gist to GW, NOV 24, 1755, GWP S4.
21. GW to Robert Stewart, to George Frazier, and to Austin Brockenbrough, NOV 18, and to Dennis McCarty (torture), NOV 22, to Joshua

Lewis, to William Bronaugh, to AS, and GO, DEC 3, GO, Dec 22 and 23, 1755, GWP S2 L1; Hog to GW, DEC 17, 1755, GWP S4.

22. Hog to GW, NOV 19, and Stewart to GW, DEC 5, 1755, GWP S4; GW to Hog, DEC 27, and GO, DEC 29, 1755, GWP S2 L3.

23. GW to AS, NOV 27, 1755, GWP S2 L1; AS to GW, DEC 3, 1755, GWP S4.

24. GW to Charles Dick, GO, Memorandum, and Instructions for Dick, all SEP 6, 1755, GWP S2 L1; Dick to GW, SEP 6, 1755, GWP S4.

25. GW to AS, NOV 28, 1755, GWP S2 L1.

26. GW to Powell Hazel, Impress Warrant, OCT 10, to John Carlyle, OCT 16, GO, OCT 16 and 29, to AS and to Dick, OCT 29, to Commissary Jones, OCT 31, and to Sergeant David Wilper (Woelper), NOV 1, 1755, GWP S2 L1; GW, GO, DEC 30, 1755, GWP S2 L3; Carlyle to GW, OCT 17, and Peter Hog to GW, DEC 17, 1755, GWP S4.

27. GW to RD, OCT 8, GO, OCT 17 and 18, and to Andrew Lewis, OCT 18, 1755, GWP S2 L1.

28. GW to RD and to JR, DEC 5, 1755, GWP S2 L1; JR to GW, DEC 16, 1755, GWP S4.

29. GW to Commissary Jones, OCT 20, to Allan McLean, OCT 26, and to Andrew Lewis and others, OCT 27, 1755, GWP S2 L1.

30. GW to Walker, NOV 11 and DEC 3, 1755, GWP S2 L1; AS to GW, NOV 7 and 29, Walker to GW, NOV 26, DEC 4, 17, and 26, and Peter Hog to GW, DEC 17, 1755, GWP S4.

31. GW to Hog, SEP 24, and to Alexander Boyd, NOV 1, 1755, GWP S2 L1.

32. GW to Boyd, NOV 1, 1755, GWP S2 L1; Hog to GW, NOV 3, 1755, GWP S4.

33. Hog to GW, NOV 26, 1755, GWP S4; GW to Boyd, DEC 3, 1755, GWP S2 L1, and to Hog, DEC 27, 1755, GWP S2 L3. GW typically spelled the man's name *Hogg*, but it is *Hog* in his will.

34. GW to Hog, DEC 27, 1755, GWP S2 L3.

35. John Martin to GW, AUG 30, 1755, GWP S4; GW to RD, SEP 11, 1755, GWP S2 L1.

36. William Fleming to GW, NOV 26, Hog to GW, NOV 29, AS to GW, Nov 29 and DEC 3, 1755, GWP S4.

37. GW to AS, DEC 3, 1755, GWP S2 L1.

38. GW to RD, DEC 5, 1755, GWP S2 L1.

39. GW to Captains Savage and McKenzie, DEC 16, GO, DEC 25, 1755, GWP S2 L1; GW, GO, JAN 8, 1756, GWP S2 L3.

40. GW, GO, DEC 20, 1755, GWP S2 L1; GW to AS, DEC 28, 1755, GWP S2 L3. On Steuben, GW, and training, see Clary, *Adopted Son*, 165–71, and Clary, *Inspectors General*, 33–51.

41. GW, GO, SEP 19 and OCT 18, and to AS, NOV 17, 1755, GWP S2 L1; AS to GW, SEP 17, 1755, GWP S4.

42. GW to RD, OCT 8 and 11, 1755, GWP S2 L1.

43. RD to GW, OCT 18, and WF to GW, OCT 20, 1755, GWP S4; Winthrop, *Military Law and Precedents* 1:19–20.

44. GW, GO, OCT 23, and to Robert Spotswood, OCT 31, 1755, GWP S2 L1.
45. Freeman 2:141–42; GW to AS, NOV 18, 1755, GWP S2 L1; AS to GW, NOV 22, 1755, GWP S4.
46. GW to RD, DEC 5, 1755, GWP S2 L1.
47. GW to Campbell, DEC 11, 1755, GWP S2 L1; and GW, GO, DEC 28, 1755, GWP S2 L3.
48. GW, GO, DEC 26 and 29, and to AS, DEC 28, 1755, GWP S2 L3.
49. GW to Ashby, DEC 28, 1755, GWP S2 L3.
50. GW to Colonel Martin, OCT 10, 1755, GWP S2 L1; Captain Cocks' [sic] Journal, attached to William Cocks [sic] Company of Rangers List, OCT 21, 1755, GWP S4.
51. GW to Ashby, OCT 14, and to George William Fairfax, OCT 23, 1755, GWP S2 L1.
52. GW to Bacon, OCT 26 and 28, and to Cocke and Ashby, OCT 27, 1755, GWP S2 L1.
53. AS to GW, DEC 23, 1755, GWP S4; GW to Cocke, DEC 28, and to Ashby, DEC 29, 1755, GWP S2 L3.
54. Hog to GW, SEP 23, OCT 6 and 13, 1755, GWP S4; GW to Hog, SEP 24, 1755, GWP S2 L1.
55. GW to Boyd and to Commissary Walker, NOV 18, 1755, GWP S2 L1; Hog to GW, NOV 26, 1755, GWP S4.
56. GW to Hog and to Commissary Dick, NOV 18, 1755, GWP S2 L1; Hog to GW, NOV 29, 1755, GWP S4.
57. Hog to GW, DEC 17, 1755, GWP S4; GW to Hog, DEC 27, 1755, GWP S2 L3.
58. AS to GW, SEP 6 and DEC 3, 1755, GWP S4; GW to Robert Hunter Morris, JAN 1, 1756, GWP S2 L3.
59. AS to GW, SEP 25 and 27, OCT 4, 1755, GWP S4; GW, Memorandum, OCT 7, to Cocke, to Ashby, and to William Vance, OCT 10, and to RD, OCT 11, 1755, GWP S2 L1.
60. GW, Public Notice on Indian Raids, OCT 13, 1755, GWP S2 L1; WF to GW, OCT 20, 1755, GWP S4.
61. AS to GW, NOV 7, and Gist to GW, NOV 24, 1755, GWP S4.
62. GW to Montour, SEP 19 and OCT 10, 1755, GWP S2 L1.
63. GW to Gist, OCT 10, 1755, GWP S2 L1.
64. GW to RD, OCT 17, 1755, GWP S2 L1.
65. GW to Gist, OCT 18, 1755, GWP S2 L1.
66. GW to Andrew Lewis, OCT 27, 1755, GWP S2 L1; Gist to GW, NOV 1, 1755, GWP S4.
67. GW to AS, DEC 3, and to RD, DEC 5, 1755, GWP S2 L1; RD to GW, DEC 14, 1755, GWP S4.
68. GW to various officers, SEP 11–15, Memorandum, SEP 15, GO, SEP 17–18, Memorandum, OCT 2 and 5, and to various officers, OCT 1–10, OCT 20–23, GO, OCT 26–27, and others, GWP S2 L1. While GW was

touring, his name was put up for election as a burgess from Frederick County, possibly without his knowledge, and in any case with not much time to campaign, and he lost. AS for one was outraged at his defeat, but he promised better luck next time. Longmore, *Invention*, 36–37; AS to GW, DEC 23, 1755, GWP S4.

69.   GW to AS, SEP 20, 1755, GWP S2 L1; AS to GW, OCT 4, 1755, GWP S4.
70.   GW to AS, NOV 28, and to RD, DEC 5, 1755, GWP S2 L1.
71.   AS to GW, DEC 9, 1755, GWP S4.
72.   RD to GW, DEC 14, and JR to GW, DEC 16, 1755, GWP S4.
73.   GW to RD, DEC 5, 1755, GWP S2 L1; GW to AS, DEC 28, 1755, GWP S2 L3; RD to GW, DEC 14, AS to GW, DEC 21 and 23, GWP S4.
74.   AS to GW, DEC 26, 1755, GWP S4.
75.   GW, GO, JAN 9, 1756, GWP S2 L3.

CHAPTER NINE

1.   On JUN 7, 1889, Harrison moved weekly inspections from Sundays to Saturdays, giving soldiers a day and a half of rest. The order cited proclamations to that effect by presidents Washington and Lincoln, which officers had uniformly ignored. An order as commander in chief automatically became part of the regulations and so could not be defied. Clary, *Inspectors General*, 320–22.
2.   GW to AS, and to Thomas Waggoner, JAN 9, GO, JAN 10 and 14, to William Cocke, to Robert Stewart, to Mordecai Buckner, and After Orders, JAN 14, 1756, GWP S2 L3.
3.   AS to GW, JAN 18 and 31, 1756, GWP S4.
4.   GW to Thomas Waggoner, to Robert Stewart, General Instructions for the Recruiting Officers of the Virginia Regiment, JAN 9, to Thomas Walker, to David Bell, to Peter Hog, to Alexander Boyd, JAN 10, to George Frazier, to Charles Lewis, JAN 27, to AS, FEB 1, to John Blagg, to John Deane, FEB 2, 1756, GWP S2 L3; John Carlyle to GW, JAN 12; Charles Lewis to GW, JAN 25, AS to GW, JAN 31, Hog to GW, FEB 3, William Hughes to GW, FEB 12, Landon Carter to GW, FEB 26, 1756, GWP S4.
5.   GW to RD, JAN 14, 1756, GWP S2 L3; RD to GW, JAN 22, 1756, GWP S4.
6.   Proceedings of Court of Inquiry, GW's endorsement, and AS to GW, JAN 16, 1756, GWP S4.
7.   RD to GW, JAN 22, 1756, GWP S4.
8.   Nicholas to GW, JAN 23, JR to GW, JAN 27, AS to GW, JAN 31, 1756, GWP S4; GW to Charles Lewis, JAN 27, 1756, GWP S2 L3.
9.   GW to AS, FEB 1, 1756, GWP S2 L3.
10.   GW to RD, FEB 2, 1756, and n.7, GWP S2 L3; Freeman 2:158.
11.   Chew to GW, MAR 4, 1756, GWP S4; Freeman 2:159–64.

12. Shirley to GW, MAR 5, 1756, GWP S4; Flexner, *GW Forge*, 147–48.
13. Sharpe to Commanding Officer, MAR 8, AS to GW (2 letters), MAR 29, 1756, GWP S4.
14. AS to GW (2 letters), MAR 29, 1756, GWP S4.
15. Shirley and GW quoted Flexner, *GW Forge*, 148; GW, GO, After Orders, and to John Blagg, APR 7, 1756, GWP S2 L3; Ferling, *Ascent*, 32.
16. AS to GW, JAN 31, 1756, GWP S4; GW to RD, APR 7, 1756, GWP S2 L3; Calloway, *Shawnees*, 26–29; Grenier, *First Way*, 124–25.
17. GW to RD, JAN 14 and APR 7, 1756, GWP S2 L3; RD to GW, JAN 22, and Hog to GW, APR 3, 1756, GWP S4.
18. RD to GW, APR 8, 1756, GWP S4; GW to RD, APR 7, 1756, GWP S2 L3.
19. AS to GW, MAR 29 (2nd letter), Dumas to Donville, MAR 23, and WF to GW, APR 14, 1756, GWP S4; GW to Dinwiddie and enclosures, and to JR, APR 7, 1756, GWP S2 L3.
20. GW to JR, and to AS, APR 7, to John Blagg, APR 8, to David Bell, APR 10 and 11, to John Mercer, APR 12, GWP S2 L3; AS to GW, MAR 29 (2nd letter), Horatio Sharpe to RD, MAR 30, William Withers (RD's secretary) to GW, APR 15, 1756, GWP S4.
21. RD to GW, Ashby to Henry Vanmeter and Thomas Waggoner, APR 15, 1756, GWP S4; GW to RD, APR 22, 1756, GWP S2 L3.
22. GW to Mercer, APR 15, to RD and to JR, APR 16, to RD, to Henry Harrison, and After Orders, APR 19, to several officrs, and GO, APR 20, 1756, GWP S2 L3.
23. Minutes of Council of War, GW to Thomas Fairfax, to militia lieutenants of Prince William and Fairfax counties, to several officers, APR 21, Minutes of Council of War, GW to Henry Harrison, and to Ensign Hubbard, APR 23, 1756, GWP S2 L3.
24. RD to GW, APR 23, 1756, GWP S4; GW, GO, to RD, APR 24, to Henry Harrison, to AS, APR 26, 1756, GWP S2 L3.
25. RD to GW, APR 26, 1756, GWP S4; GW to RD and to JR, APR 27, 1756, GWP S2 L3.
26. GW to RD and to JR, APR 24, 1756, GWP S2 L3; RD to GW, APR 29, 1756, GWP S4.
27. GW, Evening Orders, MAY 3, GW, GO, to several officers, MAY 4, to Robert Stewart, MAY 10, GO, MAY 11, Minutes of Council of War, MAY 14, to several officers, MAY 16–17, to Robert Spotswood, MAY 19, Proclamation, MAY 24 (approximate), to William Cocke, JUN 4, 1756, GWP S2 L3; RD to GW, May 3 and 8, Hog to GW, MAY 14, AS to GW, May 19, 29, and 31, 1756, GWP S4.
28. GW to RD, MAY 3, 1756, GWP S2 L3.
29. RD to GW, JUL 12 and AUG 19, Robert Stewart to GW, JUL 30 and 31, Thomas Waggoner to GW, AUG 21, 1756, GWP S4; GW to RD, AUG 4 and 14, GWP S2 L3, and GW to AS, OCT 23, 1756, GWP S2 L4.
30. GW to King Blunt, Captain Jack, and the Rest of the Tuscarora Chiefs, AUG 1, and to RD, AUG 4, 1756, GWP S2 L3.

31. RD to GW, AUG 20 and SEP 30, and Andrew Lewis to GW, OCT 28, 1756, GWP S4; GW to AS, SEP 6, to RD, SEP 8, GWP S2 L3, and to RD OCT 10, 1756, GWP S2 L4.

32. GW to Captain Johnne and Other Chiefs of the Catawbas, OCT 28, 1756, GWP S4; GW, GO, OCT 28, and to RD, NOV 9, 1756, GWP S2 L4.

33. Jacobs, *Appalachian Indian Frontier*, passim.

34. GW, GO, May 13, to JR, AUG 5, 1756, GWP S2 L3; Peter Hog to GW, MAY 14 and 17, and JUN 26, Virginia Assembly Military Committee, Decisions Regarding Colonel Washington's Accounts, AUG 18, and RD to GW, AUG 21, 1756, GWP S4.

35. GW to JR, AUG 5, 1756, GWP S2 L3.

36. WF to GW, APR 14, RD to GW, MAY 8 and AUG 19, Robert Stewart to GW, JUL 23, AS to GW, JUL 25, JR to GW, DEC 31, 1756, GWP S4; GW to RD, MAY 3 and 23, AUG 4 and 14, to Robert Stewart, MAY 10, and GO, MAY 18, GWP S2 L3, and GW to RD, NOV 8, 1756, GWP S2 L4.

37. RD to GW, DEC 15 and 27, 1756, GWP S4; GW to RD, DEC 19, 1756, GWP S2 L4.

38. GW to RD, SEP 28, 1756, GWP S2 L4.

39. RD to GW, DEC 15 and 27, and JR to GW, DEC 17, 1756, GWP S4.

40. RD to GW, APR 7 and 8, and MAY 8, 1756, GWP S4; GW to RD, MAY 3, 1756, GWP S2 L3.

41. GW, GO, APR 13, MAY 9, JUN 1 and 23, JUL 8, 9, and 21, AUG 1, After Orders, MAY 1 and 18, JUL 6, to RD, MAY 3, AUG 14, to Henry Woodward, MAY 5, to William Cocke, JUN 4, GWP S2 L3, and GW to RD, SEP 23, 1756, GWP S2 L4; RD to GW and Death Warrant for Nathan Lewis, MAY 8, Robert Stewart to GW, JUN 20 and 23 and JUL 3, 1756, GWP S4.

42. RD to GW, SEP 30, DEC 10 and 15, 1756, GWP S4; GW to JR, NOV 9, to RD, DEC 4, 10, and 19, and to Captain Bosummith, DEC 8, 1756, GWP S2 L4.

43. GW, GO, JUL 6 and 7, 1756, GWP S2 L3.

44. WF to GW, AUG 13, and RD to GW, AUG 21, 1756, GWP S4; GW, GO, and to RD, AUG 14, 1756, GWP S2 L3.

45. GW, GO, AUG 21, GWP S2 L3, and to RD, SEP 23, 1756, GWP S2 L4, are but two examples. GOs for "divine services" appeared every week throughout the summer and fall.

46. GW to Thomas Fairfax, APR 19 and AUG 29, GO, MAY 15 and 16, to RD, MAY 23 and AUG 4, Memorandum, JUL 13, GWP S2 L3, to RD, OCT 10, and to JR, NOV 9, 1756, GWP S2 L4; WF to GW (quotation), MAY 13, n.73 to GW to RD, MAY 23, 1756, GWP S2 L3; RD to GW, MAY 27, JUL 1, and OCT 26, WF to GW, JUL 10 and AUG 13, 1756, GWP S4.

47. GW, GO, APR 21, 1756, GWP S2 L3; WF to GW, MAY 4, 1756, GWP S4; Freeman 2:198n, reporting a thorough search of the record, finding the last mention on MAY 23.

48. GW to JD, and to JR, both APR 7, 1756, GWP S2 L3.

49. RD to GW, APR 15, and GW, Proposal for Organization of the Vir-

ginia Regiment, APR 16, 1756, GWP S4; GW to RD, APR 16, 1756, GWP S2 L3.

50. JR to GW, APR 17, RD to GW, APR 23, May 8 and 27, WF to GW, APR 26, Carter to GW, APR nd, 1756, GWP S4; GW to RD, and GO, MAY 23 and JUN 2, to Henry Woodward, MAY 24, GWP S2 L3.

51. GW to Robert Stewart, JUN 2, to RD, AUG 4 and SEP 8, to JR, AUG 5, to David Bell, SEP 6, GWP S2 L3, and to RD, SEP 28, 1756, GWP S2 L4; RD to GW, JUN 12 and AUG 19, and JR to GW, AUG 19, 1756, GWP S4.

52. RD to GW, JUN 12 and JUL 1, 1756, GWP S4; GW to RD, JUN 25, 1756, GWP S2 L3.

53. GW, GO, JUL 11 and 12, to John McNeill, JUL 21, to RD, AUG 4, 1756, GWP S2 L3.

54. GW to AS, AUG 5 and SEP 6, to RD, SEP 8, 1756, GWP S2 L3; RD to GW, AUG 19, WF to GW, SEP 3, 1756, GWP S4.

55. GW to RD, SEP 8, GWP S2 L3, and to RD, SEP 23, 1756, GWP S2 L4; RD to GW, SEP 8, 13, and 30, NOV 16, John McNeill to GW, OCT 31, 1756, GWP S4; Hening, *Statutes at Large* 7:61.

56. Virginia General Assembly, Building of Forts, MAR 12, 1756, GWP S4; GW, GO, JUL 30, 1756, GWP S2 L3.

57. GW to RD, AUG 4 and 14, and to JR, AUG 5, 1756, GWP S2 L3; RD to GW, AUG 19, 1756, GWP S4.

58. JR to GW, AUG 19, RD to GW, AUG 21, 1756, GWP S4; GW to AS, SEP 6, GWP S2 L3, and SEP 28, and to JD, SEP 23, 1756, GWP S2 L4.

59. RD to GW, SEP 30, 1756, GWP S4; GW to AS, OCT 23, 1756, GWP S2 L4.

60. RD to GW, OCT 26, 1756, GWP S4.

61. Minutes of Council of War at Fort Cumberland, OCT 30, GW, Remarks on the Council of War, NOV 5, GW to RD, NOV 9, and Loudoun to RD, NOV or DEC 1756, GWP S2 L4.

62. Virginia Council Proceedings on Frontier Defense, NOV 15 and DEC 9, RD to GW, NOV 16 and DEC 10, 1756, GWP S4; GW to RD, NOV 24, DEC 2 and 10, and to various officers, DEC 17, 1756, GW S2 L4.

63. GW to RD, DEC 19, 1756, GWP S2 L4; RD to GW, DEC 27, 1756, GWP S4.

64. RD to GW, MAY 8 and JUN 12, 1756, GWP S4; GW to AS, MAY 18, 1756, GWP S2 L3.

65. GW to RD, JUN 25 (2 letters), Minutes of Council of War at Fort Cumberland, JUL 10, GW to several officers, JUL 21 and 22, 1756, GWP S2 L3; RD to GW, JUL 1, WF to GW, JUL 10, 1756, GWP S4.

66. Robert Stewart to GW, JUL 23, Proceedings of Council, Augusta County Militia Officers, JUL 27, AS to GW, AUG 1, Thomas Waggoner to GW, and Proceedings of Council of War, both AUG 10, 1756, GWP S4; GW to Robert Stewart, JUL 27, to Thomas Waggoner, JUL 29, to RD, AUG 4, and to various officers, AUG 5, 1756, GWP S2 L3.

67. GW to various officers, AUG 12–13, and to RD, AUG 14, 1756, GWP S2 L3; RD to GW, AUG 19, 1756, GW S4.

68. GW to RD, SEP 23 and 28, NOV 9, to AS, OCT 23, 1756, GWP S2 L4; RD to GW, SEP 30 and NOV 16, 1756, GWP S4.

69. AS to GW, MAR 29, 1756 (2nd letter), GWP S4.

70. RD to GW, APR 7 and 8, WF to GW, APR 14, JR to GW, APR 17, 1756, GWP S4.

71. GW to RD, APR 18, 1756, GWP S2 L3.

72. WF to GW, APR 14 and 26, Landon Carter to GW, APR 21, Charles Carter to GW, APR 22, RD to GW, APR 23, 1756, GWP S4.

73. Sharpe to Shirley, APR 10, 1756, quoted Freeman 2:171; WF to GW, APR 26, RD to GW, APR 29, 1756, GWP S4.

74. Charles Carter to GW, APR 27, Landon Carter to GW, APR nd, JR to GW, MAY 3, WF to GW, MAY 9, 13, and 20, 1756, GWP S4; GW to RD, MAY 3, 1756, GWP S2 L3.

75. Freeman 2:195–97.

76. RD to GW, MAY 27, 1756, GWP S4; RD to Abercromby, MAY 28, 1756, quoted ibid., 2:197; WF to GW, AUG 13, 1756, GWP S4.

77. Freeman 2:198–99; RD to GW, JUN 12, 1756, GWP S4; GW to JR, AUG 5, 1756, GWP S2 L3.

78. JR to GW, AUG 19, RD to GW, AUG 21, Carlyle to GW, DEC 2, GWP S4; GW to RD, AUG 14 and SEP 23, to George Mercer, DEC 20, 1756, GWP S2 L4; Flexner, *GW Forge*, 163.

79. Quoted Freeman 2:209, and photocopy of the *Gazette* 210–11; Flexner, *GW Forge*, 154; Virginia Regiment Officers to GW, NOV 12, 1756, GWP S4.

80. John Kirkpatrick (quoted) to GW, SEP 22, William Ramsey to GW, SEP 22, Augustine Washington to GW, OCT 16, JR to GW, NOV 16, 1756, GWP S4; GW to RD, OCT 10, Address of the Officers of the Virginia Regiment to the Worshipful the Speaker & Gentlemen of the House of Burgesses, DEC nd, GW to JR, DEC nd, 1756, GWP S2 L4.

81. RD to GW, SEP 13, OCT 26, NOV 16, 1756 GWP S4; GW to RD, NOV 24, 1756, GWP S2 L4.

82. GW to RD, DEC 19, and to JR, DEC 19, 1756, GWP S2 L4; JR to GW, DEC 19 and 31, 1756, GWP S4.

CHAPTER TEN

1. As fantastic as it seems, this really happened. Most accounts follow that of J. L. Motley, the nineteenth-century historian of Dutch independence; see O'Connell, *Of Arms and Men*, 118–19, on the influence of this incident on the developing tradition of coolness under fire among European aristocratic officers.

2. The principal biography is Pargellis, *Lord Loudoun*; see sketches in Freeman 2:237–38 and Ferling, *Ascent*, 3–39. Portraits are in Parkman, *Montcalm*, and Anderson, *Crucible*.

3. Officers of the Virginia Regiment to Loudoun, FEB nd, 1757, GWP S2 L4.

4. GW to Loudoun, JAN nd, 1757, GWP S2 L4.

5. GW to Cunningham, FEB 2, 1757, GWP S2 L4; Cunningham to GW, FEB 27, GWP S4.

6. RD to GW, FEB 2, 1757, GWP S4; Flexner, *GW Forge*, 173. The publication was *Memorial Containing a Summary View*.

7. Freeman 2:238–40; Flexner, *GW Forge*, 174–75.

8. Chew to GW, MAR 14, and Minutes, Provincial Governors Conference at Philadelphia, MAR 15–23, 1757, GWP S4.

9. GW to RD, MAR nd, 1757, GWP S2 L4; Flexner, *GW Forge*, 174–75.

10. RD to GW, JAN 26, Robert McKenzie to GW, FEB 18, Thomas Bullitt to GW, FEB 19, John Hall to GW, May nd and JUN 1, 1757, GWP S4.

11. Virginia Regiment Officers to RD, APR 16, and GW to RD, APR 16, 1757, GWP S2 L4.

12. GW to RD, JAN 12, MAY 30, JUN 10 and 27, JUL 10, SEP 7, to JR, JUL 10, to John Stanwix, MAY 28, 1757, GWP S2 L4; Carlyle to GW, JAN 22, RD to GW, JAN 26, APR 5, MAY 23, JUN 6 and 27, SEP 2, OCT 14, JR to GW, APR 21, JUN 29, JUL 18, John Kirkpatrick to GW, JUL 21, SEP 17, Andrew Lewis to GW, SEP 1, William Ramsey to GW, SEP 3, Alexander Boyd to GW, DEC 6, 1757, GWP S4.

13. GW to RD, JAN 12, 1757, GWP S2 L4; RD to GW, JAN 26, 1757, GWP S4.

14. Proceedings of General Courts Martial, Fort Loudoun, MAY 27, JUL 15 and 26, WF to GW, JUL 17, RD to GW, JUL 18, JR to GW, JUL 18, Horatio Sharpe to All and Every of the Officers Both Civil & Military in Baltimore County, JUL 26, Sharpe to GW, JUL 27, GWP S4; GW to RD, JUL 10, 11, and 12, to John Stanwix, JUL 15, to Horatio Sharpe, to Ensign Fell, and to Ensign Crawford, JUL 20, 1757, GWP S2 L4.

15. GW to John Stanwix, JUL 30, to RD, AUG 3 and 27, 1757, GWP S2 L4; RD to GW, SEP 2, 1757, GWP S4.

16. RD to GW, SEP 2, OCT 24, Stanwix to GW, SEP 19, Robert Stewart to RD, NOV 9, 1757, GWP S4; GW to RD, SEP 17, 1757, GWP S2 L4.

17. JR to GW, APR 21, 1757, GWP S4; GW to RD, APR 29, JUN 10 and 12, AUG 27, to JR, JUL 19, to Officers of the Virginia Regiment, JUL 29, 1757, GWP S2 L4.

18. Robert Stewart to GW, SEP 27, 1757, GWP S4; GW to RD, OCT 5 and 9, to John Stanwix, OCT 8, Memorandum and Statements of Property Seized under Warrants, OCT 6, 1757, GWP S2 L4. GW told Stanwix that the quartermaster had been a sergeant in royal service for many years and appeared worthy of the assignment in the Virginia Regiment.

19. RD to GW, JAN 26, Buxton Gay, Deposition by Richard Davis, Justice of the Peace for the County of Baltimore, APR 20, JR to GW, APR 21, 1757, GWP S4.

20. JR to GW, APR 21, 1757, GWP S4; GW to RD, APR 29, 1757, GWP S2 L4.

21. RD to GW, MAY 16 (2nd letter) and 23, 1757, GWP S4; GW to RD, MAY 24, 1757, GWP S2 L4.

22. GW to RD, MAY 24 and JUN 12, to Joshua Lewis, JUN 6, to John Stanwix, JUN 15, 1787, GWP S2 L4; Richard Bland to GW, JUN 7, 1757, GWP S4.

23. WF to GW, JUN 19 and JUL 1, 1757, GWP S4; GW to RD, JUN 27, to Henry Lee, JUN 30, to Andrew Lewis, JUL 1, to Charles Carter and to Henry Fitzhugh, JUL 2, to John Stanwix, JUL 8 and 15, 1757, GWP S2 L4.

24. AS to GW, APR nd, 1757, GWP S4. On political difficulties caused by GW's loose talk about New Englanders in 1775, see Clary, *Adopted Son*, 65.

25. GW to RD, MAY 24 and JUL 11, and to Robert McKenzie, JUL 29, 1757, GWP S2 L4.

26. GW to RD, JAN 12, APR 5 and 16, Minutes of Council of War, APR 16, GW to AS, APR 17, 1757, GWP S2 L4; RD to GW, JAN 26, APR 5 and 7, WF to GW, MAR 31, 1757, GWP S4.

27. GW to RD, JAN 12, MAY 30, JUN 27, SEP 24, 1757, GWP S2 L4; RD to GW, JUN 6, JUL 13, 1757, GWP S4.

28. Clement Read to GW, MAR 15, WF to GW, MAR 22 and 31, RD to GW, APR 5 and 7, GWP S4; GW to RD, APR 16, 1757, GWP S2 L4.

29. JR to GW, APR 21, WF to GW, MAY 6, RD to GW, MAY 23, 1757, GWP S4.

30. GW to RD, MAY 24 and 29, to John Stanwix, MAY 28, 1757, GWP S2 L4.

31. GW to RD and to JR, MAY 30, 1757, GWP S2 L4.

32. GW to Andrew Lewis, JUN 3, to John D. Wilper, JUN 7, to RD, JUN 10 and 12 (2nd letter), to JR, JUN 10, to Robert McKenzie, JUN 11, to James Baker, JUN 12, to John Stanwix, JUN 28, 1757, GWP S2 L4; RD to GW, JUN 6 and 16, William Denny to John Stanwix, copy to GW, JUL 7, 1757, GWP S4; Atkin to Governor Sharpe, JUN 30, quoted n.19 to GW to JR, MAY 30, 1757, GWP S2 L4.

33. GW to RD, APR 29, JUN 10 and 12 (2nd letter), to John Stanwix, JUN 15, 1757, GWP S2 L4; Baker to GW, JUN 10, 1757, GWP S4.

34. GW to Stanwix, JUN 15 and 20, 1757, GWP S2 L4; Atkin to GW, Virginia Regiment Officers to GW, both JUN 19, 1757, GWP S4.

35. Dagworthy to GW, JUN 14 and 17, WF to GW, JUN 17, 1757, GWP S4; GW to RD, Minutes of Council of War, and GW, Memorandum and Return, GW to various officers, to Dagworthy, and to several county lieutenants, all JUN 16, 1757, GWP S2 L4.

36. Stanwix to GW, JUN 18, Alexander Beall to GW, JUN 19, WF to GW, JUN 19, John Kirkpatrick to GW, JUN 18, 1757, GWP S4; GW to Beall, JUN 20, to Stanwix, JUN 21, to RD, JUN 21, and to various militia officers, JUN 21 and 24, 1757, GWP S2 L4.

37. Stanwix to GW, JUN 22 (1st letter) and JUL 14, WF to GW, JUN 26, RD to GW, JUN 27, Dagworthy to GW, with Deposition of John Street, both

JUL 10, 1757, GWP S4; GW to RD, JUN 27, to Stanwix, JUL 8, 1757, GWP S2 L4.

38. Stanwix to GW, JAN 13, JUN 15, JUL 8, Fielding Lewis to GW, FEB 7, 1757, GWP S4; GW to RD, JUN 10, to Stanwix, JUL 8, 1757, GWP S2 L4. Stanwix became a brigadier at the end of 1756 and a major general in 1759. He resigned from the army in MAY 1760 to become lieutenant governor of the Isle of Wight and was lost at sea in DEC 1765.

39. RD to William Pitt, MAR 22, 1757, in Freeman 2:244; RD to GW, APR 7, 1757, GWP S4.

40. GW to RD, APR 29, 1757, GWP S2 L4.

41. RD to GW, MAY 16, 1757 (2 letters), GWP S4; GW to JR, JUN 10, 1757, GWP S2 L4.

42. GW to Stanwix, JUN 15 and 28, to JR, JUL 10, 1757, GWP S2 L4.

43. GW to RD, JUL 10, 1757, GWP S2 L4; RD to GW, JUL 18, 1757, GWP S4.

44. RD to GW, APR 5 and 7, JR to GW, APR 21, 1757, GWP S4.

45. GW to Stanwix, MAY 28, and to RD, JUN 10, 1757, GWP S2 L4; Stanwix to GW, MAY 23, RD to GW, JUN 6, 1757, GWP S4.

46. RD to GW, JUN 27, John Hall to GW, JUL 5, Stanwix to GW, SEP 19, 1757, GWP S4; Anderson, *Crucible*, 204–07.

47. All quotes Parkman, *Montcalm,* 328–31; see also Anderson, *Crucible,* 303–05.

48. Parkman, *Montcalm,* 329–30.

49. Stanwix to GW, JUL 11, RD to GW, JUL 18, WF to GW, JUL 20, Lewis Stephens to GW, SEP 20, 1757, GWP S4; GW to Stanwix, JUL 19 and 30, GW to RD, AUG 27 and SEP 17, 1757, GWP S2 L4.

50. GW to RD, SEP 24, OCT 5, 9, and 24, to Stanwix, OCT 8, to JR, OCT 25, 1757, GWP S2 L4; RD to GW, NOV 2, JR to GW, NOV 3, Robert Stewart to RD, NOV 9, 1757, GWP S4.

51. Vaudreuil to Minister, FEB 13, 1758, in Stevens and Kent, *Wilderness Chronicles,* 109–10.

52. Mercer to GW, AUG 17 and NOV 2, AS to GW, AUG 20, 1757, GWP S4.

53. GW to RD, JUL 12 and AUG 3, to Officers of the Virginia Regiment, and to various captains, JUL 29, to Stanwix, JUL 30, 1757, GWP S2 L4; RD to GW, JUL 13 and 18, 1757, GWP S4.

54. GW to Joshua Lewis, AUG 3 and 4, to RD, AUG 27, 1757, GWP S2 L4.

55. RD to GW, AUG 13 and SEP 2, 1757, GWP S4; GW to RD, AUG 27, GWP S2 L4.

56. RD to GW, SEP 2 and 24, 1757, GWP S4; GW to RD, SEP 17, 1757 (2 letters), GWP S2 L4.

57. RD to GW, SEP 1 and 2, Thomas Gage to GW, OCT 15, James Cunningham to GW, OCT 16, George William Fairfax to GW, OCT 17 and DEC 6, William Henry Fairfax to GW, DEC 9, 1757, GWP S4; GW to RD, SEP 17, 1757, GWP S2 L4. George William followed the same route but failed.

58. RD to GW, SEP 24 and NOV 2, Rutherford to GW, NOV 22, Robert Stewart to GW, NOV 24, 1757, GWP S4; GW to RD, OCT 5 and 24, 1757, GWP S2 L4.
59. GW to RD, JUL 10, AUG 3, and SEP 17, to Stanwix, JUL 15 and 30, 1757, GWP S2 L4; RD to GW, JUL 13 and AUG 8, WF to GW, JUL 17 and AUG 6, Stanwix to GW, JUL 18 and AUG 1, Atkin to GW, JUL 20, 1757, GWP S4.
60. Johnson to Governor William Denny of Pennsylvania, SEP 25, Denny to GW, OCT 9, RD to GW, NOV 2, 1757, GWP S4; GW to James Roy, OCT 23, 1757, GWP S2 L4.
61. GW to RD, SEP 17, 1757, GWP S2 L4; RD to GW, OCT 24, 1757, GWP S4.
62. GW to RD, OCT 5 and NOV 5, 1757, GWP S2 L4; RD to GW, NOV 14, 1757, GWP S4.
63. Freeman 2:264; William Ramsey to GW, JUL 15 and 30, John Kirkpatrick to GW, JUL 21, WF to GW, JUL 20, Stanwix to GW, AUG 1, RD to GW, OCT 19, 1757, GWP S4; GW to RD, JUL 11, OCT 5 and 24, to Stanwix, JUL 30, to JR, OCT 25, 1757, GWP S2 L4.
64. Freeman 2:265–66; JR to GW, NOV 3, 1757, GWP S4.
65. GW to RD, NOV 5, 1757, GWP S2 L4; RD to GW, NOV 2 and 14, 1757, GWP S4.
66. Stewart to RD, NOV 9, and to Stanwix, NOV 24, RD to Stewart, NOV 15, Craik to GW, NOV 25, 1757, GWP S4.
67. Anderson, *Crucible*, 212–14, Pitt to Governors in North America, DEC 30, 1757, quoted 226.

CHAPTER ELEVEN

1. Anderson, *Crucible*, 235–39.
2. Pitt to Governors, DEC 1757, in n.19 to GW to John Blair, MAY 28, 1758, GWP S2 L5; ibid., 227; Parkman, *Montcalm*, 331–32.
3. Freeman 2:306–07, 312–13, Forbes to Bouquet, MAY 19, 1758, quoted 2:332n. Bouquet's formidable intellect is reflected in his *Historical Account of the Expedition*, published anonymously in 1766.
4. Mason to GW, JAN 4, Blair to GW, FEB 5, 1758, GWP S4; GW to Blair, JAN 30, 1758, GWP S2 L4; Fleming, *Intimate*, 12–13.
5. Robert C. Nicholas to GW, FEB 6, Stanwix to GW, MAR 10, 1758, GWP S4; GW to Blair, FEB 20, to Stanwix, MAR 4, 1758, GWP S2 L4.
6. Blair to GW, JAN 25, FEB 5, APR 9, Gist to GW, FEB 3, 1758, GWP S4; GW to Blair, JAN 31 and APR 2, 1758, GWP S2 L4.
7. John Baylis to GW, JAN 30, Nathaniel Thompson to GW, FEB 20, Charles Smith to GW, FEB 23, 1758, GWP S4.
8. John Smith to GW, MAR 2, Stanwix to GW, MAR 10, 1758, GWP S4; GW to Stanwix, MAR 4, 1758, GWP S2 L4.

9. Brady, *Martha Washington*, 52–62; Fleming, *Intimate*, 20–23; Clary, *Adopted Son*, 53–54; Freeman 2:278–302, 312; Flexner, *GW Forge*, 188–93.

10. Humphrey Knight to GW, JUN 15, JUL 13, AUG 2 and 24, SEP 2, John Patterson to GW, JUN 17, AUG 13, SEP 2, William Poole to GW, JUL 9, Christopher Hardwick to GW, JUL 11, AUG 3 and 26, SEP 3, John Carlyle to GW, JUL 14 and 15, AUG 8 and 22, SEP 1, Charles Smith to GW, JUL 20, George William Fairfax to GW, JUL 25, AUG 5, SEP 1 and 15, 1758, GWP S4. GW kept replies to these reports out of his official letterbook, as they were purely personal.

11. GW to Blair, APR 9, to Stanwix, MAY 4, 1758, GWP S2 L4; Forbes to Pitt, JUL 10, 1758, quoted Freeman 2:308.

12. GW to Blair, APR 9, 1758, GWP S2 L4; Blair to GW, APR 9, GWP S4.

13. GW to Blair, APR 9 and 17, to Stanwix, APR 10, to St. Clair, APR 12, 1758, GWP S2 L4; Blair to GW, APR 9, James Baker to GW, APR 10, 1758, GWP S4.

14. GW to Stanwix, APR 10, 1758, GWP S2 L4.

15. GW to St. Clair, APR 12 and 18, to Gage, APR 12, 1758, GWP S2 L4; St. Clair to Commanding Officer at Winchester, APR 13, 1758, GWP S4.

16. GW to Blair, APR 17 and 24, 1758, GWP S2 L4; Proceedings of Council of War, APR 24, Blair to GW, MAY 3, Warner Lewis to GW, MAY 5 and 6, George Mason to GW, MAY 6, 1758, Proceedings of the Court of Inquiry against Peter Steenbergen, MAY 3, William Woodford to GW, MAY 17, 1758, GWP S4.

17. GW to Andrew Lewis, APR 21 and 26, to Blair APR 24 and 26, to AS and to Thomas Waggoner, both APR 24, to Thomas Gist, APR 26, GWP S2 L4, to St. Clair, MAY 1, 1758, GWP S2 L5; AS to GW, APR 22, Thomas Waggoner to GW, APR 30, 1758, GWP S4.

18. Mathew Talbot to Clement Read, MAY 3, Blair to Henry Lee (and to other militia officers), copy to GW, MAY 4, 1758, GWP S4.

19. GW to Blair, APR 17, to St. Clair, APR 18, GWP S2 L4, to David Franks, MAY 1, 1758, GWP S2 L5.

20. St. Clair to GW, APR 20, 1758, GWP S4; GW to Forbes, APR 23, GWP S2 L4, to St. Clair, APR 27, 1758, GWP S2 L5.

21. Thomas Basset to GW, APR 27, 1758, GWP S4; GW to St. Clair, MAY 1, 1758, GWP S2 L5.

22. GW to St. Clair, MAY 4, to Blair, MAY 4 and postscript MAY 10, to JR, MAY 10 and enclosed Minutes of Council of Officers, MAY 9, to Andrew Lewis, MAY 21, 1758, GWP S2 L5; Blair to GW, MAY 15, John Blagg to GW, MAY 11, 1758, GWP S4; St. Clair to Bouquet, MAY 27, 1758, quoted Freeman 2:309.

23. John Norton to GW, MAY 9, Blair to GW, MAY 11, Mason to GW, MAY 16, 1758, GWP S4.

24. St. Clair to GW, MAY 7 and 14, Blair to GW, MAY 15, 1758, GWP S4.

25. GW to Andrew Lewis, MAY 24, 1758, GWP S2 L5.

26. Thomas Waggoner to GW, MAY 10, Henry Lee to GW, MAY 16, Ruther-

ford to GW, JUN 6, 1758, GWP S4; GW to Blair, MAY 4, postscript MAY 10, 1758, GWP S2 L5.

27. Halkett to GW, MAY 4, Joseph Collins to John Bates, William Mead to Matthew Talbot, and Bedford County Settlers' Statement about Indian Raid, all May 8, Timothy Dalton Affidavit on Indian Raid, May 9, Pinkney Hawkins to Clement Read, MAY 10, Talbot to Red, MAY 10, 11 and 12, William Calloway to GW, MAY 15, Thomas Bullitt to GW, MAY 21, Blair to GW, MAY 24, 1758, GWP S4; GW to St. Clair, MAY 4 and 11, to Blair, MAY 4, to Halkett MAY 11, 1758, GW S2 L5.

28. Anderson, *Crucible*, 268.

29. St. Clair to GW, MAY 24, 1758, GWP S4; GW to AS, and to Andrew Lewis, both MAY 24, 1758, GWP S2 L5.

30. GW to Blair, MAY 28, 1758, GWP S2 L5. The next item in his letterbook was JUN 14.

31. St. Clair to GW, JUN 13, 1758, GWP S4; GW to St. Clair, JUN 14, and to Thomas Waggoner, JUN 15 and 19, to Thomas McClanahan and to Francis Fauquier, both JUN 19, 1758, GWP S2 L5.

32. GW to Fauquier, JUN 17, 1758, GWP S2 L5; Fauquier to GW, JUN 25, 1758, GWP S4.

33. St. Clair to GW, JUN 18, 1757, GWP S4.

34. GW to Forbes, JUN 19, 1758, GWP S2 L5; Halkett to GW, JUN 25, 1758, GWP S4.

35. St. Clair to GW, JUN 22, 1758, GWP S4; GW to St. Clair, JUN 23 and 26, to William Byrd, to Smith, to Rutherford, to Armorer Henry, and to Commanding Officer North Carolina Detachment, all JUN 24, to Thomas Waggoner, JUN 26, 1758, GWP S2 L5. Stationing the rangers at Fort Loudoun turned out to be a mistake. It was not the kind of duty they had signed up for, and they took out their frustrations on the citizens, and by drinking and deserting. Jacob Hite to GW, JUN 19, Charles Smith to GW, JUL 1, Rutherford to GW, JUL 2, 1758, GWP S4.

36. Note 19 to GW to Blair, MAY 28, 1758, GWP S2 L5; Flexner, *GW Forge*, 193–94; Brumwell, *Redcoats*, 264–89.

37. Bouquet to GW, JUN 27 and JUL 1, AS to GW, JUN 28, 1758, GWP S4.

38. John Armstrong to Bouquet, JUN 28, and Glen to Bouquet, JUL 5, 1758, both quoted Freeman 2:323n.

39. GW to Bouquet, JUL 3, 1758 (1st letter), GWP S2 L5.

40. GW to Bouquet, JUL 3 (2nd letter) and 7, AUG 24, to Francis Halkett, JUL 16, to St. Clair, AUG 13, 1758, GWP S2 L4; Bouquet to GW, JUL 14, AUG 10 and 21, Robert Stewart to GW, AUG 4, St. Clair to GW, AUG 9, 1758, GWP S4.

41. GW to Bouquet, JUL 7, 1758, GWP S2 L5; AS to GW, JUL 14 and AUG 2, Bouquet to GW, AUG 17, 1758, GWP S4.

42. Halkett to GW, AUG 2, Stewart to GW, AUG 8, Bouquet to GW, AUG 23, 1758, GWP S4; GW to Stewart, AUG 11, to Bouquet, AUG 21, 1758, GWP S2 L5.

43. Robert Rutherford to GW, JUL 20 and 31, Charles Smith to GW, JUL 20, 26, and 30, AUG 5, 15, 22, and 27, 1758, GWP S4.

44. Bosomworth to GW, JUL 7, 1758, GWP S4.

45. GW to Bouquet, JUL 7, 16, and 28, to Fauquier, JUL 10, 1758, GWP S2 L5; Bouquet to GW, JUL 14 and AUG 17, Fauquier to GW, JUL 20, Christopher Gist to GW, JUL 20, 1758, GWP S4.

46. Vaudreuil to Minister, JUL–OCT 1758, quoted Parkman, *Montcalm*, 387; GW to Bouquet, JUL 13 (2nd letter), AUG 24, 1758, GWP S2 L5; Robert Stewart to GW, JUL 23, AS to GW, AUG 2, Bosomworth to GW, AUG 9, Bouquet to GW, AUG 17 and 30, 1758, GWP S4.

47. Bouquet to GW, JUL 14, 1758, GWP S4; GW to Bouquet, JUL 16, 1758, GWP S2 L5.

48. GW to Bouquet, JUL 24, AUG 19 and 24, 1758, GWP S2 L5; Colbey Chew, Journal of Trip to Fort Duquesne, AUG 7–19, with Chew to GW, AUG 22, Bouquet to GW, AUG 21 and 23, 1758, GWP S4.

49. GW to Bouquet, JUL 3, 1758 (1st letter), GWP S2 L5.

50. GW to Bouquet, JUL 3 (1st letter) and 13, to Francis Halkett, JUL 16, to AS, JUL 16, 1758, GWP S2 L5; Forbes to Bouquet, JUL nd, 1758, quoted Parkman, *Montcalm*, 383; Bosomworth to GW, JUL 11, Bouquet to GW, JUL 11 and 14, AS to GW, JUL 13, 1758, GWP S4.

51. Gabriel Jones to GW, JUL 6, John Kirkpatrick to GW, JUL 6 and 21 ("dull barbecues"), James Wood to GW, JUL 7, Edward Snickers to GW, JUL 19, AS to GW, JUL 19, Robert Rutherford to GW, JUL 20 and 26, John McNeill to GW, JUL 24, Charles Smith to GW, JUL 24 and AUG 5, Robert Stewart to GW, JUL 25, 1758, GWP S4; GW to Bouquet, JUL 19 and 21, to James Wood ("too sparing"), JUL nd, 1758, GWP S4.

52. Parker, "Anglo-American Wilderness Campaigning"; Forbes, memorandum, nd, to Pitt, JUL 10, to Bouquet, AUG 9, 1758, all quoted Brumwell, *Redcoats*, 141.

53. Parkman, *Montcalm* 2:133ff; Freeman 2:324–26.

54. AS to GW, JUL 6, Bouquet to GW, JUL 8 and 11, 1758, GWP S4; GW to Bouquet, JUL 7 and 9, to Fauquier, JUL 10, 1758, GWP S2 L5.

55. Merrell, *Into American Woods*, 242–49.

56. Forbes to Bouquet, JUN 10, 1758, quoted Anderson, *Crucible*, 267–68; Joseph Chew to GW, JUL 17, Bosomworth to GW, JUL 24, 1758, GWP S4; GW to Bouquet, JUL 21, 1758, GWP S2 L5.

57. Glen to GW and Byrd, JUL 19, Bosomworth to GW, JUL 20, 1758, GWP S4.

58. Mercer to GW, JUL 12, Bouquet to GW, JUL 14, John Kirkpatrick to GW, JUL 21, 1758, GWP S4; GW to Bouquet JUL 13 (1st letter), 16, 19, 21, and 24, 1758, GWP S2 L5; Bouquet to Forbes, JUL 21, and James Young to R. Peters, JUL 23, 1758, both quoted Freeman 2:323.

59. Bouquet to GW, JUL 24 and 27, AS to GW, JUL 27, 1758, GWP S4; GW to Bouquet, JUL 25 and 28, 1758, GWP S2 L5; Bouquet to Forbes, JUL 26, 1758, quoted Freeman 2:326.

60. Robert Rutherford to GW, JUL 31, 1758, GWP S4; Robert Munford to Theodorick Bland, AUG 4, Forbes to Bouquet, AUG 9, Fauquier to Byrd, AUG 17, 1758, all quoted Freeman 2:328–30.

61. Bouquet to Forbes, JUL 31, 1758, quoted Freeman 2:327; GW to Bouquet, AUG 2, 1758, GWP S2 L5.

62. Halkett to GW, AUG 2, Robert Stewart to GW, AUG 5, 1758, GWP S4; GW to Halkett, AUG 2, to Bouquet, AUG 6 and 7, 1758, GWP S2 L5.

63. Forbes to Bouquet, AUG 9, to Abercromby, AUG 11, 1758, quoted Freeman 2:328–29.

64. Bosomworth to GW, AUG 9, Bouquet to GW, AUG 10, 1758, GWP S4; GW to Walker, AUG 11, 1758, GWP S2 L5.

65. GW to St. Clair, AUG 13, to Bouquet, AUG 13 and 18, 1758, GWP S2 L5; Walker to GW, AUG 14, Bouquet to GW, AUG 17, William Ramsey to GW, AUG 17 and 19, 1758, GWP S4.

66. Bouquet to GW, AUG 21 and 26, John Carlyle to GW, AUG 22, Bosomworth to GW, AUG 23, Kirkpatrick to GW, AUG 23, 1758, GWP S4; GW to Bouquet, AUG 24, 1758, GWP S2 L5.

67. GW to Bouquet, AUG 28, 1758, GWP S2 L5; Bouquet to GW, AUG 30, 1758, GWP S4.

68. Gipson, *Victorious Years*, 247–60; Anderson, *Crucible*, 270–71; Forbes to Bouquet, AUG 18, 1758, quoted Parkman, *Montcalm*, 388; Bosomworth to GW, AUG 23, 1758, GWP S4.

69. GW to JR, SEP 1, and to Fauquier, SEP 2, 1758, GWP S2 L5.

70. JR to GW, SEP 13, Fauquier, *Speech of the Honorable Francis Fauquier*, SEP 14, copy forwarded with Fauquier to GW, SEP 16, "The Humble Address of the Council," and "The Humble Address of the House of Burgesses," both SEP 18, William Ramsey to GW, OCT 17, 1758, GWP S4; Hening, *Statutes at Large* 7:171; GW to Fauquier, SEP 28, 1758, GWP S2 L5.

71. GW to Bouquet, SEP 10, to Forbes, SEP 12, 1758, GWP S2 L5; Forbes to Bouquet, SEP 4, 1758, quoted Freeman 2:332; Gist to GW, SEP 3, Bouquet to GW, SEP 4, Gist to GW, SEP 4, 1758, GWP S4.

72. William Ramsey to GW, SEP 3 and 12, AS to GW, SEP 9 and 14, 1758, GWP S4; Forbes to Bouquet, AUG 20 and SEP 4, 1758, and St. Clair, nd, quoted Freeman 2:332.

73. AS to GW, SEP 9 and 13, Hugh Mercer to GW, SEP 10, 11, and 15, Forbes to GW, SEP 16, 1758, GWP S4; GW to George Mercer, SEP 9, to Forbes, SEP 12, to Fauquier, SEP 15, 1758, GWP S2 L5; Harry Gordon to Bouquet, SEP 10, Edward Shippen to His Father, SEP 15, Forbes to Bouquet, SEP 17, 1758, all quoted Freeman 2:332n, 333.

74. Accounts of this include Freeman 2:335–29; Flexner, *GW Forge*, 197–99; Fleming, "George Washington in Love"; and Fleming, *Intimate*, 13–18.

75. William Ramsey to GW, SEP 12, Fauquier to GW, OCT 7, 1758, GWP S4; GW to Fauquier, SEP 25, 1758, British officer quoted n.76, and Bouquet quoted n.81, GWP S2 L5.

76. Forbes to Bouquet, SEP 23, 1758, quoted Freeman 2:335.
77. GW to Forbes, OCT 8, 1758, and n.84, GWP S2 L5.
78. Forbes to R. Peters, OCT 16, 1758, quoted Freeman 2:351–52.
79. Freeman 2:352–54; Forbes to Bouquet, OCT 15 and 25, and to Pitt, OCT 20, 1758, quoted Parkman, *Montcalm*, 396; Robert Stewart to GW, OCT 17, 22, 24, and 25, William Ramsey to GW, OCT 17, 1758, GWP S4.
80. Anderson, *Crucible*, 274–81, Forbes to Richard Peters, OCT 16, 1758, quoted 274–75.
81. Forbes to Pitt, OCT 20–27, 1758, quoted Freeman 2:355; GW to Fauquier, OCT 30, 1758, GWP S2 L5; Anderson, *George Washington Remembers*, 22–23; Fauquier to GW, NOV 4, 1758, GWP S4.
82. Freeman 2:357–58; Flexner, *GW Forge*, 216–17; Bullitt quoted Ferling, *Ascent*, 43; Anderson, *George Washington Remembers*, 23, Forbes to Abercromby, NOV 17, 1758, quoted 59 n.67.
83. GW to Forbes, NOV 15, 16, 17 (2 letters) and 18, 1758, GWP S2 L5; Bouquet to GW, NOV 16, Halkett to GW, NOV 21, 1758, GWP S4; Freeman, 2:358–64; Flexner, *GW Forge*, 217–19.
84. GW to Fauquier, NOV 28, 1758, GWP S2 L5.
85. GW to Fauquier, DEC 2, 1758, GWP S2 L5.
86. Bouquet to William Allen, NOV 25, 1758, quoted Freeman 2:366.
87. GW to Fauquier, DEC 9, to Forbes, DEC 30, 1758, GWP S2 L5; Robert Stewart to GW, DEC 12, 20, 29, and 31, James Craik to GW, DEC 20, 1758, GWP S4; Anderson, *George Washington Remembers*, 23–24.

ENVOI

1. 1st Virginia Regiment Officers to GW, DEC 31, 1758, GWP S4.
2. GW to Captain Robert Stewart and Gentlemen Officers of the Virginia Regiment, JAN 10, 1759, copy in Flexner, *GW Forge*, 349–50, from original in Rosenbach Library, Philadelphia.
3. Andrews, *For President's Eyes*, 6–12.
4. Weigley, *History*, 63; Maurer, "Military Justice Under Washington"; Clary, *Adopted Son*, 101–02; Chinard, *Washington as French*, 49–51, 65.
5. Clary, *Adopted Son*, 155–62.
6. GW quoted ibid., 53; Anderson, *Crucible*, 291–93.
7. Brady, *Martha Washington*, 63–65; Fleming, *Intimate*, 19–20; Clary, *Adopted Son*, 53–54.
8. Gipson, *Victorious Years*, 293–96; Titus, *Old Dominion*, 196–99; Anderson, *Crucible*, 323–24; Robinson, *American Forts*, 39–42.
9. Clary, *Adopted Son*, 55–56, GW quoted 55; Achenbach, *Grand Idea*; Flexner, *GW Forge*, 227–345; Ellis, *His Excellency*, 35–72.
10. Anderson and Cayton, *Dominion*, 146–47; Alberts, *Charming Field*, 57; Flexner, *GW Forge*, 293–97; GWD 1:192 n.52.

11. Flexner, *GW Forge*, 317; Anderson and Cayton, *Dominion*, 105–06.
12. Anderson and Cayton, *Dominion*, 451 n.3; Hogeland, *Whiskey Rebellion*; Clary, *Inspectors General*, 79–81.
13. GW to AS, JUL 20, 1776, quoted Anderson, *War That Made*, xix; Rosemarie Zagarri, "Washington's 'Remarks' in Context," in Anderson, *George Washington Remembers*, 89–107; Zagarri, *David Humphreys' 'Life.'*
14. GW to AS, JUL 20, 1776, quoted Anderson, *War That Made*, xix; GW to Lafayette, MAY 10, 1786, FGW 28:420–25; Boller, *Washington and Religion*.
15. GW to François-Jean, comte de Chastellux, APR 25, 1788, GWP S2 L15.
16. Quoted Flexner, *GW Forge*, 340–41.

BIBLIOGRAPHY

Note: Libraries, archives, museums, historic sites, and other institutions important to the subject of this book are cited in the Acknowledgments. Newspaper, newsletter, and "gazette" articles are cited in the chapter Notes only; the same is true of articles included in books listed in the Bibliography.

ARCHIVAL COLLECTIONS

The chief source of original documentation used for this book was the George Washington Papers at the Library of Congress, now available in their entirety online at the Library's website, loc.gov.

There is another substantial collection of Washington's papers at the University of Virginia, which is nearing completion of a publication, in scores of volumes, of every surviving word that Washington wrote, with remarkable indexing and Internet access. Many of his writings pertinent to this volume, however, are available in the earlier efforts of Sparks, Fitzpatrick, and Jackson and Twohig, cited below.

PUBLISHED ORIGINAL SOURCES: BOOKS

Anderson, Fred, editor. *George Washington Remembers: Reflections on the French and Indian War.* Lanham, Maryland: Rowman & Littlefield, 2004.

Anonymous [Henry Bouquet]. *An Historical Account of the Expedition Against the Ohio Indians in the Year MDCCLXIV Under the Command of Henry Bouquet, Esq.* London: Reprinted for T. Jefferies, Geographer to His Majesty at Charing Cross, 1766.

Barr, Daniel P., editor. *The Boundaries Between Us: Natives and Newcomers Along the Frontiers of the Old Northwest Territory, 1750–1850*. Kent, Ohio: Kent State University Press, 2006.

Bland, Humphrey. *A Treatise of Military Discipline* . . . 5th edition. Dublin, 1743.

Bonin, "Jolicoeur" Charles. *Memoir of a French and Indian War Soldier.* Edited by Andrew Gallup. Westminster, Maryland: Heritage Books, 2007.

Brock, R. A., editor. *The Official Records of Robert Dinwiddie, Lieutenant-Governor of the Colony of Virginia, 1751–1758.* 2 volumes. Richmond: Virginia Historical Society, 1883–1884.

Chinard, Gilbert, editor and translator. *George Washington as the French Knew Him: A Collection of Texts.* New York: Greenwood, 1940.

Crozier, William A., editor. *Virginia Colonial Militia, 1651–1776.* Baltimore: Southern, 1954.

Darlington, William M., editor. *Christopher Gist's Journals, with Historical, Geographical and Ethnological Notes and Biographies of His Contemporaries.* Westminster, Maryland: Heritage Books, 2006.

Fauquier, Francis. *The Speech of the Honorable Francis Fauquier, Esq., His Majesty's Lieutenant-Governor, and Commander in Chief, of the Colony and Dominion of Virginia: to the General Assembly [September 14, 1758].* Williamsburg: William Hunter, 1758.

The Federalist: A Commentary on the Constitution of the United States, Written by Alexander Hamilton, James Madison, and John Jay. New York: Tudor, 1947.

Fitzpatrick, John C., editor. *The Last Will and Testament of George Washington and Schedule of His Property.* Mt. Vernon, Virginia: Mount Vernon Ladies Association of the Union, 1939.

———, editor. *The Writings of George Washington, from the Original Manuscript Sources.* 39 volumes. Washington: Government Printing Office, 1931–1944.

Ford, Worthington C., editor. *The Writings of George Washington.* 14 volumes. New York: G. P. Putnam's Sons, 1889–1893.

Franklin, Benjamin. *The Autobiography of Benjamin Franklin.* New York: Penguin Putnam, 2001.

Franklin, Julian Boyd, editor. *Indian Treaties Printed by Benjamin Franklin, 1736–1762.* Philadelphia: Pennsylvania Historical Society, 1938.

Gist, William M. D., editor. *Christopher Gist's Journals with Historical, Geographical, and Ethnological Notes and Biographies of His Contemporaries.* Cleveland: Arthur H. Clark, 1893.

Grenier, Fernand, editor. *Papiers Contrecoeur et autres documents concernant le conflit anglo-français sur l'Ohio de 1754 à 1756.* Quebec: Les Presses Universitaires Laval, 1952.

Grotius, Hugo (Huig van Groot). *The Law of War and Peace [De Juri Belli ac Pacis].* Translated by Louise R. Loomis. Roslyn, New York: Walter J. Black, 1949.

Hall, Charles C., editor. *Gen. Braddock's Defeat: Contemporary Reports and Later Remembrances: A Compilation of Articles from the Colonial Gazettes, London Magazines and Later Memoirs Relative to General Braddock's Defeat at the Battle of the Monongahela.* Capon Bridge, West Virginia: The Fort Edwards Foundation, 2005.

Hamilton, Charles, editor. *Braddock's Defeat*. Norman: University of Oklahoma Press, 1959.

Hening, William W., editor. *The Statutes at Large: Being a Collection of All the Laws of Virginia From the First Session of the Legislature, in the Year 1619*. 13 volumes. New York, Philadelphia, Richmond: various publishers, 1819–1823.

Jackson, Donald, and Dorothy Twohig, editors. *The Diaries of George Washington*. 6 volumes. Charlottesville: University Press of Virginia, 1976.

Jacobs, Wilbur R., editor. *The Appalachian Indian Frontier: The Edmund Atkin Report and Plan of 1755*. Lincoln: University of Nebraska Press, 1967.

Kent, Donald H., editor. *Contrecoeur's Copy of George Washington's Journal for 1754*. Harrisburg: Pennsylvania Historical and Museum Commission, 1952.

Kopperman, Paul E., compiler. *Braddock at the Monongahela*. Pittsburgh: University of Pittsburg Press, 1977.

The Manual Exercise, as Ordered by His Majesty, in 1764. London, 1764.

McDowell, William L. Jr., editor. *Colonial Records of South Carolina: Documents Relating to Indian Affairs, 1754–1765*. Columbia: South Carolina Department of Archives, 1958.

A Memorial Containing a Summary View of Facts, with Their Authorities. In Answer to the Observations Sent by the English Ministry to the Courts of Europe (Translated from the French). A translation of *Mémoire contenant le précis des faits, avec leurs pièces justificatives pour servir de réponse aux observations envoyées par les ministres d'Angleterre, dans les cours de l'Europe* [Paris: npub, 1756]. Translated and published in London, reprinted New York: H. Gaine, 1757.

Moore, Charles, editor. *George Washington's Rules of Civility and Decent Behavior*. Boston: Houghton Mifflin, 1926.

Mulkearn, Lois, editor. *George Mercer Papers Relating to the Ohio Company of Virginia*. Pittsburgh: University of Pittsburgh Press, 1954.

Narratives of the French & Indian War: Ranger Brown's Narrative, The Adventures of Robert Eastburn, the Journal of Rufus Putnam, Provincial Infantry, Orderly Book and Journal of Major John Hawks on the Ticonderoga-Crown Point Campaign. Eyewitness to War Series. np: Leonaur, 2008.

Padover, Saul K., editor. *The Washington Papers*. Norwalk, Connecticut: Easton, 1955.

Pargellis, Stanley, editor. *Military Affairs in North America, 1748–1765*. New York: Appleton-Century, 1936.

Peyser, Joseph L., editor. *Jacques Legardeur de Saint-Pierre: Officer, Gentleman, Entrepreneur*. East Lansing: Michigan State University Press, 1996.

Sargent, Winthrop, editor. *The History of An Expedition Against Fort Du Quesne in 1755 Under General Edward Braddock*. Philadelphia: Lippincott, 1856.

Sparks, Jared, editor. *The Writings of George Washington*. 12 volumes. Boston: Tappan & Dennet, 1834–1837.

Stevens, Sylvester, and Donald H. Kent, editors. *Journal of Chaussegros de Léry*. Harrisburg, Pennsylvania: Works Progress Administration, 1940.

———, editors. *Wilderness Chronicles of Northwestern Pennsylvania*. Harrisburg, Pennsylvania: Works Progress Administration, 1941.

Walpole, Horace. *Memoirs of the Reign of King George the Second.* 3 volumes. Lon-
    don: Colburn, 1847.
Washington, George. *Journal of Major George Washington, Sent by the Hon. Robert
    Dinwiddie, Esq., His Majesty's Lieutenant-Governor, and Commander in Chief of
    Virginia, to the Commandant of the French Forces on Ohio. To Which Are Added,
    the Governor's Letter, and a Translation of the French Officer's Answer.* Williams-
    burg: William Hunter, 1754.
Zagarri, Rosemarie, editor. *David Humphreys'"Life of General Washington" with
    George Washington's "Remarks."* Athens: University of Georgia Press, 1991.

PUBLISHED ORIGINAL SOURCES: PERIODICALS

Bunford, Samuel, editor. "The Ohio Expedition of 1754." *Pennsylvania Maga-
    zine of History and Biography* 18 (1894–1895):43–50.
Davis, N. Darnell, editor. "British Newspaper Accounts of Braddock's Defeat."
    Pennsylvania Magazine of History and Biography 23 (1899):310–28.
Harrison, Fairfax, editor. "With Braddock's Army: Mrs. Browne's Diary in Virginia
    and Maryland." *Virginia Magazine of History and Biography* 32 (1924):305–20.
"Illustrative Documents Descriptive of the Defeat of Major-General Edward
    Braddock." American Antiquarian Society *Proceedings,* New Series 19
    (1908):293–301.
"Journal de Joseph-Gaspard Chaussegros de Léry." *Archives de Québec* (1927–
    1928):372–373.
"Journals of the Council of Virginia in Executive Sessions, 1737–1763." *Virginia
    Magazine of History and Biography* 14 (1906–1907):225–45.
McAnear, Beverly, editor. "Personal Accounts of the Albany Congress of 1754."
    Mississippi Valley Historical Review 39 (1953):735–45.
Schutz, John A., editor. "A Private Report of General Braddock's Defeat." *Penn-
    sylvania Magazine of History and Biography* 79 (1955):374–77.
Stotz, Charles M., editor. "A Letter from Wills' Creek—Harry Gordon's Ac-
    count of Braddock's Defeat." *Western Pennsylvania Historical Magazine* 44
    (1961):129–36.
"The Treaty of Logg's Town, 1752." *Virginia Magazine of History and Biography*
    13 (1905–1906):143–74.
Walsh, Richard, editor. "Braddock on July 9, 1755." *Maryland Historical Maga-
    zine* 60 (1965):421–27.
Wilson, J. Cook, editor. "The Campaign of General Braddock." *English Histori-
    cal Review* 1 (1886):149–52.

SECONDARY SOURCES: BOOKS

Achenbach, Joel. *The Grand Idea: George Washington's Potomac and the Race to the
    West.* New York: Simon & Schuster, 2004.

Alberts, Robert C. *A Charming Field for an Encounter: The Story of George Washington's Fort Necessity.* Washington: Department of the Interior, 1975.

Alden, John R. *Robert Dinwiddie: Servant of the Crown.* Charlottesville: University of Virginia Press, 1973.

Anderson, Fred. *Crucible of War: The Seven Years' War and the Fate of Empire in British North America, 1754–1766.* New York: Vintage, 2001.

———. *The War That Made America: A Short History of the French and Indian War.* New York: Penguin, 2005.

———, and Andrew Cayton. *The Dominion of War: Empire and Liberty in North America, 1500–2000.* New York: Penguin, 2005.

Andrew, Christopher. *For the President's Eyes Only: Secret Intelligence and the American Presidency from Washington to Bush.* New York: HarperCollins, 1995.

Arno, Stephen F., and Stephen Allison-Bunnell. *Flames in Our Forest: Disaster or Renewal?* Seattle: Island Press, 2002.

Ashburn, Percy M. *A History of the Medical Department of the United States Army.* Boston: Houghton-Mifflin, 1929.

———. *The Ranks of Death: A Medical History of the Conquest of America.* Edited by Frank D. Ashburn. New York: Coward-McCann, 1947.

Asprey, Robert B. *War in the Shadows: The Guerrilla in History.* 2 volumes. Garden City, New York: Doubleday, 1975.

Audet, Francois-Jean. *Jean-Daniel Dumas: Le Héro de la Monongahéla.* Montreal: Ducharme, 1920.

Axelrod, Alan. *Blooding at Great Meadows: Young George Washington and the Battle that Shaped the Man.* Philadelphia: Running Press, 2007.

Bailey, Kenneth P. *The Ohio Company of Virginia and the Westward Movement, 1748–1792: A Chapter in the History of the Colonial Frontier.* Glendale, California: Arthur H. Clarke, 1939.

Baker-Crothers, Hayes. *Virginia and the French and Indian War.* Chicago: University of Chicago Press, 1928.

Barbour, Michael G., and William Dwight Billings, editors. *North American Terrestrial Vegetation.* Second edition. New York: Cambridge University Press, 1999.

Beveridge, N. E. [pseudonym of Harold L. Peterson]. *Cups of Valor.* Harrisburg, Pennsylvania: Stackpole, 1968.

Bird, Harrison. *Battle for a Continent.* New York: Oxford University Press, 1965.

Boatner, Mark M. III. *Encyclopedia of the American Revolution.* New York: David McKay, 1974. Third edition, Mechanicsville, Pennsylvania: Stackpole, 1994.

Boller, Paul F. Jr. *George Washington and Religion.* Dallas: Southern Methodist University Press, 1963.

Boorstin, Daniel J. *The Americans: The Colonial Experience.* New York: Random House, 1958.

Borneman, Walter R. *The French and Indian War: Deciding the Fate of North America.* New York: HarperCollins, 2006.

Brady, Patricia. *Martha Washington: An American Life.* New York: Viking Penguin, 2005.

Brandes, Ray, editor. *Troopers West: Military and Indian Affairs on the American Frontier.* San Diego: Frontier Heritage, 1970.

Brockett, Franklin Longdon. *The Lodge of Washington: A History of the Alexandria Washington Lodge, No. 22, A. F. and A. M. of Alexandria, Virginia.* Alexandria, Virginia: George E. French, 1876.

Brookhiser, Richard. *Founding Father: Rediscovering George Washington.* New York: Free Press, 1996.

Browning, Reed. *The Duke of Newcastle.* New Haven: Yale University Press, 1975.

Brumwell, Stephen. *Redcoats: The British Soldier and War in the Americas, 1755–1763.* New York: Cambridge University Press, 2002.

Burns, James MacGregor, and Susan Dunn. *George Washington.* New York: Times Books, 2004.

Calloway, Colin G. *The Shawnees and the War for America.* New York: Viking Penguin, 2007.

Chadwick, Bruce. *George Washington's War: The Forging of a Revolutionary Leader and the American Presidency.* Naperville, Illinois: Sourcebooks, 2004.

Chartrand, René. *Colonial Troops, 1610–1774.* Oxford, United Kingdom: Osprey, 2002.

———. *The Forts of New France in Northeast America, 1600–1763.* Oxford, United Kingdom: Osprey, 2008.

———. *The French Soldier in Colonial America.* Bloomfield, Ontario: Museum Restoration Service, 1984.

———. *Monongahela 1754–55: Washington's Defeat, Braddock's Disaster.* Oxford, United Kingdom: Osprey, 2004.

Clary, David A. *Adopted Son: Washington, Lafayette, and the Friendship That Saved the Revolution.* New York: Bantam Dell, 2007.

———. *Fortress America: The Corps of Engineers, Hampton Roads, and United States Coastal Defense.* Charlottesville: University Press of Virginia, 1990.

———. *The Inspectors General of the United States Army, 1777–1903.* Washington: Department of the Army, 1987.

———. *These Relics of Barbarism: A History of Barracks and Guardhouses of the United States Army, 1800–1880.* Harpers Ferry, West Virginia: National Park Service, 1985.

Cleland, Hugh. *George Washington in the Ohio Valley.* Pittsburgh: University of Pittsburgh Press, 1955.

Coil, Henry Wilson. *A Comprehensive View of Freemasonry.* Revised edition, Richmond, Virginia: Macoy, 1998.

Corwin, Edward S. *French Policy and the American Alliance of 1778.* Princeton, New Jersey: Princeton University Press, 1916. Reprinted, Gloucester, Massachusetts: Peter Smith, 1969.

Crocker, Thomas E. *Braddock's March: How the Man Sent to Seize a Continent Changed American History.* Yardley, Pennsylvania: Westholme, 2009.

Cubbison, Douglas R. *The British Defeat of the French in Pennsylvania, 1758: A Military History of the Forbes Campaign Against Fort Duquesne.* Jefferson, North Carolina: McFarland, 2010.

Cunliffe, Marcus. *George Washington: Man and Monument*. Boston: Little, Brown, 1958.

Danson, Edwin. *Drawing the Line: How Mason and Dixon Surveyed the Most Famous Border in America*. New York: Wiley, 2001.

Danziger, Edmund J. Jr. *The Chippewas of Lake Superior*. Norman: University of Oklahoma Press, 1979.

DeConde, Alexander. *Entangling Alliance: Politics and Diplomacy under George Washington*. Durham, North Carolina: Duke University Press, 1958.

Dederer, John. *War in America to 1775: Before Yankee Doodle*. New York: New York University Press, 1990.

Dowd, Gregory Evan. *War Under Heaven: Pontiac, the Indian Nations, and the British Empire*. Baltimore: Johns Hopkins University Press, 2002.

Dupuy, R. Ernest. *The Compact History of the United States Army*. Revised edition. New York: Hawthorn Books, 1961.

Eccles, W. J. *The Canadian Frontier, 1534–1760*. Albuquerque: University of New Mexico Press, 1983.

Ekirch, Arthur A. Jr. *The Civilian and the Military*. New York: Oxford University Press, 1956.

Ellis, Joseph. *His Excellency: George Washington*. New York: Knopf, 2004.

Faÿ, Bernard. *George Washington: Republican Aristocrat*. Boston: Houghton-Mifflin, 1931.

———. *The Revolutionary Spirit in France and America*. Translated by Ramon Guthrie. New York: Harcourt, Brace, 1927.

Ferling, John. *The Ascent of George Washington: The Hidden Political Genius of an American Icon*. New York: Bloomsbury, 2009.

———. *The First of Men: A Life of George Washington*. Knoxville: University of Tennessee Press, 1983.

———. *A Leap in the Dark: The Struggle to Create the American Republic*. New York: Oxford University Press, 2003.

———. *A Wilderness of Miseries: War and Warriors in Early America*. Westport, Connecticut: Greenwood, 1980.

Fischer, David Hackett. *Champlain's Dream*. New York: Simon & Schuster, 2008.

Fleming, Thomas. *The Intimate Lives of the Founding Fathers*. New York: Harper-Collins, 2009.

Flexner, James Thomas. *George Washington and the New Nation (1783–1793)*. Boston: Little, Brown, 1970.

———. *George Washington: Anguish and Farewell (1793–1799)*. Boston: Little, Brown, 1972.

———. *George Washington in the American Revolution (1775–1783)*. Boston: Little, Brown, 1968.

———. *George Washington: The Forge of Experience (1732–1775)*. Boston: Little, Brown, 1965.

———. *Washington: The Indispensable Man*. Boston: Little, Brown, 1974.

Fortescue, J. W. *A History of the British Army*. 2 volumes. London: Macmillan, 1910.

Fowler, William M. Jr. *Empires at War: The French and Indian War and the Struggle for North America, 1754–1763.* New York: Walker, 2005.

Freeman, Douglas Southall. *George Washington.* 7 volumes. New York: Scribner, 1948–1957.

Frégault, Guy. *Canada: The War of the Conquest.* Translated by Margaret M.Cameron. Toronto: Oxford University Press, 1969.

Gallay, Alan. *The Indian Slave Trade: The Rise of the English Empire in the American South.* New Haven: Yale University Press, 2002.

Gallup, Andrew, and Donald Shaffer. *La Marine: The French Colonial Soldier in Canada, 1745–1761.* Bowie, Maryland: Heritage Books, 1992.

Ganoe, William A. *History of the United States Army.* Revised edition. New York: Appleton-Century, 1942.

Gipson, Lawrence Henry. *The Victorious Years, 1758–1760.* New York: Knopf, 1967.

———. *The Years of Defeat, 1754–1757.* New York: Knopf, 1968.

———. *Zones of International Friction: North America, South of the Great Lakes Region, 1748–1754.* New York: Knopf, 1939.

Gottschalk, Louis R. *The Era of the French Revolution (1715–1815).* Cambridge, Massachusetts: Houghton-Mifflin, 1957.

———, and Donald Lach, with the collaboration of Shirley A. Bill. *Toward the French Revolution: Europe and America in the Eighteenth-Century World.* New York: Charles Scribner's Sons, 1973.

Grenier, John. *The First Way of War: American War Making on the Frontier, 1607–1814.* New York: Cambridge University Press, 2005.

Hamilton, Edward P. *The French and Indian Wars: The Story of Battles and Forts in the Wilderness.* Garden City, New York: Doubleday, 1962.

Harding, Richard. *Amphibious Warfare in the Eighteenth Century: The British Expedition to the West Indies, 1740–1742.* London: Boydell, 1991.

Harkin, Michael E., editor. *Native Americans and the Environment: Perspectives on the Ecological Indian.* Lincoln: University of Nebraska Press, 2007.

Higginbotham, Don, editor. *Reconsideration of the Revolutionary War: Selected Essays.* Westport, Connecticut: Greenwood, 1978.

Hill, Jim Dan. *The Minute Man in Peace and War: A History of the National Guard.* Harrisburg, Pennsylvania: Stackpole, 1964.

Hodge, Frederic, editor. *Handbook of American Indians North of Mexico.* 2 volumes. Washington: Bureau of American Ethnology, Smithsonian Institution, 1907–1910.

Hofstra, Warren R., editor. *George Washington and the Virginia Backcountry.* Madison: University of Wisconsin Press, 1998.

Hogeland, William. *The Whiskey Rebellion: George Washington, Alexander Hamilton, and the Frontier Rebels Who Challenged America's Newfound Sovereignty.* New York: Scribner, 2006.

Houlding, J. A. *Fit for Service: The Training of the British Army, 1715–1795.* Oxford, United Kingdom: Oxford University Press, 1981.

Hughes, Quentin. *Military Architecture.* New York: St. Martin's, 1974.

Hunter, William A. *Forts on the Pennsylvania Frontier, 1753–1758*. Harrisburg: Pennsylvania Historical and Museum Commission, 1960.

Huntington, Samuel P. *The Soldier and the State: The Theory and Politics of Civil-Military Relations*. New York: Vintage, 1964.

Isaacson, Walter. *Benjamin Franklin: An American Life*. New York: Simon & Schuster, 2003.

Jacobs, Wilbur R. *Diplomacy and Indian Gifts: Anglo-French Rivalry Along the Ohio and Northwestern Frontiers, 1747–1763*. Palo Alto, California: Stanford University Press, 1950.

James, Albert P., and Charles M. Stotz. *Drums in the Forest*. Pittsburgh: Historical Society of Western Pennsylvania, 1958.

Jennings, Francis. *The Ambiguous Iroquois Empire: The Covenant Chain Confederation of Indian Tribes with the English Colonies from Its Beginnings to the Lancaster Treaty of 1744*. New York: Norton, 1984.

————. *Empire of Fortune: Crowns, Colonies, and Tribes in the Seven Years War in America*. New York: Norton, 1988.

————, and others, editors. *The History and Culture of Iroquois Diplomacy*. Syracuse, New York: Syracuse University press, 1985.

Johnson, Michael G., and Richard Hook. *Encyclopedia of Native Tribes of North America*. Buffalo, New York: Firefly Books, 2007.

Keegan, John, and Richard Holmes. *Soldiers: A History of Men in Battle*. New York: Viking, 1986.

Kennett, Lee. *The French Armies in the Seven Years' War: A Study in Military Organization and Administration*. Durham, North Carolina: Duke University Press, 1967.

Kent, Donald H. *The French Invasion of Western Pennsylvania, 1753*. Harrisburg: Pennsylvania Historical and Museum Commission, 1954.

King, J. C. H. *Thunderbird and Lightning: Indian Life in Northeastern North America, 1600–1900*. London: British Museum, 1982.

Knollenberg, Bernhard. *George Washington: The Virginia Period, 1732–1775*. Durham, North Carolina: Duke University Press, 1964.

Koenig, William J. *Americans at War, from Colonial Times to Vietnam*. New York: Putnam, 1980.

Koentz, L. K. *Robert Dinwiddie: Servant of the Crown*. Glendale, California: Arthur H. Clarke, 1941.

Krech, Shepart III. *The Ecological Indian: Myth and History*. New York: Norton, 2000.

Langguth, A. J. *Patriots: The Men Who Started the American Revolution*. New York: Simon & Schuster, 1988.

Leach, Douglas Edward. *Arms for Empire: A Military History of the British Colonies in North America, 1607–1763*. New York: Macmillan, 1973.

Leckie, Robert. *The Wars of America*. 2 volumes. New York: Harper and Row, 1968.

Lengel, Edward G. *General George Washington: A Military Life*. New York: Random House, 2005.

Lewis, Thomas A. *For King and Country: The Maturing of George Washington, 1748–1760.* New York: HarperCollins, 1993.

Longmore, Paul K. *The Invention of George Washington.* Charlottesville: University Press of Virginia, 1999.

Manegold, C. S. *Ten Hills Farm: The Forgotten History of Slavery in the North.* Princeton, New Jersey: Princeton University Press, 2009.

Martin, James Kirby, and Mark Edward Lender. *A Respectable Army: The Military Origins of the Republic, 1763–1789.* Arlington Heights, Illinois: Harlan Davidson, 1982.

McCardell, Lee. *Ill-Starred General: Braddock of the Coldstream Guards.* Pittsburgh: University of Pittsburgh Press, 1958.

McClung, Robert M. *Young George Washington and the French and Indian War, 1753–1758.* Chicago: Linnet, 2002.

McConnell, Michael N. *A Country Between: The Upper Ohio Valley and Its Peoples, 1724–1774.* Lincoln: University of Nebraska Press, 1999.

Merrell, James H. *Into the American Woods: Negotiators on the Pennsylvania Frontier.* New York: Norton, 1999.

Merrill, James M., editor. *Uncommon Valor: The Exciting Story of the Army.* Chicago: Rand McNally, 1964.

Millis, Walter. *Arms and Men: A Study in American Military History.* New York: Putnam, 1956. Reprinted, New York: New American Library, nd.

Morgan, Robert. *Boone: A Biography.* Chapel Hill, North Carolina: Algonquin, 2007.

O'Brien, Conor Cruise. *First in Peace: How George Washington Set the Course for America.* Cambridge, Massachusetts: Da Capo, 2009.

O'Connell, Robert L. *Of Arms and Men: A History of War, Weapons, and Aggression.* New York: Oxford University Press, 1989.

O'Meara, Walter. *Guns at the Forks.* Englewood Cliffs, New Jersey: Prentice-Hall, 1965.

Pargellis, Stanley. *Lord Loudoun in North America.* New Haven: Yale University Press, 1933.

Parker, Geoffrey. *The Military Revolution: Military Innovation and the Rise of the West.* New York: Cambridge University Press, 1988.

Parkman, Francis. *Montcalm and Wolfe: The French and Indian War.* 2 volumes. 1884. Reprinted, 2 volumes in 1, New York: Da Capo, 1984, 2001.

———. *Musket & Tomahawk: A Military History of the French & Indian War, 1753–60.* np: Leonaur, 2007.

Peckham, Howard H. *The Colonial Wars, 1689–1762.* Chicago: University of Chicago Press, 1964.

Pyne, Stephen J. *Fire in America: A Cultural History of Wildland and Rural Fire.* Princeton, New Jersey: Princeton University Press, 1982.

Raphael, Ray. *Founders: The People Who Brought You a Nation.* New York: New Press, 2009.

Rasmussen, William M. S., and Robert S. Tilton. *George Washington: The Man Behind the Myths.* Charlottesville: University Press of Virginia, 1999.

Reinhardt, George C., and William R. Kinter. *The Haphazard Years: How America Has Gone to War.* Garden City, New York: Doubleday, 1960.

Richter, Daniel K. *Facing East from Indian Country: A Native History of Early America.* Cambridge, Massachusetts: Harvard University Press, 2001.

——. *The Ordeal of the Longhouse: The Peoples of the Iroquois League in the Era of European Colonization.* Chapel Hill: University of North Carolina Press, 1992.

——, and James H. Merrell, editors. *Beyond the Covenant Chain: The Iroquois and Their Neighbors in Indian North America, 1600–1800.* Syracuse, New York: Syracuse University Press, 1987.

Ridley, Jasper. *The Freemasons: A History of the World's Most Powerful Secret Society.* New York: Arcade, 2001.

Roberts, Allen E. *George Washington: Master Mason.* Richmond, Virginia: Macoy, 1976.

Robinson, Willard B. *American Forts: Architectural Form and Function.* Urbana: University of Illinois Press, 1977.

Robitaille, Georges. *Washington et Jumonville.* Montreal: Le Devoir, 1933.

Rogers, Alan. *Empire and Liberty: American Resistance to British Authority, 1755–1763.* Berkeley: University of California Press, 1974.

Ross, John F. *War on the Run: The Epic Story of Robert Rogers and the Conquest of America's First Frontier.* New York: Random House, 2009.

Sadosky, Leonard J. *Revolutionary Negotiations: Indians, Empires, and Diplomats in the Founding of America.* Richmond: University of Virginia Press, 2010.

Schwartz, Barry. *The Making of an American Symbol.* New York: Free Press, 1987.

Shy, John. *Toward Lexington: The Role of the British Army in the Coming of the American Revolution.* Princeton, New Jersey: Princeton University Press, 1965.

Silver, Peter. *Our Savage Neighbors: How Indian War Transformed Early America.* New York: W. W. Norton, 2008.

Silver, Timothy. *A New Face on the Countryside: Indians, Colonists, and Slaves in South Atlantic Forests, 1500–1800.* New York: Cambridge University Press, 1990.

Smith, Louis. *American Democracy and Political Power: A Study of Civil Control of the Military Power in the United States.* Chicago: University of Chicago Press, 1951.

Sparks, Jared. *The Life of Washington.* Boston: Tappan and Dennet, 1843.

Spaulding, Oliver Lyman. *The United States Army in War and Peace.* New York: Putnam, 1937.

Stanley, George F. G. *New France: The Last Phase, 1744–1760.* Toronto: McClelland and Stewart, 1968.

Starkey, Armstrong. *European and Native American Warfare, 1675–1815.* Norman: University of Oklahoma Press, 1999.

Stewart, Omer C. *Forgotten Fires: Native Americans and the Transient Wilderness.* Edited and updated by Henry T. Lewis and Kat Anderson. Norman: University of Oklahoma Press, 2002.

Taylor, Alan. *The Divided Ground: Indians, Settlers, and the Northern Borderland of the American Revolution.* New York: Knopf, 2006.

Tilberg, Frederick. *Fort Necessity National Battlefield Site, Pennsylvania.* Washington: National Park Service, 1954.

Tillson, Albert H. Jr. *Accommodating Revolutions: Virginia's Northern Neck in an Era of Transformations, 1760–1810.* Charlottesville: University of Virginia Press, 2010.

Titus, James. *The Old Dominion at War: Society, Politics, and Warfare in Late Colonial Virginia.* Columbia: University of South Carolina Press, 1991.

Vale, Thomas, editor. *Fire, Native Peoples, and the Natural Landscape.* Seattle, Washington: Island Press, 2002.

Volwiller, Albert T. *George Croghan and the Western Movement, 1741–1783.* Cleveland, Ohio: Arthur H. Clarke, 1926.

Waddell, Louis M., and Bruce D. Bomberger. *The French and Indian War in Pennsylvania, 1753–1763: Fortification and Struggle During the War for Empire.* Harrisburg: Pennsylvania Historical and Museum Commission, 1996.

Wainwright, Nicholas B. *George Croghan, Wilderness Diplomat.* Chapel Hill: University of North Carolina Press, 1959.

Wallace, Anthony F. C. *The Death and Rebirth of the Seneca.* New York: Knopf, 1970.

Ward, Harry M. *Major General Adam Stephen and the Cause of American Liberty.* Charlottesville: University Press of Virginia, 1989.

Ward, Matthew C. *Breaking the Backcountry: The Seven Years' War in Virginia and Pennsylvania, 1754–1765.* Pittsburgh: University of Pittsburgh Press, 2003.

Weigley, Russell F. *History of the United States Army.* New York: Macmillan, 1967.

Weslage, C. A. *The Delaware Indians.* New Brunswick, New Jersey: Rutgers University Press, 1972.

White, Richard. *The Middle Ground: Indians, Empires, and Republics in the Great Lakes Region, 1650–1815.* New York: Cambridge University Press, 1991.

Wiencek, Henry. *An Imperfect God: George Washington, His Slaves, and the Creation of America.* New York: Farrar, Straus and Giroux, 2003.

Williams, T. Harry. *The History of American Wars from Colonial Times to World War I.* New York: Knopf, 1981.

Winthrop, William. *Military Law and Precedents.* 2 volumes. Second edition, Washington: Government Printing Office, 1920.

SECONDARY SOURCES: PERIODICALS

Boone, C. De B. "Braddock's Campaign and Its Lessons." *The United Service Magazine,* New Series 39 (1909):88–93.

Boucher, Ronald L. "The Colonial Militia as a Social Institution: Salem, Massachusetts, 1764–1775." *Military Affairs* 37 (1973):125–30.

Bowman, Larry G. "Virginia's Use of Blacks in the French and Indian War." *Western Pennsylvania Historical Magazine* 53 (1970):57–63.

Clayton, T. R. "The Duke of Newcastle, the Earl of Halifax, and the American Origins of the Seven Years' War." *Historical Journal* 24 (1981):573–84.

Dahlinger, Charles W. "The Marquis Duquesne, Sieur de Menneville, Founder of the City of Pittsburgh." *Western Pennsylvania Historical Magazine* 15 (1932):3–33, 121–51, 219–62.

Eid, Leroy V. " 'A Kind of Running Fight': Indian Battlefield Tactics in the Late Eighteenth Century." *Western Pennsylvania Historical Magazine* 71 (1988):147–71.

———. "National War Among the Indians of Northeastern America." *Canadian Review of American Studies* 16 (1985):125–54.

Ekirch, Arthur A. Jr. "The Idea of a Citizen Army." *Military Affairs* 17 (1953): 30–36.

Ferling, John. "Soldiers for Virginia: Who Served in the French and Indian War?" *Virginia Magazine of History and Biography* 94 (1986):312–32.

Fleming, Thomas. "George Washington in Love." *American Heritage* 59 (2009):42–51.

Greene, Jack P. "The Case of the Pistole Fee." *Virginia Magazine of History and Biography* 66 (1958):399–422.

Harden, William. "James Marbury, of Strathy Hall, Comrade in Arms of George Washington." *Georgia Historical Quarterly* 1 (1917):77–98.

Hildeburn, Charles R. "Sir John St. Clair, Baronet, Quarter-Master General in America, 1755 to 1767." *Pennsylvania Magazine of History and Biography* 9 (1885–1886):1–14.

"Indian Wars in Augusta County, Virginia." *Virginia Magazine of History and Biography* 2 (1894–1895):397–404.

Karsten, Peter. "The American Democratic Citizen Soldier: Triumph or Disaster?" *Military Affairs* 30 (1966):34–40.

Ketcham, Ralph L. "France and American Politics, 1763–1793." *Political Science Quarterly* 78 (1963):198–223.

Kopperman, Paul E. "The British Command and Soldiers' Wives in America, 1755–1783." *Journal of the Society for Army Historical Research* 4 (1982):14–34.

———. " 'The Cheapest Pay': Alcohol Abuse in the Eighteenth-Century British Army." *Journal of Military History* 40 (1996):445–70.

Lacock, John K. "Braddock Road." *Pennsylvania Magazine of History and Biography* 38 (1914):1–37.

MacLeod, Daniel. "Daniel-Marie Lienard de Beaujeu, 1711–1755. *Dalhousie Review* (1973):296–309.

Mahon, John K. "Anglo-American Methods of Indian Warfare, 1676–1794." *Mississippi Valley Historical Review* 45 (1958):254–75.

Martin, Ronald D. "Confrontation on the Monongahela: Climax of the French Drive into the Upper Ohio Region." *Pennsylvania History* 37 (1970): 133–50.

Maurer, Maurer. "Military Justice Under General Washington." *Military Affairs* 28 (1964):8–16.

McCleskey, Turk. "Rich Land, Poor Prospects: Real Estate and the Formation of a Social Elite in Augusta County, Virginia." *Virginia Magazine of History and Biography* 98 (1990):460–62.

Morton, Louis. "The Origins of American Military Policy." *Military Affairs* 22 (1958):75–82.

Nichols, Franklin T. "The Organization of Braddock's Army." *William and Mary Quarterly,* 3rd Series 4 (1947):130–33.

Pargellis, Stanley. "Braddock's Defeat." *American Historical Review* 40 (1936): 253–69.

Richter, Daniel K. "War and Culture: The Iroquois Experience." *William and Mary Quarterly,* 3rd Series 40 (1983):528–59.

Russell, Peter E. "Redcoats in the Wilderness: British Officers and Irregular Warfare in Europe and America, 1740–1760." *William and Mary Quarterly,* 3rd Series 34 (1978):629–52.

Savory, Reginald. "The Convention of Ècluse, 1759–1762: The Treatment of Sick and Wounded, Prisoners of War, and Deserters of the British and French Armies During the Seven Years' War." *Journal of the Society for Army Historical Research* 42 (1964):60–70.

Schlebecker, John. "Braddock's Defeat." *Ohio State Archaeological and Historical Quarterly* 58 (1949):171–84.

Shea, John D. G. "Daniel Hyacinth Mary Lienard de Beaujeu." *Pennsylvania Magazine of History and Biography* 8 (1884):121–28.

Spaulding, Oliver L. Jr. "The Military Studies of George Washington." *American Historical Review* 29 (1924):675–80.

Steele, Ian K. "Hostage-Taking 1754: Virginians vs Canadians." *Journal of the Canadian Historical Association* 16 (2005):49–73.

———. "Shawnee Origins of Their Seven Years' War." *Ethnohistory* 53 (2006):657–87.

———. "When Worlds Collide: The Fate of Canadian and French Prisoners Taken at Fort Niagara." *Journal of Canadian Studies* 39 (2005):3–39.

Stewart, Andrew. "Was Gen. Braddock Shot Down by One of His Own Army?" *The New York Times,* October 19, 1913.

Tasse, Joseph. "Memoir of Charles de Langlade." *Wisconsin State Historical Society Collections* 7 (1876):123–87.

Wall, Cecil. "George Washington: Country Gentleman." *Agricultural History* 43 (1969):1–6.

Wright, John W. "Corps of Light Infantry." *American Historical Review* 31 (1926):459–61.

Yaple, Robert L. "Braddock's Defeat: The Theories and a Reconsideration." *Journal of the Society for Army Historical Research* 46 (1968):194–201.

SECONDARY SOURCES: OTHER

Cory, Rory McKenzie. "British Light Infantry in North America in the Seven Years War." Ph.D. Dissertation, Simon Fraser University, 1993.

Fowler, David J. *Guide to the Sol Feinstone Collection of the David Library of the American Revolution.* Washington Crossing, Pennsylvania: The David Library of the American Revolution, 1994.

Grenier, John Edward. "The Other American Way of War: Unlimited and Irregular Warfare in the Colonial Military Tradition." Ph.D. Dissertation, University of Colorado, 1999.

Harrington, J. C. *New Light on Washington's Fort Necessity: A Report on the Archeological Explorations at Fort Necessity National Battlefield Site.* Richmond, Virginia: Eastern National Park and Monument Association, 1957.

Pachero, Josephine F. "French Secret Agents in America, 1763–1778." Ph.D. Dissertation, University of Chicago, 1950.

Parker, K. L. "Anglo-American Wilderness Campaigning, 1754–64: Logistical and Tactical Developments." Ph.D. Dissertation, Columbia University, 1970.

Sypolt, Larry N. *Fort Necessity Civilian Conservation Corps Camp SP12.* Farmington, Pennsylvania: Fort Necessity National Battlefield, 1988.

Strach, Stephen G. "A Preliminary Documentary Review of Historical Notations of the Great Meadows, 1740–1970." Typescript, Fort Necessity National Battlefield, 1987. Published 2001 on the National Park Service website, nps.gov.

Thomas, Tom, and Margaret DeLaura. *Fort Necessity National Battlefield Pennsylvania: Historic Resource Study.* Denver, Colorado: National Park Service, 1996.

ACKNOWLEDGMENTS

The historian pounding on his keyboard does not work alone. Behind him stand the dedicated staffs and volunteers who guard our documentary, material, and published heritage. Without their labors, the historian would be at a loss, and our culture would have no memory. I offer my sincerest thanks to the people of the following organizations who have been so helpful in this and relevant earlier projects. I tip my hat in particular to the technical wizards in most of them who make more and more material available every year over the Internet. In particular, thanks to the staff of the Library of Congress who have published the George Washington Papers on line.

Libraries, archives, and other research institutions: the Library of Congress, Washington, DC; the University of Virginia Libraries, Charlottesville; the Mount Vernon Ladies Association, Mount Vernon, Virginia; the Paul Horgan Library of the New Mexico Military Institute, Roswell; the Roswell Public Library, Roswell, New Mexico; the Library of Eastern New Mexico University at Roswell; the Golden Library of Eastern New Mexico University, Portales; the Zimmerman Library of the University of New Mexico, Albuquerque; the National Archives, Washington, DC; Indiana University Library, Bloomington; U. S. Army Military History Institute, Carlisle Barracks, Pennsylvania.

Historic sites and museums: Fort Necessity National Battlefield, Pennsylvania; George Washington Birthplace National Monument, Virginia; George Washington Masonic National Memorial, Alexandria, Virginia; Independence National Historical Park, Philadelphia, Pennsylvania; Colonial National Historical Park, Virginia; Roswell Museum and Art Center, Roswell, New Mexico; Brandywine River Museum, Chadds Ford, Pennsylvania.

Several individuals also contributed advice, information, or other assistance. Bea Clary, Jim Donovan, John Elsegood, Roger Labrie, and Jay Miller graciously agreed to read part or all of an early draft of the manuscript, and offered many helpful comments. Candace Jordon of the Roswell Museum and

Art Center helped track down historic illustrations. Thanks to my agent, Jim Donovan, for making the project happen; and to my editor, Roger Labrie, who with the brilliant and creative staff of Simon & Schuster turned a pile of paper into what you hold in your hands.

As always, my fondest thanks to my long-suffering but eternally patient quartermaster general, my wife, Beatriz Clary, who as with previous projects endured my rambling discourses on what was escaping from the notes. This army of one could not begin to march without her, nor slog on through the struggle without her continuing support. She is really the one who keeps the guns in action.

For whatever is worthy of merit in this book, credit belongs to all of these good people. Fault for whatever falls short is entirely my own.

INDEX

ABOUT THE AUTHOR

DAVID A. CLARY is the author of *Adopted Son: Washington, Lafayette, and the Friendship That Saved the Revolution; Eagles and Empire: The United States, Mexico, and the Struggle for a Continent;* and *Rocket Man: Robert H. Goddard and the Birth of the Space Age.* The former chief historian of the U.S. Forest Service, Clary has taught history at the university level and lives in Roswell, New Mexico, with his wife, Beatriz.